W9-ADO-779

# The Queen's Library

MATERIAL TEXTS

*Series Editors*

Roger Chartier          Leah Price

Joseph Farrell          Peter Stallybrass

Anthony Grafton     Michael F. Suarez, S.J.


A complete list of books in the series
is available from the publisher.

DC
108.3
.B73
2011

# The Queen's Library

Image-Making at the Court
of Anne of Brittany, 1477–1514

Cynthia J. Brown

UNIVERSITY OF PENNSYLVANIA PRESS

PHILADELPHIA • OXFORD

Copyright © 2011 University of Pennsylvania Press

All rights reserved. Except for brief quotations used for
purposes of review or scholarly citation, none of this book
may be reproduced in any form by any means without
written permission from the publisher.

Published by
University of Pennsylvania Press
Philadelphia, Pennsylvania 19104-4112

Printed in the United States of America on acid-free paper

1 3 5 7 9 10 8 6 4 2

Library of Congress Cataloging-in-Publication Data
Brown, Cynthia Jane.
    The queen's library : image-making at the court of Anne
of Brittany, 1477–1514 / Cynthia J. Brown.
        p.   cm. — (Material texts)
    Includes bibliographical references and index.
    ISBN 978-0-8122-4282-9 (acid-free paper)
    1. Anne, of Brittany, Consort of Louis XII, King of
France, 1467–1514—Library. 2. Books and reading—
History—To 1500. 3. Books and reading—History—16th
century. 4. Queens—Books and reading—Political
aspects. 5. Women—Books and reading—Political aspects.
6. Women and literature—Political aspects. 7. Women
History—Middle Ages, 500–1500. I. Title.
DC108.3.B76    2010
944'.027,dc22                                    2010004559

*Dedicated to my mother, Jane B. Bundy*

# CONTENTS

# ILLUSTRATIONS

# Introduction

I begin my investigation with a revealing image. The stunning miniature that appears in the lavishly illuminated royal copy of the French translation of Petrarch's *Remèdes de l'une ou l'autre Fortune* (BnF ms. ffr. 225) features Anne of Brittany holding her rather adult-looking four-year-old daughter, Claude of France, on her lap, surrounded by ladies of the court (fol. 165r) (Figure 1).[1] One of the few extant images of Anne together with Claude, future queen of France herself,[2] this portrayal of the queen, her daughter, and her circle of *dames d'honneur* seemingly venerates the females of the French court as its own self-contained unit. Yet, staged at the lower left section of the miniature, below the larger, more imposing figure of Reason and the accusatory figure of her husband, King Louis XII, backed up by his male protégés (including Cardinal Georges d'Amboise), Anne of Brittany and Claude of France are not in fact presented here in all their glory, as one might have expected. For in its mise en scène of Louis XII's confrontation with Reason in the context of "Adverse Fortune,"[3] this visual rendition of Petrarch's chapter on "Being a King Without Son" conveys contemporary royal anxieties about the lack of a male heir.[4] Whether or not this scenario is directly related to the recent death of the royal couple's three-week-old son,[5] this image confirms that just five years after Anne's marriage to her second husband, Louis XII, and four years after the birth of their daughter Claude, considerable concern had surfaced at the French court about the absence of a male heir.[6]

The text that accompanies the BnF fr. 225 miniature reinforces this visual staging of royal apprehensions through the voice of *Douleur* (Sorrow). Presumably the French king's alter ego, she complains at length about the lack of a male successor. Yet *Rayson* continuously responds with arguments demonstrating that the absence of a male heir has its advantages.[7] Thus, the text offers critical insight into the scene depicted in the miniature, in which *Rayson* essentially consoles the French king, who seems to take to task his own wife and daughter. Indeed Anne's portrayed position is a humble one—her eyes

1. Francesco Petrarch, *Les Remèdes de l'une ou l'autre Fortune* (translation), Paris BnF ffr. 225, fol. 165r: Louis XII confronts Reason about the absence of a male heir. Bibliothèque Nationale de France.

are cast down—one that contrasts with most other images of the queen I discuss below in which she appears alone or alongside one of her husbands in regal splendor and in a dignified pose. Depicted in this miniature as a female unit that essentially emblematizes Anne of Brittany's failure in her most anticipated function as royal spouse, mother and daughter appear at first glance to be visually celebrated, but are in fact pictorially and textually questioned.

In the end, *Rayson*'s argument as presented in the accompanying text implicitly supports the status quo, and even offers hope that God will rectify the situation.[8] However, this supposedly consolatory text-image combination belies court realities. For the absence of a male heir to the French throne would, despite *Rayson*'s efforts to provide solace in this translation of Petrarch's famous work,[9] continue to weigh on the royal couple.[10] In a sense, *Rayson*'s silence in this passage about female offspring suggests that producing a daughter had little bearing on a ruler's current power or on the future force of the realm.[11]

In reality, the marriage of a royal daughter could impact the future of the kingdom, and the designation of a husband for Claude proved in fact to be another particularly sensitive issue during Anne's queenship. While one of the French queen's few powers involved matching appropriate husbands with the females at her court, in particular her own daughters, Anne would ultimately lose her battle to marry Claude to a non-French prince in an effort to protect the independence of her duchy of Brittany. Although the queen orchestrated Claude's engagement to Charles of Luxembourg of the House of Austria through the 1504 Treaties of Blois, Louis XII outwitted his wife, manipulating circumstances that led to Claude's engagement in 1506 and ultimate marriage in 1514 to his successor, the future Francis I (for details, see Chapter 2).

Our introductory image, then, invokes a number of issues critical to this study: the political dynamics of the images of women in books; the tensions associated with late medieval and early modern queenship, including expectations concerning male heirs and daughters' marital unions; the sharing of book spaces by royal spouses; and the importance of the text-image relationship in interpreting books. Many of these issues pertain as well to those works in which Anne of Brittany and her female contemporaries are placed textually and visually in a less ambiguous, more venerated light. For example, the entire *Genealogie d'Anne Duchesse de Bretagne*, written by Disarouez Penguern "en l'honneur et louange de ladicte dame" [in honor and in praise of the said lady][12] consists of the verbal construction of her genealogical tree. Completed in 1510,[13] Penguern's description of Anne of Brittany seated atop her family

tree[14] more than counterbalances the negative image of Anne and Claude in
BnF ms. 625:

> Or maintenant est en l'arbre assise
> Tout au plus hault en royal parement
> Entre deux roys, ses espoux, en tel guyse
> Qu'il estoit dit tout au commancement
> Depuis que Dieu crea le firmament:
> Ne se trouua dame tant honnoree
> Qui ait vesqu tant vertueusement,
> Des bonnes meurs douee et decoree.
>
> Les hystoires, croniques anciennes
> Font mension de Iudich et de Helaine
> Et de plusieurs aultres de vertuz plaines;
> Des sibilles Saba et Polixenne,
> Hester, Lucresse, Susanne et Vienne.
> Mais la royne duchesse souueraine
> Les excede trestoutes et chascune
> Qui ait esté ne tient a present regne:
> Si treslouable n'y eust iamais aulcune. (fol. 42r)

[Now she is seated in the tree at the very top in royal glory between
two kings, her husbands, in such a manner that it was said at the
beginning, since God created the firmament: there was never
found another lady so honored who has lived so virtuously, [and
is] instilled and decorated with good manners. Histories, ancient
chronicles mention Judith and Helen and many other females
filled with virtue; the sibyls, Sheba and Polixena, Esther, Lucretia,
Susanna and Vienna. But the sovereign queen duchess surpasses
each and every one of them who ever reigned or still does so: never
was any of them as laudable as she.]

In this work, in which Anne is extensively glorified and favorably compared to
the famous women of mythology and biblical history, a subject of further discussion in subsequent chapters, no anxieties surface about the absence of a male
heir.[15] It does not appear to be an issue in a work commissioned by and made
for the French queen alone, one whose aim was to exalt the duchess of Brittany's

Breton ancestry and her unusual status as twice-crowned queen of France. By the same token, most other images of the queen that appear in the books examined here feature her in unambiguously laudatory light: she is either enthroned beside the French king, strategically placed alone on the throne in a place of honor receiving a book, or, in another honorable pose, and in some cases, she faces the spectator directly and authoritatively. And yet the very context of these images may shade the meaning of the illustration. One such example commemorates the very engagement of Claude and Francis mentioned above, for this illustration embodies certain complexities and contradictions associated with the political stakes of this event, in particular for the French queen.

The engagement miniature, which appears on folio iv of Jean d'Auton's *Chroniques de Louis XII* (BnF ms. ffr. 5083) (Figure 2), features the newly engaged couple surrounded by a host of church officials and court figures, with Louis XII and his entourage prominently staged above the proceedings. Anne of Brittany, positioned in the lower register in the privileged location at the royal right, stands out because of her crown and her stunning red dress as she places her right hand on her daughter's right arm. The realities behind the scenes of this dramatic political staging, however, point to the truly troubling nature of this family portrait for the French queen. Any informed viewer of this scene would have known about Anne's strong resistance to the marriage of Claude and Francis of Angoulême and her long-term rivalry with Louise of Savoy, the one figure with whom she is made to share symmetrical placement in the illustration: Louise stands at the right with her left hand placed on her son's left arm and, as in Anne's case, her dress is held by a court attendant, while her female entourage stand behind her. What this illustration was designed to project to the book owner—and indeed to the public at large, whether or not they actually viewed this miniature—was the image of unified royal support behind the union of Claude and Francis, an event that ultimately addressed earlier concerns about royal succession. However, since historical documents confirm that Anne of Brittany's power in this matter was completely undermined and that her goals lay elsewhere, it is likely that she would have disagreed with the miniature's portrayal of her support for the engagement. Created, however, by Louis XII's chronicler about and for the king himself, Jean d'Auton's account and this and other images in the royal manuscript, which sought above all to glorify Louis' role in French political affairs, doubtless privileged not only the king's point of view over the queen's, but also the royal propaganda machine that controlled the very image of court life that was projected to the outside world.

2. Jean d'Auton, *Chroniques*, Paris BnF ffr. 5083, fol. 1v: The Engagement of Claude of France and Francis of Angoulême (May 1506). Bibliothèque Nationale de France.

These text-image associations set the stage for my exploration of the larger issues surrounding female modes of empowerment in late-medieval Europe. My investigation of the cultural reconstruction of the images of noble women such as Anne of Brittany is based in large measure on the books that defined them, those they commissioned, those dedicated to them (and sometimes to their husbands), those they inherited and those received as gifts. In the belief that such books are virtual repositories of late medieval image-making in both verbal and visual terms, I consider the manuscripts, often elaborately decorated, and early printed books making up the libraries of Anne of Brittany and her female contemporaries as cultural artifacts that embody signs of contemporary harmonies and tensions—among books producers, authors, book owners, readers, and society in general—and that provide insight into how women's roles as political strategists and cultural figures were translated by and for those in their entourage and the world at large.[16]

A study of the production of books for and about females can shed new light on the imagery of women of power by providing answers to questions about how, why, and by whom works were conceived and assembled for them and related designated audiences. Perhaps more than any recent scholar Anne-Marie Legaré has produced a critical series of publications that deal directly with many of these issues. Her in-depth research into the libraries of Jeanne de Laval and Charlotte de Savoie, and comparative discussion of the collections of Margaret of York and Margaret of Austria[17] are complemented by her recently edited volume, *Livres et lectures de femmes en Europe entre Moyen Âge et Renaissance*, which presents fascinating studies of a wide-ranging number of females involved in book production and acquisition during the late medieval and early Renaissance period.[18] Much of this research examines how women inherited books from their fathers and mothers, brought books to their marriage as part of their dowries, borrowed books from their husbands,[19] and received books as gifts.[20] In addition, we learn that the acquisition of libraries by women in the late Middle Ages was often a mimetic impulse.[21] Given the inevitable sharing of— and even confusion over—books read and/or owned by spouses of rank, it is also necessary to study a husband's collection or the library of a couple to assess properly what might have figured in a woman's library.[22] Elizabeth L'Estrange, who discusses the transmission of the *Heures de Fitzwilliam* from mother to daughter, summarizes the challenges of such research in the following terms:

Contrairement aux hommes, peu de femmes étaient propriétaires de livres et la plupart des lectrices que nous pouvons étudier

aujourd'hui proviennent presque exclusivement de l'aristocratie et/
ou d'une communauté religieuse. Il faut également rappeler le fait
que les propriétaires féminins ne choisissaient pas toujours leurs
propres manuscrits: souvent, des textes dévots et enluminés—
comme les livres d'heures—étaient offerts aux femmes par leurs
conseillers ou leurs parents (masculins et féminins), afin de les
encourager à bien se conduire. De ce fait, un "double bind" (double
contrainte) se présente au chercheur qui voudrait comprendre les
goûts et les intérêts des lectrices au Moyen Âge.[23]

Much research explores the preponderance of books of devotion in females' libraries, which often served as vehicles of social exchange among
them.[24] Hanno Wijsman describes the library of Jeanne d'Artois as "une
collection typiquement féminine,"[25] a culturally constructed library that
features above all devotional and moralistic works, whereas, according to
Marie-Françoise Damongeot-Bourdat, the library of Marie de Bretagne, abbess of Fontevraud in the mid-fifteenth century, contained an unexpectedly
diverse collection of books, some of which may have made their way to Anne
of Brittany through her father.[26] We also learn that the library of Marguerite de Bavière, who borrowed many literary and moralistic books from her
husband, John the Fearless, as well as that of Marie de Luxembourg were not
typical "female" collections.[27] Legaré, while reminding us that 80 percent of
Margaret of York's library contained devotional works, states nonetheless that
the collections of her female contemporaries had much more balanced proportions of religious and secular works. In fact, Margaret of Austria "semble
avoir elle-même voulu donner à sa collection une dimension politique contri-
buant à affirmer son pouvoir et son rôle public en tant que régente."[28] This
assessment suggests that Margaret was inspired more by the establishment of
male rather than female libraries.[29] A discussion of the women of power and
book production, of influential women and the act of reading necessarily in-
tersects with research on female patronage and medieval queenship.[30] In both
cases, she maintains a certain (visual) power as patron and marriage broker.

The insightful article by Colette Beaune and Élodie Lequain on "Marie
de Berry et les livres"[31] provides a useful reference point for this study. The
authors examine the different kinds of reading Marie de Berry would have
made of BnF ms. ffr. 926, a collection of both devotional and political texts,
and the way in which the manuscript book itself "participe incontestablement
de cette entreprise de construction d'une héritière incontestable" and how the

duke of Berry "fit de sa fille un modèle à une époque où la reine Isabeau, très attaquée, ne pouvait plus guère l'être, et où la dauphine Marguerite de Guyenne était encore bien jeune" (59). Indeed, in this 1406 manuscript, Marie de Berry is figured as the ideal lady, "lettrée, bonne, vertueuse et dévote" (59). Thus, we see how well before Anne of Brittany, books designed for females were used not only for their moral instruction, but also to promote their virtues and image as noble women. It is significant that despite the devotional-political mix of texts in this manuscript, in the end the message relayed to and about Marie de Berry was a restrictive one:

> Une bonne femme ne doit aller qu'en sa maison, au moutier et au sermon. Elle ne doit mie aller de maison en maison, ni voir la "joliveté" d'un monde qui est synonyme de tentation. Il faut donc se tenir "closement" en sa chambre en oraison, car qui est "disclose" de coeur et de corps risque l'enfer. Bonne prude femme doit être comparable à une pierre car celle-ci ne se meut et ne meut autrui pour chose que l'on dise ou qu'on lui fasse. Un idéal statique silencieux qui est peu practicable pour une laïque pourvue de responsabilités familiales et politiques. . . . Il faut à la fille du duc de Berry participer à la gloire des lys en restant "estrange au monde," soutenir la croisade sans quitter son oratoire. Le livre est l'instrument indispensable à ce programme irréalisable. Il est un instrument de perfection, l'interlocuteur privilégié de l'âme dévote. Dieu est à l'origine du livre, c'est avec lui qui est toujours présent contrairement au confesseur, qu'il faut dialoguer. Le livre est le maître, l'âme dévote le disciple qui doit lui ouvrir son coeur. Le livre est "arbre de vie," il est médecine spirituelle. (60–61)

Many details about the works associated with Anne of Brittany's library corroborate this research. As in the case of her female predecessors and contemporaries, it is often difficult to distinguish her books from those of her husbands.[32] Past and recent research also confirms that, like other women's collections, a significant portion of Anne's library consisted of devotional works.[33] Much work has been carried out on the beautifully decorated books of hours made for her, most notably the famous *Grandes Heures d'Anne de Bretagne* (BnF ms. lat. 9474) illuminated by Jean Bourdichon.[34] In many cases, these devotional books display extraordinary artistic decoration that only a royal figure could have afforded. Such an exceptional outlay of funds and special attention given to the ornamentation of her books of devotion all but confirm Anne of Brittany's predilection for the book as an important vehicle for religious and moral instruction, but also as a precious objet d'art. There is little doubt that a certain manifestation of power—cultural, if not political—must have been thought to reside in the creation, possession, and perusal of such beautifully illuminated books.

Yet many decorated books associated with Anne of Brittany fall into more secular categories as well, although book scholars have considered this dimension of her library less often.[35] It is to these that I devote most of my analyses. Considering the nondevotional books that figured centrally in the life of Anne of Brittany and her contemporaries, my study aims to assess female modes of empowerment through an examination of how the demands of a patriarchal and aristocratic society influenced the creation and reception of literary and artistic images in those works.

Thanks to the recent work of Michael Jones, Pascale Thibault, and others,[36] scholars have had access to studies of the book manuscripts in Anne's collection as well as the books themselves. Drawing from this research, I offer an updated catalogue of Anne of Brittany's library, which includes the printed books she acquired (see Appendix). In fact, the relationship between her manuscript and printed works often surfaces as a special subject of interest in my discussion in the chapters below. Concentrating on the secular works in Anne of Brittany's library, I suggest that political motivations associated with court interest in and debates about women's character often explain how the twice-crowned French queen acquired books in a conscious or unconscious imitation of her rivals Margaret of Austria and Louise of Savoy, whose collections were nonetheless more extensive.

Even more than how and why women acquired and constituted book collections in the late medieval and early modern periods, what interests me here are various physical aspects of their books, including the images, especially those of women, contained in these works owned and read by women. Alison Stones, who examines portraits of women in thirteenth-century manuscripts,[37] demonstrates that although little is known about women as commissioners or owners of books earlier in the Middle Ages (especially when they were not queens), our knowledge of these details increases with time and better documentation.[38] My examination of portraits and other illustrations of women in books in the late fifteenth and early sixteenth centuries provides insight into the relationship between female images and female book ownership and their political import in these works.

Regardless of their context, all these images constitute complex representations. As cultural constructions of the artists who made them, they may have in turn been constructors of the worlds they ostensibly represented, as Jane Taylor and Lesley Smith maintain.[39] Others such as Lena Liepe, who examines the production, spatial/visual, textual and functional aspects of illustrations in her work on the epistemology of images, corroborate these same claims:[40]

> In a post-structuralist and materialist theory of visuality, images
> are seen as agents in history, as articulations of social processes
> that in themselves constitute and influence those processes. Images
> are formed by the cultural system they represent, but they also
> partake in the formation of this system, a formation that works
> as an ideological authorization. This means that images should
> be interpreted not only as mere illustrations reflecting historical
> processes; they are in themselves historical processes that contribute
> to the culturally defined self-comprehension of an epoch . . . images
> are systems of meaning, made to be read and internalized as part
> of the ideological process that constitutes a culture. The images can
> function in accordance with the dominant ideology or against it,
> but they always are related to it in one way or another.

It is not only an investigation of the intricacies and incongruities of the visual depiction of women in late medieval and early Renaissance books that leads to a better understanding of their cultural and political roles at the time. An examination of literary imagery in the accompanying texts and its relationship with the book's visual program also offers unexpected insights into the dynamics of female power in late medieval and early Renaissance Europe. Indeed, an understanding of the relationship between text and image in these volumes and of the emblems, symbols, allegories, and other visual and verbal signs that figure centrally therein is crucial to a discussion of late medieval women of power. Again, this relationship is not one-dimensional or one-directional, as Brigitte Buettner argues in her study of systems of signification in *Boccaccio's "Des cleres et nobles femmes"*. She astutely recognizes that images both provide the text with a concrete reality and recompose, reshape, and rework it through complicated and sometimes contradictory representations. In his work on thirteenth-century illustrations, Michael Camille has also discussed the conflict or tension between text and picture, stating that "It is a relationship built on a disruptive difference, a mutual incompatibility of two codes vying for the reader's attention and generating subtle nuances of meaning in the process."[41]

Therefore, uncovering and analyzing the very complexities and contradictions of the verbal and visual imagery of women of power are major concerns of my discussion. To do so, I draw from research in a number of disciplines, including not only the history of the book, literary analysis, late medieval and early modern history and art history, but also material culture and female personification theory. By taking into account the manner in which the iconographic representation of females in books making up the libraries of late medieval and early modern women of power in Europe both interfaced with and contested the historical, literary, and cultural documents they decorated, my analysis aims to uncover the potential conflict that surfaced in male-authored, male-illustrated works for and about women. My study of the choice, orientation, and design of images in these works, whether textual, visual, or an association of the two, often reveals an ambivalence about the male representation of women of power in late medieval and early Renaissance Europe that brings to the surface heretofore unexamined allusions to continued court debates about the vices and virtues of women. Moreover, I analyze not only the texts contained in these books and the relationship between the text and image or other dimensions of the paratext of those volumes associated with Anne of Brittany and her contemporaries (especially those they actively commissioned or received). I likewise consider carefully prologues and dedications, for perhaps more than any other paratextual element, they offer the clearest insight into the dynamics of the male poet-female patron relationship and other dimensions of the bookmaking process in which women's role became so prevalent. Many of these serve as key sites of analysis in my discussion below.

The correspondence between rituals of entry and departure frames my investigation, which opens with an analysis of the events that often marked the public's first contact with women of power, coronations and urban entries, and concludes with an investigation of their final viewing at the time of their funerals. The often dazzling accounts produced to commemorate these occasions are nothing less than codicological performances that set the stage for a discussion of what one might call the "politics of the page" in books for and about females of rank. Through a new reading of the text and paratext of the books associated with Anne of Brittany and her contemporary female counterparts, I not only open a new lens onto the workings of the female patronage system during the late fifteenth and early sixteenth centuries, the maternal and marital expectations of queens at the time, the culture of court ladies, the fascination with "famous women," and continuing debates between men and women about female virtues, but also uncover the real, perceived, and projected image of women of power.

Chapter 1 explores female royal entries and the festival books that commemorated and reconstructed these stagings of women of rank into orchestrated performances that blended religious and political symbolism and allegories. The promotion of female virtues in these events and related narratives served as didactic guides to the moral behavior expected of the protagonists of these ceremonials and readers of their translation into words and images.

Building on the historical reconstruction of women of power examined in Chapter 1, Chapter 2 explores the female patronage system, whereby male authors and artists exalted their female benefactors. Concentrating on the literary and iconographic reconstruction of women in allegorical works associated with Anne of Brittany and her contemporaries, I demonstrate how political tensions at the court involving males were often represented and resolved through female personification allegory, a literary device that mediated between examples of powerful females and contemporary realities about women's roles. The manipulation of gender and personification in a key literary text, Jean Marot's *Voyage de Gênes*, sheds new light on underlying sexual and political tensions between king and queen and between Breton and French interests at the time, which ultimately signaled a mise en question of female empowerment.

Chapter 3 investigates the association between works about famous women, construed as defenses of women, and the patronage relationship in books dedicated to prominent women at the French court. Here I argue that textual ambiguities in Boccaccio's *De mulieribus claris* and its French translations point to an ambivalence about women of power among male authors writing for female patrons. Tensions among bookmakers, authors, and dedicatees, uncovered through a study of Antoine Vérard's edition of the *Nobles et cleres dames*, are directly related to court debates about female virtues and vices. In addition, prefatory claims in support of females by Antoine Dufour are not always borne out by his *Vies des femmes célèbres*, for verbal and visual images in these works both glorify and contest realities about females. Actual court debates turn into a literary defense of women in *La Vraye Advocate des dames* by Jean Marot, whose shrewd staging of a female defense lawyer secured him a court position.

The artistic and literary intensity associated with Octovien de Saint-Gelais's translation of Ovid's *Heroides* and the manner in which female patrons were involved in its dissemination, explored in Chapter 4, mark a shift in interest in the continuing debate over female virtues from commanding to defenseless women. Nonetheless, the replacement of Ovid's bereaved heroines with contemporary female portraits (Anne of Brittany, Louise of Savoy), the association of them with the symbols of women of power (Louise of Savoy, Anne of Brittany), the literary staging of the French queen herself as an Ovidian heroine or the insertion of Anne of Brittany and her contemporaries (Anne de Beaujeu, Margaret of Austria) into works of mourning are coupled with an exaltation of grieving women in stunning (visual) fashion.

In Chapter 5, I investigate issues related to the obsequies of and final tributes to women of rank, in particular Anne of Brittany, and their reconstitution in book form by numerous court protégés. These include public protocol and the cultural codification of grief; the dramatic staging of mourners and the mourned in real life and in commemorative works; the political exploitation of signs, symbols, and texts at the time of public mourning; the literary exploitation of male and female allegorical voices of sorrow; and the interrelated role of epideictic and visual rhetoric. Even in works of unqualified adulation, tempered by manifestations of sorrow, hidden strains are nonetheless perceptible among rival court writers vying for renewed court status, and they are coupled with implicit competitions between the manuscript and printed forms of reproduction. Thanks to new bookmaking technologies, tributes to one queen (Anne of Brittany) were easily recycled for another (Claude of France).

In my discussion below, I often provide only an English translation of the original Middle French text, especially if the passage is long, descriptive, and available in a modern publication. I provide the original French text, especially when not easily accessible, with my own English translation, unless otherwise noted. In the transcription of unedited texts, all spelling has been maintained, abbreviations have been resolved, the distinction between *i* and *j*, *u* and *v* has been regularized, the cedilla is used as in modern French and the elision of vowels is indicated by an apostrophe. Punctuation and the use of capital letters follow modern norms.

By examining more closely and rereading with a different kind of critical eye the dynamics inherent in the books of Anne of Brittany and her contemporaries, we can better understand the complexities and contradictions that characterized the involvement of women in late medieval and early Renaissance book production and the ways in which their power was defined and promulgated by men. The underlying harmonies and tensions of these collaborations shed new light on a heretofore unexplored dimension of the *Querelle des femmes*.

# CHAPTER ONE

# Rituals of Entry:
# Women and Books in Performance

## The Staging of Anne of Brittany's Virtues:
## Guillaume Fillastre's *Toison d'Or*

The stunning illustration that opens Anne of Brittany's copy of Guillaume Fillastre's *Toison d'Or* (Figure 3), one of her earliest acquired books, sets the stage for my analysis of female images and power in late medieval and early Renaissance France through an investigation of coronations and entry rituals. The visual drama played out in this liminal miniature contrasts sharply with the images of a vulnerable French queen that I examined above in the Introduction, for it does not harbor the ambiguities of the *Remèdes de Fortune* and *Chroniques de Louis XII* miniatures. What this illustration portrays is the French queen in all her virtuous glory in a dramatic performance whose allegorical configuration anticipates (or echoes) the Parisian entry theaters created in her honor in 1492 and 1504. The context of these *tableaux vivants*, however, brings to staged images of the queen a more ambiguous quality, which I will examine more fully below.

The large, beautifully decorated two-volume set of the *Toison d'Or*, currently housed at the BnF as manuscript ffr. 138–39 and dating from Anne of Brittany's first reign,[1] contains perhaps the most unusual liminal miniature found in any of Anne's books. Given the large dimensions of manuscript 138 itself (485 by 360 mm.), the size of the image featuring Anne is particularly impressive. Unlike other liminal illustrations associated with the French queen, it does not depict a dedication scene, perhaps because manuscript 138 contains the author's original dedication to Charles, duke of Burgundy, and

3. Guillaume Fillastre, *Toison d'Or, Paris*, BnF ffr. 138, fol. 1v: Anne of Brittany engages with the Theological and Cardinal Virtues. Bibliothèque Nationale de France.

presents the verbal and visual history of the Golden Fleece, which involved a series of combats and military exploits embraced by the Burgundian duchy in its heyday.[2] Nonetheless, it is Anne's prominently displayed presence in the opening miniature that both honors her and decidedly marks the book as hers. Its particular staging of the queen and a host of personified female virtues anticipates or echoes the many allegorical scenarios she viewed along her 1492 and 1504 Parisian entry routes. Not only do a Breton shield and Anne's arms appearing on folio 223v of manuscript 138 confirm that this was the French queen's book. Anne of Brittany's association with Charles VIII is also repeatedly displayed in emblematic terms throughout the volume, for many of its folios bear elaborately painted initials A and S, referring to both queen and king.[3] In fact, the architectural frame of the liminal miniature bears the same emblematic allusions, for the illustration is encircled in varying degrees of complicated interwoven patterns by Anne of Brittany's famous *cordelière*,[4] from which hang blue or gold S's and mauve or gold letters A's on all four sides, themselves interconnected in varying ways. This insistent coupling of king and queen through the repeated intertwining of royal emblems and initials in the margins of the *Toison d'Or* manuscript resurfaces in living color on the 1492 Paris entry theater stages.

The illustration itself is quite remarkable. Anne stands at the right in a beautiful red dress and her traditional black veil headdress facing the three Theological Virtues, Faith, Hope and Charity, and the four Cardinal Virtues, Temperance, Fortitude, Prudence, and Justice, all attired in different but attractive garb. The symbol associated with each personified figure is located on or near her, and each virtue's name is indicated on a banderole.[5] These dynamics imitate Anne of Brittany's position during her 1492 entry through Paris as a spectator halting before the allegorical scenarios staged in her honor. Her lovely, young-looking face and the appearance of some of her golden hair underneath her coif all but confirm that the miniature dates from her early years as queen. Staring at the virtues to the left, Anne dominates the right section of the interior space in which the allegory is staged, because she both stands alone and is significantly larger than the personified virtues at the left. Suggesting affirmation and perhaps even dialogue through her gestures, the queen holds her delicate left hand slightly upward, while her right index finger points straight up. Below the lower frame, between the queen's and king's initials and Anne's *cordelière*, two levels of gold letters inscribed on a blue field form the phrase A SE ME RANS // POVR IAMAIS A [To this one I render myself forever].[6] Just as texts were staged as part of the allegorical scenarios presented during her Parisian entries, so too the visual and verbal dimensions of Anne's illustrated book dialogue with each other. While conceivably a pun on the S (se) and A initials decorating the miniature's frame [To S (that is, Charles VIII), A (that is, Anne) gives herself forever], this statement verbally translates the visual allegory staged above: Anne's device and gestures suggest that she consciously embraces and embodies divinely inspired virtuous behavior personified through the female agents across from her. Like them, she stages and performs her life, with her own symbols providing additional details about her queenship. To the queen's right, a blue banderole with gold writing that reads "O cest la bonne fin" [Oh, 'tis the right end] verbally confirms the wisdom of Anne's moralistic choices, and a banderole at the left above the allegorical figures from which the hand of God points to Anne, bearing the words DIEV LE ARRA A GARANS [God will have it as guarantee], provides religious authorization of Anne's virtues.[7]

More than any other illustration found in Anne of Brittany's library, the moralistic message of this miniature directly honors the French queen as a purveyor of multiple virtues. A didactic image that anticipates some of the entry theaters examined below, it nevertheless stands out in its portrayal of a demonstrative queen figure. In contrast to the Medea figure lurking behind the narrative of the *Toison d'Or*, a figure that would reappear in entry theaters and books about famous women in Anne's possession, the French queen as portrayed in the miniature of BnF ffr. ms. 138 assumes the commendable behavior of positive biblical models—although her persona is in the end inextricably intertwined with the king's throughout the manuscript.

Unfortunately, no details exist about Anne's acquisition of this work. Was it a gift made in her honor? Did the queen herself commission the manuscript book or participate in some way in the decision about its decoration and illustration? Although we are unable to answer these questions,[8] it is clear that the queen, her husband, and/or someone else in her entourage understood the importance of depicting Anne's association with virtues in verbal and visual terms. This, after all, was the comportment expected of a queen, a behavior that Anne herself may have more naturally embraced than others. The virtues featured throughout Fillastre's *Toison d'or*—*magnanimité, justice, prudence, fidelité, patience,* and *clémence,* two or three of which coincide with those associated with Anne of Brittany in ms. 138's liminal image—may well have inspired the miniaturist, who, through his illustration of Anne's embracing of the seven Christian virtues, created a strong tie between the original author's history of the Golden Fleece and the queen's copy of the work. Certainly, many of the volumes in the queen's library consisted of subjects of a religious or moralistic nature.[9] As we will learn in Chapter 3, however, the French queen, along with her contemporaries, remained fascinated with negative and positive female exempla from past mythology and history as well.

Anne of Brittany's static staging in the *Toison d'Or* miniature gives way to a decidedly more active and more complex staging during her and her female contemporaries' *sacres* and royal entries. While the coronation itself reflected the joint organization of the Church and royal court, a queen's entry, especially through France's capital, involved the cooperation of city and court officials.[10] In both instances, the performance of the queen herself figured centrally in the related festivities, although, like the conduct of officials around her, her actions, appearance, and behavior were consciously orchestrated and controlled according to protocol.[11] As convention dictated, the queen would make her entry through Paris following her coronation at Saint-Denis to the adulation of its citizens. The latter both reveled as she and her entourage traversed the capital city and viewed staged theaters in her honor along the entry route.[12] Thus, the queen was at once the protagonist of her own living theater in its movement through the capital city and a spectator of dramatic presentations, often of an allegorical nature, that portrayed her relationship to the city and kingdom. Thanks to the redactors of numerous entry accounts, or what Helen Watanbe-O'Kelly calls festival books,[13] commemorating these events, contemporary readers had access to spectacles they may not have witnessed and present-day scholars are able to reconstruct to a certain degree these ceremonials. Indeed, the queen's status as viewer and viewed as she processed through France's capital and citizens' staging of her relationship to city and kingdom in street theaters along her entry route provide rich material for an investigation of the harmonies and tensions surrounding the ways in which the court and the Parisian citizenry defined her role. Watanabe-O'Kelly offers sage advice on this score:

It is . . . necessary to consider the festival book as a textual genre, to see it within the context of the early modern court. . . . To treat the festival book purely as a window on the festival, to regard it as a straight factual account of what actually happened and not to examine it as a phenomenon in its own right, leads inevitably to a misunderstanding of both the festival itself and the festival

book. . . . the festival book comes into being because, like the
festival itself, it fulfills, for the court or the city that commissioned
it, a function as part of the panoply of power. (3)

That the dynamics of power relationships surfaced directly or indirectly in
these festivals and festival books lies in the fact that such events and their
commemorations often took place during times of change.[14] The coronation
of queens, for example, more often than not, followed upon the marriage of
the French king, whose new mate frequently hailed from a foreign realm as
part of a peace treaty.[15]

   Alone among all French royal females, Anne of Brittany, twice crowned
queen (1492, 1504), made her entry twice into Paris; each event was commemorated in a festival book.[16] The coronation and entry of her successors,
Mary Tudor (1514) and her own daughter Claude of France (1517), for whom
special festival books were made, followed suit. Of a more unusual dynamic
is the account of the coronation of Anne of Brittany's cousin Anne de Foix,
as queen of Hungary, which the French queen herself commissioned. The
visual, cultural, and rhetorical dynamics of the real-life celebratory stagings
in honor of these women are, I would argue, consciously or unconsciously
rearticulated and refashioned not only in their festival accounts, but also in
other books commissioned by or dedicated to these women of power. More
often than not, it is through the literary mise en scène of personified (female)
figures, like those in the *Toison d'Or* miniature, that this interpenetration of
the theater and the book occurs. In some of the volumes that I examine in
this chapter, manuscript illuminations of the events, embellished by personalized decorations, beautifully complement the written account, providing
their own codicological drama of the coronation festivities and often functioning as instruments of propaganda in their own right. I thus consider these
and the books examined in subsequent chapters as "books in performance"
and I seek to uncover how they staged women of power.

## Political and Religious Stagings
## of the Queen in Her 1492 Parisian Entry

The anonymous imprint, *Le Sacre d'Anne de Bretagne à Saint-Denis en 1492*
(BnF Rés. 8° Lb[28] 13), and André de la Vigne's personalized account of
Anne of Brittany's coronation at Saint-Denis and entry into Paris in 1504

(Waddesdon Manor MS 22), serve as the point of departure for this reconstruction of "women in performance." While Anne of Brittany figures as the centerpiece of each panegyric, their different formats yield significantly different results, offering evidence of the conflicting representations of females that were often created and projected by male image-makers and confirming Watanabe-O'Kelly's claim that "Instead of the festival book telling us what actually happened on the day and providing a straightforward window on the event, it tells us rather about the political aims, the allegiances and rivalries, the fears and anxieties of a particular court or city, as they are expressed in that festival" (15). While the accounts I study contain real-life events, the inevitably selective nature of these actions resulted in differing portraits of the royal figure.

On 8 February 1492, following the December 1491 marriage of the Duchess Anne of Brittany and king of France as a result of a peace treaty she negotiated upon the impending defeat of Brittany by the forces of Charles VIII,[17] Anne was crowned queen at Saint-Denis.[18] The next day, following the reception of a delegation of Parisians at the outskirts of Paris, Anne and her entourage proceeded through the city from the Saint-Denis Gate to the Palais Royal. At different stations, dramatic stagings were presented on raised platforms for the queen's diversion.[19] These entry theaters embodied not only tributes to the queen but also consciously or unconsciously documented concerns of the Parisians and underlying tensions between city and kingdom.

Jean Nicolaï's manuscript account (BnF ffr. 24052, fols. 418–25) as well as an anonymous narrative of these events printed by Jean Trepperel in 1492 (BnF Rés. 8° Lb[28] 13), which closely resembles Nicolaï's version, allow us to reconstruct the different stages of this spectacle.[20] While Anne herself may not have owned a copy of this record, that fact that it was propagated in printed form reveals the accessibility of this cultural document to the general populace. Printed for public consumption, this account of Anne's first coronation stands out for its conscientious identification of participants and witnesses (ll. 1–72), especially ecclesiastical figures, and its focus on the different stages of the *sacre*, including the presentation of royal symbols—the crown, scepter and hand of justice (ll. 41–42). The authors thus reminded French subjects of just who the people in power were and what instruments authorized their power.

Of note are the subtler signs of the transfer of female power at this time. Throughout the coronation and entry rituals as well, Anne of France (also known as Anne of Beaujeu), duchess of Bourbon and the king's sister, who had served as regent during Charles VIII's minority, was ever-present, playing a key supporting role to the new queen. "Madame de Bourbon" lent a hand in guiding Anne of Brittany as she entered the Saint-Denis Church (ll. 20–22, 28), helped seat her during the coronation mass (ll. 55–57), and was positioned next to the queen's litter as it approached Notre Dame (ll. 299–301, 306–9). Despite the rather strained relationship between Anne of Brittany and her sister-in-law,[21] who had repeatedly challenged Brittany's autonomy during her regency, Anne of France was stepping back before the new queen, as protocol dictated, observing and aiding her own replacement as the most highly ranked female at court.

Thus, as protagonist of the politico-religious drama that comprised the coronation itself, the queen, placed on center stage, sat on a royal throne richly decorated in gold and silk material that itself stood on a raised platform (see ll. 43–50). However, the original crown, too heavy for Anne of Brittany, had to be held in place on her head during the ceremony by Monseigneur d'Orléans (ll. 51–53), an action symbolically portraying Anne of Brittany's political dependence on French male nobles—and perhaps even prefiguring her difficulties with some of them—and anticipating her second marriage with this figure of support (the future Louis XII).[22] No king needed his crown held by another or replaced by a lighter crown, like the queen (ll. 60–65), at least according to extant accounts. Although a sovereign in her own right as duchess of Brittany, Anne's political status was to change dramatically as French queen.

Just as the coronation had blended religious and political ritual and symbolism through the presence and participation of witnesses from the Church and the royal court, so too the theaters erected along Anne's entry route into Paris offered political and religious interpretations of her assimilation into the French kingdom. Inspired by the recent resolution of the conflict between Anne and Charles, the allegorical play at the Saint-Denis Gate staged Peace's victory over War—rather than France's over Brittany—to the approval of the allegorical ensemble of Church, Nobility, Merchant Class and Labor, accompanied by *Franc Vouloir* (Free/Bold Will), symbolizing France, and *Seure Alliance* (Sure/Secure Alliance), representing Brittany. Presumably designed as a mythological counterpart to Charles VIII and his recent military victory over Brittany—would this scene have offended the newly crowned queen in any way or merely amused her?—a bearded giant representing Hercules stood atop the Saint-Denis Gate and decapitated the seven-headed Cerberus with a large sword (ll. 158–68). The combined allegorical and mythological staging at the Saint-Denis Gate thus diplomatically reconfigured the way in which queens in general, and Anne of Brittany in particular, were often integrated into their husband's realms: through negotiated marriages resulting from peace treaties between military adversaries.[23]

Complementing this staging of the sociopolitical make-up of the French kingdom, the Ponceau Fountain entry theater, articulated around five fleurs-de-lis from which water flowed, offered the welcoming city's self-representation (ll. 169–97). Focusing on its own virtues, rather than those of its female guest, and adopting allegory and acrostics as rhetorical tools that would be subsequently deployed for the queen and her new husband, the Parisians boasted of their renown through the display of their city's name in yellow letters, each one displayed on a red pillar atop of which stood a personified abstraction—*Paris, Amour, Raison, Justice,* and *Science*—accompanied by a cultural or historical figure or institution.[24] *Paris* then recited verses of welcome (vv. 25–35) that also explicated the meaning of the scene to the queen as she passed by.

Counterbalancing these two political *échafauds* [scaffoldings] of the new royal relationship and the city itself at the beginning of the queen's entry was a *tableau vivant* of the queen alone at the last station, the entrance to the Palais Royal (ll. 287–94). Here Anne of Brittany's joint coat of arms, held up by a flying stag and ox above the stage, complemented the figure of the queen on stage holding the city's gift of a ship, symbol of Paris. This unusual portrayal of the French queen alone, who was more often than not paired with her husband in such entry scenes, recalls the *Toison d'Or* illustration and anticipates a number of miniatures that opened manuscript books dedicated to Anne of Brittany, which I analyze throughout this investigation. Indeed, Anne of Brittany's viewing of entry theaters as she processed through Paris in 1492—and later in 1504—could be understood in metaphoric terms as her perusal of a decorated manuscript book.[25] I will return to this analogy shortly.

All but one of the remaining entry theaters in honor of Anne of Brittany's 1492 coronation incorporated both biblical and current political themes.[26] For example, the mise en scène at the Painters' Gate implicitly alluded to the royal couple's recent marriage through the staging of King Solomon's search for and crowning of a spouse (ll. 208–27), a necessarily revised version of history that downplayed the original French-Breton hostilities. Featured with his entourage in the process of securing a judicious marital union,— identified as a "seure alliance," the same term used to personify Brittany at the Saint-Denis Gate—Solomon's actions doubtless reminded Parisian citizens of

Charles VIII's own marital decision and perhaps helped them (and Anne)
forget the critical distinction that military pressures had no counterpart in
the biblical account.[27]

At Saint-Jacques-de-l'Hôpital, an actor playing Charlemagne, mounted
on a horse fifteen hands high, bearing symbols of his empire and the king's
and queen's arms, addressed the queen and then rode to Notre-Dame Cathedral (ll. 228–47). Gordon Kipling suggests that Charlemagne designated the
king's chivalric prowess and imperial designs. He adds: "Manifestations of
the king's personal glory are specially designed to enforce the queen's relative
humility. . . . queens are always encountering epiphanies of their husbands'
glory."[28] Indeed, Anne of Brittany's staged presence through direct and indirect representation was nearly always accompanied by that of the Charles
VIII, despite the fact that the king himself was, by protocol, generally absent
from these celebrations. By contrast, organizers of French kings' entries rarely
incorporated the queen into their stage designs.

This dynamic was borne out in 1492 by the entry theater at the Châtelet,
which staged royal justice. Here the queen's cortège halted before a platform
with three prophets on each side predicting the advent of Christ, their Latin
words inscribed on scrolls they were holding. On center stage, the king and
queen, surrounded by their entourages, flanked the figure of Justice herself.[29]
Kipling analyzes the relationship between king and queen at this staging in
the following way:[30]

> the Queen's femininity . . . ultimately relegates her to . . . a
> supporting role. . . . When Anne of Brittany entered Paris as the
> consort Queen of Charles VIII (1492), she, too, saw herself sitting
> in a Throne of Justice beside her royal spouse. The imagery of the
> Virgin's heavenly coronation is unmistakable. But the six prophets
> who attend this Throne of Majesty ensure that Charles, rather than
> Anne, will claim the symbolic focus of interest. . . . The pageant
> accordingly takes the manifestation of Charles VIII as King of
> Justice as its theme; Anne's *adventus* merely provides the occasion
> for his epiphany. (309)

The refrain of a double ballade written for the occasion and displayed
on stage at the Châtelet, "De veoir le lis acompaigné d'ermynes" [To see the
lily accompanied by ermines],[31] verbally reminded literate viewers of Anne's

dependence on Charles as well. Even specific attention directed at the queen alone in two stanzas provides her with moralistic advice:

N'amenez plus en jeu Panthasillee,
Menalippe ne toute sa puissance,
Que nul n'alegue aujourduy plus Medee,
Semyramus, Dido ne leur chevance,
—Celles ont eu d'aulcuns biens joÿsance—,
Veu qui n'ont faict nulles oeuvres divines.
Laissés les la, prenés rejouÿsance
De veoir le lis acompaignié d'ermynes.

C'est icy la saige royne de Saba,
Qui le roy Salomon a visité;
C'est l'humble Hester qui Asuerus ama
Pour sa beauté et grande humilité;
C'est icy Judic qui en transquilité
A mis son peuple et osté de ruÿnes,
Qui desormais aura jocondité
De veoir le lis acompaignié d'ermynes. (vv. 64–79)

[Do not bring Penthesilea into play any longer, or Menalippa or all her power. Let no one any longer invoke Medea at the present time, or Semiramis, Dido or their wealth—they have enjoyed many riches—given that they have not accomplished any divine deeds. Let them be; rejoice instead in seeing the lily joined by ermines. Here you see the wise queen of Sheba, who visited King Solomon. Here is the humble Esther whom Asuerus loved for her beauty and great humility. Here is Judith, who brought her people tranquility and lifted them out of ruins. From now on she will have happiness in seeing the lily joined by ermines.]

While mythological comparisons with the new French queen are invoked in flattering fashion, the poet carefully distinguishes between powerful and aggressive female warriors or rulers of Antiquity, who are best forgotten—Penthesilea, Medea, Semiramis, and Dido—and more commendably behaved biblical women—the wise Queen of Sheba, the humble Esther, and the rescuer Judith—with whom he implicitly couples Anne of Brittany. The appearance of these famous and infamous women of the past in connection with the French queen and her female contemporaries remained a central theme in her cultural life, one examined more fully in Chapters 3–4. This particular distinction reflects an underlying tension regarding the assimilation of foreign queens in general and Anne of Brittany in particular into the French kingdom. More closely aligned with mythological female warriors and leaders in her capacity as an independent duchess of Brittany and adversary of France prior to her negotiated marriage to Charles VIII, the poet of these verses provides Anne with models to emulate that would be less confrontational, more humble and/or more supportive of her husband and his subjects. Thus, although Anne receives singular attention through a poem composed and staged for her and directly addressed to her at the Châtelet entry theater, these words of advice and counsel offered by the city to the queen through mythological analogies assume a didactic tone. Echoing one of the overarching themes of the 1492 entry, the refrain returns again and again to Anne's coupling with the king:

> Tresexcelente princesse soubz la nue,
> Dame royalle, tu as evidens signes.
> Quel joye on a de ta noble venue,
> De v[e]oir *le lis acompaigné d'ermynes*. (vv. 88–91, my emphasis)

> [Most excellent princess beneath the heavens, royal lady, you see manifest signs. What joy we have upon your noble arrival to see *the lily joined by ermines*.]

We observe, then, different levels of women in performance at the time of Anne of Brittany's 1492 coronation and Parisian entry. The queen herself was protagonist of a moving theater viewed by Paris citizens as it wended its way through the streets of Paris, accompanied by her sister-in-law in a new supporting role. The queen's comportment during this procession, like that of Anne of France, would have been dictated by royal protocol. At the same time, Anne of Brittany joined her subjects as spectator of allegorical scenarios that staged aspects of her own political history through predominantly female personifications and literal stand-ins for the queen herself, roles acted by Parisians according to theatrical protocols. The insistent coupling on entry stages of the new queen with the king, whose own qualities were emphasized in this tribute to Anne of Brittany, was accompanied by advice specially addressed to the queen through the use of biblical models. The *Toison d'Or* miniature examined above suggests in fact that Anne assimilated this message, internalized it, integrated it into her life, and then had the image of herself reigning among Christian virtues visually restaged.

Several issues associated with Anne of Brittany during this entry ritual—marriage, motherhood (see n. 29), the definition of queenship, famous women, female vices and virtues—would repeatedly resurface throughout her lifetime. My literal and metaphoric reading of her "book(s) of life" seeks to expose the underlying contradictions that emerge from the texts and images in her library as well as that of her female contemporaries. Just like the *tableaux vivants* of Anne's Parisian entry, the issues of greatest concern to Anne, the French court, and her subjects were most often articulated in allegorical form.

## The Image of Noble Women in Marriage Ceremonials: Anne de Foix and Anne of Brittany

Subsequent to Anne of Brittany's 1492 coronation ceremonies, but prior to her 1504 *sacre*, the French queen was associated with a spate of royal activities that were rendered into memorable book accounts: her marriage in 1499 to Louis XII, commemorated through a volume of Plutarch's *Discours sur le mariage de Pollion et Eurydice* dedicated to Anne of Brittany herself (1499), to which I will return; the reception in Blois of Philip, archduke of Austria, and his wife Joan of Castille (October 1501);[32] and the marriage of Anne de Foix to Ladislaus of Hungary in September 1502. Anne of Brittany commissioned Pierre Choque, her Breton herald, to redact an account of the receptions and festivities surrounding the coronation and marriage of her cousin, Anne de Foix, to King Ladislaus. This commission reminds us of Anne of Brittany's significant role in the selection of a wife for Ladislaus,[33] a contribution that figured among the few powers the French queen possessed.[34] As the first known coronation book to have been acquired by the French queen,[35] it underscores Anne's personal interest in the commemoration of such royal events,[36] and may well have inspired the specially made manuscript version of André de la Vigne's account of Anne of Brittany's second coronation in 1504 that the author offered the French queen (see below).

Choque's account of Anne de Foix's coronation has come down to us today in two unusual versions that complement each other. BnF ms. ffr. 90 contains seven fragile, large-sized folded folios of vellum, each decorated with series of coats of arms, although blank spaces intended for other images remain.[37] Folio 5 alone, which unfolds out to four times the size of one folio, bears some 70 coats of arms, making it a veritable poster of heraldic signs (Figure 4). At the top of this large folio are featured three arms, that of Louis XII, the joint arms of Anne of Brittany as French queen, and the arms of Brittany. Indeed, these folios were originally configured as a scroll akin to a roll of heraldic signs.[38] The large dimension of the unfolded folios may have been consciously adopted to reflect the grandeur of the subject.

In editing Choque's text in 1861, Leroux de Lincy realized that the manuscript folios of the two-part narrative were transposed in ms. 90. The account actually begins on folio 5 and opens with Choque's salutation to Anne of Brittany, followed by a description of Anne de Foix's reception in Crema (13 July), Brescia (16 July), Verona (18 July), Vicenza (22 July), Padua (25 July) and Venice (1–5 August) during the first stage of her journey through Italy.[39] A closing note to the French queen, dated 17 August, ends on folio 7. Folios 1–4 provide an account of Anne de Foix's peregrinations through the territories of the Hungarian king. It opens with another dedication to Anne of Brittany, followed by details about her cousin's departure by boat from Venise (20 August), her welcome in Segna (23 August) and Zaghreb (5 September), her reception in Alba Regia (Albregast) by Ladislaus (September 27), which preceded her marriage, coronation and related festivities there (29 September), and her arrival in Buda (3 October) for a royal feast (6 October). Choque addresses Anne of Brittany again at the end of his account, which is dated 16 December 1502. Whether BnF ms. 90 was actually the queen's personal copy is difficult to confirm, although Leroux de Lincy assumes that Choque's claims to having transcribed and painted the coats of arms in the version he offered the queen pertain to this manuscript.[40]

The British Library houses a partial version of Choque's account: folios 69r–78v of Stowe manuscript 584 contain a nearly complete version of the second stage of Anne de Foix's coronation journey, namely the passage through Hungarian territories from late August to early October 1502.[41] Unlike the BnF manuscript, however, Stowe 584 is decorated with nine miniatures as well as two sets of coats of arms, those of the French royal couple (Louis XII and Anne of Brittany) and those of the Hungarian royal couple (Laudislaus and Anne de Foix). This latter display across the top of folio 69r and again following the dedication on folio 69v visually confirms the dynamics

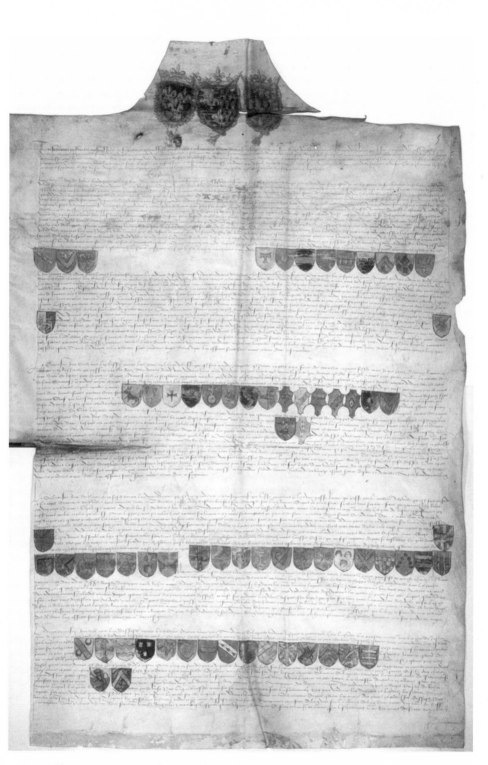

4. Pierre Choque, *Discours sur le voyage d'Anne de Foix*, Paris BnF ffr. 90, fol. 5r: Opening folio with royal arms and arms of princes. Bibliothèque Nationale de France.

of political alliances between foreign queens and kings, such as that of Louis XII and Anne of Brittany, and Anne de Foix and Ladislaus. The arms of both females, once married, incorporated into half of their escutcheons their husband's emblems, which themselves remained unchanged subsequent to their nuptials. In other words, it was the queen, more often than not hailing from a foreign territory, who was integrated into her husband's realm emblematically and politically. As we learned above, Anne of Brittany was actually her first husband's military and political enemy prior to their union. Anne de Foix's marriage, on the other hand, was part of an alliance between France, Hungary, and Venice against the Turks and Habsburgs.

Two sets of relationships associated with these events and their manuscript record figure centrally in our analysis in this chapter of women in performance: the author's function as the queen's hired writer and actual witness of and participant in the international ceremonies he describes and the underlying association between the commissioner of this account and its subject—between the two cousins named Anne who were both queens married to kings of foreign territories. Indeed, the often subtly wrought, complex relationships between female benefactors and male authors and illustrators lie at the crux of my investigation of female empowerment in early sixteenth-century France.

Numerous passages in this account inform us about Choque's relationship to his patroness. In closing the first section of his narrative, the author makes it clear that Anne of Brittany commissioned him to write the work: "it was your pleasure to commission me to come on this present voyage and inform you about the honors made for this lady" (185). In his dedication to the second part of his narrative, Anne of Brittany's herald at arms adds:

en ensuivant vostre commandement et exersant mon office au
moins mal que j'ay sceu comprandre et faire, vous ay fait savoir
de ces honneurs et accueil faictz a tres haulte, tres puissante, tres
excellante princesse et ma très redoubtée dame, Madame Anne de
Fouex. (422)

[in obeying your command and exercising my duty in the least
poor way that I know how to do, I have informed you about these
honors and the welcome made to the most noble, most powerful,
most excellent princess and my most revered lady, Madame Anne
de Foix.]

In addition, Choque emphasizes in both of his dedications to Anne that her interest in noble and solemn things (166, 422), especially those resulting from virtuous behavior, and the details about marriage alliances and related honors motivated his account. Choque's second dedication reiterates the centrality of virtuous deeds in his patron's life.[42] In yet another manner that echoes the 1492 Châtelet entry theater and the liminal miniature in the *Toison d'Or* manuscript, Anne of Brittany's own virtuous behavior is acknowledged by her protégé.

Focusing on his own court status and artistic talents, Choque reveals at the end of the first section of his account that he is a "new officer" who has both written the text and painted the images in the manuscript he offers the queen (185). He adopts similar terms at the end of the second part of his work, adding that linguistic difficulties hampered his endeavor:

> Ma souveraine dame, il vous plaira m'avoir pour excusé, s'il y a quelque chose mal couchée et mise soit en escripture ou autrement ; et moy pardonner pour tant que leur langaige est estrange et que n'ay sceu du tout sçavoir les faitz du pays comme si eusse entendu leur langaige. Et une autre foys je mecteray peine a myeulx faire, à l'aide de Dieu. (439)

> [My sovereign lady, please excuse anything poorly stated and written or otherwise expressed and pardon me, since their language is foreign (strange) and I was unable to learn the facts about the country as I would have been able to do had I understood their language. And another time I will strive to do better with God's aid.]

Thus, in the rhetorical fashion of the times, the court chronicler exalts his patroness while minimizing, if not belittling, his own literary talents. Of unusual note, however, is the Breton herald's contribution as illustrator of his own account.[43] Less unusual, but nonetheless noteworthy, is the active participation of Choque, or Bretaigne, as he identifies himself, in Anne de Foix's receptions and coronation rituals to which he makes several references throughout his narration. His role as royal representative entails the display of his benefactor's arms. For example, Choque describes his role in Alba Regia, the site of Anne de Foix's marriage and coronation (my emphasis):

> The aforementioned lady descended accompanied by Duke Lorens, son of the king of Bosnia, by the bishops of Nytice and Zaghreb,

and by many great lords and prelates; and before them walked
the officers in arms Agenetz, at the right, and myself at the left,
wearing the coats of arms of France and Brittany, and your arms on
a standard and depicted in the heraldry of a queen-duchess. (428)[44]

Except in this passage and his dedications to Anne of Brittany, Choque almost
always references Anne of Brittany in association with Louis XII, whether in
the context of their official representatives (167),[45] the display of their coats
of arms,[46] which reappear as symbols of power on the manuscript pages in
both the BnF and BL manuscripts and in the manuscript miniatures of Stowe
584, along with those of the king and queen of Hungary, or their letters of
authorization that were officially presented by various ambassadors (433). As
the queen's ersatz eyewitness, Choque also transmits his astonishment at the
magnificent sights he beholds, repeatedly registering his observations in the
most superlative of terms.[47]

Anne de Foix's perspective was different than that of Pierre Choque, who
sought to regale his patroness with accounts of royal splendor. As in the 1492
festival book of Anne of Brittany's coronation and Parisian entry, there is little
mention of the new Hungarian queen's personal reaction to the extraordinary
events surrounding her marriage and coronation in the author's account. According to Jean d'Auton's contemporary remarks, however, Anne de Foix was
very reluctant to leave France for Hungary. While these underlying tensions
were recorded in his chronicles,[48] implicitly demonstrating how much women
were pawns in European political affairs, no sign of such disharmony surfaces in Choque's rendering of her marriage voyage. This distinction between
the two accounts underscores the contradictions between the official face
displayed during royal ceremonials and the underlying emotions of the individual, a situation that was doubtless all the more traumatic for the women
undergoing dramatic life changes in the process. Nonetheless, as these accounts suggest, despite behind-the-scene tensions, the public performances
of these royal women were carefully controlled and codified. Indeed, these
female performances constituted dramas about kingdoms as much as, if not
more than, the parading of individual noble women. Unfortunately, Anne
de Foix died just four years after her marriage, having successfully fulfilled
her expected role of bearing offspring, a daughter and son, to the previously
thrice-married but childless Ladislaus.

Like her cousin, the queen, in 1492, although in even more elaborate
fashion, Anne de Foix played the role of protagonist on the center stage of a

moving theater as she and her entourage traveled through the various towns and cities of Italy and the Hungarian territories. Generally speaking, her entries through the different Italian cities resembled French entries in that the different groups of specially attired townspeople came to greet the queen outside of their city. In fact, the numbers of citizens turning out to welcome Anne de Foix during her journey from France to Hungary were stunning, although they were likely exaggerated for effect: 4,000 greeted her outside the city gates of Vicenza (172), 5,000 outside Padua (174), more than 12,000 were on the scene in Venice (177), and up to 10,000 men appeared in Veglia to protect the queen against any potential Turkish threats (424). Escorted by her greeters into the various cities, which were often decorated in the queen's honor, Anne de Foix was, like her French counterparts, nearly always protected by a canopy carried over her head as she wended her way through the streets of each town.[49] Some cities proudly displayed their specialties, such as the relics of Padua (175) and the city treasure of Venice (181). Following her entry, each city regaled the guest of honor with a banquet, music, dance, and other forms of entertainment. Unlike French entries, however, transport on water figured among the queen's mode of travel.[50] Not only did she travel in all forms of boats,[51] but entertainment was occasionally staged on boats as well. Choque thus sought to dazzle the French queen through his account of this extraordinary series of celebrations.

The receptions in Anne de Foix's honor included dramatic presentations much like those Anne of Brittany viewed along the entry route into Paris in 1492, but of a slightly different nature. Vicenza's theatrical reception, for example, staged three examples of female power: politico-religious, politico-allegorical, and physical. At the first site, angels in red tunics emblazoned with the arms of France, Brittany, Foix, and Hungary, and perched on the branches of a tree of Jesse, welcomed the Hungarian queen. Above the Virgin Mary, featured in the tree's center, a crowned Lady Nobility, dressed in gold, offered Anne de Foix the city's greetings, service, and support, while wishing that her marriage might serve all of Christianity (173). At a second site, the Hungarian queen-to-be and her cortege viewed a scene of Fortune's wheel: twelve bejeweled, crowned queens stood on a large, continuously turning wheel, signifying that they were joined together to destroy adverse Fortune (173). At another site, each of three beautiful teenage goddesses dressed in revealing red satin dresses, wearing jewels and displaying hair so long it touched the ground, conveyed her power to the guest of honor (173–74). Thus, a female alliance to destroy adverse Fortune, and the power of youth and beauty aimed to provide Anne de Foix with its service and support. Unlike the 1492 stagings in Anne of Brittany's honor, here females alone, including Anne de Foix's alter egos, are exalted. Subsequently, she is celebrated more as a mate of Ladislaus than in association with political personified figures, like her cousin.

Venice's entry performances, unique in Anne de Foix's travels, given their geographic location, were, however, politically charged, with repeated references to the Turkish threat. A series of stunning maritime stagings featured exotically dressed characters in various alliances and configurations. The royal boat itself in which she traveled served as a dramatic platform with some 240 richly dressed and bejeweled female dancers greeting the queen as she entered the boat and performing during her voyage (177). Not only did 1,500 other vessels filled with nobles accompany the royal boat (178), but several provided entertainment as well. On one boat, three crowned queens with sword in hand, signifying France, Hungary, and Venice, victoriously defeated three Turks, the appearance and coronation of a lady dressed in French style suggesting that Anne de Foix figured centrally in the political alliance against the Turks.[52] In a galley bearing ladies dressed in Moorish costumes, one queen paid homage to another queen dressed *à la française*, stating that she wished to become her heiress (179–80), while another political staging of women showed Venice honoring France. As a theatrical finale, two boats appeared alongside that of Anne de Foix, one displaying the banners and coats of arms of the triple alliance. Rather than the allegorical entry theaters in Anne of Brittany's Parisian ceremonials, Anne de Foix witnessed stagings of symbols and emblems or her alter egos in Italy, with women figuring centrally among the performers.

Venice's banquet in honor of the Hungarian queen (182–85) provided a third kind of dramatic entertainment through a striking variety of dinner courses mounted on numerous chariots:[53]

The third course was a triumphant chariot filled with greens;
the fifth was a nude siren painting herself; the sixth a wild man
holding a ducal shield, the hat serving as crest, in the other hand
Hercules' club, then a flask of gold, a lion, then a two-headed
siren with two tails, a man at arms, three goddesses, a fountain
with lions' faces, a bear, a crocodile, a dolphin in the sea, three
goddesses holding their veils and several ships in the form of
carrickes, galleys, or swifts, several kinds of lions, dragons, snakes,

cities and towers. And this day were counted 400 men at the
banquet carrying the aforementioned fictional scenes, cups, flasks,
saucers and other courses of gold and silver. (183)

Following the meal itself, other exotic figures and animals appeared in various scenarios, including political stagings of a topsy-turvey world threatened
with the Turkish menace, suggesting that the new alliance associated with
Anne de Foix's marriage would join together to destroy the Turks (183).

In contrast to her lavish reception in Venice, Anne de Foix's entries in
Hungarian territory were less ostentatious but no less welcoming.[54] Choque's
description of the marriage and coronation ceremonies is surprisingly brief
(432–33), perhaps due to the language barriers mentioned earlier, although he
elaborates upon the royal feast in Buda (434–35), whose remarkable beauty
he notes.[55]

In Stowe 584, miniatures of a mediocre quality depicting this second
stage of the queen's travels offer visual details that complement the text. Besides the two series of arms representing France, Brittany, Foix, and Hungary
that open the manuscript and reappear at the end of Choque's address to the
queen, the reader also discovers visual renditions of the real-life and theatrical
stagings, absent from BnF ms. 90, but frequently announced in the narrative
itself. A full-page miniature (70v) features a crowned Ladislaus in an exterior
setting near the sea, along with an enormous crowd of men with banners
bearing coats of arms. This illustration sets the stage for the illustration of
Anne de Foix's arrival in Alba Regia. In yet another dramatic setting on the
water, she appears on horseback in the middle of an entourage of men (and
two females), dressed in gold brocade and wearing a black headdress made
fashionable by Anne of Brittany (71v) (Figure 5). Many men hold banners,
including a large one bearing Ladislaus's arms. Two of Anne of Brittany's
heralds bear the French queen's arms on their capes. Other miniatures depict
scenes that stirred Choque, who was doubtless desirous as well of conveying
to his patroness their particularly foreign or exotic nature.[56]

While Choque's repeated descriptions of the ceremonials surrounding
Anne de Foix's travels through Italian and Hungarian territories echo those
of other royal entries, underscoring the interchangeability of the royal figure
in procession at the time, he occasionally singles out the Hungarian queen's
special assets, calling attention to her remarkable beauty (433). He also depicts
an intimate moment when, upon meeting her husband for the first time,
Anne de Foix acknowledges Ladislaus's superiority by kneeling before him

5. Pierre Choque, *Discours des ceremonies du sacre et mariage d'Anne de Foix*, London, British Library Stowe 584, fol. 71v: Anne de Foix arrives in Alba Regia to meet King Ladislaus of Hungary. © The British Library Board, Stowe 584.

three times, an action likely dictated by protocol. Her inadvertent blushing at this moment is quickly glossed over by Choque as if to direct attention away from a slight faux pas in order to focus instead on the queen's innate nobility:

> On this day the king was dressed in a garment of red tooled velour, with a silk cap of various violet shades. The aforementioned lady knelt three times, once at the beginning of the carpet, once ten feet from the king, the other when the king held out his hand to her. And the lady changed color. But it is impossible that any lady could offer a more noble profile and bearing than she, for she showed clearly on this day that she was of royal issue. (429)

Unlike stagings surrounding Anne of Brittany's reception by the Parisians in 1492, the various urban ceremonies welcoming Anne de Foix in 1502 celebrated and blessed her anticipated love encounter with Ladislaus before their first, very public meeting. For example, a scenario in Vicenza featured Cupid sitting atop Fortune's wheel, turning another world with his foot, while two accompanying angels sang *"Benedictus qui venit"* to the queen (173). At another site along the same entry route, the god of love offered golden apples to Anne de Foix as she passed by to promote good fortune, renown, and wealth.[57] In Venice too, the queen viewed the god of love in another welcoming pageant:

> The first was a galley on which there was a god of love upon a pillar decorated with greens, who pointed to the aforementioned lady, saying these words: *Embrace love.* Below him stood ladies dressed in Italian style and doctors holding books, each of them stating that the only life [worth living] was that of lovers. And they also found [this idea] in writing. (178)

At the lavish banquet thrown by the Venetians in Anne de Foix's honor, Cupid appeared yet again as part of a series of the *tableaux* described above.[58] As the grand finale of this banquet entertainment, Anne de Foix was treated to the famous drama of Paris's seduction of Helen, with both Cupid and Venus playing roles in its staging (183–84). Although a somewhat ambiguous choice of a love story to depict in Anne de Foix's honor, given its tragic ramifications, the legend nonetheless bore relevance to the current celebration, because of the similar coupling of a foreign queen and king, the beauty of the young royal female, and the love between the two mythological characters. Indeed, Helen figured among the "famous women" whose biographies circulated at the French court and around Europe at the time (see Chapters 3–4). The repeated allusions to Cupid and, by implication, to the anticipated love match between the new king and queen in these entry theaters may have been inspired by Italian tradition, since no such signs appeared in earlier entries of French queens or during Anne's reception in Hungarian territories. Nonetheless, echoing the many visual references he must have witnessed in the Italian *tableaux vivants*, Choque explicitly describes the king's attachment to his bride at the end of his account: "Le Roy ayme bien la Royne. Et jamais à Royne n'auroit esté signé apoinctement de douaire par les seigneurs du pays fors à elle" [The king likes the queen very much. And a dower never would have been granted to any other queen] (438).

Unlike the marriage ceremony of Anne de Foix, a public event for which Choque provides a detailed account, little information about the 1499 nuptials of Anne of Brittany and Louis XII in Nantes has come down to us. However, the absence of political hostilities between the two spouses—in fact, Louis XII had earlier supported Anne against Charles VIII[59]—and Anne's more powerful position as an independent duchess of Brittany significantly altered the negotiations for and dynamics of her second marriage, in comparison with the first.[60]

Although not recording the particulars of the wedding of Anne of Brittany and Louis XII in 1499 or focusing on Anne as a queen in procession, an exquisitely decorated manuscript belonging to the French queen, currently housed in the National Library of Russia in Saint Petersburg,[61] offers an interesting display of females and marriage advice to newlyweds.[62] Ms. Fr. Q. v. III.3, which contains the translation of Plutarch's *Discourse on the Marriage of Pollion and Eurydice* by Jean Laudet, a native of Nantes,[63] bears Anne of Brittany's coat of arms, supported by two angels, on folio 46.[64] While Laborde (132) and Aulotte (610) both claim that the manuscript belonged to Louis XII (132), the presence of Anne's arms on the last folio suggests rather that it was her book, as Voronova and Stergligov believe (189). Eleven half-page miniatures by Jean Pichore, who painted a number of other works for the French court at this time,[65] punctuate the treatise with visual renditions of Plutarch's advice. As in many of the Italian entry pageants staged for Anne de Foix, the frontispiece miniature (IV) portrays an allegory with Venus on center stage.[66] Here she stands nude (partially covered with a transparent veil)

on a pedestal in the very middle of a room, accompanied by the three Graces
in contemporary dresses, positioned at the upper left. In the lower left, Mercury interacts with the goddess, while Lady Persuasion at the right, dressed
in red, points with her left hand to Venus. Voronova and Sterligov claim
that "This miniature illustrates the main idea of the text in allegorical form:
Mercury, messenger of the Gods, explains that a marriage must be based on
love (Venus in the centre) accompanied by the Three Graces (women on the
left). The woman on the right symbolizes a sense of responsibility, an essential
attribute of marriage" (189).[67] The exquisite miniature offers visual confirmation of Plutarch's first precept:

> Here begins the first precept containing a beautiful comparison
> representing three things necessary in marriage, that is, eloquence,
> persuasion and mutual grace. Indeed, the Ancients applied and
> created the simulacrum and statue of the god Mercury, ambassador
> and interpreter of the gods' will, near that of the goddess Venus,
> because pleasure and nuptial desire require above all else prayer
> and discussion exchanged between the man and woman joined in
> marriage.[68]

Plutarch's text offers marital advice to both men and women, although the
majority of his precepts target the bride rather than the groom, suggesting that
this particular manuscript book may have been a wedding gift destined to teach
Anne moralities about her conduct as a wife during her second marriage.

The miniature on folio 42r, which accompanies the following advice of
Plutarch, displays a double portrait of Anne and Louis:[69]

> Plato advised old men to be particularly respectful of the young,
> so that the young should respect them in turn. Where the old are
> shameless, he says, there is no modesty or reverence in the young.
> A husband should keep this in mind, and respect no one more than
> he does his wife. The bedroom will be her school of discipline or
> immorality. A husband who enjoys pleasures which he prohibits in
> his wife is like a man who tells his wife to fight the enemy to whom
> he has himself surrendered.[70]

According to Nicole Hochner (253), this illustration provides scenes before
and after the marriage of Anne of Brittany and Louis XII, although Laborde

interprets this miniature more generally as a depiction of how the husband should maintain respect toward his wife (133). Both of these interpretations are relevant if we consider the scene at the left as a visual depiction of Louis XII's modesty and respect toward Anne of Brittany—perhaps this even represents the marriage scene—while the right-hand illustration, situated inside the nuptial chamber alluded to in the precept, features a two-way exchange of ideas between the king and the queen, confirmed by both of their "talking hands." The importance of couples' sharing in discussion is the hallmark of Plutarch's work from the outset. Perhaps these images were intended to evoke the author's addressees, Eurydice and Pollianos, as well, through an assimilation of Louis XII and Anne of Brittany to this mythological couple.

Whatever Pichore's exact motivation in painting this miniature, we, unlike the couple's contemporaries who would not have seen this book, view the royal couple in an intimate setting, that of the conjugal bedroom. Unlike the entry accounts discussed elsewhere in this chapter, which reconstructed public events, including Anne de Foix's marriage to King Ladislaus, this book commemorating Anne of Brittany's marriage to Louis XII was at once more intimate and more moralistic. The introductory lines of Laudet's sixteenth-century translation of Plutarch, cited by Aulotte (610–11), confirm the intimate nature of many of these marital recommendations (my translation):

> Plutarch's *Discourse on the Marriage of Pollianus and Eurydice,*
> briefly gathered and organized in short chapters and texts by
> similarities so that you may more easily commit [them] to memory
> and forever remember them. Hoping and begging that the muses,
> ladies of peace, harmony and concord, might aspire to your
> Venus, that is, to your matrimonial union and coupling, and show
> themselves propitious and favorable to it. To them it is no longer
> convenient or easy to tune sweet harp or other musical instrument,
> save the consonance and concord that belongs to the marital state
> and domestic relationship through sweet and gracious speech and
> philosophical harmony.

Besides advice about sexual coupling, however, Plutarch's precepts, which include moralistic counsel to females very much in tune with the late medieval mentality, present in literal form the importance of women's virtuous behavior, whose more abstract image we saw earlier in the *Toison d'Or* liminal miniature of Anne of Brittany's association with Christian virtues.[71] Thus, the

*Discours sur le mariage de Pollion et Eurydice* represents a different kind of display of women in performance, for it is not based on staged public processions of females. Rather it offers a private, more intimate portrait of a royal marriage with images depicting a series of interior scenes, more appropriate than public spaces for the transmission of Plutarch's marital advice to the French counterparts of Pollianus and Eurydice, but especially to the bride.

## The Literary Reconstruction of Queens: Anne of Brittany's and Claude of France's Parisian Entries (1504, 1517)

Although Anne of Brittany married Louis XII, successor of her first husband, in January 1499, just nine months after Charles VIII's death, it was nearly six years later that she was officially crowned for the second time and made her entry into Paris.[72] The delay may have had more to do with the king's image than the queen's, for Anne's coronation and entry into Paris in November 1504 were apparently intended to reinforce the prestige, authority, and ultimate legitimacy of Louis XII in reviving popular support for the monarch,[73] in light of recent political setbacks and the king's fragile health that had weakened the image of his royal court and power.[74] Scholars have also suggested that Anne of Brittany counted on her coronation to assert her authority at court, in particular vis-à-vis Maréchal de Gié, who had implicated her in an incident for which he had been accused of lèse-majesté.[75] Thus, as suggested earlier, festivals and festival books often came into being at times of instability and crises. Anne's second *sacre* may have also been organized to celebrate the renewal of the engagement of her daughter Claude of France and Charles of Luxembourg, the future Charles V, through the Treaties of Blois (22 September 1504).[76] Whatever the exact motivation for these festivities, the shaping of the political image of the king, the queen, or both royal figures, figured centrally in the court's organization and realization of the ceremonies surrounding Anne of Brittany's coronation in 1504. However, the city's participation in the entry ritual was not necessarily inspired by the same concerns.

André de la Vigne, the French queen's secretary, authored the principal account of his benefactor's coronation and entry into Paris in 1504; it was subsequently transcribed, illustrated, and dedicated in a finely prepared manuscript to the queen herself.[77] Housed today in the Rothschild Collection at Waddesdon Manor in England, manuscript 22 is an exquisite volume illuminated by a Parisian artist known as the Master of the *Chronique Scan-daleuse*.[78] La Vigne's written testimony accounts for the events, personalities, and actions surrounding Anne of Brittany's second coronation at Saint-Denis in great detail (ll. 11–407).[79] He reports the welcome extended to the queen outside of Paris by the many city dignitaries (ll. 391–698),[80] carefully identi-fies the many nobles making up the royal cortege as it proceeded through Paris, noting the ordered change in city personnel privileged enough to hold up the canopy over the queen's head (ll. 703–930), mentions Anne's official reception at Notre Dame (ll. 980–95), and describes the banquet held in her honor at the Palais Royal (ll. 1001–1164). Substantially more informative than the printed festival book of her 1492 coronation and Parisian entry, Waddes-don ms. 22 also furnishes an illustrated version of the ceremonials through marginal decorations and three miniatures that depict the critical stages of this celebration: the crowning of Anne of Brittany at Saint-Denis (2), her arrival at the Saint-Denis Gate (76), and the "souper" following her entry (108). Even more than the earlier Nicolaï and Trepperel entry accounts, this festival book was a phenomenon in its own right. Its verbal reconstruction of events, including the *tableaux vivants* staged along the queen's entry route and descriptions of the processions and their participants, above all of Anne of Brittany herself, is dramatically interpreted through decoration and full-page illustrations. This dialogue between textual and artistic expression on nearly every folio of the commemoration book contrasts decidedly with the extant 1492 accounts, which targeted a bourgeois readership, as it takes on a more panegyric tone.

A study of the limited details provided by La Vigne about the entry the-aters presented along the rue Saint-Denis in Anne of Brittany's honor (ll. 709, 939–79) leads to the conclusion that they were considerably less personalized than those created on the occasion of Anne of Brittany's first coronation or those organized for her successors, Mary Tudor and Claude of France. Absent from nearly all the stagings in 1504 were personal allusions to the queen or her function, as the city focused more on its own institutions and corporations. What explains this striking absence of symbolism personally linked with the queen? Was it a conscious response on the part of the entry organizers to the king's scandalous divorce from Jeanne de France in order to marry Anne?[81] Were the Parisians less supportive of celebrating a queen who had already been crowned once? Did the city resist involvement because of the costs incurred during preparations for a postponed entry two years earlier?[82] Did the citizens of Paris simply lack the necessary time to organize a more personalized entry, since they had been accorded only a month lead time for preparations?[83] Or was it the absence of any overall coordination of the entry stagings?[84]

Whatever the answer, a measurable distance between royally sanctioned and urban-generated images sets the 1504 entry theaters apart from those of Anne's first entry as Charles VIII's queen in 1492 and from the entries of her two successors. Thus, whereas the *tableaux vivants* staged to celebrate Anne of Brittany's coronation in 1492 had imparted an individualized political message associated with the peace resulting from France's military defeat of Brittany and her union with Charles VIII (Saint-Denis Gate) and a personalized staging that featured the queen alone (Palais Royal), those marking Anne's second entry into Paris welcomed the queen in a fashion visibly less engaging and less directly adapted to her political and social role. Only the *mystère* presented at the Painters' Gate was designed with any personalized allusions. Here, Anne's supposedly strong biblical heritage was staged to remind Parisians about her innate virtue (ll. 951–57). Spectators, including the queen, discovered the life and virtues of five biblical women named Anne in this entry theater: *Helcana* (Hannah, Anne), mother of Samuel and wife of Elkanah, who had been sterile for a long time (1 Samuel 1: 1–2); Anne, wife of the elder Tobias, known for her charity and compassion; Anne, wife of the younger Tobias, who was also the mother of Sarah; Anne, daughter of Samuel, who had predicted the advent of Christ; and Saint Anne, mother of the Virgin Mary.[85] An actor punctuated his explanation of the *tableau* (vv. 22–46) with praise for Anne herself, whose behavior emulated that of her namesakes:

> Semblablement Anne, royne de France
> Par sa bonté, par sa magnificence,
> Jusques icy, tant yver comme esté,
> A preservé son peuple de souffrance,
> Dont aujourduy pour vraye obeyssa[n]ce
> Paris sans per en fait solempnyté. (vv. 40–45)

> [Similarly Anne, queen of France, through her goodness and
> generosity, up to this time, as much in winter as summer, has kept
> her subjects from suffering; therefore today, in true obedience, Paris
> without peer solemnly celebrates her.]

On the one hand, given that two of the Annes depicted on stage—the mothers of Samuel and of the Virgin Mary—had had difficulties conceiving, it is

possible that the organizers of this entry theater were also implicitly referring
to the queen's failure to produce a male heir up to that point in time and hope
that she might now give birth to Louis XII's successor. No offspring had survived her first marriage with King Charles VIII, and Anne and Louis XII had
only a daughter, Claude, born five years earlier (October 1499). La Vigne's
court-sanctioned account, on the other hand, avoids all mention of such an
association in its abbreviated description of this entry theater. Such popular
anxiety about Louis XII's successor thus underscores a distinction, if not tension, between the royal and municipal reconstructions of the queen.[86]

This staging at the Painters' Gate, where an actor represented the queen
in the middle of five biblical Annes, reminds us of the potentially confusing coincidence of certain characters on stage and the queen herself who, as
spectator of her alter ego, also played the dramatic role of the star of her own
entry, like the Parisians acting in her name on stage. Beautifully dressed,
decorated, and glorified, Anne of Brittany, placed at the center of her own
narrative, was thus staged like the personifications of the living theaters that
she viewed. All her actions, like those of the actors re-presenting her, were pre-
determined. This dynamic anticipates the reading process the queen would
make as reader-spectator of her manuscript book containing the account of
her entry, for the close ties between the literal and metaphoric at the time of
the entry were subsequently reproduced in a "dialogue" between text, image,
and marginal ornamentation in ms. 22, as I detail more fully below.

All the other entry theaters created in Anne's honor in 1504 were more
site specific in subject matter. No visual political statement whatsoever about
her queenship was conveyed by the municipal authorities in these stagings.
Rather than defining how the city perceived Anne's queenship, as had been
the case in 1492, they presented what defined the city and its guilds and organizations. At the Saint-Denis Gate, for example, Parisians constructed their
self-image in terms commonly adopted to represent royalty, borrowed from
courtly literature itself. The city literally and metaphorically opened itself up
to the queen by displaying the allegory of the Heart of Paris: the personified
figures of Honor and Loyalty were perched inside a large heart supported by
Justice, Clergy, and Commoner (ll. 714–20),[87] as an actor delivered verses of
welcome to Anne (vv. 4–21). While water flowed from "la representacion" (l.
940) [the image? the statue?] of a small nude child to Parisian spectators at
the Ponceau Fountain *échafaud* (ll. 939–44), two other entry theaters reenacted religious dramas. The Confraternity of the Passion presented the drama
of the Transfiguration and other scenes from the Passion at the Trinity (ll.

945–49) and a mystery play of the Three Kings' adoration of the infant Jesus was staged at the Saint-Innocents (ll. 964–65).[88] Kipling's suggestion that this religious theme "reminded Anne of Brittany of her duties as mother of the future king" (315) implies that this entry theater may have consciously or unconsciously echoed the Painters' Gate scenario.[89]

The orderly visual performance of the French queen's *sacre* and procession through Paris in 1504[90] was as filled with protocol, symbolism, and role playing as the performances she viewed along the entry route, often portrayed through female personifications. Like urban actors figuring her persona, Anne of Brittany played a role according to script and expectations.

After the queen viewed the entry theater staged at the Palais Royal,[91] ecclesiastics, university professors, and students welcomed her at Notre-Dame. La Vigne furnishes many details about the participants at the banquet (ll. 1025–91) given in the queen's honor at the Palais Royal, the lavish and multiple courses served at the "souper" (ll. 1091–1112), the exquisite dinnerware and utensils employed for the occasion (ll. 1129–42), and the entertainment (ll. 1154–61). Although the latter did not approach the extravagance of Anne de Foix's banquet in Venice, La Vigne's assessment of the event was nonetheless filled with superlatives: "Car j'ose dire et affirmer pour verité que depuis le temps que entrees de roys et de roynes en France se font, ne fut veue plus belle compaignye ensemble que lors elle estoit" [For I dare say and affirm that, in truth, during all the times we have had kings' and queens' entries in France, never was there seen such beautiful company together as was the case on this occasion] (ll. 1112–15).

In documenting the staged events associated with Anne's coronation and entry, the literary and artistic reconstruction found in manuscript 22 functions explicitly as a testimonial to court ritual. Whereas the city, not the queen, took center stage in the 1504 entry theaters—Anne of Brittany was essentially replaced by religious characters or urban-centered personifications—author and artist of the queen's special manuscript account downplayed the city's theatrical contribution to the cultural event in order to capitalize on celebratory images of Anne and the display of her symbols and emblems. Indeed, manuscript 22 is a document about political performances that also embodies performance, for the unique configuration of its physical properties produces a codicological drama that reinforces the text's cultural assumptions. Through a coordinated verbal and visual reconstruction of the queen's coronation and entry into France's capital city in her specially prepared coronation book, author and illustrator place Anne of Brittany on center stage. On the border of

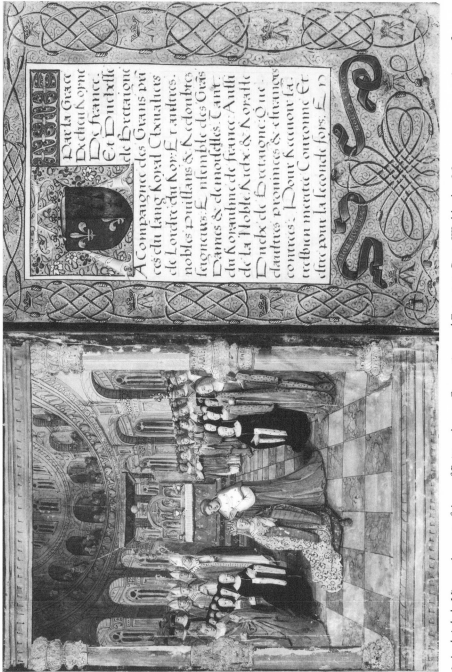

6. André de la Vigne, *Account of Anne of Brittany's 1504 Coronation and Entry into Paris*, Waddesdon Manor ms. 22: p. 2: Anne of Brittany's Coronation at Saint-Denis; p. 3: Opening folio of La Vigne's account. Accession No. 917; Andre Delavigne; Description of the Coronation of Anne of Brittany; Fifteenth Century. Waddesdon, The Rothschild Collection (The National Trust). Photo: Mike Fear. © The National Trust, Waddesdon Manor.

the real-life spectacle and of La Vigne's reduction of it into the language and royal ideologies of the times, the images and decorative signs and symbols play an enlightening role in the reconstitution of the ceremonial.

The three miniatures that embellish the manuscript book depict the most decisive moments of this regal and political drama. In the scene of the queen's coronation (Figure 6), the dramatic juxtaposition of gold and red on center stage isolates into their own political unit Anne of Brittany and the king's closest advisor, Cardinal Georges d'Amboise, who crowns her.[92] Other nobles and ecclesiastics witnessing the ritual—many of whom are dutifully identified by La Vigne in his account—constitute a secondary cast of characters,[93] while spectators in the distant balcony share the perspective with the reader of the manuscript.

Anne's prominent position above her entourage as she arrives on a litter before crowds at the Saint-Denis Gate is highlighted in the second miniature of ms. 22 by a horizontal band of gold (Figure 7). Her crowned head, toward which all witnesses' eyes gaze, dominates the image by its position at its center, framed as it is by the four poles holding up the canopy over her head, which effectively isolate the queen from others depicted in the illustration. As in the frontispiece, a supporting cast of "actors" assembled around the queen, each of whom La Vigne identifies in the accompanying text, forms a second tier of participants, while spectators situated further back from the entourage follow the procession from neighboring streets and the windows of adjacent buildings. In the left background, the allegorical entry theater of the Heart of Paris staged at the Saint-Denis Gate by Paris organizers is partially visible. As in La Vigne's text, however, a sociopolitical hierarchy dictates the artistic focal points.

In the third miniature, which portrays the banquet hall at the Palais Royal, similar textual and visual laws apply. Like her crown, the gold backdrop behind the guest of honor at once accentuates Anne's unique status and separates her from the other diners, while other women (the widows) at the great marble royal table, although sitting slightly apart from Anne of Brittany, are more closely staged near the queen than the other banquet tables for the men, many of whose backs are turned to the viewer (Figure 8). Thus, visually corroborating La Vigne's celebratory text, these three illustrations place the author's patroness on center stage, while visually maintaining the sociopolitical hierarchy revealed in the written account.

Like the miniatures, the decoration on several leaves of manuscript 22, such as the folio facing the opening illumination of the queen's coronation (Figure 6), reinforces La Vigne's effort to present the queen as the

7. André de la Vigne, *Account of Anne of Brittany's 1504 Coronation and Entry into Paris*, Waddesdon Manor ms. 22: p. 76: Anne of Brittany begins her entry into Paris at the Saint-Denis Gate; p. 77: Folio facing the illustration of Anne of Brittany's entry into Paris. Accession No. 917; Andre Delavigne; Description of the Coronation of Anne of Brittany; fifteenth century. Waddesdon, The Rothschild Collection (The National Trust). Photo: Mike Fear. © The National Trust, Waddesdon Manor.

8. André de la Vigne, *Account of Anne of Brittany's 1504 Coronation and Entry into Paris*, Waddesdon Manor ms. 22: p. 108: Banquet at the Palais Royal in Honor of Anne of Brittany; p. 109: Folio facing the illustration of the banquet at the Palais Royal. Accession No. 917; Andre Delavigne; Description of the Coronation of Anne of Brittany; fifteenth century. Waddesdon, The Rothschild Collection (The National Trust). Photo: Mike Fear. © The National Trust, Waddesdon Manor.

protagonist of his entry book account. Just as the French queen dominates the book's miniatures, so too her name and symbols generate and govern the opening lines of the text. The most arresting image is the decorated letter A in pink on a flowered gold background that ushers in the first word of the text and the most prominent name of the book—ANNE. The arms of the queen, which partially cover this large initial, dialogue with the scene depicted in the facing miniature to the left (Figure 6), echoing the fleurs-de-lis on the altar of the church of Saint-Denis. By the same token, Anne's heraldic device in the margins at the right, the crowned letter A, resonates with the main object of interest in the scene to the left, the crown that Georges d'Amboise places on the queen's head. Multiple images of the *cordelière*, Anne's personal emblem, painted in blue like her other symbols, likewise fill the gold margins.

Throughout his verbal account La Vigne carefully tracks these and related symbols, such as the royal scepter and hand of justice:

> And so, my lord the Legate [Georges d'Amboise] . . . placed in her right hand the royal scepter of France and in her left the hand of justice, and this having been done . . . he placed on her very worthy and felicitious head the crown of my lord Saint Louis, king of France. . . . [B]ecause the said crown was so heavy, it was placed on a square piece of gold material before the aforementioned lady, and a lighter and less heavy one was placed on her head. Likewise, the rod of justice was given to the lord Charles, my lord of Bourbon, count of Vendôme, and the royal scepter to Louis, my lord of Bourbon, prince of Tallement, who held them at their sides before her while the Mass was performed. . . . And likewise, next to the great altar there was prepared another one of the chapel ornaments of the aforementioned lady, namely an image on golden cloth memorializing the Crucifixion, decorated with lilies and crowned ermines with the letters L and A, also crowned and intertwined with *cordelières*. (ll. 300–350)

At her coronation, then, the French queen was associated with conventional royal symbols controlled by designated males of the court and an artifact that united her personal emblems (ermines and *cordelières*) with that of French royalty (lilies) and Christ (crucifix). The margins of the opening folio of text in ms. 22 thus literally reenacted the symbolism of the coronation visually depicted on the opposite folio and verbally invoked in La Vigne's text.

The illuminator of ms. 22 again succeeded in rendering into artistic terms La Vigne's verbal description of Anne's litter as she entered Paris through another "dialogue" between the Saint-Denis Gate miniature and the margins on the facing folio (Figure 7). Indeed, La Vigne's very description of the decorated litter bearing the queen through the capital city clearly inspired the artist:

> The throne and all of the aforementioned litter down to the ground were covered in a very rich cloth of gold frize on frize with about a half-foot border of white satin, and over it, red velour cut away and notched with interlaced *cordelieres* with love ties and letters from her device, [all designed] with the most original skill. (ll. 798–805)

He filled the margins on the facing folio with intertwined *cordelières* and crowned initial As that echo the crown on the queen's head in the miniature. As on the first folio of the text, which opened with the name of the queen, a large initial A in pink covered with Anne of Brittany's coat of arms initiates La Vigne's description of the queen's entry through Paris on the folio facing the second miniature in an orchestrated dialogue between text and image that imitates the rigorous order of the actual procession itself the day of Anne's entry through Paris. This time, however, the queen's emblems are painted in gold leaf on margins of a stunning royal blue.

The artist of Waddesdon Manor ms. 22 sets up a similarly striking relationship between the third miniature, namely the banquet scene and the marginalia on the facing folio (Figure 8). The two sections of the queen's arms, fleurs-de-lis and ermines, which again decorate the inside of the first initial, a pink capital P, which opens the text (109), are echoed in the elaborate pattern of diamonds in the margin.[94] This dizzying diagonal pattern of crisscrossing symbols is so complex and stunning that it rivals the 20-line text transcribed on the folio.

The richness of Waddesdon Manor manuscript 22's visually striking miniatures and decorated margins echoes La Vigne's verbal descriptions of the queen's appearance on her coronation day. The author emphasizes Anne's sumptuous apparel (ll. 95–100), the precious stones decorating her headdress (ll. 101–6), the crown on her head (ll. 379–80), and the expensive jewels she wore:[95]

> She wore at her neck, made by marvelous craftsmanship, a neck piece of other large multi-faceted diamonds, which was worth some

forty to fifty thousand écus. The collar consisted of large, new and original pearls . . . she wore certain other singular rings on the solemn occasion of the extravagant ritual, like a sovereign princess and queen of marvelous force, which together were probably worth and valued at the sum of 100,000 écus or more. (ll. 107–16)

The chronicler's account reaches a rhetorical and poetic paroxysm in his summary description of the stunning glitter of the jewelry displayed by all the female participants in the queen's entourage:

As for the appearance of the thick chains, large collars, neck pieces, bracelets, brooches, rings, ornaments, hems with devices, large pearls, large diamonds, rubies, sapphires and other substantial things that they wore to dignify their angelic faces, they were adorned, enriched, and decorated with such a great abundance and such good quality of [these jewels] that they seemed to be nymphs or goddesses descended from heaven rather than worldly creatures. (ll. 193–200)

Equally dazzling are the qualities attributed to Anne of Brittany by La Vigne, who often employs catalogues of her superlatives in describing his benefactor's virtues:

Then . . . the most exalted, prized and esteemed lady of the world, in triumph, magnificence, excellent acclaim, praise, honor and everlasting glory, dignified in her comportment, assured in her manner and generous magnanimous solemnity, began to walk forward. (ll. 374–82)

The queen's manner likewise conformed to the impressive nature of her dress and ornaments. Like the directors of the theaters along the queen's Parisian entry route and her publicity agents for the French court, La Vigne contributes to the dramatic glorification of Anne of Brittany's image through his stunningly elaborate descriptions.

While flattering his benefactor through his dazzling account, La Vigne maintains a very low individual profile throughout his report. In fact, although he notes in the introduction to this account that "J'ay tout escript en ce petit traicté" [I've written everything in this little treatise] (v. 5),[96] it is not until the last folio of his manuscript book that the chronicler steps forward to identify himself in an acrostic:

D ame d'onneur, royne par excellence
E t duchesse de grant magnifficence
L a plus digne qui fut onc en noblesse,
A vous je viens soubz toute reverance
V ous apporter l'euvre qu'en vostre absence
I 'ay faite ainsi, selon ma petitesse.
Gardez la bien, car a vous je l'adresse,
N on a aultre, pour plaisir voluntaire,
E t n'oubliez vostre humble secretaire. (vv. 50–58)

[Lady of honor, queen *par excellence* and duchess of great magnificence, the most worthy who ever was a noble, I come to you in all reverence to bring you the work that, in your absence, I have thus prepared, according to my little talent. Protect it well, since I address it to you, not to any other, for your voluntary pleasure, and do not forget your humble secretary.]

Adopting a discrete, albeit traditional, strategy, La Vigne verbally and visually articulates his relationship to Anne of Brittany through his vertical signature, which engenders horizontal praise of the queen.[97] As he associates Anne of Brittany with aristocratic qualities, notably honor and nobility, that are reminiscent of those personified figures appearing on the Saint-Denis Gate entry theater stage, La Vigne directly beseeches his benefactor to protect and support his work. Implicitly embodied in this nine-verse stanza that closes the narrative of Anne's 1504 coronation and Parisian entry, then, is reference to the fundamental interdependence between the patroness financially supporting her court protégé and the court writer, who redacts works to please his benefactor and to advertise her virtuous reputation. Although succinct, these verses essentially define the poet-patroness relationship of the times. We will see it played out with slight variations in subsequent chapters.

In the end, Anne of Brittany, as subject and recipient of Waddesdon Manor ms. 22, would most likely have read and seen herself positioned in flattering fashion not only at the center of the royal universe reconstructed in the manuscript account of her entry into Paris in 1504, but also as separate from and above her subjects. Through a distortion of perspectives that downplayed the contributions of Parisian citizens through the entry theaters, the queen performed the exclusive role of protagonist in her—and her husband's—politically staged drama. Its highlights recall not only the highly public and publicized rituals surrounding her coronation in 1492, but also those involving her cousin Anne de Foix two years earlier. Yet, Anne of Brittany's verbal and visual performances on the pages of the 1504 festival book, rendered as closely interwoven artistic systems, are articulated in much more dazzling albeit consciously constructed fashion.

To a certain degree, the 1504 celebrations and account of them offer less a sense of Anne of Brittany's uniqueness than insight into the role she played as queen in the mythology of royal imagery. Nevertheless, it was Anne of Brittany herself who was doubtless involved in securing memorial records of these momentous events. The results of her personally initiated commission of a decorated manuscript record of Anne de Foix's coronation celebrations in 1502 may well have inspired patroness and protégé to conceive of a festival book on the occasion of her own coronation just two years later. Even though there is no documented evidence that Anne of Brittany actually commissioned the Waddesdon Manor ms. 22 containing La Vigne's account, its costly and personalized decoration all but confirms that the court, and likely the French queen herself, paid for the decorated manuscript. If so, this suggests that Anne of Brittany sanctioned the panegyric mode of festival books—why wouldn't she?—that reconstructed in coordinated word and image her most dramatic place on the public stage.

Although Anne of Brittany had died by the time of the coronation and Parisian entry of her daughter thirteen years later, her spirit was nonetheless most present during the ceremonials for Claude of France in several ways. First, in his accounts of the 1517 celebratory events that he directly addressed to Claude,[98] Pierre Gringore, doubtless repeating official terminology, refers to Claude of France by adopting a title that includes her mother (and father): "Madame Claude, queen of France, daughter of the most Christian king Louis XII of this name and of Madame Anne of Brittany, twice crowned queen of France (ll. 2–4).[99] Second, the arms of Claude, featured prominently during her entry, were differently configured but nonetheless similar to those of her mother, since both were simultaneously queen of France and duchess of Brittany. Indeed, ermine symbols of Brittany decorated Claude's overgarment and bodice (App. IV, ll. 150–63, 160–62) and *cordelières*, another emblem inherited from Anne of Brittany, appear on the raised throne on which she sat during her coronation (App. IV, ll. 64, 66) as well as on her litter as she made her way through Paris (ll. 104–5). The day before her coronation, Claude paid special tribute to her deceased mother and father upon entering the church at Saint-Denis:

> And that evening she came to the aforementioned church to pray and say orisons in great devotion and contemplation over the tomb and statue of her father and mother, and not without tears and lamentations. (App. IV, ll. 43–46)

In addition, Claude wore an exquisitely decorated cape that had been given to her by her mother for her coronation ceremony:

> And among other masterpieces was a cape sewn with little leaves of gold onto silver cloth, filled with beautifully fashioned ermines in the formed of raised animals, all completely covered with raised pearls; and so life-like were these ermines that they lacked only movement. And everyone said that this was the most expensive cape they had ever seen and that the queen's mother, Madame Anne of Brittany, now deceased, had given it to the queen and commanded that it be carried to Saint Denis where her body lies. In front of this cape, in the middle of the clasp, is inserted a large ruby of great value. (App. IV, ll. 132–41)

Finally, the entry theater staged in Claude's honor in 1517 at the Châtelet, the seat of royal justice, featured Anne of Brittany's genealogy as an example of law- and custom-abiding ancestors. Although royal genealogies often figured in entry theaters during kings' entries to authorize their accession to the throne, their appearance during a queen's entry, especially ancestral trees depicting a female lineage, was rare.[100] While describing in elaborate detail the complicated allegory presented at this site and drawing associations for the reader between the genealogy on center stage and the allegorical scenario erected below, Gringore's account nevertheless offers fewer details about the Breton genealogical tree on view (ll. 419–23) than the anonymous version:[101]

> Then, the aforementioned lady arrived at the Châtelet of Paris where she found a tree with many branches, like a Tree of Jesse, on a large scaffolding. In the upper branches were a crowned king and queen, representing the king and queen, and on each side of

these branches were several princes, princesses, kings and dukes
of Brittany, demonstrating the line and genealogy from which the
aforementioned lady arose. (App. IV, ll. 623–28)

The miniatures in the anonymous accounts associated with this mise
en scène corroborate the verbal description by featuring the royal couple,
Francis I and Claude of France, in the upper branches of the tree (Figure 9).
Kipling (69–71) identifies Anne of Brittany with her two husbands, Charles
VIII and Louis XII, and the other figures as Anne of Brittany's ancestors in
the branches below. However, whereas Anne-Marie Lecoq suggests that this
entry theater figures the French queen as having "un grand rôle de modéra-
teur à jouer dans l'exercice de la justice royale" (387), Kipling interprets it
instead as a political statement about France's aim to absorb Brittany:

> The pageant thus describes the subordination of the Tree of
> Brittany to the laws and customs of France. As a symbol of royal
> nativity, the pageant is more about the birth of French nationhood
> than it is about Claude's symbolic birth as Queen . . . it foresees the
> eventual, formal incorporation of Claude's duchy into the French
> crown. (71)

Although Anne of Brittany and her ancestry were consciously and visually
invoked by Parisian citizens to celebrate her daughter's coronation, the integration of the duchy of Brittany into the French kingdom was still at issue,
even though Claude had already granted her husband control over it.[102]

Claude's entry resembles her mother's in many other respects. In fact,
municipal preparations for Anne of Brittany's entry in 1504 served as a model
for the coronation festivities of her daughter in 1517 (and for those of her immediate successor in 1514, Mary Tudor).[103] Like her mother at the 1492 and
1504 coronations, Claude of France sat on a raised platform.[104] Widows also
figured prominently in the procession of royals,[105] the queen's apparel was
conscientiously described, and participants and chroniclers alike paid special attention to the display of symbols of royal power, including the crown,
scepter and hand of justice, and ring.[106] As during Anne of Brittany's two
coronations, the heavy crown had to be held on Claude of France's head,
this time by the lord of Alençon.[107] In addition, the order of participants was
carefully controlled and their identification dutifully enumerated as the same
stages of the ritual were followed:[108] the arrival of city authorities to greet the

9. *Le Sacre, couronnement et entrée de Madame Claude Royne de France* (anonymous), Paris, BnF ffr. 5750, fol. 45r: Entry theater staged at the Châtelet in honor of Claude of France on May 12, 1517 depicting her maternal ancestry. Bibliothèque Nationale de France.

queen outside of the city and their return back into the city along with the
queen and her entourage, the entry theaters staged at the same seven sites in
the queen's honor, her reception at Notre Dame and the banquet held in her
honor.[109] In a sense, then, Claude of France served as a symbolic replacement
of the previous queen, a situation rendered all the more dramatic given her
lack of political power in comparison with the king's. While she underwent
the same ritual, Claude was relegated to life behind the scenes more than
her mother, in part because she lived a shorter life and as queen functioned
above all as a producer of babies. Her public profile was minimized not only
because of her almost constant pregnant condition, but also because of the
more dominant presence of her mother-in-law, Louise of Savoy, at court.[110]
Just as Anne of France had played a role as a leading female of the court during Anne of Brittany's two ceremonials, so too Louise of Savoy figured as
a major player—and an even more prominent presence—in events during
Claude's coronation. Both royal and urban image-makers placed the duchess
of Angoulême in a central position during the *sacre*, and she was directly or
indirectly represented on two entry theater stages as well.[111]

Although the multifaceted allegorical *tableaux vivants* erected along the
queen's entry route into Paris consisted of a more coordinated effort than in
1492 and 1504, given that one theater organizer had been hired (Gringore),
and although they featured more individualized messages than during Anne
of Brittany's 1504 entry, these entry theaters were not as often personalized
for the queen herself as for other royal personalities. Several staged allegories
were associated solely with the king,[112] while actors representing the king
and queen enthroned side by side appeared on raised platforms at two sites,
the Châtelet and the Trinity, where the queen's particular virtues were emphasized.[113] The final entry theater, which involved a dialogue between Saint
Louis and his mother Blanche de Castille, implicitly invoked the relationship
between Francis I and his mother, rather than his wife.[114] Louise of Savoy's
political dominance at court was thus visually reenacted during Claude's
entry to such a degree that she nearly upstaged her daughter-in-law.

Three other female-centered entry theaters, those staged at the Saint-Denis
Gate, Ponceau Fountain and Saint-Innocents, featured Claude of France in
revealing ways that both hark back to issues associated with her mother, Anne
of Brittany, namely the anticipation of male heirs, and to themes concerning
famous women of the past that I examine more fully below in subsequent
chapters. At the entry theater at the Saint-Denis Gate, the queen, or rather
the actor playing her part, stood in the center, surrounded on both sides by six

biblical women, each exemplifying a different virtue: Sarah (loyalty), Rachel (amiability), Rebecca (prudence), Esther (modesty), Deborah (good learning), and Leah (fertility). The queen's central position among these famous biblical women confirmed her incarnation of these very female virtues, many of which overlapped with the four Cardinal Virtues featured on the lower stage of the *échafaud*, Prudence, Justice, Magnanimity, and Continence.[115] Reminiscent of the *Toison d'Or* miniature of Anne of Brittany's embrace of the seven virtues,[116] the four virtues personified in the 1517 Saint-Denis Gate entry theater also doubled as the four royal widows of France, namely Louise of Savoy, Anne of France, Margaret of Lorraine (duchess of Alençon), and Mary of Luxembourg (countess of Vendôme). In addition, an analogy between Claude's and the Virgin's coronation was made explicit through the live-action crowning of the queen figure by a mechanical dove descending from above. Thus, somewhat reminiscent of the staging of the five biblical Annes during Anne of Brittany's 1504 Parisian entry, although involving much greater detail and multilayered meaning, the 1517 entry theater at the Saint-Denis Gate strongly reinforced those virtues expected of noble females in general and of the French queen in particular.

Elaborating upon the first entry theater's theme of fertility through the character of Leah, Gringore's scenario at the Ponceau Fountain focused on the queen's reproductive qualities. The crowned female with two young girls in a garden of lilies, accompanied by the display of Pauline verses about the king's planting of the kingdom and the queen's multiplication of its fruit, obviously alluded to Claude's role as bearer of children, above all a male heir.[117] Having already borne the two daughters represented in the Ponceau Fountain staging, Louise (1515) and Charlotte (1516), Claude would go on to give birth to a male heir to the throne nine months later (Francis).[118] Thus, unlike her mother, Claude was exceedingly prolific, producing seven children, including a future king, before her premature death in 1524 at age twenty-three. In fact, Claude's sustained role as childbearer not only kept the French queen away from political decision-making, perhaps conveniently so, but may well have contributed to her early death as well.[119] Of note is the king's symbolic presence in this staging—his salamander emblem and the queen's ermine emblem appear together among French royal fleurs-de-lis beneath the fountain in the miniatures featured in copies of the anonymous manuscript version. In addition, the figure representing the queen cites the following verses that emphasize her husband's contributions and her willingness to follow suit in playing her accompanying role:

Le Tres Crestien a planté ce vergier
Semé de liz, qu'il garde de danger
Par sa vertu triumphalle et puissance.
De l'enroser et de le soullaiger
Preste je suis et me y vueil heberger.
Tout noble cueur y vit en asseurance;
Il plaise a Dieu de y donner a croissance.
Je m'y deduys d'honneste cueur courtoys
Treshumblement comme royne de France,
Multipliänt ce beau jardin françoys. (vv. 23–32)

[The very Christian (king) has planted this orchard sown with
lilies, which he protects from danger through his triumphant
virtue and power. I am ready to water it and care for it and wish to
reside here. Every noble heart lives there in security; it pleases God
to help it grow. I very humbly delight in being queen of France
with an honest, courteous heart, multiplying this beautiful French
garden.]

Thus, as in the entry theaters staged in honor of Anne of Brittany, the French
queen is almost always presented in association with the king.

The royal family was depicted in completely different fashion in the
entry theater erected at the Saint-Innocents site in 1517, however. The upper
stage featured open hearts inside of which three female personifications represented Divine Love (in the center) and Natural Love and Conjugal Love on
each side, each associated with the king's arms of France, his mother's arms
of Savoy, and the queen's arms respectively. This entry theater thus made
clear that Claude's role as one of three symbolic figures of love in the French
kingdom was shared—and, as it turned out, superseded—by her mother-in-
law. On the lower stage, biblical and historical *exempla* glorified each kind of
coupling: David and Abigail, whose story represented divine love; Corialanus
and his mother Veturia, who brought peace to Rome through her maternal
love; and the faithful Julia and Portia, who chose suicide over life without
their mates, all classic examples of conjugal love. Echoing the famous biblical women exalted in the opening entry theater at the Saint-Denis Gate,
the female figures staged here again provided positive examples of virtuous
behavior and even sacrifice.

The appearance of these famous women in performance alongside the personified religious virtues in this and adjacent stagings offered spectators a measure of those qualities expected of all women and exemplified by the leading female of the kingdom, the queen of France. This public display of personified virtues and famous biblical and mythological females along the queen's Parisian entry route in 1492, 1504, 1514, and 1517 reflects above all cultural (male) expectations concerning female comportment in everyday life, thereby serving as a form of social control of women of all classes. It also had the effect of reducing any distinction between the public performance of the queen and the allegorical "staging" of her supposed virtues. It is likely that in most cases these women accepted such roles, even willingly acceding to royal and social needs and hopes. Yet underlying tensions did surface in other contexts. We learned, for example, that Anne de Foix strongly but futilely resisted the court's arrangement of her marriage to King Ladislaus of Hungary. In fact, Anne of Brittany's decisive role in this decision and her commission of a festival book to commemorate the events surrounding Anne de Foix's marriage and coronation underscore her "complicity" in this royal world of ceremonies and socially dictated codes of comportment.

Controlled by male-defined public relations strategies and protocols at the time of their very public ceremonies and reconstructed by male chroniclers in a variety of festival books, the women in performance examined here, in particular Anne of Brittany, Anne de Foix, and Claude of France, were essentially agents of propaganda who abided by established performative codes as they dutifully played out their roles in dazzling fashion on the center stage of their respective kingdoms—in these carefully chosen moments. That we possess little sense of the thoughts of these female protagonists on such occasions all but confirms the conscious avoidance of individualized reactions in these coronation ceremonies and commemoration books. The stylized performances of these royal women before and alongside of similarly staged female personifications, however, sheds light on the public's and the court's expectations of them. The embodiment of the Cardinal and Theological Virtues in addition to the production of male heirs, both "ideals" that tended to keep queens in their place and in the background politically, were the images projected by and acceptable to officials and citizens alike, rather than the promotion of women wielding power.

Although lacking in political clout, just like most of her predecessors and immediate successors,[120] Anne of Brittany had, nonetheless, more of a political voice in affairs of state than many of her female cohorts, at least during her second reign—although Louise of Savoy came to wield substantial political power, without ever having been queen. Anne's shared control of Brittany with Louis XII and, ironically, perhaps her very failure to produce male heirs may have contributed to her greater presence on the political stage. But just how powerful was the French queen and duchess of Brittany? What about the status of her female contemporaries? We will gain further insight into these questions as we explore the implications of the performances of other political and literary female figures appearing in the books making up the libraries of women of power in the following chapters.

# CHAPTER TWO

# Female Patronage and the Politics of Personification Allegory

Expanding upon the historical reconstruction of women in entry perfor- mances, which we examined in Chapter 1, this chapter explores the dynam- ics of female patronage relationships, which involved the praise of a feminine benefactor by male authors and artists, through an analysis of the literary and iconographic reconstruction of women in allegorical works. Anne of Brittany, one of the most prominent patrons of the arts during her lifetime, and her support of numerous court protégés figure centrally in this discus- sion. The French queen's secondary textual and iconographical role in André de la Vigne's *Ressource de la Chrestienté* (1494) typifies her presence in books associated with her queenship during Charles VIII's reign.[1] And yet, the author's use of female personification allegory[2] in the *Ressource* anticipates his portrayal of the French queen ten years later in his account of her corona- tion and Parisian entry in 1504, analyzed in Chapter 1. Thus, the allegorical portrayal of political entities during Anne of Brittany's first reign ultimately foreshadows a real-time political representation of the queen during her second reign.

Anne's more prominent profile in books dating from her second marriage—images of the queen alone appear more frequently—may well reflect her increased political authority as administrator of Brittany, a role her first husband had assumed. The French queen's greater maturity and increased economic status further enabled her to commission more of her own books at the time of her marriage to Louis XII, as Maulde La Clavière confirms:

La reine Anne de Bretagne usait royalement des gros revenues
de son duché personnel et de son douaire; et, comme elle
ne redoutait point le luxe ni la flatterie, les lettres, l'art, les
industries artistiques trouvèrent auprès d'elle un accueil sans
rival. Quant au roi, il dépensait moins largement, parce qu'il
se considérait comme un économe du denier populaire, mais il
encouragea spécialement l'histoire, qu'il s'agît d'histoire ancienne
ou moderne, des origines fabuleuses de la dynastie ou des faits
contemporains.[3]

Indeed, court artists often dedicated works to the queen that glorified her
husband's exploits. While such tributes to the king obviously honored Anne
as well through association, these authors also seemed to be targeting King
Louis XII—as both potential audience and patron—through the queen. For
example, the special vellum copy of Antoine Vérard's edition of Claude de
Seyssel's *Louenges du roy* (1508) juxtaposes an opening miniature featuring
the author's presentation of his work to Anne with a verbal dedication of his
writing to the king himself. In a similar vein, the *Dyalogue de Vertu Militaire
et Jeunesse Françoise*, dedicated to the French queen by Jean Lemaire de Belges
in 1511, lauds Louis XII as an example of military virtue, while associating the
queen with *Dame Vertu militaire* herself. Thus, while evidence suggests that
Anne of Brittany controlled the literary patronage system at the French court
more resolutely in her second reign, during which time she often appears
alone, both verbally and visually, as designated dedicatee or commissioner of
the books written and decorated for her, she frequently ends up sharing center
stage with her royal partner as well.

These dynamics motivate one of the best-known works about Louis
XII's military accomplishments, Jean Marot's *Voyage de Gênes*, which the
author offered to the French queen in an exquisitely decorated manuscript
(BnF f.fr. 5091) around 1507. Not only did the king figure centrally as a
protagonist in Marot's chronicle, but his visual presence dominates the
dedication manuscript as well. An analysis of Marot's conscious attempt
to please Anne of Brittany with this military and political account through
the exploitation of female personification allegory uncovers unexpected associations between the author's dedicatee and the work's principal literary
characters. This discussion sets the stage for an examination of James Paxson's theory that, as textual and fictional personifications came to imitate

10. André de la Vigne, *La Ressource de la Chrestienté*, Paris, BnF ffr. 1687, fol. 1v: Dedication of the manuscript to King Charles VIII by the poet. Bibliothèque Nationale de France.

the forms of actual women, real women were increasingly treated like personified agents.

## Female Personification Allegory in a King's Narrative: La Vigne's *Ressource de la Chrestienté*

Among the most elaborately decorated books associated with Anne of Brittany is the royal manuscript copy of La Vigne's *Ressource de la Chrestienté* (BnF ffr. 1687), whose dedication by the author to Charles VIII is officially recorded in the opening full-page miniature. La Vigne on bended knee offers his book to the king, who sits enthroned in a semipublic space before seven male witnesses (Figure 10). The arms of the king, the queen, and the dauphin[4] adorn the miniature frame on this first folio, while the entire surface of the margins surrounding the text on each folio bears a series of four related emblematic designs that are repeated throughout the manuscript: gold fleurs-de-lis on a blue field, designating the king of France; black ermines on a silver background, representing Anne of Brittany (Figure 11); blue dolphins (*dauphins*) encircling either fleurs-de-lis or ermines, symbolic of the dauphin; and finally a combination of these three designs in diagonal bands (Figure 12).[5] This visual tribute to the king and his family in a manuscript book that contains no dedicatory prologue essentially serves as a form of dedication.[6] Thus, in a manuscript book in which Charles VIII dominates verbally and visually—it is after all a work for and about him—visual references to his family are intimately interwoven with his own. However, the allusions to Anne of Brittany are limited to emblematic form. Folios bearing her ermine symbols in the margins are always framed by those of the king and those of the dauphin, such that "she" is always surrounded by the two men in her life. Nonetheless, those folios that bear Anne of Brittany's ermine symbols alone remind the reader that Charles VIII's identity was closely affiliated with that of the queen. He may have governed Brittany during their marriage, but it was she who had brought the duchy to him through marriage.

Just as the queen's visibility is limited to emblematic representation in this manuscript, so too is her textual presence. The narrator makes a brief allusion to Anne of Brittany by describing the union of ermines and a *cerf volant* in the Garden of France (the French court) that he witnesses, a transparent reference to the marriage of Anne and Charles VIII in 1491. Worth noting

11. André de la Vigne, *La Ressource de la Chrestienté,* Paris, BnF ffr. 1687, fol. 2v: Margins with Anne of Brittany's black ermine emblems. Bibliothèque Nationale de France.

12. André de la Vigne, *La Ressource de la Chrestienté*, Paris, BnF ffr. 1687, fol. 23v: Flanked by *Dame Chrestienté* and *Noblesse*, *Magesté Royalle* speaks. Bibliothèque Nationale de France.

is La Vigne's omission of any reference to the military confrontation between France and Brittany that concluded with the 1491 nuptials:[7]

> On the other side there was a cluster of noble, expensive and much sought-after little animals called ermines which, some three years earlier, through the will and consent of the aforementioned Lady Nobility and the fervent and singular love that the ermines had for the noble fleurs-de-lis, had entered the said garden and had such acquaintance, alliance and intimacy with the so-called fleur-de-lis that they could touch, embrace and hug it as much and often as they wished. (ll. 117–24)

In a manuscript in which the queen's presence is reduced to visual and textual symbolism, her name is never mentioned, whereas Charles VIII's name appears frequently in highlighted form.

The textual and iconographical dynamics of manuscript 1687 contrast completely with those of La Vigne's 1504 *Sacre et Couronnement d'Anne de Bretagne*, which, as we learned in Chapter 1, was dedicated and exclusively devoted to the queen herself. The entire decorative program of a work that inaugurated her second reign places Anne of Brittany at its center both literally and figuratively, without any mention whatsoever of the king. The greater political authority Anne wielded during her second marriage, in particular involving her administration of Brittany, is reflected not only in the decision to prominently stage her second coronation, but also in the confection of the sumptuous manuscript record of it.[8] Nevertheless, the display of Anne's persona during these ceremonials served to embellish the image of the French king and his government as much as that of the queen. And yet, in redacting his account of the queen's coronation and "voyage" through Paris in 1504, La Vigne obviously borrowed substantially from his earlier poem about Charles VIII's own anticipated voyage, his military expedition, into Italy in 1494. It is through his allegorical program in the *Ressource de la Chrestienté* that La Vigne's two very different works intersect and find a shared literary expression and perspective.

In the *Ressource* the reader discovers, along with the narrator, several personified figures, whose feminine or masculine gender is, not surprisingly, determined by the linguistic gender of their titles: *Chrestienté*, *Noblesse*, and *Magesté Royalle* are identified as "Dames" both in the text and in the accompanying historiated initials, whereas *Je ne sçay qui* and *Bon Conseil* are staged grammatically and visually as males. While the female personifications dominate the allegorical stage, they embody an implicit political tension between their gender and the entity they represent. *Dame Chrestienté*, for example, stands for the Church (especially in the Holy Lands), a politico-religious institution governed by men, and *Dame Noblesse* represents the aristocratic class, a sociopolitical entity managed by males. The masculine personifications in the *Ressource* play less abstract roles. *Bon Conseil* designates the king's advisors who support his foreign policy in 1494—a planned expedition to Naples and subsequent crusade to Jerusalem—whereas *Je ne sçay qui* speaks for those hostile to Charles VIII's proposed military mission into Italy;[9] his political opposition to royal policy is strongly refuted by *Bon Conseil*. The ten finely executed historiated initials that punctuate this series of speeches offer exquisite scenes of the poet-narrator[10] and the allegorical characters whose interactions he observes and subsequently records.[11]

The most ambiguously constructed figure in the *Ressource de la Chrestienté* is *Magesté Royalle*, who represents not an institution or political concept but a particular male, the king himself, Charles VIII. In a series of historiated initials, she sits enthroned at the center of the court (Figure 12), just like the king in the dedication miniature that opens manuscript 1687 (Figure 10). Moreover, *Magesté Royalle*'s words are literally engendered by acrostics forming the name of the French king and a prayer in his honor that identifies him as well.[12] Adopting aggressive and threatening words, *Magesté Royalle*'s militaristic speech signals her readiness to take up arms for a crusade in defense of *Dame Chrestienté* (ll. 720–43, vv. 1364–1434) with the support of nobles, which she subsequently obtains, thanks to *Dame Noblesse*. Thus, *Magesté Royalle*'s call to arms aims to defend *Dame Chrestienté* with the aid of *Dame Noblesse* (ll. 1435–44). Unlike the male allegorical figures who oppose each other's political agendas, the three female personifications are mutually supportive of each other.

Even though she is the principal figure of the narration, the physical description of *Magesté Royalle*, like that of the two male personifications, receives little attention. In fact, this female allegorical character visually recalls the depiction of Charles VIII in the opening dedicatory miniature: wearing a crown and royal apparel, she holds a scepter in her right hand[13] and, enthroned in imposing fashion, she too is surrounded by courtiers. Moreover, La Vigne's narrator verbally emphasizes *Magesté Royalle*'s royal attributes of power (ll. 128–35), rather than focusing on her beauty and clothes, as he does in portraying *Dame Noblesse*.

In the end, political authority in manuscript 1687 of the *Ressource de la Chrestienté* is visually and poetically transferred from the male, Charles VIII, depicted in the dedicatory miniature, to the female, *Magesté Royalle*, the central allegorical figure in numerous historiated initials, whose call to arms represents the work's climax and raison d'être.[14] She promises to protect a political institution governed by men (the Church) but personified by a woman (*Dame Chrestienté*), thanks to the intervention of another allegorical female (*Dame Noblesse*), who symbolizes the men surrounding the king in the dedication scene. In many ways, then, *Magesté Royalle* is an androgynous figure. Contemporary writers and readers obviously accepted as a purely literary phenomenon this internal contradiction in the allegorical representation of political power of the time, for these rhetorical dynamics are never mentioned or questioned. Nonetheless, in a France governed for years by the Salic law, the literary attribution of power to female characters (*Magesté Royalle*, *Dame Noblesse*) inevitably involved the staging of political tensions between men and women, no matter how camouflaged they might have been through custom, ceremony, and expectations. Although never analyzed in terms of political enmity (as ll. 117–24 quoted above [69] confirm), the marriage of Charles VIII and the young Anne of Brittany did in fact result from a confrontation of enemies—the French king attacked Anne and the forces of her duchy—and, more precisely, from the capitulation of the female sovereign before her male adversary.

In striking contrast to *Magesté Royalle*, *Dame Chrestienté*, the very tearful and troubled lady (ll. 128, 139), provides the reader a conventional portrait of a grieving woman (vv. 208–16), who, despite her noble origins, is unable to defend herself.[15] Powerless against the Turkish onslaught, she can only lament her situation and appeal to others for aid. From the beginning, the narrator describes *Dame Chrestienté* as a lady of most noble and impressive background, who laments alone, like a poor lost lamb, in this desert (ll. 26–27).

Again in contrast to the depiction of *Magesté Royalle*, the reader is much more aware of the physical appearance (ll. 28–47) of *Dame Chrestienté*, which suggests a certain voyeurism on the part of La Vigne, or rather of the centuries-old allegorical tradition from which he borrows, in which female personifications are often elaborately dressed up in aristocratic attire through the intermediary of the narrator, or *acteur*. La Vigne presents Lady Christianity from all angles, focusing on her general nature, gestures, and comportment (ll. 29–30) in order to portray the nobility of this figure through her

physical qualities, behavior, and dress. *Dame Chrestienté's* remarkable countenance (l. 31), in particular her pleasing and amiable face (ll. 42–43), offers
a sense of her external and internal make-up alike, because her sweetness is
manifest in both emotional and moral terms. The use of hyperbole reinforces
the image of a lady of such extraordinary demeanor and beauty that she can
belong only to the divine world (ll. 43–44).[16] In a stunning dialogue between
text and image, the rhetorical and poetic embellishment adopted by the author to describe Lady Christianity's astonishing exterior and interior beauty
reflects the sumptuous decoration that surrounds the text on every folio of
manuscript 1687.

La Vigne's evocative literary language finds its most developed expression
in the portrait of *Dame Noblesse* (ll. 82–108), an embroidered version of his
descriptions of *Magesté Royalle* and *Dame Chrestienté*. Like Lady Christianity who comes from noble heritage, Lady Nobility too is "de hault arroy" [of
noble ligneage] (l. 83). But La Vigne amplifies this trait in his poetic prose
through a remarkable accumulation of past participles—"descendue, yssue,
propaganee et prymogenitee de l'ymperialle, royalle et pryamyde lignee troy-
enne" [descended, issued, propagated and first born of the imperial, royal and
Trojan pyramid and line] (ll. 84–85)—and adjectives: "en beaulté, pulcritude,
doulce, amyable, courtoise, humble, begnigne et gracieuse" [sweet, amiable,
courtly, humble, benign and gracious in beauty, in pulchritude] (ll. 85–86).
Expanding the enumerations used in his portrayal of Lady Christianity, La
Vigne has his narrator emphasize the role of *Dame Noblesse*—thereby indirectly flattering his noble audience as well—whose beauty is inextricably
associated with her royal attire, jewels, and headdress:

> Triumphantly wearing a dress of gold material in the most elegant
> style, lined with ermine fur, embroidered with gold and enriched
> with precious stones and pearls. Hanging round her neck like
> scarves, she wore thick necklaces, large chains of gold of a great
> price and weight. Her head was adorned and decorated with a
> headdress made of fine gold in the modern fashion. (ll. 86–70)

The crown of Lady Nobility is also more elaborate and exotic than that worn
by *Dame Chrestienté* and *Magesté Royalle* (ll. 90–94). In addition, La Vigne
builds on descriptions of his other personified figures in adopting superlatives reminiscent of Other-Worldly Celtic characters in courtly romances as

well as an abundance of other details to describe *Dame Noblesse*'s physical beauty and her related intellectual and moral qualities (ll. 94–102).[17] Like *Dame Chrestienté*, *Dame Noblesse* is touched by the hand of God, who has elected her to preserve and defend the excellent and deific fleur-de-lis planted in the middle of the garden (ll. 104–8).

La Vigne's emphasis on the beauty and virtues of *Dame Noblesse* suddenly veers away from expected female attributes to describe her martial qualities that make of her a Christian Minerva, in particular her nobility, prowess, wisdom, and ability as a victorious military goddess (ll. 102–4).[18] *Dame Noblesse* thereby embodies the most noble feminine traits of *Dame Chrestienté* but also certain conventionally masculine characteristics of *Magesté Royalle*. What appears to distinguish the vulnerable female figure (*Dame Chrestienté*) from the two strong female personifications (*Magesté Royalle*, *Dame Noblesse*) is the lack of physical and moral power to take action.

Thus, through the use of personification, intensified through superlatives, hyperboles, enumerations and metaphoric and symbolic analogies, André de la Vigne transforms sociopolitical tensions among French males at the end of the fifteenth century into an allegorical scenario dominated by women of power who resolve these very hostilities. While Anne of Brittany herself appears in only a minor visual and textual role in manuscript 1687, La Vigne's allegorical construction of women in this book dedicated to Charles VIII generally flatters the female sex, while anticipating the literal representation of the French queen that he will provide in his account of her coronation and royal entry into Paris ten years later, following her second marriage. For example, the queen's sumptuous clothes in 1504 resemble those of *Dame Noblesse* (ll. 95–100, 106–8); the precious stones decorating the queen's headdress and the dazzling jewels recall those of her allegorical predecessors as well. In addition, in each of the three manuscript miniatures of her coronation book (Figures 6–8). Anne of Brittany sits or stands at the center of all activity, like *Magesté Royalle* in the scenes painted in manuscript 1687. That the queen's name, Anne, visually and verbally engenders La Vigne's verbal account of the coronation echoes the textual and pictorial use of the Charles VIII acrostics in manuscript 1689.[19] This rhetorical connection between the literary representation of allegorical characters in the *Ressource* and the literal portrayal of Anne of Brittany in the coronation account, reinforced by the exquisite illustrations in each work, is critical for an understanding of the French court's publicity machine that sought to enhance its own reputation and reinforces its self-image through a carefully presented illustration of its members, a system adroitly exploited by La Vigne himself.

## Praise of the King in Manuscript Books for the Queen

Like La Vigne's *Ressource de la Chrestienté*, Seyssel's *Louenges du roy Louys XIIe de ce nom* and Lemaire's *Dyalogue de Vertu Militaire et Jeunesse Fran-çoise*, which date from Anne of Brittany's second reign, glorify her husband's military heroics. Unlike the *Ressource*, they are both dedicated to the French queen, providing additional confirmation of her prominent role as a court patron at this time.

An influential member of the king's council from 1498 on, Claude de Seyssel penned several books lauding Louis XII's military and political actions. While his position afforded him privileged access to the king, to whom he dedicated his works, including the *Louenges* (published in 1508 by Vérard),[20] Seyssel also offered luxury copies to others, thereby assuring that his own credentials as author circulated as much as his tribute to the king. Indeed, Anne of Brittany received a personally prepared volume of the *Louenges*, housed today in the BnF as Rés. Vélins 2780.[21] While maintaining his lengthy dedication to Louis XII, which also figured in the paper copies of the publication,[22] Seyssel had the original presentation woodcut of a cleric offering his book to the French king on folio 1v replaced in Anne's copy by a specially made miniature depicting the queen as the sole dedicatee receiving the book from Seyssel (Figure 13).[23] The black ermine symbols on gray background symbolizing Brittany that decorate the frame around the miniature echo those covering the throne on which Anne of Brittany sits[24] and her arms that appear in the lower margin. The queen's mantel consists of gold fleurs-de-lis on a blue field, while the bodice of her gold dress beneath features black ermines on a white background. Staged in this symbolic endorsement of the French-Breton alliance, Anne of Brittany is accompanied by a female entourage: four *dames d'honneur* appear at her left, one of whom has "talking hands" that depict her involvement in the dedication scene. More unusual in a dedication miniature featuring Anne of Brittany alone is the presence of four male figures. Standing to the right of the kneeling author, whose own stature is rather diminished, they likely designate Seyssel's following.

Thus, the queen's association with the manuscript as dedicatee is visually

13. Claude de Seyssel, *Louenges du roy Louys XIIe de ce nom*, Paris, BnF Rés.
Vélins 2780, fol. 1v: Dedication of the book to Anne of Brittany by the author.
Bibliothèque Nationale de France.

and emblematically promoted in the liminal miniature, while the king dominates Seyssel's dedication and text. Dedicatory honors are thereby shared as
Anne of Brittany is identified as the reader of this specially made book that
glorifies her husband.[25]

A similar dynamic characterizes BnF ms. ffr. 25295, a collection of Jean
Lemaire's works dating from July 1, 1511 that begins with his *Dyalogue de
Vertu Militaire et de Jeunesse Françoise.* The beautifully decorated folio that
opens the manuscript (3v), which is entirely devoted to Anne's symbols and
insignia, visually sets the stage for Lemaire's verbal dedication of the *Dyalogue* to the queen (Figure 14).[26] Her motto *Non mudera* dominates the upper
register, while her coat of arms, encircled by her famous *cordelière* symbol,
figures centrally on the folio. In the lower register appears a complementary
iconographical representation: a white ermine stands on a plot of grass before
blooming fleurs-de-lis.[27] Thus, from the opening page, multiple combina-
tions of Anne of Brittany's emblems mark the manuscript book as hers.

Lemaire's dedication to Anne of Brittany, however, offers homage to
both the queen and the king:

> Ce dyalogue, treshaulte, tresexcellente princesse et ma
> tresredoubtée dame, Madame Anne, par la grace de Dieu royne
> de France et duchesse de Bretaigne, je vous presente en toute
> humblesse pour donner exhortation à ung chascun jeune et
> vertueux seigneur de la langue françoise de tendre à choses
> plushaultaines et plus memorables, à l'exemple des preux et vaillans
> princes tant du temps passé que moderne, mesmement du roy,
> nostre sire treschrestien et tresvictorieux. Si ne doit aucun prendre
> à desdaing les admonitions de Vertu, ny en trop grand licence les
> excuses de Jeunesse. (1)[28]

> [This dialogue, most noble, most excellent princess and my most
> revered lady, Madame Anne, by the grace of God Queen of France
> and Duchess of Brittany, I present to you in all humility, in order
> to exhort every young and virtuous lord of the French language
> to attain the most noble and memorable things, following the
> example of courageous and valiant princes as much from times
> past as present, including that of our king, our very Christian and
> very victorious lord. And no one should disdain the admonitions of
> Virtue nor give too great license to the excuses of Youth.]

14. Jean Lemaire de Belges, Collection of the author's works, opening with the *Dyalogue de Vertu Militaire et de Jeunesse Françoise*, Paris, BnF ffr. 25295, fol. 3v: The staging of Anne of Brittany's symbols and emblems. Bibliothèque Nationale de France.

Again, it is not surprising that court writers sought to honor the queen through association with her husband. Such dedications seem to confirm that Anne may have been a more sought-after benefactor than the king, presumably because she was more supportive of literary patronage. It was thus through the queen that court poets sought to reach the king's eyes and ears with their writings in praise of his actions. This dynamic seems especially relevant in the *Dyalogue*, in which *Dame Vertu militaire* (Lady Military Virtue) mourns the fact that [*Dame*] *Jeunesse Françoise* (French Youth) no longer supports her. The striking similarities between *Dame Chrestienté*'s complaint in La Vigne's *Ressource*, *France*'s in Chartier's *Quadrilog invectif*, and that of *Vertu militaire* suggest that the author consciously invoked these familiar intertextual echoes. Lemaire, however, goes on to describe not only the allegorical relationship between his two female personifications but also the association between his literary creations and Anne of Brittany, whose announced aural reception of his allegorical scenario suggests it may have originally been staged:[29]

> Vertu est dame et maistresse des nobles hommes, et Jeunesse est sa
> ministre. Toutesvoies obeit plus aucunefois le cheval au varlet que au
> maistre, s'il n'est de generosité souveraine. Maintenant orrez-vous,
> s'il vous plaist, deviser lesdictes deux dames, de l'une desquelles vous
> est affine, et de l'autre regente, ouquel estat prosperant le largiteur de
> toutes graces vous conserve longuement. (1)

> [Virtue is the lady and mistress of noble men and Youth is her
> minister. However, the horse on many an occasion obeys his valet
> more than his master, if there is no generosity from the sovereign.
> Now please listen to the discussion of these two ladies. You are
> an ally [a relative] of one of them and ruler of the other. May the
> provider of all graces preserve you for a long time in this prosperous
> state.]

No other author at Anne of Brittany's court goes so far in explicitly associating his dedicatee with his female personification allegory; she appears to be not only the ally of Military Virtue, but almost her alter ego. Lemaire sheds further light on his literary invention of this personified character: "Dame Vertu militaire, enclose ymaginativement et potenciallement en ung corps trespuissant qui represente l'estat universel de la noblesse françoise" [Lady

Military Virtue, enclosed imaginatively and powerfully in a very strong body, who represents the universal state of French nobility] (1–2).[30] *Vertu* herself is conscious of her own physicality, stating that she is a "prisoner" in her beautiful and noble body (2) and "enclosed" in her body (3). Like *Magesté Royalle*, *Vertu Militaire*'s external appearance receives little attention. It is rather her inner androgynous-like virtues that she privileges, as she compares herself to great male military heroes of the past by enumerating her strengths: she contains in her body's frame the presence of an Alexander, the grace of a Jason, Caesar's dignity, Hector's body size, Absalom's head of hair, the force of Achilles (3). Despite all her inherent masculine force, however, *Dame Vertu militaire*, like *Dame Chrestienté* before her, cannot defend her cause alone; she can only grieve at her vulnerability, caused by *Jeunesse*'s lack of support (3). The blatant defense of her own pleasures, good looks, and youth on the part of *Jeunesse*, the negative personification in the debate, ultimately leads to atonement when she is presented with the noble example of Louis XII:

> Prens ton exemple a ce fort conquerant,
> Loys le grant, douziesme de ce nom.
> Ne vantons plus aucun prince ou tirant
> Jadis errant renommée querant,
> Car ton garant obtient meilleur renom.
> Son confanon, sans autre compaignon,
> Mais sans Dieu non, a dompté les Ytalles,
> Et reprimé fureurs sacerdotalles.
>
> En son jeune aaige il commença
> De planter fruictz que ores il menge.
> Prouesse et vertu l'adressa;
> N'oncques de puis ne se lassa
> De repulser vice et laidenge. (8–9)

[Take as an example this strong conqueror, the great Louis XII; let us no longer boast of any prince or tyrant formerly in quest of renown, since your guarantor [Louis XII] obtains greater fame, his banner without any other companion, but without God, no, tamed Italy and repressed sacerdotal wrath. In his youth he began to plant fruit, which now he eats; prowess and virtue came to him and never since has he ceased attaching vice and evil.]

As in the *Ressource*, political tensions at the court involving males—here, the absence of military support for the king on the part of young men—are dissected in the *Dyalogue*, represented through female personification allegory, and then resolved through debate, with one of the disputants acceding to the other's logic.

The ballade following the *Dyalogue* serves to link the first poem about the French king's need for military support from French youth and the last work, which treats Louis XII's confrontation with Pope Julius II without any mention whatsoever of the queen.[31] Lemaire's praise of past political nobles who sought out the example of history (*A la louenge des princes & princesses qui ayment la science historialle*)—through chroniclers their own reputations flourished—is a transparent celebration of his own role as court writer. The author's third-person allusion to male and female aristocrats in the opening verse suggests he is targeting the French king and queen, a strategy reinforced by the examples he offers of legendary men and women (Hector, Penelope, Camille) whose actions have been regaled by past historians. As he flatters his readers through implicit comparisons with past great leaders who were inspired by historical example and who sponsored writers of history, Octavian and Mecenas serve as models for Louis XII, while Amalasunthe, queen of the Ostrogoths, who ruled during the minority of her son (526–35), whom she taught to read and write,[32] is most readily comparable to Anne. To complete his series of past and present analogies, Lemaire sets himself up as the continuator of the tradition of the greatest classical authors of myth and history, Virgil, Homer, and Livy. Reminding us, however, that this ballad in particular, like the manuscript book, has been dedicated to Anne, the poet explicitly addresses the envoy to the French queen, placing her on center stage through a celebration of her love of history, while implicitly suggesting that it is he who can spread word of her reputation through his literary talents as historian:[33]

> Princesse heureuse, ainsi comme la brasme
> Se meurt sans eaue, aussi le cueur s'affame
> A qui ne plaist des histoires la cresme.
> Mais vous l'aymez, par quoy vous aurez fame
> Resplendissant trop plus que nulle gemme. (12)

> [Blessed princess, just as the bream dies without water, so too is the heart of (s)he who is not interested in the best history starved. But

you love history, for which reason you will gain fame that glitters much more than any other gem.]

As Armstrong and Britnell suggest, this work, along with others in ms. 25295, figured centrally in Lemaire's efforts to obtain patronage at the French court (IV–VI) and doubtless inspired Anne to hire Lemaire de Belges as a court writer. Indeed, she subsequently commissioned him to write a chronicle of the history of Brittany.

Through the deployment of poetic instruments, including female personification allegory, and paratextual means, such as a visual rendition of Anne's emblems on the opening folio and a dedication to the queen, Lemaire's manuscript book for Anne of Brittany embodies a range of instruments used to flatter and honor his future patron, all the while lauding her husband's political achievements.

## Political Tensions and Contradictions in Jean Marot's *Voyage de Gênes*: Ambiguous Images of Female Modes of Empowerment

Like Lemaire's and Seyssel's manuscript books dedicated to Anne of Brittany, Jean Marot's *Voyage de Gênes* is a work that treats the heroic deeds of Louis XII but is offered solely to the French queen. Reminiscent of La Vigne's account of Charles VIII's Italian expedition in 1494–95, the *Voyage de Naples*, much of Marot's work consists of a *prosimetrum* chronicle of Louis' exploits during his victory over Genoa in 1507. Whereas La Vigne had kept his prewar allegorical narrative about internal political conflicts (*Ressource de la Chrestienté*) separate from his straightforward account of the French expedition after the fact (*Voyage de Naples*), Jean Marot, sought to entertain and divert his benefactor by combining his chronicle with an allegorical staging of characters. Gender ambiguities are associated this time with the enemy, *Gênes*, and her children, but female figures are hardly characters of strength and action. Personified figures are again manipulated to present conflict, but with the shift in political perspective, the particular role of females in this scenario is significantly more detrimental. Nonetheless, magnificent miniatures of these allegories dramatically set off the manuscript Marot dedicated to Anne, BnF ffr. 5091.

The 1,306 verses and 100 prose lines of the *Voyage de Gênes* recount in

detail one of the most publicized political events in Louis XII's reign up to
that point: the revolt of Genoa against French rule in a popular uprising in
1506 and France's success in quelling the city's vigorous resistance through
armed force, culminating in the French king's victorious entry into Genoa on
April 29, 1507.[34] The majority of the eleven miniatures decorating BnF ms.
ffr. 5091 depict these military skirmishes and triumphs. However, by fram-
ing his chronicle with an allegorical staging of *Gênes* admonishing her three
children, who are uncooperative in supporting her resistance to the French
king (vv. 125–298), and her enlightened conversion to *Raison* following her
defeat (ll. 39–100; vv. 861–1306), Marot embellishes his eyewitness account of
the king's victory over the Italian city to suit the taste of his dedicatee, Anne
of Brittany. Adopting a self-deprecating tone and vocabulary in his prologue,
like many contemporary court poets, the author confirms this conscious desire to cater to the French queen's tastes when he alludes to his effort to please
her in the following manner:

> Combien soit en faire ou en dire que trop petite chose puisse
> ma povre simplicité, toutesfoys congnoissant qu'à droit tout bon
> serviteur se doit esvertuer à son povoir soit en matieres graves ou
> aultrement de faire chose plaisante à l'oeil, recreative à l'esperit,
> consolative au diuturnel travail de son maistre ou maistresse, j'ay à
> diverses instances pourpensé de coucher par escript la magnanime
> victoire du roy trescrestien Loys XIIe, par luy obtenue en l'an mil
> cinq cens et sept au moys de may contre les Genevoys ses rebelles
> selon le vray effect sans adjunction ainsi que je l'ay continuellement
> veu suyvant son excercice tant à l'exploict que apres jusques à son
> retour. (ll. 1–12)

> [Although my poor simplicity can be only too little of a thing in
> action or in word, nevertheless recognizing that every good servant
> by right should strive within his power, either in serious subjects or
> otherwise, to create something pleasing to the eye, agreeable to the
> mind, comforting to the daily trials of his master or mistress, I have
> several times thought about recording the magnificent victory of the
> most Christian king Louis XII, achieved by him in May 1507 against
> his rebel Genoans according to the truth without any addition, just
> as I continually saw it in witnessing his activity, including both his
> actual exploits and their aftermath up to his return.]

That the author refers to pleasing the queen through visual means suggests that he knew his transcribed work was to be illustrated. Indeed, Jean Bourdichon, one of the queen's favorite court painters and well known as miniaturist of the *Heures d'Anne de Bretagne*,[35] produced the exquisite miniatures in ms. 5091. Marot obviously "set his sights" on both members of the royal couple, with whom he enjoyed a special relationship. Secretary to the queen, he also figured as part of the king's entourage during his military expedition to Genoa in 1507. While his poetic chronicle was designed to comfort his patroness, the passage cited above confirms that it was Marot's idea to write and dedicate the work to Anne. Although the queen does not seem to have commissioned this particular composition, as was sometimes the case, it was probably expected that as her secretary Marot would furnish her with writings in her honor. Unlike La Vigne's dedicatory comments in his account of the queen's 1504 coronation and entry into Paris, which the poet had modestly restricted to a few verses at the end of his work (see above, 53) and Lemaire's relatively modest dedication of the *Dyalogue* to Anne, Marot provides more expansive and effusive dedicatory remarks in the prologue of his *Voyage de Gênes*. Articulating his goal of diverting the queen from the numerous demands placed upon her through his literary embellishments, while maintaining his self-deprecating posture as the queen's humble servant, Marot offers readers insight into Anne's generous support of courts artists at the time:

> Toutesfoys, me confiant en la clemence et gracieuse bonté de tous
> temps experimentée de vous, ma treshaulte dame et princesse
> Anne, par la grace de Dieu Royne de France, Duchesse de
> Bretaigne et cetera j'ay prins conclusion de descrire non en tel stille
> qu'il appartient, mais seulement en lourde et par trop basse forme
> ainsi que la grosseur de mon petit entendement la peu comprendre,
> pour seullement par quelque bien petite espace d'heure les grandes
> cures et solicitudes de voz esperitz entreoublier. Parquoy, ma dame,
> desirant par toutes voyes cercher moyens d'acomplir chose qui
> vous soit agreeable, toutesfoys indigne et incapable de ce faire, je
> Jehan Des Marestz, vostre povre escripvain, serviteur treshumble
> des vostres treshumbles et tresobeyssans serviteurs, vous presente
> ce mien petit ouvrage à vous et non aultre voue et desdie, vous
> suppliant tant et si treshumblement comme faire le puys que à gré
> plaise, à l'humanité de vostre grace, ainsi que avez de l'heure de

voz premieres intelligences jusques à ce jour continuellement fait, le recepvoir. (ll. 19–38)

[Nevertheless, relying on the clemency and gracious goodness you have always shown, you, my most noble lady and princess Anne, by the grace of God Queen of France, Duchess of Brittany, etc., I decided to describe [this event] not in the appropriate style but only in a heavy and too lowly form such as the turgidity of my little mind can understand it, in order to, if only for a short time, help you forget the great cares and preoccupations of your mind. That is why, my lady, wishing to find the means to create something that will please you in every way possible, but nevertheless unworthy and incapable of doing so, I, Jean Marot, your poor writer, present to you this little work of mine; to you and no other I offer and dedicate it, begging you as ever so humbly as I can that it please you to receive it willingly, according to the humanity of your grace, just as you have continuously done from the hour you were born until this day.]

Four miniatures of the drama of personified figures invented by Marot to please the queen present Bourdichon's visual re-creation of the poet's allegorical narrative frame (fols. 6r, 27r, 34v, 37v).[36] One presents a weeping female dressed in black and seated upon a throne in a room that is similarly draped in black; both her robe and the wall hangings are flecked with silver tears (Figure 15). Before her stand two men held back by a disconsolate woman. Another illustration offers the reader an equally imposing scene, in which the same female mourner now lies on a bed inside a dark room draped in the same black pattern as in the previous illustration; she is surrounded by an old man and two grieving women (Figure 16). These two miniatures initially seem out of place in a work that celebrates King Louis XII's recent victory over Genoa. And yet a closer examination of the miniatures and careful reading of the accompanying text confirm that the funereal drama played out in these images constitutes an allegorical staging of the defeat of the king's enemy, namely *Gênes*, or the city of Genoa herself. The attempts of two of Genoa's sons, *Marchandise* (Merchant Class) and *Peuple* (the People), to console her are checked by *Honte* (Shame), thereby leading to her suicidal state. In a life-saving gesture, *Raison* (Reason) intervenes, chasing away *Raige*, *Douleur* (Grief), and *Desespoir* (Despair). With her aid and enlightenment, Genoa

15. Jean Marot, *Le Voyage de Gênes*, Paris, BnF ffr. 5091, fol. 27r: *Gênes* laments before *Marchandise* and *Le Peuple* whose hands are held by *Honte*. Bibliothèque Nationale de France.

16. Jean Marot, *Le Voyage de Gênes*, Paris, BnF ffr. 5091, fol. 34v: *Gênes* laments before *Raige*, *Douleur* and *Désespoir*, whom *Raison* comes to chase away. Bibliothèque Nationale de France.

17. Jean Marot, *Le Voyage de Gênes*, Paris, BnF ffr. 5091, fol. 37v: *Gênes* thanks *Raison*. Bibliothèque nationale de France.

enters the *Chambre de Vraye Cognoissance* (the Chamber of True Knowledge), where she finds peace, stability, and repose (Figure 17).[37] In literal terms, Genoa ends her resistance to the foreign invader from France and succumbs to the domination of Louis XII. Or, as Jean Marot's partial interpretation implies, Genoa, having finally come to her senses, gratefully accepts the judicious rule of the French victor. She has thus been converted to his ways. Metaphorically speaking, the nervous breakdown and near suicide of a woman, translated visually and verbally into a scenario of grief and mourning,[38] are transfigured into allegorical form so as to contrast all the more dramatically with the king's triumphant expedition to Italy.

This scenario from the *Voyage de Gênes* serves as a key text in my discussion of the corpus of works I am examining, because its images dramatically evoke certain contradictions and ambiguities concerning the representation of late medieval women of power in French books written for and about them. Through an examination of the gender of mourning and of private and public activity, the manipulation of grammatical genders, and the relationship between text and image, I aim to uncover the underlying sexual and political tensions in the depiction of females in the *Voyage de Gênes*. Far from the source of delight or consolation that it is purported to be, this work, I argue, served as an "ideological carrier,"[39] that is, an agent in the construction of the female gender that restricted women to interior spaces, mourning, and prayer. It is Marot's ingenious reworking of martial events into a literary scenario more palatable for the queen, namely the narrative of a military confrontation between a historical male figure and an allegorical female character, that sets the stage for the surfacing of latent tensions in this work.

Marot's dedication of the elaborately decorated manuscript 5091 to Anne of Brittany was obviously intended to be a gesture of homage, as the opening miniature of the poet on his knee offering the book to his patroness confirms (Figure 18). Indeed, his subservient position contrasts with the imposing, authoritative pose of the queen, who is surrounded in this image by a number of women representing her entourage, reminiscent of the dedication miniature in Anne's special copy of Seyssel's *Louenges du roy Louys XIIe*.[40] And yet, despite this visual exaltation of the queen in her empowered state as a benefactor, an image corroborated by Marot's accompanying verbal self-deprecation, as expressed in his dedication to the queen, considerable ambivalence about the role of women is transmitted by the manuscript book's author as well as its artist.

The images of Louis XII and his forces in ms. 5091 are consistently

18. Jean Marot, *Le Voyage de Gênes*, Paris, BnF ffr. 5091, fol. 1r: Jean Marot offers his completed book to Queen Anne of Brittany. Bibliothèque Nationale de France.

spectacular and grandiose. Seated astride his horse outside the gates of Alexandria upon his departure from the city (15v), before his vast number of troops gathered on the outskirts of Genoa, as urban delegates request his clemency (20v), and surrounded by his entourage as it escorts him through Genoa in his triumphant entry (22v),[41] the French king figures at the center of military and political activity.[42] While it is not surprising that focus is placed on Anne of Brittany's husband in a work that celebrates his victory, the staging of a female protagonist in countervailing images is unusual and stands in sharp contrast to the depictions of the king. This tension can be explained in historical terms by the fact that a foreign power was making his entrance into a reluctantly supportive city, but the details of the literary reconstruction of this event yield an ambiguous scenario for the medieval and modern reader.

What is most visually striking throughout the queen's manuscript copy of the *Voyage de Gênes* is the conspicuous differentiation between the illustrations of the victorious battles and entries, which literally and gloriously portray King Louis XII in very public spaces filled with crowds, and the miniatures depicting the allegorized tale of the domineering, then dolorous and depressed, and finally reborn figure of Genoa, all of which are located in increasingly constricted interior spaces, with a diminishing number of actors.[43] The scenes of Genoa move from semipublic council rooms, the first with windows (Figure 19), the second without (Figure 15), to her bedroom (Figure 16), and finally to the private chapel presumably located near her chambers (Figure 17). She simultaneously progresses from an enthroned position to a bedridden state to bended knee. Thus, Genoa's status as a haughty (*superbe*) city is both visually and verbally reversed. This juxtaposition of manuscript illuminations of majestic exterior settings and of confining interior spaces ever so subtly explores the implication that the male king has successfully invaded the territory and space of the female adversary.[44] But this violation is made explicit in an extraordinary passage in one of Genoa's speeches in which she draws this analogy in the most violent of terms, that of the rape of a virgin:[45]

Ainsi vaincue, palle, blesme, adollée,
De desespoir presque toute affollée,
Contrainte fuz de luy ouvrir ma porte
Et, neantmoins que jamais maculée
N'avoyt esté, fut lors despucellée,
Car jamais homme n'y entra de la sorte. (vv. 897–902)

19. Jean Marot, *Le Voyage de Gênes*, Paris, BnF ffr. 5091, fol. 6r: *Gêne* addresses her children, *Noblesse*, *Marchandise* and *Le Peuple*. Bibliothèque Nationale de France.

[Thus vanquished, pale, wan, afflicted, almost completely
diminished by despair, I was forced to open my door to him and,
although I had never been sullied, I lost my virginity then and
there, for never had a man entered in that fashion.]

Alluding to the idea of constriction and constraint in both visual and verbal
terms, and to the king's forced entry in textual terms alone—note Marot's
exploitation of the familiar metaphor of the "open door" for the "open body"
of the woman—this manuscript book collocates literal imperialist tropes of
the dominating French male who triumphs and allegorical renditions of the
resistant female enemy who is sexually assaulted and battles depression and
suicide before finding supposed consolation by capitulating to the foreign
victor.

Such images of rape in the context of war during the Middle Ages, while
usually sympathetic to the victim and critical of the assailant, could be quite
ambivalent, according to Diane Wolfthal, since sexual violation by soldiers
was often considered legitimate. Wolfthal points out that women surviving
rape were often expected to undergo a process similar to mourning (182), and
that medieval images tended to offer evidence of a bleak aftermath to the
experience involving shame, suicide, and death (184). Both Marot and Bourdichon thus adopted conventional iconography in their portrayal of Genoa in
the queen's manuscript, while legitimizing the king's violation of the female
figure.

The one image in the *Voyage de Gênes* that can be construed as conjoin-
ing the allegorical world of the female ruler-victim with the literal space of
invading male royal power is the Genoa entry scene itself, which presents
adoring girls and admiring female spectators looking out windows along the
entry route,[46] as Louis XII, clad in military attire, makes his way through the
city streets.[47]

A disconcerting dimension of the manuscript book's entire staging—at
least for the postmodern reader—especially in light of the author's advertised
aim of providing Anne of Brittany with pleasant, entertaining, and comforting distraction from the daily demands of her life (ll. 4–6), is the expectation that Marot's female dedicatee will sympathize with and celebrate the
violator. There is no doubt that the French queen would have supported her
husband first and foremost. That he is portrayed as a violator, however, subtly
undercuts his role as victor. Such a focus, which points up the contradiction
between authorial intention and textual realities, suggests that the *Voyage de*

*Gênes* may have really been a book made by men for men—the author and artist were presumably "speaking" through the queen to the king—since the monarch's implicit comforting of the converted Genoa and the author's supposedly consoling words to Anne of Brittany are seriously undermined by antifeminine representations. As we learned above in this chapter, a number of other books associated with the French queen likewise appear to be volumes that targeted the king through her.

These underlying sexual tensions in the *Voyage de Gênes* manuscript are reinforced not only by the author's offhand sexist remarks, whose conventional nature doubtless rendered them barely noticeable—Marot, for example, refers to the women of Milan as "si belle marchandise [such lovely merchandise]" (v. 829)[48]—but also by a curious gender distortion. For Genoa's children and subjects, *Noblesse*, *Marchandise*, and *Peuple*, are all textually and visually depicted as males,[49] despite the fact that only one of the words used—*Peuple*—is of the masculine grammatical gender. Author and artist have colluded in depicting the agents of the aristocratic and bourgeois classes, *Noblesse* and *Marchandise*, as well as *Peuple*, in masculine and, we may suspect, more authoritative bodies. Only when they fail to stand up for her against the French king does Genoa reconfigure two of her children in feminine terms—but in derogatory fashion—as she labels her spineless sons, *Marchandise* and *Peuple*, effeminate: "O lasches cueurs, effeminez enffans" [Oh cowardly hearts, effeminate children] (v. 1008).[50]

By contrast, *Gênes* visually and textually retains the feminine grammatical form of her name, as she plays the role of the admonishing mother and enemy ruler. The pejoratively labeled *Honte* likewise maintains her feminine grammatical identity, precipitating Genoa's depression through association with her two cowardly sons and sending her into a state of deep grief. Both text and image recount how Genoa repeatedly breaks into tears and experiences fainting spells, laments her fate, and suffers fits of despair that lead her to near suicide.[51] As characters personified in female form in accordance with the grammatical gender of their names, *Rage* and *Douleur* too participate in this grieving. The only male figure involved in this mourning process is the monstrous old man portraying *Désespoir*, who is associated with suicide and insanity, in a rather terrifying description (ll. 55–71).

Corroborating Paul Binski's assessment of lamentation in medieval art, namely that "gestures of despair" were considered to be female attributes and that the "codification of grief" was usually "the special preserve of women,"[52] one of the implicit ideological codes of this manuscript book is that mourning and depression are more appropriately associated with females. But grieving assumes a negative valence in this particular work, whose aim is to justify and celebrate the French king's victorious assault on and entry into Genoa. Moreover, whereas it was men who had played the role of mourners in the historically anchored versions of Louis' entry into Genoa,[53] Jean Marot recasts this episode in almost exclusively feminine terms in his allegorical re-creation of the moment. With the exception of *Désespoir*, those forces resisting submission to French direction and guidance—*Gênes*, *Honte*, *Rage*, and *Douleur*—are depicted as females in mourning, albeit in stunning miniatures in which the grieving and feeble *Honte* tries to intervene and the pattern of black tears decorating Genoa's mourning clothes spill over onto the blanket on her bed and is repeated on all the walls of her bedchamber.

By contrast, male enemy forces, Genoa's children, demonstrate less offensive behavior vis-à-vis the French, by cooperating with the foreign ruler. For example, *Noblesse*, betraying his mother and brothers, is in fact France's ally from the start (vv. 51–72, 133–64), whereas *Marchandise* and *Peuple* easily surrender to the French (vv. 1017, 1928–37). Not only are gender lines readily crossed by collaborating author and artist for political expediency, but female figures in the *Voyage de Gênes* have essentially no redeeming value—until *Raison* makes her brief appearance at the end. Although depicted as a female, however, *Raison* is actually associated with masculine victory, in perhaps an unconscious allusion to the conventional medieval alliance of males with reason and females with emotions.

Curiously, another allegorical staging of Genoa as a grieving woman in a contemporary narrative related to Louis XII's mission in Italy offers a positive portrait of the personified city. In the *Complaincte de Gennes sur la mort de dame Thomassine Espinolle, Genevoise, dame entendyo du roy*, Jean d'Auton recounts the death of Louis XII's Genoese female acquaintance who, believing the French king had died in 1505, succumbed to death herself out of grief. The city of Genoa accorded Thomassine an elaborate funeral.[54]

I would like to step back briefly here to discuss the negatively valenced female personifications of the *Voyage de Gênes* by invoking the enlightening studies of Cristelle Baskins ("Trecento Rome: The Poetics and Politics of Widowhood") and James Paxson ("Personification of Gender"). In the first place, Marot's dramatization of *Gênes* in the allegorical staging he inserts into his *Voyage de Gênes* to please Anne of Brittany recalls the tradition of widowed Rome discussed by Baskins. Although not textually described as a widow—Genoa's husband is never mentioned[55]—she has been abandoned by her children and displays in verbal and visual terms extensive signs of mourning. In reminding us that allegory "allows for the convergence of volatile and contradictory social, political, and gendered messages" (198), Baskins's evocation of the dual identity of Rome in triumph and in mourning anticipates that of Genoa in the *Voyage de Gênes*. Rome, with distorted facial expression, streaming hair, and the tearing of her clothes to expose her chest in the fourteenth-century *Panegyric to King Robert of Anjou* is shown, like Chartier's *France* and La Vigne's *Dame Chrestienté*, "in a pitiful condition, not capable of action herself but inspiring salvation through the intervention of male authority" (201–2). Baskins astutely uncovers the underlying sociopolitical problematic of this widow iconography, contextualizing it with contemporary social practices:

> The personification of Rome, in the *Panegyric to King Robert of Anjou* or in the frescoes commissioned by Cola di Rienzo, registers a crisis over the management of widows in the Trecento. The depiction of widowed Rome recalls traditional women's mourning but also its taint of excess, of uncontainable emotion and potential violence. Late medieval texts and images of widowed Rome fuse sorrow, rage and desire; in so doing they contribute to the projection of threat, which in turn excuses efforts to control and discipline the disorderliness associated with widowhood. On the local level, the widow threatens family disintegration and economic well-being; the widowed city shows in macroscopic form how the community is threatened and how it requires a collective response. The vivid expressiveness of widowed Rome indicates more than just naturalism or pictorial skill; it speaks in that secretive language that Gordon Teskey finds integral to the political risk and political care of allegory. (208–9)

In the end, Baskins's analysis of Rome in late medieval texts and art calls attention to the use of female personification allegory to explore contemporary political tensions:

> Allegorical imagery, so often analyzed within Art History as a puzzle with universal meanings to be deciphered, is better understood as an equivocation responding to the specific historical and political contingencies of its production. (209)

Paxson too builds his ideas about personification on the female city. He accepts the grammar-identity argument as explanation of "the . . . femininity of personified characters in the allegory produced in the late Middle Ages" (153)—that is, the fact that most personified figures were female, because most abstract nouns in Latin and French tended to be feminine. But he extends that argument to propose a complementary theory that takes into account rhetorical, semiological, and ideological structures, which, in a number of respects, resonates with the text under discussion here.

Paxson traces the association of the female gender and personified forms back to the famous *Rhetorica ad Herennium* (first century B.C.E.), in which the definition of personification was built around the example of a speaking female city, an observation of double significance in our analysis of Genoa (my emphasis):

> Personification consists in representing an absent person as present, or in making a mute thing, or one lacking form articulate, and attributing to it a definite form and language or a certain behavior appropriate to its character, as follows: "But if this *invincible* city should now give utterance to her voice, would she not speak as follows? 'I, city of renown . . . am now vexed, O citizens, by your dissensions'." (cited by Paxson, 153)

In its development from a science of oratorical prowess and persuasion to "a massive inventory of tropes and figures" (165) by the first century A.D., Rhetoric became divided into a positive, honest, cultural practice associated with the masculine and a negative, deceptive, indulgent one associated with the feminine. Paxson describes this evolution in the following terms:

> In the act of persuasion, plain speech gets "dressed up" or "mantled," often to the detriment of the direct, the normal, the masculine, the healthy. Although the discourse of oratory existed as a masculine enterprise *par excellence* (one complementary to society's martial arts), tropes and figures more and more became sheer "ornaments" in a "cosmetic" economy of verbal production. (166)

Thus, at the same time that personification had become the rhetorical trope of embodiment, because it was constituted according to features of cloth-ing, facades, cosmetics, and even concealment, the "dressed-up" speech of

Rhetoric was beginning to provoke negative associations with females. Inevitably, actual personifications in narratives were, as Paxson puts it, "forced to adopt female bodies" (172). Moreover, since personification involved the creation of speakers, it was talkative women who, by default, came to figure as the signs of prosopopeia (177–78). This automatic linking of females to dressed-up personifications and to ornamental rhetorical tropes in increasingly derogatory fashion may in fact have helped promote the culture, or "discourse," of misogyny (154) that R. Howard Bloch describes in *Medieval Misogyny and the Invention of Western Romantic Love* as a persistent force in ancient and medieval literature.

While male personifications figured increasingly in late medieval allegories—accompanied on occasion by the gender distortions I alluded to earlier—the deep-seated, often negative associations drawn between females and personified forms in earlier medieval culture are still very much alive in Marot's *Voyage de Gênes*, by virtue of the fact that the central female allegorical figures are made by the author to speak and act excessively and inappropriately, at least until the dénouement. In a sense, Jean Marot's work still bears the traces of the transition from classical to medieval Rhetoric through its deconstruction of the *invincible* female city promoted in the *Rhetorica ad Herennium* into a weak, personified Genoa, who is not only violated and conquered, but also whose discourse is, prior to conversion, implicitly self-indulgent and emotionally excessive. Unlike the *Gênes* of Auton's tribute to Thomassine Espinolle with whose grief the audience is meant to sympathize, Marot's *Gênes* has appropriated the negative and threatening attributes of the widowed Rome described by Baskins.

But such implicit frictions are seemingly resolved in the last illumination found in the queen's manuscript copy of the *Voyage de Gênes* (Figure 17). Here we discover a resplendent miniature of the protagonist on her knees before Reason, an encounter that marks an end to her lamentations, while contrasting with the two previous very somber scenes (Figures 15 and 16). Moreover, this scenario offers a spiritual dimension that is all but absent from Marot's text, for Reason visually resembles the Virgin Mary.[56] Attenuating the explicit violence of the textual metaphor of rape invoked earlier, this miniature situates the female protagonist in a less offensive and in fact quite familiar, controlled, and more acceptable posture, that of a woman kneeling alone in prayer within a private chapel. With the taming of Genoa as she progresses from her domineering position as an enthroned woman to one in mourning and then in enlightened prayer—doubtless a more palatable visual metaphor for her sexual and political submission to a male ruler—the *Voyage de Gênes* elucidates, consciously or unconsciously, late medieval codes concerning the appropriate portrayal of (noble) women. In fact, the illustration of Genoa in prayer before the Virgin figure anticipates Bourdichon's famous miniature of Anne of Brittany in the *Grandes Heures d'Anne de Bretagne* painted around the same period of time.

Yet, the representation of Genoa embodies an inherent ambiguity, since the reader is uncertain whether she should actually sympathize with the female enemy figure during her psychological journey from ruler to ruled, from an internally excessive state to an externally controlled one. For in addition to the metaphor of rape—a problematic image to promote in a work offered to the French queen—the literary construction of Genoa as a mourner inevitably recalls several French allegorical ancestors, such as *France* in Alain Chartier's *Quadrilog invectif* (1422) or *Dame Chrestienté* in La Vigne's *Ressource de la Chrestienté* (1494). For example, the grieving of *Chrestienté*, who in a state of dishevelment and near madness bemoans the divisive nature of her children's actions, had in this earlier work been clearly designed to elicit audience sympathy.[57] With such intertextual references in mind, Anne of Brittany's loyalty to her husband and support of his violation of a woman may have been tested—at least in literary terms—with this partially sympathetic, albeit ambiguous, portrayal of his female victim and enemy in the *Voyage de Gênes*.

Indeed, the similarity between the spaces inhabited by both *Gênes* and Anne of Brittany in this and subsequent manuscript miniatures inextricably—and unexpectedly—associates these two female figures with each other more than it does the queen with the king, which would be the more expected alliance. Like Genoa, the queen appears in the dedication miniature in a semipublic interior space, one seemingly more appropriate to women in ms. 5091 (Figure 18). On the one hand, Anne of Brittany, praised in word by Marot, is visually displayed by Bourdichon in a position of power in this miniature, as she, like innumerable patrons of this period, receives the dedicated book from the author. Furthermore, Marot's classic position on bended knee before his patroness and the focus of his eyes on her bespeak complete reverence. Anne herself appears engaged in the moment as she leans slightly forward to take the book with her right hand from the poet and, as suggested by her left hand, speaks to her protégé. On the other hand, the queen's female entourage is rather passive. The "talking hands" that often characterize witnesses' behavior during book dedications, as we saw in the dedication miniature in Seyssel's *Louenges du roy Louys XIIe*, are absent from this scene. In addition, the position of the queen's seat at floor level contrasts visually with that of Genoa whose throne is raised above her subjects in her initial presentation (Figure 19), but who essentially "pays the price" in the end by being dethroned.[58]

Anne's lower seated position in this and dedication miniatures associated with other works she received[59] thus distinguishes her from the "ruler image"[60] visually associated with Genoa in manuscript 5091 and with the queen's husband in an illuminated manuscript in which they share visual prominence.[61] These images may implicitly invoke the ritual whereby the French queen traditionally took a lower throne than the king at her own coronation.[62] In BnF ms. 5091, the miniatures illustrating female figures of power seemingly promote the idea that enthroned women in action, like Genoa, end up being cast in lower, less domineering, more interiorized roles as women grieving or submitting to a higher authority. Such an implication is all but confirmed verbally, when Marot chronicles how Louis XII's "ruler image" replaces that of Genoa, who, following her defeat, exclaims in reference to the victorious French monarch: "Et luy estant en siege magnifique / Me prononça nouvelles loix et drois" [And from his magnificent seat he pronounced to me new laws and decrees] (vv. 917–18). Genoa's words mirror historical reality, for following his entry into the defeated city in 1507, Louis XII took his place upon a throne that had been set on a large constructed platform in the courtyard of the doges' palace, consciously exploiting the dramatic power of public spectacle.[63]

The undermining of the sociopolitical status of both Genoa and, to a lesser degree of Anne of Brittany, in the queen's manuscript book resonates in another way with the remarks of Paxson. He astutely observes that at the same time that textual and fictional personifications in medieval works came to imitate the forms of actual women, "real women in the patriarchal world of early modern Europe were in many cases treated something like personified agents, lifted," as they were, "out of history," and "often deprived of significant social power and suitable ontological status by men" (172–73). It is the intersection of such underlying literary and political forces, concretized through the mutually reinforcing associations between the personified Genoa within the text and the historical figure of the French queen outside of the text, that works to keep the dedicatee of the *Voyage de Gênes*, Anne of Brittany, in her place. The subtly transparent interconnections drawn both visually and verbally between the text's protagonist and royal reader serve in the end as a literary and semiotic reminder of the queen's true position vis-à-vis her husband and France's male ruler.[64]

The dedication manuscript of the *Voyage de Gênes*, then, although written and decorated with the goal of pleasing and even comforting the French queen, offers a somewhat contradictory image of the very female to whom the work was dedicated. Superficially speaking, the image of Anne of Brittany in Marot's dedication manuscript interfaces well with the glorified portrait of French royalty commonly celebrated by male writers and artists in historical and cultural documents of the period, the one that dominates La Vigne's manuscript account of her 1504 coronation. But at a more subtle level, this manuscript book unconsciously contests the celebration of royal women through Anne's implicit affiliation with its female antiprotagonist. This and other examples of the potential conflict that surfaced in male-authored, male-illustrated works for and about noble females point to a deep-seated ambivalence concerning the representation of women of power in late medieval Europe, corroborating Caviness's suggestion that images of women bookowners in earlier centuries were sometimes made "against" rather than "for" them (106).

But why this ambivalence, especially about the French queen herself? Because, I would argue, Marot's *Voyage de Gênes* embodies not only the tensions over power and control that arose between the French king and Genoa, but also, consciously or unconsciously, the political anxiety at the heart of the royal relationship that figures literally and metaphorically in this work. In the last analysis, the *Voyage de Gênes* is a narrative about the contradictions concerning the cultural and political assimilation of noble women, especially foreign-born queens, in late fifteenth- and early sixteenth-century France. I would go so far as to suggest that the *Voyage de Gênes* is, in thinly disguised form, a recreation of the subjection of a rival duchess and the making and remaking of a queen. It is, in other words, the metaphoric narrative of Anne of Brittany's own political trajectory.

There is no doubt that issues of sovereignty lurk at the dynamic center of the work. The confrontation between Louis XII and the city of Genoa, or its feminized form *Gênes*, offers the most obvious incarnation of a late medieval and early modern *mise en question* of female empowerment. Less explicit are the allusions to past and present power struggles between the French queen and king themselves, although the correlations drawn between Genoa and Anne of Brittany encourage readers to uncover such implicit references. In evoking this latent political dimension of the *Voyage de Gênes*, I draw on the suggestive remarks made by Louise Fradenburg in "Rethinking Queenship," the introduction to her edited volume entitled *Women and Sovereignty*.[65]

Fradenburg's discussion of the ambiguous nature of the sovereignty of medieval queens finds concrete corroboration in the case of Anne of Brittany, queen to two succeeding French kings. Becoming queen only through marriage, like most of her medieval counterparts—but unlike their husbands who ascended to the throne by virtue of their own sociopolitical rank and status—Anne of Brittany implicitly accepted as a consequence of her betrothal to two French kings, a situation in which the concepts of marriage and sovereignty (or lack thereof) were inextricably intertwined. In Anne's particular case, her prior sovereignty as duchess of Brittany[66] was actually compromised through her assumption of the queenship, given that she lost control of Brittany to her first husband, interested in assimilating the duchy into the French kingdom, and that as queen of France, she could never legally reign in her own right. Anne of Brittany was essentially accorded a place at the margins of the official institutions and practices of authority in France.[67] Because she, like many other medieval queens, hailed from beyond the French kingdom, Anne was at the same time a potentially threatening external force. At once an embodiment of the unity of her people,[68] she also represented the forces that might undermine and ultimately divide them.[69] Just like other medieval queens, she was torn between conflicting loyalties by virtue of her inherited sovereignty as duchess of Brittany and her accession to the French throne as queen. Fradenburg and Parsons, among others, remind us that while a noble male's place in the medieval world was determined by a single patrilineal family tie, an aristocratic woman's place was determined by multiple family allegiances.[70] Indeed, Anne of Brittany's relationships with both Charles VIII and Louis XII were influenced to a large extent by her overarching desire for the independence of her native territory, the duchy of Brittany.

In 1491, Brittany, with Duchess Anne at its head, had been subdued by the military might of her rival, the king of France, Charles VIII. As part of the peace treaty negotiations, Anne had agreed to marry Charles. On the one hand, it was Anne herself—and not a patriarchal figure such as father or son—who had determined her own matrimonial destiny, who had negotiated her own exchange, as it were, signaling an unusually powerful role for a woman.[71] On the other hand, Anne was, in the end, forced to concede complete control over the duchy of Brittany to the king of France. While all the details are not exactly the same, the parallels between Anne and Marot's *Gênes* are nonetheless evident: a reigning female sovereign is dethroned and in "enlightened" submission renders herself to her conqueror, symbolizing the union of two sovereign territories.[72]

Upon the death of Charles VIII, however, Anne regained independent control of Brittany.[73] Finding herself in a more powerful position when marriage negotiations with Louis XII were under way,[74] Anne ensured that Brittany would not be automatically integrated into France this time around. She jealously guarded the independence of her administration in her duchy throughout the reign of Louis, who, unlike his predecessor, did not interfere with her control over it. In fact, Anne not only held separate court and maintained separate audiences with visiting ambassadors, but she also filled her entourage with more Bretons than French, repeatedly advertising the distinction she liked to make between her "ducal coronet and her regal crown."[75] John S. C. Bridge offers the following, rather chauvinistic, assessment of Anne of Brittany's priorities at this point in time. She was, according to him:

> always ready to sacrifice the unity of France to a selfish and
> short-sighted passion for the independence of Brittany. It was
> in this spirit that she had dictated the terms of her second
> marriage contract, with its numerous precautions for defeating
> French interests. In the same spirit she would pursue for years
> the project of marrying her daughter into the House of Austria
> and so preserving the independence of Brittany at the cost of
> dismembering a united France for the benefit of its most dangerous
> foe. (III, 26)

Anne of Brittany, then, representing a potentially threatening force, came to assume a political profile that resembled that of *Gênes* at the beginning of Marot's work. Like her literary counterpart, albeit in figurative fashion, Anne found herself challenged and ultimately defeated by French political forces during a number of highly charged domestic confrontations, including the betrothal of her daughter Claude. The concurrence of this political episode involving Anne herself, which dates from the period leading up to and overlapping with Louis XII's conquest of Genoa, and the redaction of the *Voyage de Gênes* (1506–7) was, I would argue, more than coincidental. As the conscious or unconscious voice of the political codes of a male-dominated society, Marot, with the visual support of Bourdichon, was implicitly offering his dedicatee a moral lesson, or reminder, of the consequences of a rebellious "foreign" queen.

It was Anne's "unwavering determination" to preserve the independence of Brittany over its absorption into France (Bridge, III, 206–7) that dictated her adamant opposition to the engagement of her daughter Claude to the French heir apparent, Francis of Angoulême. The queen's search for a "separatist settlement" through the marriage of her daughter to Charles of Luxembourg of the House of Austria, ostensibly with the support of Louis XII himself, was rewarded in September 1504 by the signing of the Treaties of Blois. Anne had, like many of her female counterparts, succeeded in wielding power through her participation in what John Parsons calls "matrimonial politics."[76] However, in spring 1506, the king broke off that engagement, because, as the monarch claimed, he could no longer resist increasing French public opposition to Claude's proposed marriage to a foreigner, an anxiety that loomed all the larger with Louis XII's recent series of near-death illnesses. Evidence reveals, nonetheless, that as early as May 1505, one entire year beforehand, Louis XII had, during the absence of Anne of Brittany from the court, made a will stipulating that if he died, the Austrian marriage treaty was to be ignored and Claude was to be wed "at home" to the French heir to the throne. Publicly, however, it was at the meeting of nobles and deputies in Tours in May 1506 that the official decision took place.[77]

Thus, in rather duplicitous fashion, the French king had his way over the wishes of his queen.[78] In fact, the official engagement of Claude and Francis was formally celebrated in May 1506, at the very moment that the city of Genoa was challenging French rule. As a consequence of this unsuccessful turn of events, Brittany was eventually absorbed into France.[79] Thus, while Parsons offers convincing evidence that matrimonial politics provided medieval queens a means to empower themselves by crossing the boundaries of the unofficial sphere to which they were limited and the official sphere in which their husbands functioned (*Medieval Queenship*, 75–76), Anne of Brittany's particular history shows how she was in fact disempowered in her efforts to control matrimonial politics and, as Bourdichon's images suggest, relegated to the marginalized, unofficial sphere of French royal activity. Even Anne's potential to serve as a regent upon the king's death—another manner in which medieval queens traditionally wielded significant power—was undermined by the designation in Louis XII's will that she serve as *co*-regent with her rival and mother of the French heir, Louise of Savoy.[80] Anne's death, however, preceded that of her husband.

One particular image in the library of Louis XII offers visual evidence of the official historic moment that marked Anne of Brittany's failure to maintain the independence of Brittany through her choice of Claude of France's husband: her daughter's engagement to the heir apparent, the future Francis I in May 1506.[81] In fact, its position as the opening miniature of the second volume of a manuscript copy of Jean d'Auton's *Chroniques* (BnF ffr. 5083, fol. IV) lends it a particularly privileged status (see Figure 2).[82] Although not of the same artistic quality as other miniatures examined above, its staging surprisingly resembles the images of entry theaters, in particular those decorating the festival books of Claude of France's coronation. In the upper register, an enthroned Louis XII with scepter in hand dominates the scene: nobles stand at the right and deputies at the left, who had supposedly demanded at the recent council of the Estates General in Tours that the king's daughter marry a French royal figure "pour le bien et utillité du royaume de France" [for the welfare and utility of the French kingdom].[83] At the center of the illustration, on the lower stage, Cardinal Georges d'Amboise, accompanied by two other cardinals, blesses the young couple, Claude of France at the left and Francis of Angoulême at the right. The mothers of each fiancé, Anne of Brittany and Louise of Savoy, each with her outside arm supporting that of her child, are depicted in symmetrical fashion—except that Anne is the only crowned female figure. In addition, a coterie of females, one of whom holds up the lower end of Anne's and Louise's dress, stands behind each mother.

As Le Fur states, "Toutes et tous sourient. Cette miniature, véritable image officielle, symbolise l'union des trois États autour du roi, pour le bonheur et la prospérité du royaume" (*Anne de Bretagne*, 114). That is, this image is meant to depict the solidarity of the people and court behind the engagement of Claude and Francis. Any evidence of Anne of Brittany's anger at Louis' manipulation of the situation, manifested in her departure for Brittany in June 1505 for some three months,[84] or of the rivalry between the French queen and Louise of Savoy at this time, are entirely absent from this liminal miniature or from Auton's accompanying account. As in other visual projections of royal figures, the court's desire to promote political interests—in this case, those of the king over the queen's—has not only taken precedence but also, as would be expected, repressed any suggestion of internal dissension over the issue.[85]

Anne's ambivalent position as both duchess of Brittany and queen of France also posed an obstacle to French internal affairs during the trial of the Maréchal de Gié, charged with high treason. Considered by Anne to be a renegade Breton, because his service to Charles VIII had led to the defeat of Anne's duchy, Gié, as leader of the opposition to the marriage of Claude and Charles of Luxembourg again seriously threatened Brittany's future sovereignty. Accused of a plot to arrest the queen upon the king's expected death,[86] tear up the treaty authorizing Claude's engagement to Charles, and marry Claude to Francis, an accusation that the king himself never seemed to take seriously, but for which Anne actively sought confirmation, Gié was convicted in February 1506 not of treason, however, but of "certain excesses and faults" (Bridge, III, 241). Nonetheless, his goal of assuring the union of France and Brittany through the marriage of Francis and Claude was ultimately achieved to the detriment of Anne's duchy. Precipitating a ground swell of public support for that union, this famous episode also coincided with the events in Genoa that would be recreated by Jean Marot in his *Voyage de Gênes* shortly thereafter.

Both historically and allegorically, then, Anne of Brittany's profile and reactions embodied the implicit contestation between the different spheres and practices of power that typified medieval queenship, with public and private, official and unofficial comportment figuring centrally in the royal equation of pomp and decorum.

Not only is there an unexpected, and doubtless unconscious, association between *Gênes* and Anne of Brittany in Marot's dedication manuscript of the *Voyage de Gênes*, but other portrayals of Anne, most of which appear in the books that figured in her library, echo the visual and verbal depictions of *Gênes* in grief, in prayer, in marginalized and controlled, enclosed spaces that punctuate MS 5091. The stunning image of *Gênes* in bed mourning, for example, could easily have illustrated Anne of Brittany's own distress over the death of her child Charles-Orland in December 1495 (Figure 16). Philippe de Commynes's description of the French queen at this moment contrasts with the more "rational" form of mourning of her first husband, King Charles VIII:

> Ledit seigneur en eut deuil, comme la raison le veut, mais peu luy
> dura le deuil; et la royne de France, duchesse de Bretagne, appellée
> Anne, en mena le plus grand deuil qu'il est possible que femme
> pust faire, et longuement luy dura ce deuil; et croy que, outre le
> deuil naturel que les mères ont accoutumé d'avoir de la perte de
> leurs enfans, que le coeur luy jugeoit quelque grand dommage à
> venir; mais au roy son mary dura peu ce deuil, comme dit est, et la
> voulut réconforter de faire dance devant elle.[87]

[The said lord grieved, as reason would have it, but his grief lasted
a short time; and the queen of France, the duchess of Brittany,
named Anne, manifested the greatest grief that was possible for
a woman to show, and her grief lasted a long time. And I believe
that, beyond the natural grief that mothers usually display at the
loss of their children, her heart condemned her to some great future
loss. But the king's grief lasted a short time, as has been said, and
he attempted to comfort her by having dancers brought before her.]

Charles's seemingly inappropriate attempts to comfort his wife[88] remind us of
Jean Marot's somewhat contradictory efforts to console Anne of Brittany by
dedicating to her his *Voyage de Gênes*, a work filled with images of lamentation, rape, and suicide.[89]

The active participation of Anne in these political events and their ultimate outcome prefigured, then, the political trajectory Marot assigned to
Genoa in his work. In much the same way that a queen could be ceremoni-
ously exalted, while state rituals simultaneously prescribed a submissive role
that secluded her from authority,[90] Marot's *Voyage de Gênes* uncovers inherent
political tensions and contradictions between male and female modes of empowerment in early sixteenth-century France. Both historically and allegorically, the queen's body, or rather that of her allegorical alter ego, had become
the site of contestation between different spheres and practices of power, between subjection and sovereignty.

The relationships analyzed above regarding Anne of Brittany, her book
and her bookmakers, and the people of France were, at the very least, tenu-
ous and ambivalent. The French queen's sociopolitical status within the book
culture itself presumably endowed her with exclusive power over the men
who authored and illustrated the books dedicated to her. After all, she held
the purse strings. And yet Anne's bookmakers served, consciously or not, as
ideological agents in the continued restriction of women's actions and powers. For it is not only that the male-endorsed associations between women
and rape, mourning and suicide, and political domination were so pervasive
in manuscript 5091. In addition, these images of women with restricted power
were presented as positive examples of female behavior. To complicate matters, Marot's rhetorical and literary systems in which personified females imitated the forms of actual women and real women were treated like personified
agents, these verbal systems that essentially sought to control female comportment, which was more often than not contrasted with that of men, were

translated by Bourdichon into stunning miniatures whose beauty endorsed that underlying message in resounding fashion.[91] At once a superficially praiseworthy representation of female royalty and an insidious sanctioning of established cultural codes that kept women of power in their place, the verbal and pictorial discourse examined in this chapter situated Anne of Brittany in a more restricted yet seemingly more acceptable place than her male counterparts. Offering, perhaps unconsciously, a moral lesson regarding her past and future political comportment, this recreation of the dynamics of the queen's own political trajectory, all but confirms that in the final analysis, Anne of Brittany was an unintended target as much as an honored recipient of the book that had been created in her name.

# Women Famous and Infamous:
# Court Controversies
# About Female Virtues

This chapter focuses on another form of literary reconstruction, namely the "famous-women" *topos*, whose wide popularity in fifteenth- and sixteenth-century Europe was generated to a large degree by the biographies in Boccaccio's *De mulieribus claris*. Translated into French in the early fifteenth century, Boccaccio's work also inspired imitations, such as Christine de Pizan's *Cité des Dames* (1404–5).[1] In the late fifteenth century, Louise of Savoy and her husband commissioned a manuscript version of one of the earlier French translations of Boccaccio's work (BnF ffr. 599). The first known edition of a French translation of Boccaccio's work (Paris: Antoine Vérard, 1493) was dedicated to Anne of Brittany. The French queen also commissioned an elaborately decorated manuscript book on this subject, Antoine Dufour's *Vies des femmes célèbres* (1504–6), which contains some ninety verbal and visual vignettes of classical, historical, and contemporary women of note, including Joan of Arc. Around the same period (1503) Symphorien Champier's *Nef des dames vertueuses*, dedicated to Anne of France, appeared in print. The writings of other court poets, such as Jean Marot and Jean Lemaire de Belges, were likewise strewn with references to famous and infamous women.[2]

Ambiguities surrounding male and female definitions of famous women as well as authors' and illuminators' reconstruction of them emerge through an examination of this corpus of writings. They offer insight into conceptions about women in late medieval and early Renaissance Europe and the manner in which the intended portrayal of females of rank by authorized male voices might have underpinned—or contested—contemporary realities. Indeed, inherent contradictions that surface in these works between the ostensible glorification of women and the literary and artistic means adopted toward that end suggest the existence of underlying tensions in male creations of works for and about women.[3]

## Boccaccio's *De mulieribus claris*: Textual and Pictorial Ambiguities

It is not surprising that the savvy Parisian bookseller-publisher Antoine Vérard chose to exploit the popular—and sometimes provocative—theme of famous women with his 1493 publication of an anonymous French translation of Giovanni Boccaccio's *De mulieribus claris*, one of the most celebrated works of the late medieval period.[4] Written for the most part in 1361–62,[5] Boccaccio's collection of 106 biographies of famous women from the classical, biblical, and medieval worlds was the first *recueil* in Western literature devoted to women alone.[6] But his catalogue of women offers an ambiguous assessment of females, at least to some modern readers, because, despite the many women he praises, Boccaccio essentially considers them to be inferior to men, due to their propensity to be unfaithful, lascivious, suspicious, avaricious, and stubborn. Some critics believe that Boccaccio's pervasive criticism of women nullifies their praiseworthy comportment and offers an ambiguous perspective vis-à-vis women.[7] Such an outlook reminds modern scholars of typical medieval male attitudes toward the opposite sex inherited from antiquity and Christian teachings.[8] Kolsky suggests, however, that the work's "extremely ambiguous" nature set the stage for a variety of future adaptations:

> By its ambiguities, Boccaccio's work constituted an extremely powerful, flexible and amenable model . . . [that] could be appropriated to vastly differing points of view; it could be shrewdly adapted to address diverse readerships, and to attend to changing social and political contexts. (4)

Indeed, several critics point out that in his *De mulieribus claris* Boccaccio actually presented women as greater intellectual and moral powers than most of his contemporaries or sources,[9] that his use of their stories as moral narratives authorized the presence of these unorthodox women in the visual arts, and that the work anticipated the Renaissance endorsement of the active participation of gifted women in art, literature, and public life.[10] Franklin's claim that "there is little doubt about *Famous Women*, either the text itself or its reception among those for whom it was written, to suggest that it would have been experienced as ambiguous or contradictory" (13) is tempered by Buettner, who straddles both camps by recognizing Boccaccio's ambivalence toward women and support of the female cause (18). Glenda McLeod (6–7) also sees both the innovative and conventional nature of Boccaccio's work. She contends, on the one hand, that the work "anticipates future links between the good woman and the good state," and, on the other, that it "is still largely conservative in its approach" (7)

It is true that in his dedication Boccaccio, although seemingly discrediting women because of their general physical and intellectual weaknesses, simultaneously praises (some of) them and claims that past oversights need to be rectified:

> If we grant that men deserve praise whenever they perform great
> deeds with the strength bestowed upon them, how much more
> should women be extolled—almost all of whom are endowed by
> nature with soft, frail bodies and sluggish minds—when they take
> on a manly spirit, show remarkable intelligence and bravery, and
> dare to execute deeds that would be extremely difficult even
> for men?
>
> Lest, therefore, such women be cheated of their just due, I had
> the idea of honoring their glory by assembling in a single volume
> the biographies of women whose memory is still green. To these
> I have added some lives from among the many women who are
> notable for their boldness, intellectual powers, and perseverance,
> or for their natural endowments, or for fortune's favor or enmity. I
> have also included a few women who, although they performed no
> action worthy of remembrance, were nonetheless causal agents in
> the performance of mighty deeds. (9–11)

And yet, while Franklin contends that it has been twentieth-century readers focusing on Boccaccio's contradictory messages who make interpretations of Boccaccio "murkier" now than they really were during the late medieval period (1), subsequent French imitators of Boccaccio, such as the anonymous translator of Vérard's edition of his work, Antoine Dufour and

Symphorien Champier, consciously adopted less ambiguous attitudes about women, at least in the prologues to their works.[11] These assessments, which I examine more closely below, confirm that well before modern skepticism about Boccaccio's representation of women, at least some early sixteenth-century French readers of his work (whether in Latin or French translation) approached his moralizing statements in the *De mulieribus claris* with a certain critical eye.

Although it is often difficult to assess the direct or indirect influence of female dedicatees such as Anne of Brittany in bringing to life this new rhetoric that questioned Boccaccio's relationship to the women whose biographies he authored, their contributions as commissioners and inspirational figures doubtless played a significant role in the cultural dissemination of Boccaccio's *De mulieribus claris* and its imitations. Through a close reading of both textual and paratextual material, I aim in this chapter to elucidate this role. As we shall learn, ambiguities in the relevant texts themselves, those that lie beyond the dedicatory prologue of these seemingly protofeminist works, point to an ambivalence about women among French male authors writing for female patrons that in the end approaches the contradictions in Boccaccio's own writing. Because such ambiguities lie (hidden) within the text itself, these imitators may well have conceived their prologues and subsequent texts differently, perhaps expecting that their work would not actually be read by their female dedicatees much beyond their protofeminist dedications. Furthermore, adherence to social codes by male artists creating works for female patrons may have been a subconscious force at work at the same time as expectations that their imitations of Boccaccio would ultimately reach a male audience.

In addition to the contradictions between ideas expressed in the prologue and the text proper in the various French translations and imitations of his work that lie beyond the internal contradictions of Boccaccio's *De mulieribus claris*, another form of female image-making creates an additional layer of ambiguities: the illustrations of the women themselves. Many of the decorated fifteenth-century French manuscript versions of the *Cleres et nobles femmes* feature dedicatory images of the author offering his book to his female dedicatee, who is surrounded by a number of ladies of her court. At least three of them open with a miniature of Boccaccio as an individual author at work.[12] Thus, there existed a visual juxtaposition of—and sometimes competition between—these two visions, that of the author as independent creator and that of the author beholden to—or at least somehow dependent on—his patroness. In his study of varied and conflicting manuscript and printed imitations of Boccaccio's *De mulieribus claris* in late fifteenth- and early sixteenth-century Italy,[13] Kolsky describes a kind of identification between court writers and their female patrons:

> Courtier-writers of the Renaissance often found that their own situations bore resemblances to the powerlessness of high-ranking elite women: like such women, the courtiers tended to lack financial means and independence; they were objects of condescension, and they were obliged to assert a place for themselves, their skills, and their aspiration within the court system . . . the male writing subject can be seen negotiating the significance of "woman" in order to consolidate his own authority as an arbiter of the feminine. (227)[14]

Just how much this same phenomenon might have characterized the writers at Anne of Brittany's court remains to be seen. Although the French queen did not "lack financial means" like the Italian Renaissance women Kolsky discusses, there may nevertheless have been a similar vying for literary (and economic) power vis-à-vis the French queen among male poets penning works about women, a topic she must have overtly favored. Because this desire among court poets to impress the queen often entailed attracting the attention of the king as well, Anne of Brittany and her contemporaries obviously served as conduits to their more powerful husbands. We learned in Chapter 2 above that such was the case for the *Voyage de Gênes*.

In the series of French manuscripts of Boccaccio's *De mulieribus claris*, the multiplication of the positive, albeit less commonly executed image of female patronage, which portrays the male author kneeling before his patroness, doubtless enhanced the image of women at the time. Since the visual reading of an illustrated book manuscript likely preceded a textual reading (and may have been the raison d'être for its commission or purchase), one could argue that this positive staging of female patrons in many of these miniature versions may have had a countereffect on some of the ambiguities surfacing in Boccaccio's and later translators' texts.[15] But what if these positive illustrations of females dominating the court scene and literary enterprise were excised and replaced by the more conventional dedicatory scene of men?

All of these issues surface in the context of Vérard's 1493 edition of the

*Nobles et cleres dames*, whose translator claimed to draw inspiration directly from Anne of Brittany. But before an analysis of this edition, a brief discussion of this work's translator is in order.

To better contextualize our discussion of the Vérard edition, dedicated to Anne of Brittany, I wish first to examine briefly a slightly earlier manuscript version of the French translation, B.N. ffr. 599, one belonging to the Family B textual tradition. According to Bozzolo (25), the text was probably copied in the third quarter of the fifteenth century, before 1467, that is, during the lifetime of Jean d'Angoulême. However, it was illuminated after 1488 for Charles, count of Angoulême and his wife Louise of Savoy (94) with "peintures très soignées," which Paul Durrieu attributed to Robinet Testard (93). This manuscript figures in the inventory of books made upon the death of Charles in 1496 and is described in the first entry in the following manner: "C'est assavoir le libvre de *Jehan Boucasse*, escript en parchemin et à la main, historié et tourné à or et azur, couvert de veloux cramoysi garny de fermoers, aux armes, l'un de monseigr et l'autre de madame" [That is to say, the book of Giovanni Boccaccio, written by hand on parchment, historiated and painted in gold and azure, covered with red velour garnished with clasps, bearing arms, one of [the duke] and the other of [the duchess].[16] What is somewhat confusing are the two slightly different interpretations of the arms featured on folio 2v of the manuscript, beneath an exquisite dedication miniature. Are they the joint arms of Charles and Louise, or the arms of Louise herself? While Bozzolo claims the decoration and illumination were carried out "pour Charles d'Angoulême et sa femme Louise de Savoie, dont les armes mi-parties sont peintes au f. 2v," both Ségemaud and Paulin Paris, cited by Ségemaud, are clearer in their claim that the "ouvrage [fut] exécuté pour Louise de Savoie, dont les armoiries décorent la première vignette" (70). Mary Beth Winn also recognizes the arms as those of Louise de Savoie.[17] Given the 1496 inventory reference to the manuscript as having been "historiée," it does appear that the manuscript was illuminated by the inventory date of 1496, whether it was for the couple or for Louise herself.[18] At the very least, this is one of the French translations of the work that directly involved the arms of a woman, all other known manuscript translations having been commissioned by men. This copy is housed today in the BnF as ffr. 599.

While very few other indications in the manuscript call attention to Louise of Savoy as the commissioner or reader of ms. 599, there are two unusual features that set it apart from other known manuscripts of the French translation. Although the miniature depicting Boccaccio's dedication of his work to

Andrea Acciaiuoli appears at the beginning of the dedicatory prologue, as is the case with many other manuscript copies,[19] no author portrait appears at the beginning of the author's prologue that follows. Instead, we find the author image on fol. 94v, at the beginning of the *Recapitulation*, or Boccaccio's conclusion to the work.

Of more interest is the actual dedication miniature itself, which receives privileged status as the liminal illustration of the work. Except for one feature, this exquisite image offers a scene that commonly appeared in the French translation manuscripts of the *Cleres et nobles femmes* (Figure 20): a seated, crowned female, who, in this case, is dressed in an ermine-decorated bodice and gold skirt and surrounded by two young female attendants, receives a closed blue-bound book with two clasps from a man, presumably Boccaccio, who kneels before her dressed in a red robe and gray fur-lined sleeves. But one figure here does not appear in other dedication miniatures: an older woman with white headdress and gold chain across her body stands on the dedicatee's left, holding up her right hand and placing her left hand on the right shoulder of the kneeling author-figure. Whom does this figure represent? Could it be Louise of Savoy herself, portrayed as an intermediary figure in the transition from the Italian dedication scene to the updated version of the French translation? Unlike illuminations of Louise after 1496, however, she is not portrayed in black dress, suggesting that if it is she, the scene was painted before the 1496 death of her husband. But why does she appear so old? This is neither historically accurate nor flattering. And what of the young lady attendant standing on the dedicatee's right who puts her hand on the knee of the crowned figure? Neither the older woman nor young girl appears in the other known manuscript versions of the French translation. Since the age of these two figures is an issue, perhaps another explanation pertains. Could it be that the older figure in the dedication scene in fact represents the original dedicatee, Andrea Acciaiuoli, who serves as the intermediary figure between Boccaccio and the new recipient of the French translated version of the work, the seated figure, Louise of Savoy herself? Her crown would then correspond to that of a duchess, and the young female with a hand on the enthroned figure's knee might then represent Margaret, Louise's daughter. If that were the case, however, either the dedication miniature would date from a later period in the early sixteenth century, since Marguerite was born in 1494, or it would be an odd representation of a girl who could not have been more than two years old in 1496. At this point, neither explanation is completely satisfactory. If the older figure represents Andrea Acciaiuoli, then the kneeling

20. Giovanni Boccaccio, *Cleres et nobles femmes*, Paris, BnF ffr. 599, fol. 2v: Dedication miniature. Bibliothèque Nationale de France.

figure would not be Boccaccio, but perhaps someone else associated with the confection of the book, such as the translator or miniaturist (Testard). Might the older woman represent instead one of Boccaccio's case studies, that is, one of his own female characters, instead of a dedicatee figure?[20]

As for the illustrations of Boccaccio's subjects, the 111 miniatures that appear throughout the manuscript owned by Louise of Savoy (and her husband) diverge pictorially from those of the early fifteenth-century copies of the French translation. For example, BnF mss. 12420 (ca. 1402) and 598 (ca. 1403) offer extensive narrative scenes in their miniatures. By contrast, a large proportion of the illustrations in ms. 599 feature women as single figures with a focus on half to three-fourths of their bodies, providing a broader, and even less enigmatic, perspective on Boccaccio's biographies, because they often incorporate numerous other characters related to the individual story. Thus, each individual female in ms. 599 is more greatly magnified than in other extant manuscripts.[21] While it would be speculative to read into this artistic style a particular predilection on the part of Louise of Savoy herself, it is noteworthy that this manuscript places more attention on portraits of Boccaccio's women than miniatures of the other versions of the work. These figures anticipate those of the *Heroides* in Louise of Savoy's manuscript copy of Octovien de Saint-Gelais's translation of Ovid's work, the *XXI Epistres d'Ovide*, especially BnF ffr. 875, which Testard also illuminated (see Chapter 4 for a discussion of this and related manuscripts).

The images of dedicatee, author, and famous women in Vérard's edition of the *Nobles et cleres dames* were considerably less striking because in the reproduction of his paper copies, he relied on a less remarkable, albeit more practical, affordable form of illustration, the woodcut. Nonetheless, this particular edition highlighted more dramatically the role of the female dedicatee than in Louise of Savoy's specially decorated manuscript of the work, resulting in interpretive complexities regarding the dedication and distribution of the work.

## Anne of Brittany as Dedicatee, Inspiration, and Informed Reader

Vérard's decision to have an anonymous French translation of Boccaccio's writing, *De la Louenge des cleres et nobles dames*, printed in 1493 reflects the strategy he frequently adopted of publishing popular works whose authors were already deceased. His printed copies of a particular text targeted a buying public of nobles and bourgeois, whereas royal clients often commissioned or purchased his luxury copies, which resembled manuscripts because they were printed on vellum and often contained both dedication miniatures and painted illustrations instead of the original woodcuts as well.[22] In fact, at least three such hybrid copies of Vérard's edition of the *Nobles et cleres dames* have come down to us today, one of which was dedicated to Anne of Brittany's first husband, Charles VIII. A comparison of the paratext of these luxury copies uncovers not only implicit tensions among their bookmakers,[23] but also ambiguities in the representation of these famous women to the designated readers of the translated work. Of particular interest here are conflicting details about fifteenth- and sixteenth-century interests in Boccaccio's *De mulieribus claris* and related debates at the French court about the relative virtues of men and women.

A comparison of the full title of Vérard's edition, *Le Livre de Jehan Bocasse de la louenge et vertu des nobles et cleres dames*, with that of the different manuscript versions of the early fifteenth-century translation reveals significant emendations.[24] First, like the title of earlier translations,[25] the original adjective *claris* has been translated into two words, *nobles* and *cleres*, although in a different order. Vérard may have constructed this title from the translator's reference in the opening lines of his dedication (my emphasis): "translaté de latin en françois le livre du tresexcellent poethe Jehan Bocasse par lui fait des vertus et louenges, fortunes et infelicités des *nobles et cleres dames*" [translated from French to Latin the book of the most excellent poet Giovanni Boccaccio made by him about the virtues and praise, fortunes and misfortunes of noble and famous ladies]. Borrowing again, perhaps, from the translator's rendering, the printed version substitutes the more courteous "dames" for "femmes" in the title, even though the colophon maintains the original term (my emphasis): "Cy finist Bocace des nobles et cleres *femmes*" [Here ends Bocaccio's *Concerning noble and famous women*]. Vérard's edition also adds "de la louenge et vertu" [about the praise and virtue] to the earlier titles of the French manuscript versions, echoing in reverse order the translator's own language, albeit in singular form. These modifications enhance the image of the females whose narratives are subsequently recounted by suggesting through a form of "false advertisement" that Boccaccio's biographies present positive images of women. Unlike most of the manuscript versions, which advertise that Boccaccio dedicated his book to the Countesse of Altavilla[26] and then provide that very dedication, Vérard eliminates mention of the original dedicatee from his title, most likely out of deference to the French queen. The

Parisian editor publicizes instead the anonymous translator's dedication of his edition to Anne of Brittany.

On the linguistic level, another series of comparisons is in order. Even though he dedicated his work to Andrea Acciaiuoli[27] and claimed in his dedicatory remarks that his work "will please women no less than men" (13), the fact that Boccaccio composed his work in Latin all but confirms that he essentially targeted a male audience. Indeed, Franklin, like Buettner before her (20), refers to *De mulieribus claris* as "a book for men about women" as well as a "guide to male behavior" (27), explaining by way of a specific example that "by redirecting the discussion of Minerva's extraordinary abilities away from the potentially dangerous reality of an intelligent flesh and blood woman to a conventional abstraction, Boccaccio could comfortably outline the attributes of wisdom as they apply to men" (47–48).[28]

The late fifteenth-century anonymous French translation of the *Nobles et cleres dames*, however, targeted a different public than Boccaccio's *De mulieribus claris* and perhaps a different readership than the earlier French manuscripts, which, as Buettner notes (20), were all commissioned by men.[29] First and foremost, because the *Nobles et cleres dames* translation was dedicated to Anne of Brittany, its first intended reader was a royal female figure. The dedicatory prologue further indicates that the queen's female entourage was targeted as well. But in its printed state, the translation would have reached a more general public of male and female readers. In fact, given the dissemination of the French manuscripts to a limited royal or noble public, it was not really until the publication of Vérard's late fifteenth-century edition that the translation was significantly publicized in France. Nonetheless, Boccaccio's original ambivalence vis-à-vis his audience would have been maintained in all the French versions.

Presumably written by the work's anonymous translator, the dedicatory prologue that Vérard incorporated into his 1493 edition of the *Nobles et cleres dames*[30] informs the reader that Anne of Brittany inspired this translation of Boccaccio's work:[31]

L'onneur et reverence de vous tressouveraine et tresdoubtee
princesse, ma dame Anne, royne de France, pource que je suis
bien tenu a vous, aprés les commandemens de mon tresdoubté
seigneur, je qui suis vostre treshumble et obeissant subget ayant
en vous parfaicte fiance, qui suis homme de tendre estude et de
feible entendement, ay a curieulx plaisir pour vous donner quelque

recreation et passe temps entre vos solicitudes temporelez translaté
de latin en françois le livre du tresexcellent poethe Jehan Bocasse
par lui fait des vertus et louenges, fortunes et infelicités des nobles
et cleres dames (a1v).

[The honor and reverence I owe you, most sovereign and most
revered princess, my lady Anne, Queen of France, because I am
obligated to you, after the orders of my very noble lord, I who am
your very humble and obedient subject with perfect faith in you,
I who am a man of slight education and feeble understanding,
I have, with heedful delight in bringing you some comfort
and distraction from your temporal demands, translated from
Latin into French the book of the very excellent poet Giovanni
Boccaccio, written by him about the virtues and praise, fortunes
and misfortunes of noble and famous ladies.]

Whereas Charles d'Angoulême and his wife Louise of Savoy commissioned
a manuscript of Boccaccio's *Cleres et nobles femmes*, perhaps around the same
period, the French queen does not appear to have requested a copy of the
work on her own initiative according to the translator's dedication. He nonetheless makes it clear that Anne's own exemplary attributes inspired him to
offer her his rendition into French of Boccaccio's famous work and perhaps
even to carry out his translation in the first place:[32]

Car, quant je considere vos faciles, doulces et celebrables meurs
et vos trescellentes honesteté et prudence, qui estes le souverain
honneur des dames, non pas seullement du royaulme de France,
mais avecques ce du monde mesurez, quant je remembre en ma
pensee l'elegance de voz parolles, ensemble la tresexcellente vertu
que avez aporté en ce royaume, lequel avez enrichy de noble
et tresexcellente lignie, de laquelle Dieu par sa saincte grace et
bonté vous a remplie au grant prouffit de tous vos sugetz, terreur
et depossession de tous les ennemys du trescrestien royaume de
France, et que finablement Dieu et nature ont mys en vous par
leur liberalité les biens et vertuz dessus ditz, j'ay prins hardiesse et
courage de diriger et adresser ceste presente translation a vostre
tressouveraine majesté. (a2r)

[For when I consider your gracious, pleasing and renowned
manners and your most excellent honesty and prudence, that
you are the sovereign honor of ladies, not only in the kingdom
of France, but measured against those all over the world; when
I remember the elegance of your speech, together with the very
excellent virtue that you have brought to this kingdom, which
you have enriched with your noble and most excellent lineage,
with which God in his holy grace and goodness has filled you
to the great benefit of all of your subjects [and] to the dread
and deprivation of the enemies of the most Christian kingdom
of France; and finally that God and nature have placed in you,
through their generosity, the above-mentioned goodness and
virtues, I have been so bold and courageous as to direct and address
this present translation to your most sovereign majesty.]

Throughout this dedication, the Vérard translator often echoes many of
the remarks Boccaccio offered to his dedicatee, without, however, acknowledging his source. In addition he elaborates upon the original, providing insight
into French court dynamics. Thus, unlike the extant manuscript translations,
all of which present and openly advertise Boccaccio's dedication to Andrea Ac-
ciauioli, the latter is absent from Vérard's version. In its place the reader finds a
dedication personalized for Anne of Brittany. Although the Vérard translator
borrows readily from the Italian author's words,[33] it is highly doubtful that
readers of the 1493 edition would have been cognizant of this fact.

In defining the queen's influence on the outcome of his translation in the
prologue, the Vérard translator bases his text on Boccaccio's, adding his personal
condemnation of critics who take translators as well as authors and "expositeurs"
to task. The fact that such defensive remarks were more likely to issue from the
pen of a veritable translator, rather than that of a publisher like Vérard, offers additional confirmation that the Parisian bookseller was not the work's translator:[34]

Et si vous est agreable que ce present livre voise en lumiere, donnés
luy hardiesse et auctorité de ce faire. Car j'ay ferme et indubitable
esperance, se ainssy vous plaist, que vos congié et auctorité royaulx
feront ceste presente translacion seure des assaulx des mauvais et
iniques detracteurs *qui tousjours ont de coustume poindre et picquer,
non pas seulement les acteurs, mais avecquez ce les expositeurs et
translateurs.* (a2v)

[And if it is agreeable to you that this present book go out into the world, grant it the courage and authority to do so. For I have the firm and certain hope, if it pleases you, that your royal license and authority will protect this present translation from the assaults of bad and wicked detractors *who are always accustomed to pricking and stinging not only authors, but interpreters and translators along with them.*]

Although the *Nobles et cleres dames* translator focuses on Anne of Brittany's protection of his work against its potential detractors in his dedication to her, it is not a one-way association, for he simultaneously praises the queen and flatters her through favorable comparison with the famous women originally staged by Boccaccio, adopting the same terms used by the Italian author in his dedication:[35]

j'ay parfaicte esperance que vostre trescelebrable nom volitera de plus en plus, par les bouches des hommes par sur la fameuse et tresclere memoire de toutes les dames illustres, cleres, et nobles du temps passé. (a2v–a3r)

[I have the singular hope that your most honored name will flutter increasingly over the lips of men above the famous and very bright memory of all illustrious, famous and noble women of past times.]

This verbal association between Anne of Brittany and Boccaccio's famous women is visually reinforced by the seventy-six woodcuts disseminated throughout Vérard's edition. Placed at the beginning of the anonymous translator's prologue, the image of a crowned lady seated on a throne before three other female court figures (Figure 21) ostensibly represents the queen, who is identified in the prologue that follows. Although not a dedicatory image like that found at the beginning of many of the manuscripts of the French translation, this illustration, doubtless a generic woodcut from the publisher's or printer's stock, resembles the earlier luxury manuscript versions of the French translation by according visual prominence to the female dedicatee, portraying her in a position of power, as she holds the scepter.[36] One of the nine images repeated throughout Vérard's edition, this same woodcut is reused to identify 21 other women or groups of women in the work.[37] These associations between the Anne of Brittany figure in the initial illustration and

Le prologue du trãflateur fur le liure de Jehã
Bocaffe par luy fait de la louenge & Bertu des
nobles et cleres dames.

Lonneur
& reuerëce
De Bous
treffouuerainet
trefdoubtee prin
ceffe ma Dame
ãne zopne de frã
ce pource q̃ ie fu
is bië tenu a Bo⁹
apres les cõmã
demës ¡De mon
trefdoubte fei ↑
gneuz ie qui fuis
Boftre trefhum

ble & obeiffant fubget ayant¡en Bous parfaicte fiance q̃
fuis hõme De tendre eftude& De feible entendement ay
a curieulx plaifir pourBous donner quelq̃ recreation et
paffe temps entreBos folicitudes téporeles; traflate De
latin en francois le liure du trefexcellent poethe Jehan
Bocaffe par luy fait des Bertus & louenges fortunes & i ↑
felicites des nobles & cleres Dames. Affin queBous ma
trefredoubtee dame ayez matiere & repliquer& alleguer
les nobles & celebzables Bertuz qui ont efte par cy deuãt
ou fexe feminin: quant les princes et p̃s Du royaume
Souldroiët en deuifãt deuãtBoftre illuftre maiefte ppo
fer les beaux faiz & Bertuz Des hões a la Diminutiõ deſ
louables Bertuz Des dames. Et iafoit ce q̃Boftre noble
clerte& trefrefplandiff ãte gloire foit fi grande par la re ↑
fplãdiffeur DeBoftre royale maiefte.et mes ãtedemët &

21. Giovanni Boccaccio, *De la Louenge des nobles et cleres dames* (Paris: for Antoine Vérard, 1493), Paris, BnF Rés. 365, fol. a1v: "Dedication" woodcut to Anne of Brittany. Bibliothèque Nationale de France.

dedicatory prologue and other famous women, such as Juno (fol. biiiv), in the body of the *Nobles et cleres dames* visually connect the French queen as a noble and virtuous woman with 20 percent of the famous women Boccaccio had examined in his work. Anne of Brittany, a living woman of renown, thereby served as an explicit verbal and visual link between the famous women of the past and those of the present.

Yet, through reuse of this same "dedicatee" illustration, doubtless necessitated because of the limited number of woodcuts illustrating females on hand, infamous women serving as negative *exempla*, such as Semiramis, Medusa, and Cleopatra, are also associated with Anne of Brittany. Vérard likely figures as a major player in the resulting contradictions between the translator's desire to flatter the queen through verbal and pictorial association with virtuous women of the past and many implicit visual connections that undermine that aim. The Parisian publisher probably helped determine which images were to match up with which biography, although such decision-making was likely based more on technical and practical rather than interpretative considerations. In fact, given that few of Boccaccio's females received completely positive assessments from their biographer, there were overall more negative or "notorious" women, to use McLeod's term (64), than virtuous women, who shared the "dedicatee" woodcut image with Anne of Brittany. Tensions surface, then, between the glorification of Anne of Brittany through the translator's laudatory remarks describing the French queen as one of the *nobles et cleres dames*, praise that is punctuated by the liminal woodcut of a reigning female court figure, and the subsequent use of the same image to depict infamous women with whom no link should properly be maintained. This visual ambivalence between dedicatee and biographical subject characterizes the text as well.

Besides placing the French queen on the same stage as famous women of the past in his dedicatory prologue, the Vérard translator also links the dissemination of Anne of Brittany's renown to the diffusion and ultimate success of his own translation. According to him, the book as physical object could more successfully promulgate word of her virtues than the queen herself: "Et que comme ainssy soit que ne puisses estre par tout par puissance corporele, ce present livre fera congnoistre vous et vos merites a ceulx qui sont presentement vivans" [And since you are unable to be physically present everywhere, this present book will make you and your merits known to those currently living] (a3r). Here the Vérard translator borrows directly from Boccaccio in advertising the public relations dimension of his work.[38] Promoting the interdependence between himself and the French queen

through the development of religious references, while elaborating upon
Boccaccio's words to his dedicatee, the Vérard translator ends up publicizing
his role—and that of his translation—in the diffusion of Anne of Brittany's
name to posterity:[39]

> Et mesmement vous fera estre eternele envers les posterités et
> generacions futures subsequentes et advenir. Et finablement
> aidant nostre Seigneur, ne serés pas seulement eue et reputee
> tresresplendissante sur et entre les nobles dames qui ont esté, et
> seront en ceste vie transsitoire et corruptible, mais avecques ce
> aprés que aurés despoullé et laissé l'abit humain de ceste mortalité
> perissable, vous serés receue en perpetuelle clarté par Celuy qui est
> largiteur des graces et biens celestez. (a3r)

> [And it will even immortalize you for posterity and future and
> subsequent generations. And finally, with the help of our Lord, you
> will not only be esteemed as most resplendent above and among
> the noble ladies that have existed and will exist in this transitory
> and corruptible life, but in addition, after you have stripped away
> and left behind the human vestment of this perishable mortality,
> you will be received in perpetual brightness by Him who is the
> provider of celestial graces and goods.]

Thus, the *Nobles et cleres dames* translator, his dedicatee, and his book, a literary, artistic, and indeed political object, were linked through their interconnected potential for fame.

But it is the manner in which the Vérard translator diverges from Boccaccio's dedication to Andrea Acciaiuoli that is most enlightening. For the
reader learns that this rendition of the *Nobles et cleres dames* was intended
to settle any clashes of male and female opinion at the French court about
the prominence of virtuous women, disputes that echo centuries-old debates
surrounding the condemnation and defense of women. In his dedication to
Anne of Brittany, the Vérard translator refers specifically to contemporary
confrontations about the respective virtues of each sex. According to him,
his translation was designed to furnish Anne of Brittany with ammunition
against the masculine position, for it supported instead the argument that
there was widespread evidence of virtuous women:

Affin que vous, ma tresredoubtee dame, ayez matiere de repliquer
et alleguer les nobles et celebrables vertuz qui ont esté par cy
devant ou sexe feminin: quant les princes et seigneurs du royaume
vouldroient, en devisant devant vostre illustre majesté, proposer
les beaux faiz et vertuz des hommes a la diminution des louables
vertuz des dames. (aIv)

[So that you, my most noble lady, may have the material to respond
and argue on behalf of the noble and celebrated virtues that have
always been embodied in the female sex: when, in discussions
before your illustrious majesty, the princes and lords of the realm
would like to put forth the great deeds and virtues of men to the
detriment of the praiseworthy virtues of ladies.]

While the actual details of such arguments are impossible to reconstruct,
we can glean significant information from this passage. The *Nobles et cleres
dames* translator was apparently reviving the memory of—and perhaps
anticipating—debates in which certain male courtiers negatively compared
the virtues of women to those of men in the presence of the queen herself.
Curiously, the reference made to *the* ("les"), not *some* ("des"), princes and lords
of the realm, suggests that all male courtly perspectives were "anti-feminist"
in this regard. If the French king himself were implied in this comment, then
the passage might well allude to an implicit tension between the queen and
king themselves over the virtues of women as compared to those of men. By
referring to the "vertus et louenges, fortunes et *infelicités* des nobles et cleres
dames" [virtues and praises, fortunes and *misfortunes* of noble and famous
ladies] (aIv) (my emphasis), the Vérard translator realized that many of Boccaccio's biographies did not support the claim of widespread female virtue
and nobility. He contends, however, that negative *exempla* offer material for
moralistic education as well and should not deter the queen from reading his
translation:

Et supposé que en recitant les beaux faitz et felicitez desdictes
dames l'acteur narre ou recite aucuns faitz impudiques ou
infelicitez desdictes dames, ce ne vous debvra mouvoir ou divertir
de la lecture de ce present livre, car la fin et intencion dudit acteur
est monstrer l'instabilité et variacion de fortune. (a2r)

[And if it happens that the author, in recounting the excellent
deeds and good actions of the above-mentioned ladies, narrates
or recites some shameful or infelicitous behavior, this should not
disturb you or divert you from reading this present book, for the
author's goal and intention is to demonstrate the instability and
variation of fortune.]

Nevertheless, the translator's claim implicitly reawakens the traditional
controversy about female readers. Should they have the right to read texts,
such as Boccaccio's, containing non-Christian ideas or pagan examples? In
other words, did women possess a critical enough mind to be able to distinguish good from evil? Borrowing the horticultural metaphor, but not the
tone, adopted in a related passage by Boccaccio, who was much more condescending through his use of the imperative voice,[40] the *Nobles et cleres dames*
translator strongly affirms Anne of Brittany's critical intelligence:

[T]ressouveraine et redoubtee dame, se vous entriés en ung vergier
ouquel eut plusieurs belles fleurs parmy ung tas de ronsses et de
espines, et vous vousissées cueillir lesdictes fleurs, vous detourneriés
avecques vos elegans et delicieux dois la pointure desdictes ronsses
et espines et par apres cueilleriés lesdictes fleurs. Pareillement,
tresredoubtee dame, vous saurez bien cueillir et retenir les choses
louables et vertueuses desdictes anciennes dames, fuir et eviter les
vicieuses. Et certes, quant aucune dame crestienne lyra quelque
chose en ce present livre digne de louenge, laquelle chose elle
congnoistra ne estre point en elle, ce luy sera cause et matiere de
eveiller son engin, affin qu'elle puisse surmonter en honnesteté,
pudicité ou autre vertu les dames gentilles et paienes. Et metra
lors ladicte dame crestienne toutes les forces et vertu de son engin
a ce qu'elle ne soit vaincu en vertu par aucune dame paiene du
temps passé. (a2v)

[Most sovereign and revered lady, if you entered an orchard where
there were many beautiful flowers among a pile of brambles and
thorns, and you wished to pick these flowers, you would, with
your elegant and delicate fingers, avert the prick of the brambles
and thorns and afterwards you would pick the flowers. Similarly,

most noble lady, you would know well how to pick and retain the laudable and virtuous things about the aforementioned ladies of the past, and to flee and avoid the vicious things. And certainly, when any Christian lady reads something in this present book worthy of praise, which thing she recognizes as not being in her, this will be the cause and reason for awakening her mind, so that she may surpass in honesty, modesty or other virtue noble pagan women. And then this Christian lady will use all the force and virtue of her mind so that she will not be surpassed in virtue by any pagan lady of times past.]

By implicitly alluding to men's anxiety about the intellectual capacities of women, the translator of the 1493 *Nobles et cleres dames* calls attention to Boccaccio's own ambiguous attitude about his famous women. As noted earlier, the Italian author's female case studies were all famous, but not necessarily virtuous: he judged many to be infamous. The Vérard translator, on the other hand, stands squarely on the side of women in general and of Anne of Brittany in particular, praising her as a reader who would know well how to distinguish virtuous behavior that should be imitated from dangerous behavior to be avoided.

Thus, in the eyes of our translator, Anne of Brittany not only played a central role in the dissemination and ultimate success of his translation. As a virtuous and wise woman who would not be derailed by negative examples of famous women described by Boccaccio, she also served as an intellectual role model for all other ladies of whom "la lecture de ce present volume pourra[it] exciter et éveiller le noble courage . . . a faire et acomplir plusieurs faiz et operacions vertueuses a l'imitacion et maniere des nobles dames anciennes" [the reading of this present volume could excite and awaken the noble heart in order to carry out and accomplish several deeds and virtuous actions in imitation of and in the manner of past noble ladies] (a2r).[41] Ultimately, Anne of Brittany, not the unenlightened dedicatee treated in more patronizing terms by Boccaccio, provides the link to and model for both ladies of the court and other females outside court circles. In the translator's mind, the French queen resembles less Andrea Acciaiuoli than Joanna, Queen of Sicily, Boccaccio's first choice of dedicatee, who, he decided in the end, was too distinguished.[42] In fact, Joanna, one of the most positively portrayed women in the *De mulieribus claris*, figures as the work's concluding biography. Both Christine de

Pizan and Antoine Dufour retained her as one of their famous women in their respective works.


## Editorial Intervention in the Praise of Women

The fact that the *Nobles et cleres dames* was successfully printed and circulated presumably among a large number of readers would have probably pleased the anonymous translator. We cannot, however, verify whether this success resulted from action taken by the queen vis-à-vis Vérard. It is nonetheless the case that the publisher's involvement in the printing of the work altered the relationship that the translator had established with Anne of Brittany in the prologue. First, Vérard never disseminated details about the translator's identity in his edition. The publisher identified Boccaccio as author of the *Nobles et cleres dames* on the title page: "Le liure de Jehan bocasse de la louenge et vertu des nobles et cleres dames trāslate & īprime nouellemēt a paris" [The book of Giovanni Boccaccio about the praise and virtue of noble and famous ladies translated and newly printed in Paris] (a1r).[43] As bookseller, Vérard would have profited from his association with the well-known Italian author by attracting a larger clientele of readers with this publicity. But advertisement of the identity of the less famous translator may have been deemed unnecessary in the publisher's quest to arouse the interest of potential book purchasers. In fact, if the translator's identity was known among some contemporaries, it may have overshadowed or at least complicated Vérard's own paratextual performance. Indeed, the absence of the translator's name created a convenient ambiguity for the publisher, whose own name—the only contemporary name associated with the publication—appeared in the colophon of the publication, followed by his bookseller's mark (fol. t5v). By suppressing the translator's name in the volume he published and identifying himself in the colophon, Vérard shared this privileged paratextual space only with the famous—but deceased—Boccaccio, placing himself in the same universe, because both had contributed to the creation of the book.[44] This manipulation on Vérard's part confirms Winn's general observation that "the publisher could pre-empt even a contemporary writer's work" (*AV*, 48). As a result, the potential confusion between Vérard's function and that of the contemporary translator in the book's creation made all the more ambiguous Vérard's relationship with the translator's dedicatee, Anne of Brittany. The reader might have easily concluded that it was Vérard who had penned the prologue and dedicated his edition to the queen.

This suppression of the translator's identity and implicit appropriation of his functions by Vérard are more dramatically evident in two of the extant hybrid versions of the *Nobles et cleres dames*. To personalize these copies dedicated to Charles VIII (Paris, BnF Vélins 1223) and Henry VII (BL C.22.c.2*), Vérard eliminated the prologue that had originally figured in the paper copies of his edition, because it was addressed to the queen, not to the kings of France or England.[45] In fact, Vérard had the first two folios of the prologue (a1r–a2r), one of which originally bore the title page (fol. a1r) and the woodcut representing the queen (fol. a1v), removed from the copies dedicated to Charles VIII and Henry VII, and the last lines of the prologue erased from the third folio (a2r).[46] In the hybrid copy destined for Henry VII,[47] a dramatic miniature of Thisbe's bloody suicide before the dead Pyramus appears on folio a2r. Even though Thisbe's biography is one of the 25 or so that are not accompanied by a woodcut illustration in Vérard's edition of the *Nobles et cleres dames*—which perhaps explains the bookmakers' decision to paint her story as the royal frontispiece—its gory rendition does set a particularly disturbing tone at the outset of the English king's copy for the rest of the famous women's biographies.

In the French king's copy, a miniature placed on the third folio depicts Vérard, not the translator, on bended knee offering a red book with gold decorations and clasps to Charles VIII, who is identified visually by his crown, enthroned position and fleurs-de-lis symbols decorating his robe, the backdrop behind his seat and the folio margins (Figure 22). The king points with his left curled finger, presumably to the publisher. Two male courtiers standing in the left background and three female figures standing in the center background witness the dedication. The substitution of this dedication scene for the generic woodcut of the queen, coupled with the removal of the anonymous translator's prologue, effectively eliminated the visual and thematic links originally established between the translator's dedicatee, Anne of Brittany, and the famous women of Boccaccio's work. It is nonetheless unusual to find women included in the king's entourage in this depiction of a book dedication.

In addition, a male and female stand in the foreground of the dedication miniature that opens Charles VIII's copy of the work. The lady, wearing a red dress, stands to the right and appears to gesture with her right hand in the direction of the dedication scene. She faces the male in the left foreground of

22. Giovanni Boccaccio, *De la Louenge des nobles et cleres dames* (Paris: for Antoine Vérard, 1493), Paris, BnF Rés. Vélins 1223, fol. 1r (a3r): Dedication of the book to King Charles VIII by the publisher. Bibliothèque Nationale de France.

the miniature who is dressed in a red hat and coat. He points with his right hand to the dedication scene as well, while looking at the woman across from him. Whom are these two figures meant to represent? While one might be tempted to identify them as Anne of Brittany and the anonymous translator, an interpretation that corresponds to the prologue's presentation of personal and political networks associated with the creation of the book, the absence of a crown on the female's head—she wears a hood-like headdress—and of more regal attire (not to mention the lack of the prologue itself) seems to preclude such an analysis. These characters are perhaps intended to depict either the original author and his dedicatee, Andrea Acciaiuoli—although Boccaccio's dedication to the duchess of Altavilla does not appear in Vérard's edition—or the Italian author and a representative figure of his famous women.

What further suggests that the characters in the foreground of the liminal miniature in Charles VIII's copy are not meant to represent the work's translator and his dedicatee is Winn's discovery (134) of an illustration of Vérard presenting a book to Anne of Brittany on the verso of a folio that contains the beginning of the prologue from the *Nobles et cleres dames* (Figure 23). This image, which must have originally been intended to decorate a special copy of Vérard's edition meant for the queen, was pasted on to another leaf and inserted into his edition of a different work, Robert de Saint Martin's *Trésor de l'âme*, which the publisher then offered the French queen as a luxury copy (Paris, BnF Rés. Vélins 350) at a later date (around 1497).

This illustration merits further examination, since it presents a different scenario than the dedication scene featuring Charles VIII. There we discovered a number of female participants in a cultural ritual that usually involved male figures alone. In this miniature, a crowned female figure sits on a throne beneath a baldaquin decorated with fleurs-de-lis; these symbols of French royalty also adorn the skirt, sleeves, and mantel of her attire and echo the symbols that ornament the folio margins. Ermines decorate her white bodice and the white fur lining of her mantel. Although neither of the edition's two prologues nor the text of the *Trésor de l'âme*, a religious treatise on the human soul by Frère Robert,[48] refers specifically to Anne of Brittany, the royal attributes associated with the principal figure in the miniature make it clear that she is meant to represent the French queen. The kneeling presenter has been identified as Vérard (Winn, *AV*, 148), the author himself, Frère Robert, having died in 1388,[49] and the last folio verso of the book bears the publisher's mark below a colophon with his name and address. Vérard's involvement

23. Robert de Saint Martin, *Trésor de l'âme* (Paris: for Antoine Vérard, c. 1497), Paris, BnF Rés. Vélins 350, fol. AA6: Dedication of the book to Queen Anne of Brittany by the publisher. Bibliothèque Nationale de France.

in the publication enterprise, confirmed textually, is thus reinforced in the dedication miniature.

In the miniature, six ladies-in-waiting staged in two groups witness the dedication of the book by the publisher to the queen, who reaches for the volume. One lady in each cluster points to the queen and another has "talking hands." Thus, the women surrounding the queen enthusiastically participate in the dedication ceremonial, with their actions directing the viewer's attention all the more emphatically to the queen.

Why did Vérard excise the dedication miniature in which he offers Anne of Brittany a copy of the *Nobles et cleres dames* and place it in another work? Why did he dedicate a luxury copy of the same edition to the king rather than the queen, when the prologue he had incorporated into the paper copies specified that Anne had inspired this translation?[50] Did Charles VIII play any role in this rather dramatic modification of dedicatees? Was there a misunderstanding between Vérard and the queen, or between the king and the queen about the creation, reproduction, and dedication of the work? Or was the actual conferral of the volume on the French king simply a more practical arrangement for all involved? Was this change of dedicatee related in any manner to the court debates over the more virtuous sex to which the translator alludes in his prologue? Despite its apparent celebration of women, did this work, or rather Charles VIII's copy of it, end up providing the king with more ammunition for the masculine opinion because of Boccaccio's many examples of infamous, rather than, virtuous women? We will never know the answer to these questions. But it is nonetheless quite curious that Charles VIII rather than Anne of Brittany received a luxury copy of Vérard's publication of the *Nobles et cleres dames* and that no trace of a manuscript or a printed copy of the work belonging to the queen has been located. It is possible, of course, that such a copy was lost.

It was nevertheless in the vellum copies dedicated to two of the most powerful men in Europe at the time that Vérard eliminated the critical contribution of both translator and queen to the creation of the *Nobles et cleres dames*. Whereas the reader of the paper edition of the *Nobles et cleres dames* could appreciate the responsibility accorded Anne of Brittany in the transmission of this translation, the power the translator accorded his female dedicatee disappeared from the volumes specially prepared for the kings of France and England. Most likely honoring royal protocol, Vérard doubtless sought to avoid any confusion or competition between queen and king. Assuming the function of author-translator and replacing the French queen with her husband, Vérard thus suppressed all association between text and female dedicatee as well as all verbal references to any controversy about the virtues and intellectual capabilities of women. In other words, in these royal copies he eliminated the contradictions and tensions lying beneath the surface of these texts in the paper copies of his edition. In the end, the modifications made to these two royal copies of Vérard's edition of the *Nobles et cleres dames*, the apparent replacement of an already prepared dedicatory miniature destined for the queen with one for the French king and ensuing actions on the part of Vérard and the French queen regarding the commission and dedication of subsequent books (see below) may well indicate the existence of tensions between the publisher and the translator's dedicatee, Anne of Brittany.

A third extant luxury copy of the *Nobles et cleres dames*, currently housed in the John Rylands Collection of the library of the University of Manchester, England as Inc. 15.E.2 (Pressmark 15883),[51] offers a decidedly different paratextual vision of the *Nobles et cleres dames*. Unlike its two vellum counterparts, this copy retains not only the title page, but, more important, the prologue penned by the anonymous translator that prominently features Queen Anne of Brittany and refers to court disagreements over female virtues. Moreover, whereas empty spaces were consciously left in the places originally designed to contain the woodcuts in the French king's copy, which were subsequently filled with small miniature scenes, the woodcuts in the John Rylands copy were actually printed in the volume, but then subsequently painted over with miniatures.[52] Although the miniaturist more or less retained the original scenario in painting over the initial woodcut of the book, slight alterations made to the image result in a significant restaging of events (Figure 24). The central figure seated on a throne and clad in a red robe continues to be portrayed as a royal figure, for she still wears a crown (with short veil beneath it) and holds a scepter in her left hand.[53] The two ladies to the right, one seated and one standing, have not been transformed except that the miniature overpainting, which adds color to the image, results in prettier faces. However, the female seated at the left, now points with her right hand to a book, absent in the woodcut, which, although rendered in awkward artistic fashion, she holds in her now raised left hand. The volume, painted in a periwinkle blue with gold clasps and gold decoration on its cover attracts the viewer's attention as much as the enthroned queen.

Thus, the original woodcut in which the female figure representing Anne of Brittany sits in regal state before her ladies-in-waiting has been transformed into a more active scenario that directs attention to the court ladies' new

24. Giovanni Boccaccio, *De la Louenge des nobles et cleres dames* (Paris: for Antoine Vérard, 1493), Manchester, University of Manchester, John Rylands Collection, Inc. 15.E.2, fol. a1v: Miniature painted over the original "dedication" woodcut. Reproduced by courtesy of the University Librarian and Director, The John Rylands University Library, The University of Manchester.

object of attention, the book. Reminiscent of frontispiece dedication miniatures that frequently open luxury medieval manuscripts, this reconstituted
image does not, however, present the traditional scenario in which a donor,
usually the book's author (but also its publisher, as we have seen), kneels before the royal figure to offer a copy of his or her completed book. Given the
history of the confection of Vérard's edition of the *Nobles et cleres dames* that
we have just reviewed, it does not seem that realistically a female figure would
have offered the volume to the queen or other dedicatee. And yet the image
does appear to illustrate just that moment. Perhaps this reworking of the
woodcut was intended to depict not the presentation of a volume to the queen
but rather an emphasis on the book itself. In this case, the artist of the John
Rylands copy, opting to retrace in color almost the entire design of the original woodcut rather than overpainting it with an entirely different image—a
strategy employed in many subsequent miniatures in the same volume—may
have sought to portray a scene that conveys the attention accorded by the
female court to the presumably newly acquired work about famous women
authored by Boccaccio. In fact, viewed in conjunction with the anonymous
translator's opening comments, this modified miniature, with its emphasis
on the veneration of the book by ladies of Anne's court, more faithfully illustrates the prologue than the generic woodcut decorating most other printed
editions of the work. The queen's physically elevated position vis-à-vis her
court in this reconstituted image emblematically figures her role as both
a female of power and an exemplary reader, whose ability to negotiate the
ambiguous material contained in Boccaccio's work would, according to the
*Nobles et cleres dames* translator, serve as a model for other women. As in
the miniature of Anne of Brittany and Vérard that eventually decorated the
*Trésor de l'âme*, instead of the *Nobles et cleres dames*, at least one member of
the female entourage is, along with the royal figure herself who points with
her right hand, depicted as an active participant in the event commemorating the arrival—and perhaps even the dedication—of the *Nobles et cleres
dames* edition at court.

  Unfortunately, it is impossible to identify the designated first owner of
this luxury hybrid copy.[54] No signs such as those found in the two royal
copies—deletion of the title page, empty spaces provided for miniatures or
decorative royal symbols—indicate that this might have been a copy specially prepared for Anne of Brittany herself. The placement of the illustration of Vérard's dedication of this work to the queen in another book, as
we learned above, makes it all the more unlikely that such a version existed.

Nevertheless, given the strong concentration of females in this scene, coupled with the book's examination of famous women, it is quite conceivable that the original owner of the John Rylands copy was a noble lady and that the miniature itself might have been tailored to represent a scene more relevant to her own experience.[55]

The second miniature in the John Rylands library copy of the *Nobles et cleres dames*, which opens the first chapter, or Boccaccio's prologue (fol. aiiiv), merits special consideration as well. This double-sized illustration makes no obvious changes to the original author-woodcut in its lower register.[56] But in the upper register, which originally featured a bearded man at the left and a nun-like female character at the right, as decorative accessory figures in the generic woodcut, the male has been replaced by a lady, clothed in a light red dress, and three other females behind her. This elimination of the male figure from the stock image obviously signals a conscious desire to focus on women in the miniature. Perhaps the artist sought to represent the very subjects of the book authored by Boccaccio, who, sitting at his desk in the lower register of the image, might then be viewed as imagining to life his famous women, some of whom appear above in the upper register. Similar modifications in the analogous miniature in the French king's copy appear to confirm this interpretation.[57]

Just as in the miniature programs of earlier French manuscripts of the *Nobles et cleres dames*, which we briefly examined above, a certain visual rivalry between the female dedicatee and male author surfaces in the opening folios of the John Rylands library copy. Emphasis in the initial image on the French queen's role in the creation and dissemination of the work is counterbalanced by a portrayal of the author at work in the following illustration.[58] In the end, both reconfigured miniatures in the John Rylands copy provide a more relevant rendering of the two prologues than the original woodcuts.[59] Because the latter were stock images from the printer's or publisher's available collection,[60] one would expect these kinds of adjustments to the generic woodcut by a miniaturist decorating a luxury copy of the French translation for a particular patron. What is noteworthy is the fact that in both the opening illustrations of the John Rylands Library copy, women are placed more prominently on stage, either through their roles as active political or cultural court figures—as a reigning female and as potential readers of the featured book—or as the subjects of a famous author's writing. An examination of the miniatures that accompany Boccaccio's biographies of famous women in the John Rylands copy uncovers similar kinds of pictorial alterations.[61]

Although Anne of Brittany's potential contribution to the creation of the *Nobles et cleres dames*—as inspirational source, literary protector, champion of female virtues, and savvy reader—was suppressed by Vérard in the two royal copies he had specially prepared; although the queen does not ever seem to have received her own specially prepared copy of this edition, given the apparent transferal of her dedication miniature to another book, Vérard did succeed four years later in 1497 in presenting Anne of Brittany a hybrid vellum copy of another work, Christine de Pizan's *Livre des Trois Vertus*, whose title in Vérard's fifteenth-century incarnation of the work is *Le Tresor de la Cite des dames selon Dame Cristine*. This printed version of another literary text in French about women composed by a deceased author featured the French queen in its prologue and dedicatory miniature. The second of only three known luxury copies that Vérard specially prepared for Anne alone,[62] this hybrid version is currently housed in the ÖNB as Ink.3.D.19.[63] We do not know whether Vérard's decision to publish and dedicate his edition of the *Trésor de la Cité des dames* to Anne of Brittany was related to the seemingly unusual modifications made to the royal copy of the *Nobles et cleres dames*. Was the publisher attempting to atone for past errors or misunderstandings through this dedication? The fact that he decided to have a work about women printed for the queen was likely a conscious tactic aimed at pleasing Anne of Brittany and simultaneously currying favor with her so that he might gain her financial backing. That Anne of Brittan had owned a manuscript version of the work since before her marriage to Charles VIII[64] suggests that the queen possessed an already existing interest in Christine de Pizan's writing. She might have even inspired Vérard's decision to print the work. However, in his personalized prologue, the only one he ever addressed to the French queen, Vérard makes no mention of Anne having commissioned an edition of the work, nor does he indicate that she motivated its publication.[65] If that had been the case, the publisher would very likely have promoted such royal associations. It appears instead that Vérard himself initiated the publication of the *Trésor de la Cité des dames*. Lauding the female whose support he doubtless hoped to secure and placing himself in a humbling position vis-à-vis her—that is, assuming the conventional pose of a court poet—Vérard dedicates the work to Anne of Brittany in the following manner:

> Et pour ce, ma treschiere et tressouveraine dame Anne, Royne de France treschrestienne, que vostre tresbenigne et royale magesté

tousjours desire veoir bonnes choses et vertueuses, je, vostre
treshumble et tresobeissant serviteur, a l'honneur et magnificence
de vostre trestriumphante souveraineté, ay fait *Le Livre des Trois
Dames de Vertus*. (ll. 12–18)

[And because, my most dear and most sovereign lady Anne, most
Christian Queen of France, your most gentle and royal majesty has
always desired to see good and virtuous things, I, your very humble
and very obedient servant, have made *The Book of the Three Ladies
of Virtue* in your honor and to the glory of your most triumphant
sovereignty.]

Although the Parisian publisher extols Anne of Brittany for her basic virtuous
impulses, the dominant tenor of his brief dedication reminds the queen above
all about her responsibility vis-à-vis her subjects of providing an example of
upright behavior. This more moralistic address to Anne of Brittany than that
of the *Nobles et cleres dames* translator not only adopts the main message of
Christine de Pizan's *Trésor de la Cité des dames*, but also that of the *Trésor de
l'âme*, which the publisher dedicated to Anne around the same date.[66] Thus,
two of the three books that Vérard specially prepared for the queen alone
were didactic treatises aimed at encouraging upstanding conduct. Although
he doubtless sought to honor Anne through this dedication of the *Trésor de la
Cité des dames* to her, Vérard actually presented it more as a moralistic lesson
than as an excuse to pay tribute to the French queen. For, as he claims in the
Prologue, the work was designed to show

comment les bonnes princesses doivent aymer et craindre Dieu
pour le premier et principal enseignement, et qu'elles doivent
prendre le bon et sainct avertissement qui vient pour l'amour et
crainte de Nostre Seigneur, avecques plusieurs beaulx et vertueux
enseignemens contenus en celui livre, ainsi que vostre tresglorifique
et beneuree dignité en lisant le livre, ou faisant lire, par maniere de
recreation pourra veoir et congnoistre. (ll. 27–34)

[how, as their first and principal lesson, good princesses should
love and fear God and should take the good and holy advice that
comes from the love and fear of Our Lord, with many beautiful
and virtuous lessons contained in this book, just as your most

renowned and prosperous nobility in reading the book, or having it
read, for your diversion will see and know.]

Vérard's address to the queen thus contrasts with the more deferential and
complimentary remarks of the *Nobles et cleres dames* translator, who, in assuming that the French queen already possessed the necessary moralistic
qualities, painted a substantially more flattering portrait of his dedicatee, because it was more forceful, inspiring, and empowering. It is likely that Vérard
assumed the queen would promote his edition of Christine's rules of conduct
to the many women at her court, whose behavior Anne of Brittany supervised
and guided.[67] However, even though Christine provided a strong didactic
structure to her work and adopted a decidedly moralistic stance throughout,
she took care to pay significantly greater tribute to Margaret of Guyenne, to
whom she dedicated her work in 1405–6. Employing far more ingratiating
language than Vérard, Christine presented the work to her young dedicatee
in more diplomatic fashion, admitting in terms that anticipate those of the
*Nobles et cleres dames* translator, rather than those of Vérard, that Margaret
was already an exemplary figure of upstanding behavior (my emphasis):

> [J]e Cristine, vostre humble servante desireuse de faire chose qui
> plaire vous peust . . . ay fait et compilé ou nom de vous et pour
> vous singulierement cestui present livre, lequel est a la doctrine
> et enseignement de bien et deument vivre aux princesses et
> generalment a toutes femmes, si que veoir le porés, s'il vous plaist
> et a y lire. . . . *nonpourtant que je soye assés certaine que ceste dicte*
> *doctrine n'ait besoing par maniere d'enseignement a vostre noble*
> *personne, qui ja est, Dieu mercy, toutte enseignie et aprinse en ce qu'il*
> *convient, ma tres redoubtee dame,* neantmains, affin que vostre noble
> coer de plus en plus se delicte asuevir la voye de bonnes meurs que
> des vostre enffance avés emprise. (3–4)[68]

> [I, Christine, your humble servant, desirous of making something
> that might please you . . . have made and compiled this present
> book in your name and for you alone, which is about the doctrine
> and teaching of living well and rightly for princesses and generally
> for all women, so that you will see, if it pleases you to read it,
> that. . . . *despite the fact that I am very certain that this said doctrine*
> *does not need to be taught to your noble person, who already has,*

*thanks to God, learned and apprehended everything that is important*
*to know in this area, my most noble lady,* nevertheless, so that your
noble heart increasingly enjoys following the path of good behavior
which, from your childhood, you have adopted.]

As in Vérard's edition of the *Nobles et cleres dames,* ambiguities surrounding
the author's and publisher's role in the making of the *Trésor de la Cité des dames*
abound, for in dedicating his edition to the French queen, the publisher appropriated the traditional role of the court poet, as we have just learned, by
writing his own dedicatory prologue to the queen and adopting Christine's
terminology in some instances.[69] In addition, Vérard had himself painted into
the dedication miniature that opens the queen's specially prepared copy of
the *Trésor de la Cité des dames,* the only known luxury copy of the edition
(Figure 25). Here we discover an illustration divided into two compartments:
a scene depicting the prologue's main characters in the upper register and the
dedication of the work to Anne of Brittany in the lower register. In the latter image, the French queen, who is positioned closest to the viewers and to
whom the work is directly presented, is the most elegantly dressed of the three
seated females, although she is not portrayed here wearing a crown, as in other
dedication miniatures in which she figures. Her identity is confirmed, nonetheless, in the dedicatory prologue that follows. The placement of the three
court ladies in this lower image may consciously echo the three Virtues, Reason, Rectitude, and Justice, depicted in the image above.[70] Whereas Vérard is
portrayed on bended knee, in the classic pose of an author presenting his work
to his patron in the lower register, the image above of the true author of the
work emphasizes the female protagonists of the narrative. Indeed the upper illustration stages the author of the *Trésor* in the pseudoautobiographical role of
narrator she has created for herself in the work's prologue. Dressed in a nun's
habit and lying on a bed, "Dame Cristine" converses with the three Virtues
surrounding her, instead of sitting at her desk in an author-portrait or dedicating her work to a patron, as was the case in nearly all the known miniatures
of Christine de Pizan.[71] The publisher has now assumed this function, as the
illustration in the lower register bears out.[72]

   Thus, in attempting to balance the role of the deceased author with his
role as living publisher, Vérard chooses simultaneously to depict Christine
as a protagonist of her own narrative and to render homage to his dedicatee,
Anne of Brittany, while presenting himself as a visually prominent and perhaps intermediary figure as well. The male bookmaker has thus interceded in

25. Christine de Pizan, *Trésor de la cité des dames* (Paris: for Antoine Vérard, 1497),
Vienna, ÖNB, Ink.3.D.19, fol. A1v: Upper Register: "Dame Christine" surrounded
by three Virtues; Lower Register: Vérard offers his edition to Anne of Brittany.
Copyright: ONB, Bildarchiv+Signatures.

the process and reconfigured the paratextual dynamics of the original book about women, composed by a woman, and intended for women.

We cannot deny the significance of the presence of Christine de Pizan's *Trésor de la Cité des dames* in Anne of Brittany's library. As the only woman author writing in French in the late medieval period, Christine de Pizan's relevance to a female readership that included Anne of Brittany cannot be underestimated. In assessing two of the works on women discussed thus far in this chapter, Winn rightly argues that

> the feminist aspect [of the *Nobles et cleres dames*] must not be
> neglected: Boccaccio's text on famous women shares with Christine
> de Pisan's treatise [the *Trésor de la cité des dames*] a focus which
> was sure to please a queen whose court was termed "une fort belle
> escole pour les Dames." (136)

The *Trésor de la Cité des dames*, a collection of moralistic teachings that was dedicated to the French queen, not commissioned by her (at least in the case of Vérard), was part of her book collection, appearing in two versions no less.[73] Indeed it is especially in Book I of her *Trésor de la Cité des dames* that Christine, commanding decidedly more literary and feminine authority than Vérard, provides advice to queens and those women at the top of the ruling classes. She urges them in rather sermonlike fashion to avoid temptation through divine guidance, cultivate all virtues, demonstrate diplomatic character by maintaining peace between their husbands and those nobles over whom they preside, be charitable, treat spouse, family and subjects well, show discretion, behave justly toward all classes, demonstrate economic resourcefulness yet be generous, and maintain the reputation of princesses in their charge. Although Vérard himself never expands his prologue comments beyond urging the queen to meet her moral obligations, Christine's wide-ranging suggestions would have proved quite relevant to Anne of Brittany in her roles as wife and mother, but also as duchess and queen, particularly in her interactions with the ladies under her charge at court, to whom Book II of Christine's work directed important counsel. What much of the counsel in the *Trésor* implies, especially in its later chapters in Book I, but which Anne's dedicator failed to emphasize, was not only the moral responsibility expected of the queen, but also the power in political and economic arenas that she wielded vis-à-vis her subjects, her court entourage, her family, and her husband.

Thus, the distinction between works that Anne of Brittany acquired herself and those that others commissioned for her or dedicated to her, often for their own advancement, should not go unnoted. This dynamic may well shed greater light on her individual interests as well as actual political power, for it appears that Anne of Brittany was more dependent on Charles VIII than on Louis XII when it came to literary patronage, perhaps because she was both relatively young and more controlled by her first husband. Her independent appearance in many more extant dedication miniatures that were produced during her second marriage than during her first upholds this theory. In point of fact, this contrast describes a later book about women in Anne of Brittany's library, Antoine Dufour's *Vies des femmes célèbres*, which I examine below.

Vérard's rather condescending tone and minimization of the French queen's authority in his dedication of the *Trésor de la Cité des dames*, coupled with his erasure of Anne of Brittany and of the praise of women offered by the anonymous translator in the two royal hybrid copies of the *Nobles et cleres dames* and the seeming displacement of a copy originally dedicated to the French queen may well explain why Anne of Brittany decided some ten years later, as the wife of Louis XII, to commission Antoine Dufour, the royal couple's future confessor, to rewrite Boccaccio's work about famous women, which he completed in 1504. Anne of Brittany's special manuscript book of the *Vies des femmes célèbres*, which treats a number of women placed on Boccaccio's literary stage, but others as well, was magnificently illuminated by Jean Pichore and completed around 1506.[74] It is currently housed in the Musée Dobrée in Nantes as MS XVII. It is telling that the French queen did not order a printed volume of this work, even in a luxury hybrid copy, and that she did not engage Vérard (who nonetheless dedicated one last work to her two years later, as we learned above) in this enterprise in any fashion. The queen's commission of the *Vies des femmes célebres* thus seems to confirm Anne's preference for manuscript books and signals perhaps her predilection for a system of book reproduction over which she maintained greater control.

## Antoine Dufour's *Vies des femmes célèbres*: The Queen's Commission

Drawing inspiration from Boccaccio's *De mulieribus claris* and perhaps from Symphorien Champier's *Nef des dames vertueuses*,[75] among other works,[76] Dufour's *Vies des femmes célèbres*, a compilation of 91 biographies of famous women from antiquity, mythology, the Bible, and medieval history, merits special consideration, because it is one of the few works containing documentation that Anne of Brittany commissioned it. Seventy-three miniatures painted by the Parisian artist Jean Pichore and his workshop collaborators illustrate most of the biographies featured in Dufour's manuscript book of seventy-six leaves,[77] leading the work's editor to declare it "parmi les manuscrits les plus remarquables qui aient été composés pour Anne de Bretagne, une fois devenue reine de France" (vii).[78] While the *Vies des femmes célèbres* offers a rather traditional and moralistic depiction of women, based as it is on familiar late-medieval paradigms that presented female models of virtue (and negative *exempla* of vice) from the past, it nevertheless imparts a certain ambivalence about that particular status quo through the shifting positions explicitly and implicitly adopted by the author vis-à-vis his patron and some of his female models.[79]

The iconography associated with Anne of Brittany in the *Vies des femmes célèbres* is, at first glance, completely female centered and female empowering. Despite the fact that the French queen is seldom explicitly lauded through Dufour's words, the opening dedicatory miniature prominently presents Anne in her roles as patron and future reader of the book (Figure 26). In a scene in the left background, Anne of Brittany commissions the *Vies des femmes célèbres* from Antoine Dufour. To my knowledge, this constitutes the only visual depiction of the queen in her role as commissioner of a work; in fact, this dimension of the book enterprise is rarely portrayed in visual terms in any decorated book. Did Anne of Brittany herself play a role in staging this particular depiction? In the right foreground scene, Anne receives the completed manuscript book from Dufour, who assumes the conventional dedication pose of an author on bended knee before his patron.[80] This kind of dedication scene is commonly replicated in dedicatory manuscripts, although more often than not a male rather than a female is placed in the position of power as the recipient of such a work.

Anne's active involvement in the commission, confection, reading, and dissemination of the *Vies des femmes célèbres* is underscored verbally as well, for in the prologue that begins immediately below the dedication scene, Dufour confirms that the French queen requested him to write the biographies in French, given that court ladies were unable to read Latin, for the purpose of overcoming idleness:

Et considéré que la plupart des nobles dames de France ne
entendent le langage latin, et congnoissant l'abisme et comble de
vertus estre en treshaulte, trespuissante et tresexcellente dame

26. Antoine Dufour, *Les Vies des femmes célèbres*, Nantes, Musée Dobrée, ms. XVII, fol. 1r: Anne of Brittany commissions the author to write the book; the author dedicates the completed book to Anne of Brittany. Cliché Chantal Hémon, musée Dobrée, Conseil général de Loire-Atlantique, Nantes.

et princesse ma dame Anne de Bretaigne, royne de France et duchesse de Bretaigne, je frère Anthoine Dufour, docteur en théologie, de l'ordre des Frères Prescheurs, général inquisiteur de la foy, par le commandement d'icelle, pour matter oysiveté, ay bien voulu translater[81] ce present livre en maternel langage, en y prenant les hystoires anciennes, loyales et véritables, pour brider la langue de ceulx qui ne ont veu ny leu que fables et mensonges. (1–2)[82]

[And given that most noble ladies of France do not understand Latin, and knowing the heights and depths of virtues to be found in the most noble, most powerful and most excellent lady and princess, my lady Anne of Brittany, queen of France and duchess of Brittany, I, Brother Antoine Dufour, Doctor in theology from the Dominican Order, General Inquisitor of the faith, by her order, to overcome idleness, wanted this present book to be translated into [our] mother tongue, in presenting its ancient, faithful and true stories, with the aim of restraining the language of those who have seen or read only fables and lies.]

Whereas Boccaccio had written his *De mulieribus claris* in Latin primarily for a male readership, as we learned earlier, and the French translations of the work were commissioned for the most part by male patrons, Dufour's *Vies des femmes célèbres* joins the *Nobles et cleres dames* in explicitly targeting a female readership. This aim appears to reflect the intervention and wishes of the queen herself, whose commission of the work may have been inspired by the complications associated with the Vérard edition of the *Nobles et cleres dames*.[83] Dufour's remarks also reveal that Anne of Brittany's motivation in requesting this work was at once of a virtuous and generous nature. This so-called "Mirror of Ladies"[84] was designed not only for her moral improvement, but, since she herself apparently knew Latin (Dufour, ix), was also destined for a wider female court public, doubtless the one represented by the ladies at the queen's side in this and other similar dedication miniatures.[85] Anne apparently supported many females from noble families with a court pension and trained them in disciplined fashion.[86] Since Anne of Brittany was known for her scrutiny of their dress, behavior, education, and entertainment, one could say that she incarnated the principles proposed by Christine de Pizan in her *Livre des Trois Vertus*, discussed above. Leroux de

Lincy describes the French queen's supervision of her female entourage in the following way:

> Anne de Bretagne avait pour les filles attachées dès leur bas
> âge à son service des soins tout particuliers; non-seulement elle
> s'appliquait à leur inspirer l'amour & la pratique de toutes les
> vertus, les stimulant & les guidant dans le travail, mais encore elle
> les soignait dans leurs maladies, les récompensait largement de leurs
> peines, & ne reculait devant aucun sacrifice pour leur procurer des
> mariages avantageux. (94–95)[87]

The prologue of the *Vies des femmes célèbres* confirms that through this commission Anne of Brittany actively sought to influence the court culture of women by providing them with models of virtuous females.

Whereas the conception and reception of Dufour's work are visually staged in the dedication miniature, with the queen, surrounded by her ladies-in-waiting, depicted as the central figure in these transactions, the prologue verbally prepares the reader's state of mind by announcing the defensive role to be taken by the author. Dufour categorically distinguishes his work from others on the subject, in particular the writings of Boccaccio and Theophrastus, who, he claims, arbitrarily blamed women, asserting that his writing is based instead on a wise, loyal, and truthful assessment of females:[88]

> Pour ce ce que la plus commune partie des hommes se adonnent à
> blasmer les dames, tant de langue que de plume, et en ont composé
> des livres, comme Bocasse, Théophraste et ung tas d'aultres, j'ay
> bien voulu cercher par les anciennes librairies à celle fin de trouver
> aucun veritable acteur qui sagement, loyallement et véritablement
> parlast d'elles. (1)

> [Since most men tend to blame women, in both their speech and
> writing, and have composed books about them, such as Boccaccio,
> Theophrastus and a lot of others, I wanted to search through old
> book collections with the goal of finding some truthful author who
> spoke wisely, loyally and truthfully about them.]

To place Boccaccio in the same category as Theophrastus, considered to be a serious misogynist by Christine de Pizan and others, constituted a stinging criticism of the Italian author. Dufour goes further when he attributes any evil inflicted by women presented in his work to the evil counsel of men associated with them:

> Ny ne vous esbayssez si, en lisant ce présent oeuvre, vous y trouvez aucunes vicieuses dames entre les bonnes; car en la généalogie et compaignie du rachater des hommes, là vous trouverez de lasches et meschans hommes. Et croy que, si les dames ont fait quelque mal, s'a esté plus pour l'instruction d'aulcuns maulvais hommes qui par aventure les admonestoient à pis faire, ainsi que vous voirrez et orrez en ce présent livre. (2)

> [Do not be astonished either if, in reading this present work, you discover in it some corrupt ladies among the good ones; for in the genealogy and assembly of men seeking redemption, you will find cowardly and wicked men. And I believe that if ladies have done any ill, it has been more because of the teaching of certain malicious men who happened to advise them to act worse, as you will see and hear in this present book.]

In the prologue, then, the author's posture is defensive of women in general. This protofeminist attitude may well reflect the thinking of Anne herself, or at the very least the perspective adopted by a male author conscious of his patron's interest in women of the past. Contradicting opinions voiced by Dufour in the actual text, however, undermine his assertions here, as we will learn below. Moreover, except for his initial conventional description of Anne of Brittany, including his reference to the "abisme et comble de vertus" found in the queen (1), Dufour never explicitly extols his patroness like some of his contemporaries. He praises her only implicitly when he claims that since the creation of the world no greater number of "good and wise ladies" can be found than at the present time:

> Car, à la vérité, il me semble que, depuys la création du monde, l'on ne trouva ung si grant nombre de bonnes et sages dames que aujourd'huy de ce temps, l'an mil cinq cens et quatre excepté celles qui miraculeusement de Dieu ont été gardées. (1)

> [For in truth it seems to me that, since the creation of the world, one has not found such a large number of good and wise

ladies as today in the year 1504, except for those who have been miraculously saved by God.]

Dufour's rather sober manner of addressing Anne of Brittany contrasts sharply with the effusive dedication that introduces the *Nobles et cleres dames* and Jean Marot's *Voyage de Gênes*. Although these two authors may have been seeking Anne's patronage, in contrast to Dufour, who was commissioned by her to write the book, the sycophantic tone of the translator's and Marot's dedicatory introductions is in fact more typical of contemporary court dedications than that of Dufour's prologue. While it would have been inappropriate for Anne to commission a work devoted to her own glory, it is also striking that Dufour did not capitalize on the obvious opportunity to pay extensive tribute to the French queen, like many other court writers. This may well confirm that Dufour was not dependent on Anne's patronage for his livelihood,[89] like Jean Marot, La Vigne, or Lemaire de Belges. Nevertheless, echoing the *Nobles et cleres dames* translator rather than Vérard in his *Trésor de la Cité des dames* prologue, Dufour assumes that his dedicatee and her entourage already possess the virtues embodied by his famous women, instead of suggesting that they will benefit from instruction through his *exempla*. In the end, Dufour chooses perhaps to venerate Anne's female entourage rather than the queen alone.

An additional statement in Dufour's prologue merits attention because it harkens back to the controversy at court about female virtues raised by the *Nobles et cleres dames* translator in his prologue some ten years earlier. In describing his aims in composing the work, Dufour mentions that he hopes not only to help his readers overcome idleness, but also to "restrain the language of those who have seen or read only fables and lies" (1–2). While less specific than the *Nobles et cleres dames* translator, Dufour nonetheless evokes the necessity of setting the record straight about the traditionally misogynistic assessment of female character.[90] This comment may well confirm that Dufour read the translator's prologue of the *Nobles et cleres dames*. In any case, the *Vies des femmes célèbres* very likely figured in continuing court debates about the respective virtues of males and females.

Anne's royal presence in the opening miniature of the *Vies des femmes célèbres* and Dufour's direct and indirect praise of her and her female entourage in his prologue are reinforced by implicit associations between his dedicatee and the models he offers her in his book.[91] Like the pictorial depiction of the queen, a number of famous women are portrayed visually as enthroned figures, a stance reminding readers of their power as political leaders of one kind or another. They include Niobe, Faustina, Irene, Theodolinda, Mathilda of Tuscany, and Joanna, queen of Naples and Sicily. Buettner's analysis of the visual staging of queens in the miniatures of BnF ms. ffr. 12420, the earliest known French translation of Boccaccio's *De mulieribus claris*, holds relevance for the *Vies des femmes célèbres* manuscript offered to Anne of Brittany over a century later:

> The *Cleres femmes*'s vision of queens is literally, rather than
> metaphorically representational. They are fictional, and of the
> distant, very distant past, when customs were certainly different,
> very different. And yet the recurrent imagery of these queens,
> ruling over male subjects, might have had quite a vivid impact on
> the viewer's imagination, even though it was without consequences
> on a social and political level. While neither Boccaccio's text nor
> the images articulate a political theory of queenship as such, this
> regal subcycle displays a remarkable variety of roles, ceremonies,
> and actions proper to this particular status. (31)

Like Boccaccio, Dufour presents the enthroned Niobe and Faustina in rather negative terms,[92] whereas he extols Irene, who reigned ten years as Empress of Byzantium (fourth c.) during her son's minority and found popular support among the Romans in contrast to her husband's and son's abuse (149–51). The three other enthroned figures provide even more inspiration as positive political models. Unequivocal praise of Joanna of Sicily (Figure 27), the last of Boccaccio's famous women, must have inspired Dufour's own tribute to her great political diplomacy, wise counsel, unparalleled generosity toward the underprivileged, and successful marriage, which places her among the most virtuous *exempla* in his work as well. Of all the famous women, this fourteenth-century ruler is chronologically and doubtless psychologically the closest to Anne of Brittany in political rank, station, and character.[93] Their appearance in each miniature is not dissimilar. Like the French queen who stands out in the dedication miniature because of her red dress (all others are dressed in black) and her seated position of honor, Joanna of Sicily, likewise featured in red, is centrally positioned on a throne in her miniature scene. The extent of her power is even more considerable than Anne's, both historically and visually, for she faces the viewer directly and only men, reacting to her in a humble and respectful manner, comprise her entourage.

27. Antoine Dufour, *Les Vies des femmes célèbres*, Nantes, Musée Dobrée, ms. XVII, fol. 75v: Joanna, Queen of Sicily. Cliché Chantal Hémon, musée Dobrée, Conseil général de Loire-Atlantique, Nantes.

28. Antoine Dufour, *Les Vies des femmes célèbres*, Nantes, Musée Dobrée, ms. XVII, fol. 73r: Mathilda [of Tuscany], Countess of Mantua. Cliché Chantal Hémon, musée Dobrée, Conseil général de Loire-Atlantique, Nantes.

Wielding even more power than Joanna of Sicily, as she sits in a more prominent position than either the emperor or the pope on each side of her, Mathilda, twelfth-century countess of Mantua, who did not figure in Boccaccio's book, likewise excels in the political arena (Figure 28). Celebrating Mathilda's support of the pope against the emperor—she was the only female defender of the Church (156)—and her renown as a chaste widow, Dufour's description provides a counterpoint to the biography of the more infamous Faustina (see n. 92):

Femme soigneuse, à mal faire craintive, à bien faire audacieuse, pensant es choses loingtaines et bien usant des prochaines, cordialle à ses amys, ingénieuse à la deffaicte de ses ennemys, orgueilleuse en contenance, passant toutes aultres en humilité de cueur et honnesteté, prudente à ouyr conseil, providente à l'exécuter, familière selon le temps, rien ne perdant de son auctorité. Humanité la conduisoyt, doulceur l'entretenoit, beaulté la décoroit, vérité l'ennoblissoit, libéralité aymer la faisoit, grandeur de cueur les plus grans en crainte tenoit. (155)

[Attentive lady, fearful of doing evil, audacious in doing good, thinking of far-off things and using well those nearby, cordial to her friends, ingenious in the defeat of her enemies, proud in her comportment, surpassing all in humility of the heart and honesty, prudent in listening to advice, provident in executing it, friendly according to the times, losing nothing of her authority. Humanity motivated her, sweetness sustained her, beauty adorned her, truth ennobled her, generosity made her loved, the most impressive greatness of heart made her feared.]

Theodolinda, absent too from Boccaccio's work,[94] is among those whose visual and verbal portrayal resonates most strongly with Anne of Brittany's character. As one of the few females enthroned in the miniature accompanying her story—a man kneels before her, offering her a volume of St. Gregory's *Dialogues* (Figure 29)—she earns one of the longest biographies in the *Vies des femmes célèbres* and, on several occasions (147, 148), is even given voice by Dufour. Like the French queen in the liminal miniature of her own manuscript book, Theodolinda is associated both with political power and intellectual pursuits. Verbal associations between the two figures abound as well. Daughter of the king of Bavaria and queen of the Lombards in the late sixth century through her marriage to Autharis, Theodolinda is a foreign-born queen who is extolled for the manner in which her subjects offered unequivocal support for her choice of a second husband as ruler, following her first husband's death. Dufour offers equally strong praise for Theodolinda's conversion of her

29. Antoine Dufour, *Les Vies des femmes célèbres*, Nantes, Musée Dobrée, ms. XVII, fol. 69v: Theodolinda. Cliché Chantal Hémon, musée Dobrée, Conseil général de Loire-Atlantique, Nantes.

husband and countrymen to Christianity and sponsorship of the construction of religious establishments. But he emphasizes her intellectual renown
as well:

> Si curieuse fut et si sage que tous les différentz des royaumes et
> des princes luy estoyent présentez pour les appointer, ce qu'elle
> faisoit aisément, sans nulle difficulté, tant qu'elle mérita lesser son
> propre nom et estre nommée par tout le monde le sage dame. Les
> philosophes n'ont treuvé que les sept sages d'Athènes, mais lisez ce
> livre: vous en trouverez plus de trente dignes de pareilles ou plus
> grandes louenges. (149)

> [She was so curious and so wise that all the disputes of the
> kingdoms and princes were brought to her for judgment, which
> she accomplished easily, without any difficulty, so much so that
> she earned the right to abandon her own name and to be called by
> everyone "the wise lady." Philosophers have found only the seven
> wise men of Athens, but read this book: you will find in it more
> than thirty [women] worthy of equal or greater praise.]

As one of the more than thirty exceptionally worthy women in the *Vies des
femmes célèbres*, Theodolinda would have reminded readers of Anne of Brittany's own profile, a "foreign" queen who nevertheless attracted much popular
support, one who survived one ruling husband and married another.[95]

Theodolinda also served as a figure linking Anne visually and verbally to
past women lauded not only for diplomatic success in the political arena but
also to those celebrated for their intellectual pursuits. For like Anne, many of
the women Dufour commends figured actively in the book culture, signs of
which fill the miniatures accompanying their vignettes. Those such as Sappho, Amalthea, Cornificia, Zenobia, Proba, and Battista Malatesta are praised
for their talents as poets or writers, while Dufour applauds the oratorical
and linguistic gifts of Hortensia, Zenobia, (Saint) Helen, Blesilla, and Proba.
Erythraea's and Albunea's intellectual contributions as sibyls earn kudos, as
do Nicostrata's invention of Roman letters and Mammea's love of books.[96]
Many are accomplished in numerous arenas, such as Zenobia, whose illustration emphasizes her prowess as a warrior, but whose biography recounts many
other virtues. Her history of wise and virtuous women is noteworthy for its
*mise en abyme* of the very production and dissemination of the *Vies des femmes*

*célèbres*, in which Zenobia herself figures as a model female, but likewise for her disparagement of men's misleading writings about women:

> Ce fut elle qui trouva la façon de mettre par hystoire les sages et
> vertueuses dames, disant que femme de cueur ne peult estre sans
> grant et bon serviteur, tant aux lettres que aux armes, et que les
> hommes par leurs faulces escriptures avoyent ainsi brouillé le papier
> des dames. (119–20)

> [It was she who found the means to put into narrative form the
> [stories of] wise and virtuous ladies, stating that a woman of heart
> cannot be without a servant, great and good in letters as much
> as at arms, and that men, through their false writings have thus
> confounded the account of ladies.]

These particular contributions of the highly praised Zenobia, whose qualities are compared favorably to those of celebrated males, such as Aristotle, Seneca, Demosthenes, and Solon (118), supplied additional ammunition to Anne and her female cohorts in their defense of women at the French court.

By the same token, Hortensia's oratorical skills before the Roman triumvirate, provides powerful language for supporters of feminine versus masculine virtues at the French court, as she defends all Roman woman against a new law limiting their freedom:

> Laquelle proposa tant honnestement et vertueusement, en
> remonstrant les grans biens que ont fait les dames et le grant mal
> qu'il aviendroit de ainsi mal les traicter, donnant aussi raison
> qu'ils ne ont point esté appellées et que nulle sentence ne peult
> estre donnée partie non ouye et que, s'il falloit alléguer les jeux
> dissoluz et la prodigalité des hommes, trop plus on auroit matière
> du contraire, disant aussi qu'il n'est riens qui garde mieulx
> un bon meuble que les dames; et, pour conclusion dist que
> invérécundement et publicquement les hommes péchoyent plus que
> les femmes. (91)

> [She proposed most honestly and virtuously, in advertising the
> great good done by women and the great evil that would occur if
> they were poorly treated, providing also the objection that they had

not been invited [to plead their case] and that no judgment can be
given if a party has not been heard and that, if one were to offer
evidence of the dissolute actions and lavish expenses of men, there
would be a great deal of material against them, saying also that
there is no one who can better keep a household than ladies; and,
in conclusion she said that men publicly and unabashedly sinned
more than women.]

Although citing the ideas of Zenobia and Hortensia through indirect discourse in these biographies, Dufour also gives voice to some 37 of his famous
women, thereby affording his literary subjects seemingly more independence
than Boccaccio. Saint Helen is one such model who, like Anne of Brittany,
according to her court writers, was motivated in reading both philosophi-
cal and religious books to avoid idleness and to learn new and foreign ideas
(122).[97] Mammea's inspiration for establishing a library doubtless recalls that
of all bibliophiles of Anne's time, including the French queen herself:

> Elle fist rédiger par escript toutes les hystoires anciennes vrayes
> et avoit son cabinet de son trésor et l'autre de ses livres à part, et
> singulièrement ceulx que Origenes et aultres hystoriographes par
> son commandement avoyent translatez. (128)

> [She had all the true and ancient chronicles written down and
> kept the compartment for her riches and the other one for her
> books separate, and especially those that Origen and other
> historiographers had translated at her command.]

Dufour's attribution of a voice to Mammea stands out because of her as-
tuteness in understanding the benefit of books over accumulated wealth for
posterity: "J'ayme mieulx mes petitz cayers que mon trésor, car à perpétuité
ilz parleront de moy, et l'autre, comme chose insensible, de mains en mains
sera aliené" [I prefer my little quires to my treasure, because they will speak in
perpetuity about me, and [my riches], like an inanimate thing, will be gradually diminished] (129). Mammea's preference for her library over her material
wealth, because her name would not be lost through her books as it would
be through her riches, underscores her consciousness—and presumably that
of Dufour, Anne, and her female entourage—of the function of books as instruments of image-making and empowerment that would be passed down to

posterity. Whereas Mammea's access to her books was direct (120), Lucretia listened to her chamber ladies reading a book about wise and virtuous ladies (65). Both experiences doubtless reenacted those of Anne of Brittany and her entourage upon the queen's acceptance of Dufour's dedication copy of his *Vies des femmes célèbres* and other books. In fact, the *Nobles et dames* translator had earlier described the queen's use of his work in these very terms, perhaps referring as well to Anne of Brittany's viewing of the images accompanying the biographies of famous women (my emphasis): "la lecture de ce present volume sera occasion de eviter oesiveté et recreation de esperit, quand vous plaira *veoir ou ouyr* les faiz celebrables des nobles dames" [And in truth, my most noble lady, the reading of this present volume will offer you the opportunity to avoid idleness and recreation of the mind, when it pleases you to *see or hear* about the celebrated deeds of noble ladies] (a2r).

Indeed, Anne's visual and verbal placement on center stage as a sovereign reigning over the women of her court and controlling the book production process in the dedication miniature of the *Vies des femmes célèbres* serves to associate her thematically with nearly one third of the 96 portraits that follow. Such visual repetition provides a coherent framework for the stories of famous women, which, although presented chronologically, are otherwise juxtaposed without connection, as Jeanneau points out (xxxvi). Dufour's choice of past models may have been determined to a large degree by the profile of his patron—and perhaps with the active participation of Anne herself.

Nevertheless, although Dufour appears in an appropriately self-effacing author-posture in the opening miniature of the *Vies des femmes célèbres*, and although he presents many of the women in a positive light, a close reading reveals that his textual voice is in fact quite interventionist, as he frequently introduces his famous women from a moralistic perspective. This can be explained in part because his work, like Boccaccio's, treats both virtuous and infamous women. As we might expect of a Dominican friar—and as Anne of Brittany herself must have expected—the author clearly distinguishes the positive from the negative *exempla* for his readers, promoting in particular Christian heroines such as Azella, Paula, and Galla Placidia as models of virtue and positioning the Virgin Mary first in his portrait gallery as the highest example of feminine rectitude. Most of these figures did not, of course, appear in the catalogue of Boccaccio, who had consciously eliminated saintly women from his biographies.[98]

In the queen's manuscript copy of the *Vies des femmes célèbres*, artist and author concurred in devoting the most attention to Mary through an elaborate series of exquisitely painted scenes surrounding the Annunciation and the longest narrative in the book about the Virgin's life.[99] She provides the measure for all the biographies that follow. At the opposite end of the spectrum are stories such as that of Medea, whose heinous crimes repel Dufour as he struggles to narrate her biography, even as a negative *exemplum*:

> Il me fasche bien de parler de ceste cy, pour la reverence des
> bonnes, mais pour enseigner les simplettes du dangier de cest
> inconvénient, au plus brief je en diray ce qu'il m'en semble. . . . Je
> me vouldroys voluntiers taire, mais il m'est du tout difficile. (38–39)

> [It greatly angers me to speak about her, because of my reverence
> for good women, but in order to teach simple women about the
> danger of this unfit person, I will say what I deem necessary in the
> briefest way . . . I would rather keep silent, but it is very difficult for
> me to do so.]

This example typifies how intrusive Dufour's first-person voice actually can be, as it inserts itself repeatedly in more than a quarter of his narratives, sometimes even vying with the speaking voice he grants to his "femme célèbre." In a more aggressive tone than in the prologue, he comes across here in a didactic mode, as he aims specifically to warn simple women against the dangers of a person like Medea. But overall, Dufour's interventions are generally much less negative than Boccaccio's, because, unlike his predecessor, he includes in his *Vies des femmes célèbres* many women who were devout Christians, and his interjections often convey his deep respect and admiration for his subjects. Dufour does not hold back his praise of a pagan woman, such as Nicostrata, as the most learned person on earth, whose invention of the Latin alphabet earns unreserved praise (45).[100]

What nonetheless gains Dufour's strongest endorsement in the end, just like Boccaccio's, are those women who remained virgins or those widows who strived, often against great odds, to remain chaste and faithful to their deceased husbands by refusing to remarry.[101] Dufour's praise centers, for example, on Diana's avowed chastity (34), Hippone's decision to drown herself rather than be raped (68–69), Dido's undying loyalty (52–54),[102] Sarah's wifely devotion (18–23), the purity of Marcia (77–78), who, as an artist, refused to paint nude women, and Paulina's chaste life following the death of her husband.[103]

The author's aggressive defense of women in his prologue is, therefore, tempered by his conservative interjections, as he promotes traditional values and roles for women. In fact, the underlying misogynist tone that sometimes surfaces in Dufour's comments belies his attribution of women's evils to men, earlier professed in the prologue, and resembles closely the perspective of Boc-caccio himself.[104] For example, Emilia's sacrifice of overlooking the blatant infidelities of her husband Scipio and actual sponsorship of Scipio's mistress following his death earn Dufour's adulation, which assumes even greater au-thority through its juxtaposition with his derision of most other women:

Posé toutesfoys que la pluspart des femmes soyent suspicionneuses, singulièrement quand il est question de la perte du droit qu'ilz doyvent avoir de leurs mariz, ceste cy, par discrétion, se monstra gentille . . . ce que ne feroyent beaucoup de femmes. (82)

[In any case, assuming that most women are suspicious, particularly when it concerns the loss of their power over their husbands, this one, through discretion, proved to be noble . . . which many women would not be.]

Such an assessment seems to fly in the face of his prologue pronouncements in defense of women. In another biography, Dufour denounces in equally fer-vent terms Sabina Poppaea's lasciviousness as the common vice of women and her use of female wiles, or "modes fémenines" (103), to deceive. In these exam-ples, Dufour's essentialist position about the female sex, which is not surpris-ing given his religious grounding and the literary traditions from which he draws, nonetheless undermines yet again the claim in his prologue about men being to blame for women's sins. In the end, although he offers less perva-sive criticism of women than his predecessor, Dufour frequently assumes the same posture as Boccaccio, whom he had criticized in his introduction. Was Dufour unconsciously hypocritical at these points in the text, while striving to please and appease his patron and audience in his prologue?[105] Whatever the answer, the author's shift from the traditional focus of a number of stories is worth noting, especially since it is precisely at the intersection of word and image that these more unusual renditions are the most striking.

The miniatures painted by Jean Pichore in Anne of Brittany's copy of the *Vies des femmes célèbres* tend to follow closely Dufour's textual representa-tions, as Cassagnes-Brouquet argues, suggesting that he was either familiar

with the text or had been given specific instructions about the visual translation of text to image.[106] For example, Pichore does not offer the conventional
image of Lucretia's death—presumably because of Dufour's voiced criticism
of suicide—but portrays instead the moment at which Lucretia's attacker as-
sails her, thereby focusing on the male perpetrator of evil (fol. 311).[107] Ignoring
another well-established iconographical tradition, while remaining faithful
to the text, Pichore presents Eve in the throes of childbirth, as Adam wor-
riedly looks on, instead of in her more traditional role of precipitating the Fall
(fol. 84).[108] In describing Eve's sin, Dufour surprisingly downplays the moment of the Fall, making no moral judgment about it whatsoever (17). Like
Pichore, Dufour focuses instead on the positive relationship between Adam
and Eve, demonstrating empathy for the pain Eve suffered in childbirth, a
punishment, of course, for her sin (18).

This unusual interpretation, appealing more to the experience of Dufour's
female readership than to the average contemporary reader, foreshadows another seemingly less conventional dimension of the *Vies des femmes célèbres*,
the author's glorification of women's courage, physical vigor, and endurance,
especially their military prowess, which implicitly evokes an androgynous
image of the ideal woman. In a significant number of cases, Dufour compares women to men in very favorable terms, most often portraying them as
the superior sex. Zenobia's comparison with Aristotle, Seneca, Demosthenes,
and Solon is matched by Irene, who surpassed her father in the art of painting (77) and Hortensia, who spoke so ingeniously that everyone thought they
were hearing her deceased father (91). Cornificia, inventor of epigrams, elicits
praise for having invented what wise men could follow only with great effort
(91). Mariamne abandoned all feminine behavior and did what few knights
in similar circumstances would have known how to do, receiving the death
blow as courageously as any man or woman before her (95–96). Triaria, for-
getting her sex and fragility, carried out what few men would have dared
undertake (108). Blesilla is as adept at Greek as Homer and at Hebrew as
Solomon (130).[109]

The most repeated visual image of women in the *Vies des femmes célèbres*
is that of the armed female combatant, for whom Dufour often expresses
enormous admiration. Dufour never condemns women for cross-dressing,
because, in point of fact, they usually dressed like men for the most respectable of reasons—to remain chaste, join their loved ones, or enter into religion. For example, Semiramis, queen of the Assyrians, held men of arms
in fear, because none surpassed her in battle (23). Hypsicrathea changed her

clothes and cut her hair, arming herself with all kinds of weapons to avoid being begged or solicited (85). Euphrosine donned the clothes of a young boy, pretending to be a eunuch, and became a monk in an abbey (134). Maria Putheolina, avoiding all feminine behavior, never drank, slept little, and was surpassed by no one in competitions and in battle (157). A contemporary of Petrarch, she elicits the following compliment from King Robert of Sicily: "Nous sommes en merveileux temps là où il fault qu'une femme en touz faits certaineux passé les hommes" [We live in a marvelous time in which a woman for certain has surpassed men in all deeds] (158). This female model is one of the many portrayed in military gear in the illustrations accompanying their biographies.[110]

Pichore, nevertheless, avoids any excessive display of female superiority over men in his miniatures, and, not surprisingly, any suggestion of androgyny. Twelve of the women Dufour lauds for their military expertise are painted with armor and/or arms, although five others who achieved celebrity in similar fashion are not thus depicted.[111] It is likely that there was little resistance to the portrayal of many of these women in military gear, because this was a conventional iconographic feature of the virtues. The highly stylized scene in which these figures are depicted rather passively standing in their armor recalls the traditional medieval iconography of personified virtues who successfully resist their enemies in their battle against vices.[112] The fact that all of these examples belonged to the historic or mythic past doubtless created a convenient cultural distance from contemporary female readers.

And yet, Dufour's *Vies des femmes célèbres* provides one compelling visual testimony to female knighthood, that of the rehabilitated Joan of Arc, who is the only female warrior depicted astride a horse in a stunningly bold, albeit awkwardly painted, pose (Figure 30). Dufour's claim that Joan had been falsely condemned for having worn armor suggests that early sixteenth-century French court circles no longer held Joan's cross-dressing in contempt, as had many of her contemporaries. And yet, this rather realistic portrait of a military woman, the very image with which the *Vies des femmes célèbres* ends, symbolized not so much Joan's military and political victories as her moral triumphs, in particular her ability to remain a virgin against all odds (165). Laura Dufresne's contention that female warriors in late medieval texts are not usually visualized in a warring posture unless the patrons of the texts are women[113] suggests that Anne of Brittany may have played even more of an instrumental role in designing the *Vies des femmes célèbres* than previously thought.

30. Antoine Dufour, *Les Vies des femmes célèbres*, Nantes, Musée Dobrée, ms. XVII, fol. 76v: Joan of Vaucouleurs [Joan of Arc]. Cliché Chantal Hémon, musée Dobrée, Conseil général de Loire-Atlantique, Nantes.

The queen may or may not have been directly involved in the decision to include Joan as a "femme célèbre" or to portray her and other famous women as military heroines in Dufour's work. But it would not have been an inconceivable gesture on her part, given that her second husband, Louis XII, had initiated a reexamination of Joan's trial transcripts around 1500 that involved a compilation of past and existing judicial records.[114] Might Anne of Brittany herself have played a role in this action? The fact that Dufour, like Christine de Pizan herself some seventy-five years earlier, describes the deed of the woman whose biography and portrait close the *Vies des femmes célèbres* as "more divine than human" (162) implies that Joan of Arc had attained the same level of mythic celebrity as her predecessors in the work and that her vignette was consciously designed to symmetrically complement the work's opening image of the Virgin. In the end, celibacy and devotion to religious ideals constitute the virtues for which Dufour most enthusiastically extols his famous women. Curiously, the author never directly associates Anne of Brittany with upstanding religious behavior in his book, although the contents of her library—a good number of the volumes in her collection were books of hours or works on moralistic subjects—and numerous contemporary images of the queen emphasize this dimension of her character.[115]

It is apparent, then, that a number of tensions underlie Antoine Dufour's *Vies des femmes célèbres*, which is not an unbiased presentation of women, and could not have been so for the reasons outlined above. The topic of famous women invited potentially conflicting views about the general character of females. Rhetorically speaking, moreover, the Dominican writer had to negotiate diplomatically a path between a discourse of respect due his female patron, a stage visually represented in the dedicatory image, and a discourse of moral instruction, which implied an assumption of superiority. Dufour, subsequently appointed confessor of both the king and the queen, clearly adopted the dominating voice and persona of a moralizing teacher. This relationship of male counselor and queen recalls that associated with the medieval tradition of the *Speculum dominarum*.[116]

Dufour's strong affiliation with ecclesiastical opinions points to an implicit tension between the Church's traditional adoption of *exempla*, especially those of powerful women, often used negatively,[117] and Anne of Brittany's commission to write about famous women. Moreover, an inherent contradiction existed between one of Dufour's major sources, Boccaccio, and his own ecclesiastical training. Not only did the author of *De mulieribus claris* adopt few examples of famous Christian women (five out of 106 biographies), but Dufour's criticism of Boccaccio in his prologue for having arbitrarily blamed women authorized him to attribute women's sins to men's evil impetus. While Dufour enthusiastically provided numerous examples of strong, assertive women, repeatedly praising the physical prowess of several of them, he also contradicted at times his prologue's claim of women's natural innocence through references to their innate propensity to deceive, seduce, and control men, an assessment that at times realigned him with the authors he claimed to correct.

In the *Vies des femmes célèbres*, despite—or because of—the focus on celebrated females of virtue, the strong presence of male authors and artists complicated the verbal and visual portrayal of women. The visual placement of Anne of Brittany on center stage in the opening dedication miniature of Antoine Dufour's commissioned work as a sovereign reigning over her court and controlling the book production process, an ideal image of the royal married lady, contrasted with the fact that Dufour's analogies between Anne and virtuous females of the past were indirect at best. Just like the entry theaters examined in Chapter 1, Anne's book served as the mirror in which she would discover models from the past and presumably find her own reflection in them. It embodied a delicate balance of male voice and female subject, of female presence and male articulation, and the verbal and visual images of Anne of Brittany and other female figures presented by Dufour and Pichore consciously or unconsciously glorified and contested the queen's authority and the virtues of women in general. The *Vies des femmes célèbres* thus affords modern scholars a glimpse into how the complex and sometimes contradictory cultural realities of the late medieval and early Renaissance periods informed the portrayal of women of rank.

## Jean Marot: The Staging of a Female Defense Attorney in the Battle of the Sexes

Ambiguities about female fame and power likewise surface in Jean Marot's *Vraye disant advocate des dames*, although in a different manner and to a much less degree than in the works examined above. It was apparently in the fall of 1506 that Marot dedicated this work to Anne of Brittany, thereby seeking for the first time to establish ties with French royal court.[118] And it was probably not coincidental that Marot sought to enter into the French queen's service by means of this protofeminist writing only two years after Dufour penned the *Vies des femmes célèbres*, whose miniatures—in the queen's copy at least—were completed by Jean Pichore sometime during the same year that Marot offered the *Vraye disant advocate des dames* to the French queen. Like the *Nobles et cleres dames* translator a decade earlier, Marot places Anne on a pedestal in his prologue dedication to the queen, explicitly associating her virtues with those of her (famous) predecessors:

[M]a treshaulte, tresexcellente, tresmagnanime souveraine
et redoubtée dame: considerant . . . que vostre haultesse et
magnanimité, dès vostre adolescence et primitive origine, a tousjours
continué de non seullement ensuivre les precedentes de vostre
haultesse, qui par leurs vertus et meritoires œuvres ont fait valloir et
fleurir l'honneur et glore du sexe femenin: mais en cheminant par
ce sentier avez tousjours travaillé et par sollicitude applicqué vostre
naturelle entente à l'augmenter, exaulcer et eslever de mieulx en plus,
en accumullant voz vertuz avec celles de voz preterites et anciennes
instructrices; joinct que vous estes la superintendente fleur de toutes
celles qui, au vergier de ce val, centre et territoire, tiennent ores
dominations, principautez et seigneuries. (94–95)

[My most noble, most excellent, most magnanimous sovereign
and revered lady: considering that your nobility and magnanimity,
from your adolescence and earliest beginnings, have always
continued not only to follow your highness's female models, who,
through their virtues and meritorious works have made the honor
and glory of the feminine sex praiseworthy and flourishing, but
also in taking this path, you have always worked and through
solicitude applied your natural understanding to augment, exalt
and increasingly elevate [it] by adding your own virtues to those of
your previous, ancient female instructors; in addition, you are the
reigning flower of all those who, in the orchard of this valley, center
and territory, hold dominions, principalities and lordships.]

Like the *Nobles et cleres dames* translator and Dufour, Marot praises the queen, through her association with all women, in both terrestial and spiritual realms:

Cognoissant par vraye experience et reduysant en l'ymaginative de
ma memoire les grandes, excellentes, admirables et infuses graces,

vertus et merites, dont de tous temps et de present la femenine
geniture et maternelle secte a esté et est douée, fulcie, decorée
et en si hault degré eslevée, que non seullement les int(f ?)eriores
monarques en sont adornées de privilleges et infiniz benefices, mais
aussi les sainctiffiées et benedictes regions celestes collaudées et
glorieusement enrichies. (93)

[Knowing through true experience and remembering the great,
excellent, admirable and infused graces, virtues and merits, with
which, in all times and at the present, the female and maternal sex
has been endowed, sustained, decorated and elevated to such a high
degree that not only are inferior monarchs adorned with privileges
and infinite benefits [through females' virtues], but the sanctified
and blessed celestial regions are also lauded and gloriously
enriched.]

Like Dufour, Marot, through his female narrator, acknowledges that the
many honorable ladies of the past have been succeeded by examples of equally
virtuous females at the present time:

Plus que jamais on voit croistre les dames
En tout honneur. Si jadiz fut des femmes
Dignes de loz, croyez qu'il en est ore
Dont il sera immortelle memoire,
Lors que les corps seront dessoubz les lames. (vv. 724–28)

[More than ever we witness an increase in ladies of great honor.
If there were women in the past worthy of praise, believe me that
there are now those who will be remembered immortally when
their bodies are beneath gravestones.]

However, Marot presents himself much more humbly in his prologue
than his contemporaries. Whereas the *Nobles et cleres dames* translator, Vérard, and, to a lesser extent, Dufour behaved in an appropriately deferential
manner in their dedications to the queen, the humility voiced by Marot, who
effaces himself in exaggerated fashion before his dedicatee, is considerably
more extreme. We already learned in Chapter 2 how Jean Marot would define
himself in an equally submissive manner vis-à-vis his dedicatee in offering

Anne of Brittany the *Voyage de Gênes* several years later (around 1507), a work
that celebrates the military exploits of King Louis XII through a political
allegory that stages personified women in ambiguous fashion. The *Advocate
des dames*, however, exalts Anne of Brittany herself and the virtuous women
among whom she figures in both the prologue and the text it introduces. But
no existing evidence indicates that the French queen actually commissioned
either of Marot works.

Like many other court writers of the time, Marot hoped to procure the
financial support of his dedicatee; he therefore defines his relationship to
her through the use of verbs and metaphors of subjection and a constructed
image of himself as a powerless writer with little talent:

Je, qui suys des petiz le moindre, emmailloté au berceau
d'ingnoscence, si peu extimable que, sans oser prendre la
hardiesse d'imprimer mon nom en mes rudes, incongruz et mal
porporcionnez escrips; pour autant qu'il a pleu à vostre liberalle
haultesse me faire eslargir et disperser des miettes tumbantes de
vostre table pour la substantation de ma povre humanité, avecques
la subjection et obeyssance qui par souveraincté vous appartient et
est deue: esperant aussi que ce pourra causer l'augmentation de mes
biensfaitz: Ay, incapax, et non digne de ce faire, entreprins de, selon
mon gros et ruralit mestier, forger et marteller sur l'encluclume [*sic*]
de mon insuffisance les harnoys, estocz, lances et escuz servans à
la deffence, louenge et victoire de l'honneur des dames. . . . En me
prosternant, en treshumble reverence et humilité, au devant des
piés de vostre haulte seigneurie, [ce dit petit livret] je vous dedie,
presente et sacriffie, vous suppliant tres humblement que, sans avoir
regart à l'incapacité et basse condition de l'acteur d'icelluy, il vous
plaise de vostre grace le prendre en gré et en recueillir ce peu que
trouverez melliflu et de savoureuse digestion: et le reste, subgect à
correction, relinquir et delaisser comme chose infructueuse et mal
cultivée, plus procedant de puerille invencion et barbare facture
que de haulte ymaginative, quadrée ne exquise taille. (94–95)

[I, who am the least of the smallest, born in the swaddling clothes
of ignorance, so little esteemed that, without daring to be so
bold as to print my name in my unpolished, irregular and poorly
measured writings; for as much as it has pleased your generous

highness to give and disperse to me crumbs falling from your
table for the sustenance of my poor being, with the subjection and
obedience which you deserve through your sovereignty; hoping
also that this can lead to an augmentation in my benefits: I,
incapable and unworthy, have undertaken, in my dull and rustic
manner, to form and hammer on the forge of my insufficiency
harnesses, swords, lances and shields serving for the defense,
praise and victory of the honor of ladies. . . . In prostrating myself
in very humble reverence and humility at the feet of your noble
queenship, I dedicate, present and sacrifice to you this little book,
begging you very humbly that, without regard for the incapacity
and low condition of its author, it might please your grace to accept
it willingly and to receive the little honey and savory digestion
you might find there. And the remainder, subject to correction,
to relinquish and abandon it as something unfruitful and poorly
cultivated, proceeding more from childish invention and ill-
informed workmanship rather than being shaped and crafted with
lofty imagination and exquisite proportions.]

This self-criticism, coupled with a hyperbolic celebration of the dedicatee ("tres
haulte . . . tresexcellente . . . tresmagnanime . . . tresredoubtée") often characterizes the Rhétoriqueurs' repertory, but Marot inflates his rhetoric in extreme
fashion. Employing language that exaggerates the lowliness of his condition
and situation vis-à-vis the queen—"Je, qui suys des petiz le moindre"—he further elevates her own position. The metaphor of infancy and the analogy that
associates him with a pet dog reinforce the pitiable image of one in great need
that Marot creates of himself much more dramatically than that offered by the
*Nobles et cleres dames* translator, without ever clearly stating, like his predecessor, that Anne of Brittany's reputation would be enhanced by his work.[119]

Marot understood well that in order to attract the attention and protection of Anne of Brittany as his patron, he had to flatter her while, at the same
time, inserting himself into the debate about women's virtues, the controversial
subject of discussion at court. Indeed, Marot confirms in the prologue of the
*Advocate* that he is defending the female sex against its slanderous detractors, as
he consciously lauds "the excellence of this very noble and magnificent sex":

Deuement adverti que pour cuider attaindre à la deffloration de
l'excellence de ce tresnoble et magnificque sexe, aucuns lasches,

abastardiz et advortez courages, muez de malicieux, damnapble et
innaturel voulloir, envieux des biens procedans plus par grace divine
que humaine, ont entreprins et de fait excecuté par leur superbe
conspiration et vicieuse machination, en desployant les dangereuses
et tresperçans allumelles de leurs serpentines et venimeuses langues,
voulloir mesdire, villipender et vituperer l'honneur des dames et le
translater et reduyre de glore à reproche. (93–94)

[Duly alerted to the fact that believing they are able to deflower the
excellence of this very noble and magnificent sex, some cowardly,
degenerate and aborted souls, transformed by malicious, damnable
and unnatural desire, envious of the goodness [of women] arising
more from divine than human grace, have undertaken and in
fact carried out by their arrogant plots and vicious machination,
using the dangerous and very piercing swords of their snake-like
and venomous tongues, their desire to speak ill about, vilify and
vituperate the honor of ladies and to translate and reduce it from
glory to reproach.]

It is as if Marot knew that in order to impress Anne of Brittany with his literary prowess as a champion of women, he not only had to evoke their excellence but also to defend them passionately by vilifying their enemies. In fact,
the author adopts the metaphoric pose of a forger of military arms against the
"deflowering" of women's virtues in this war of words, thereby defining the
terms of this battle being waged by the sexes:

Ay, incapax et non digne de ce faire, entreprins de, selon mon
gros et ruralit mestier, forger et marteller sur l'encluclume [*sic*]
de mon insuffisance les harnoys, estocz, lances et escuz servans
à la deffence, louenge et victoire de l'honneur des dames, et au
reboutement, confusion, envahyssement et totalle deffaicte de leurs
ennemys. (94)

[Incapable and unworthy, I have undertaken, in my dull and rustic
manner, to form and hammer on the forge of my insufficiency
harnesses, swords, lances and shields serving for the defense, praise
and victory of the honor of ladies and the rebuttal, confusion,
invasion and complete defeat of their enemies.]

In presenting himself as a servile subject, an incapable writer, and a weak but willing arms maker, Jean Marot emphasizes by contrast the power of his literary character, the *Advocate*, who presents her defense of women.[120]

Unlike most other narratives by Marot and his contemporaries, in which the prologue voice is transformed into a pseudofictional narrator who presents the literary text and frequently plays a role in its allegorical scenario as well, no direct tie exists between the masculine speaker of the prologue and the female lawyer who pleads the cause of women in the text itself. In point of fact, what follows the prologue is not a narrative, but rather a series of contemptuous assaults against the enemies of women and an enumeration of classical arguments in defense of their honor.[121] Whereas the author metamorphoses into the *acteur*-narrateur in the *Voyage de Gênes* after having dedicated his work to the queen, the poet in the *Advocate des dames* remains external to the text's literary scenario, choosing to replace himself with the voice of a spokeswoman.[122] Marot doubtless made a conscious decision to grant literary power to a female speaker, the only person he places on stage, to better attract the attention of the queen. Indeed, the legal argument she outlines in her monologue offers powerful ammunition for the pro-female camp in the debates about female virtue being waged at court.

What the humbled masculine voice of the prologue and the fervent female voice of the literary defense of women share is their political stance: both resolutely side with women, focusing in particular on Anne of Brittany herself as a paragon of virtue. However, Marot proves to be rather ambiguous in transferring the power of the word to his fictional character, since it is not until the last verses of the work that the reader discovers her actual identity:

Vous m'en povez croire sans que je jure,
Veu que je suis nommée, entre les femmes,
La vraye disant advocate des dames. (vv. 745–77)

[You can believe my claims without my taking an oath, given that I am named, among women, the truth-speaking female advocate of ladies.]

Since the speaker of the four initial stanzas of the text that follow the prologue (vv. 1–25) is not explicitly named, the reader assumes at first that the narrative voice is that of the prologue speaker himself. However, the identity of the *Advocate* gradually emerges through her use of pronouns (my emphasis):

> Et si ne sçay qui vous peult esmouvoir
> A concepvoir contre *nous* faulx langage,
> Fors villenie. (vv. 26–28)

[And I do not know what moves you to conceive of such false language against *us*, except vilany.]

The "nous" in verse 27 confirms that the person who speaks is a woman, not the prologue author. She subsequently identifies with mothers at the same time that she intensifies her attack against female detractors in the first lines of her "little treatise . . . or monologue" (p. 94) (my emphasis):

> Considerez que par *nous* allaittés
> Avez estez [*sic*] en vostre adolescence,
> Torchez, lavez, bercez, amaillotez,
> Amignotez, tant que de povretez
> Estes jettez en grant convallescence. (vv. 42–46)[123]

[Consider that you have been breast-fed by *us* in your infancy, you have been wiped, washed, rocked, swaddled, fawned over so much that from a state of need, you have been ushered forth into a state of great strength and vigor.]

For a passage of two stanzas (vv. 156–70), the *Advocate*, who more often than not directs her comments against male slanderers, addresses women, warning "jeunes dames" in particular against men's false promises and flattery that end up dishonoring them and alerting them to their antifeminist writings. Just like a prosecutor whose audience changes according to who is testifying, she shifts her attacks against the accused here to direct her comments to the victims.

In addition, her exploitation of rhyme schemes and verse forms cleverly reflects the tensions that the *Advocate* seeks to uncover for her readers. This poetic prowess, coupled with her adoption of juridical rhetoric, allows her to criticize effectively the false language employed by slanderers of women, thereby proving that females—at least fictional females—can defend their own cause as skillfully as men.[124] Of note is the fact that the *Advocate* never degrades herself before others, like her literary creator:

> Croyez certainement
> Que nous avons sens et entendemens,
> Et force aussi, pour cy et tous endrois
> Le nostre honneur deffendre puissamment
> Si permys fust par loix, canons et drois. (vv. 197–201)

> Comment osez vous presumer,
> Cocquars, bejaunes, descongnuz,
> Par voz faulx blasons diffamer
> Les vaisseaulx dont estes venuz?
> Quelz maulx trouvez vous en nous? Nulz.
> Tout bien vient de femenin gerre. (vv. 529–34)

> Si par foul langage
> Nous faictes oultrage,
> C'est grant cruaulté.
> A la verité,
> Loy n'auctorité
> A ce ne s'accorde.
> C'est contre equité
> Dont s(e)[i] villité
> De nous on recorde. (vv. 562–70)

> Je vueil, par raison evidente,
> Monstrer à tout bon escoutant
> La femme estre tresexcellente. (vv. 596–98)

[Believe for certain that we have reason and understanding and strength too, here and everywhere, to defend our honor powerfully, if it were permitted by canon and regular laws. . . . How dare you, proud geese, ninnies, misfits, presume through your false words to defame the vessels whence you came? What evil do you find in us? None. All good comes from the feminine sex. . . . If through foul language you do us outrage, it's a great cruelty. In truth, no law or authority agrees with this. It is unfair that vileness is what we are remembered for. . . . I wish, through plain reasoning, to prove to all good listeners that women are most excellent.]

As these verses amply demonstrate, the *Advocate*'s manipulation of the rhetorical question, which allows her to both ask and, at least implicitly, answer her own queries in defiant fashion, underpins much of her argument. This strategy reaches its zenith near the end of her defense:

Faisons nous guerre? Non, concorde.
Que vient-il de nous? Tout prouffit.
Et rigueur? Non, misericorde
Qui toute rigueur desconfit.
Le cueur? en loyauté confit.
Et la bouche, quoy? Veritable
Comme l'evangille. Il suffit
Qu'on le congnoisse en lieu notable. (vv. 571–79)

[Do we wage war? No, peace. What comes from us? All profitable things. And rigor? No, mercy, which undoes all rigor. Our hearts? Placed in loyalty. And what about our words? Truthful, like the Holy Scriptures. It is important that this be made known in notable places.]

It is not by chance that eloquence is among the most prized female attributes the *Advocate* emphasizes (vv. 202–35), a recognition that implicitly acknowledges her own talents.

Borrowing classical *exempla* adopted from previous authors such as those who penned the books already owned by Anne of Brittany and her husbands, the *Advocate* reinforces her criticism of female detractors, such as Jason, Theseus, Jean de Meun, and Matheolus, by promoting her historical and literary defenders and protectors (Tristan, Gawain, Caesar, Hector, Valerius Maximus, Orosius, Martin Le Franc, Alain Chartier). Like Boccaccio, Christine de Pizan, Dufour, and others, she also provides numerous positive examples of famous women from the past, many of whom were wrongly defamed (Minerva, Judith, Thamaris, Penthesilea, Terpsichore, Calliope, Joan of Arc, Ceres, Isis, Ariadne, Pamphile, Sappho, Deborah, Thamar, Christine [de Pizan], Dido, Esther, Penelope, Lucretia). All of the positive female *exempla*, which have figured in the works previously examined in this chapter, lead to the following defiant declaration:

> Dames sont honnestes,
> Gentes, mignonnettes,
> Doulces et plaisantes,
> Advenantes, nettes
> Trop plus que vous n'estes,
> Bestes arrogantes.    (vv. 422–27)

> [Ladies are honest, gentle, mignonne, sweet and pleasant, graceful, much more pure than you are, arrogant beasts.]

In imitation of previous defenders of women who considered the Virgin to be the female model par excellence, the *Advocate* devotes a long poem in the middle of her argument to Mary (vv. 262–321). True to the Christian arguments that she borrows, the *Advocate* offers as evidence of the superiority of women the fact that Eve was created from more noble matter than Adam, that men, not women, condemned Christ, and that a woman first discovered the risen Christ (vv. 505–23).

In the end, the flourishing of female virtues and deeds (vv. 509–20) as well as their association with peace rather than war (vv. 571–78) lead the defender of women to qualify them as a worldly treasure (vv. 525, 554–58), as she punctuates her poetic vindication of women in the simplest of terms: "Le plus grand bien, que dieu oncques donna / Et delivra à l'homme, se fut femme" [The greatest good that God ever gave and delivered to man was woman] (vv. 639–41).

Just as the Virgin Mary merits a *chant royal* in her honor (vv. 262–321), so too Anne of Brittany is celebrated in her own poetic space in the "Ballad of the Paragon of Ladies." The French queen is thereby placed in a privileged position at the end of the *Advocate des dames*, echoing Joan of Arc's position as the last famous woman in Dufour's *Vies des femmes célèbres*. The ballad's refrain,"Royne d'honneur, exemplaire des bonnes" [Queen of honor, exemplary among all good ladies] allows the *Advocate* to recapitulate her long argument. Moreover, Marot adopts the technique of the acrostic, earlier deployed by La Vigne to emphasize the identity of Charles VIII in the *Ressource de la Chrestienté* as well as his own name in the account of Anne's coronation, in order to visually extol his dedicatee's name: ANNE DE BRETAJGNE

ROYNE DE FRANCE.[125] Although BnF ms. ffr. 1704 was not necessarily the copy of the poem offered to Anne of Brittany,[126] the enhancement with blue and red colors of the vertical letters forming the queen's name, which literally engenders a poetic celebration of her own virtues, enriches the *Advocate*'s words at the end of ms. 1704, while visually exalting the French queen's identity.[127]

The envoy of Anne's personalized ballade merits special attention as well. Like Marot in his prologue, the *Advocate* creatively deploys military vocabulary in a recapitulation of her defense of women in these verses. For she femininzes traditionally masculine-centered vocabulary and coins a new word—*chevaleureuses*—thereby placing on stage an arresting image of female knights that is accentuated by its location at the rhyme (my emphasis):

> A ceste cause vous, langues venimeuses,
> Ne parlez plus pour exceder noz bournes,
> Car nous avons, comme *chevaleureuses,*
> Escu d'honneur, exemplaire des bonnes. (vv. 720–23)

> [For this cause, you, venomous tongues, speak no longer in
> exceeding our limits, for we have, like *female knights,* our own
> shields of honor, exemplary of all good women.]

Metaphorically reshaping the image of a female lawyer into that of a female warrior in defense of the female sex, this final message compellingly conveys the sense that women do not need male writers or combatants to defend them. Except, of course, that the *Advocate*'s words were actually penned by a male poet.

In her closing argument, the *Advocate*, having alerted female victims to the methods of their detractors and berated all guilty male parties, turns to the jury, to that undecided panel of male judges, to persuade them to disregard all slanderers of women, who, she claims, in taking up Christine de Pizan's rhetorical strategy, resort to their behavior in revenge for having been rejected:

> Pour tant, seigneurs, gentilz et mecaniques
> De ces braguars n'escoutez plus les ditz,
> Et me croyez que telz mots sophistiques
> Viennent de gens de dames escondis,

Qui, ce voyans de leur grace interdis,
A leur pouvoir desgorgent tout injure. (vv. 739–44)

[However, lords, both noble and ordinary, listen no longer to
what these gallants say, and believe me that such false words come
from men rejected by women, who, seeing themselves deprived of
female grace, do everything in their power to retaliate against such
affronts.]

In this manner, Marot's fictional character openly joins the real-life court
debate about the virtues of the female sex alluded to earlier by the *Nobles et
cleres dames* translator and Dufour.

Strategically humbling himself before the French queen in his dedication of the *Advocate des dames* to Anne of Brittany, Jean Marot also submits
to his literary character, the *Advocate*, by transferring to her his defense of the
female sex. This shrewd tactic makes Marot's argument on behalf of women
in general and Anne of Brittany in particular all the more compelling, because the *Advocate*'s ability to identify with women (with "nous"), like that
of Christine de Pizan in her argument against the defenders of the *Romance
of the Rose*, is dramatically more authoritative than the words of a male. To
place on stage a fictional female character in such imposing fashion, without
permitting her to lower herself before the men she condemns, allows Marot
to boldly defend the female cause and challenge traditional male attitudes
about women while, at the same time, maintaining his carefully fashioned
image of a humble writer in need of the queen's patronage. Marot is indeed
clever, for while effacing his presence and replacing his voice with that of a
female lawyer, the author, unlike the *Nobles et cleres dames* translator, Vérard
or Dufour in their dedications to Anne of Brittany, makes the tacit case that
it is the French queen in point of fact who needs this male poet to effectively
promote her virtuous image and that of other women precisely because he
knows how to manipulate male and female voices for the right cause. Marot
proved successful in adopting this ingenious strategy, for he subsequently
obtained a position at Anne of Brittany's court.

My analysis in Chapter 3 of the words and images of male poets, publishers, and artists in works about famous women has uncovered ambiguities surrounding women's character, power, intellectual proclivities, and
image. The moralizing, occasionally flattering, but more often patronizing
dimension of Boccaccio's *De mulieribus claris* was inevitably transmitted

in the French translations of his work throughout the fifteenth century. However, the tone of the Italian author's male-controlled, third-person narratives of women's lives was considerably attenuated in the 1493 edition of the *Nobles et cleres dames* through the substitution of Boccaccio's dedication to the Countess of Altavilla with the anonymous translator's protofeminist dedication to Anne of Brittany. The resultant incongruities in the *Nobles et cleres dames* between prologue and translated text, between woodcuts representing the enthroned queen and those depicting both virtuous and notorious women of legend, may have been related to conflicting dedication materials involving King Charles VIII, Queen Anne of Brittany, and the publisher Antoine Vérard as well as the court debates over the superior virtues of men or women.

A decade later, Antoine Dufour's *Vies des femmes célèbres*, whose composition may have stemmed from these earlier tensions, rewrote the work of Boccaccio and his imitators by directly or indirectly adopting the protofeminist ideas found in the prologues of the *Nobles et cleres dames* (and Symphorien Champier's *Nef des dames vertueuses*). Maintaining the moralistic stance originally embraced by Boccaccio, Dufour nevertheless provided more positive biographies of famous females, in part by staging more virtuous examples worthy of his own admiration and in part by granting first-person status to many of his famous women. Honorably staged in the liminal miniature of the Musée Dobrée manuscript XVII, Anne of Brittany's inspiration doubtless prompted the modifications Dufour made to the famous woman *topos* and motivated the creation of Pichore's extraordinary illustrations of other celebrated females miniatures in this manuscript book that the queen herself commissioned.[128]

Jean Marot's dedication of *La Vraye disant advocate des dames* to the French queen around the same period (1504) further implies that Anne of Brittany's interest in manuscript books promoting female virtues and empowerment had become well established during her second marriage to Louis XII. However, instead of narrating a series of legendary women's biographies, like many of his predecessors and contemporaries, Marot chose to integrate the famous women *topos* into the first-person speech of one fictional female defense lawyer to whom he ceded the power of the word, while carefully maintaining the pose of the queen's humble servant. Fusing the visual and verbal veneration of his anticipated patroness, the author, along with the artist of BnF ms. 1704, sought simultaneously to highlight her name vertically and her virtues horizontally through the use of an acrostic. Anne's positive reception of this literary strategy was subsequently translated into Marot's appointment at her court.

Whether celebrated for their virtuous deeds or maligned for their infamous actions, the famous women that were staged in the works of Boccaccio and his translators and imitators, including the *Nobles et cleres dames* translator, Antoine Dufour, and Jean Marot, lived a fascinatingly diverse range of experiences in historical, biblical, mythical, legendary, and literary contexts. However, one particular genre of illustrious females soon emerged as distinctive figures of attention: famous women in mourning. Chapter 4 explores this more specialized class of (famous) females in works dedicated to women of power.

# CHAPTER FOUR

# Famous Women in Mourning: Trials and Tribulations

Many of the famous women depicted in word and image in the works of Giovanni Boccaccio, Antoine Dufour, and Jean Marot included women in mourning, widows and females who, grieving at the loss or departure of their loved ones, often withdrew from society or even resorted to suicide. The verbal and visual images of women in mourning in books belonging to Anne of Brittany and her cohorts, however, derived not only from literary *topoi*, but also from historical realities. The French queen greatly grieved over the death of her children and her first husband, as we learned above. We will also discover her presence in other books of sorrow eulogizing the demise of court figures. Anne of France became one of the most famous royal widows following the death of her husband, Pierre, duke of Bourbon, in 1503. Like her, Louise of Savoy was a prominent court widow who never remarried following the death of her husband Charles, count of Angoulême, in 1496. Both figured prominently among the widowed participants in Anne of Brittany's and Claude of France's Parisian entries in 1504 and 1517, as we learned above in Chapter 1. It was Margaret of Austria who experienced widowhood more often and perhaps even more grievously than her contemporaries, for she lost two husbands (Juan of Castille in 1497 and Philibert of Savoy in 1504) and was abandoned by another, Charles VIII himself, to whom she had been engaged since she was a child, when he married Anne of Brittany in 1491. Unlike the French queen whose widowhood lasted just a few months, but like Anne of France and Louise of Savoy, Margaret of Austria chose to remain a widow the rest of her life.

Building upon the notion that the literary reconstruction of famous women is repeatedly expressed through images of grief, Chapter 4 analyzes the verbal and visual portraits of women in Octovien de Saint-Gelais's popular translation of Ovid's *Heroides, Les XXI Epistres d'Ovide,* and Anne of Brittany's portrayal as a grieving woman awaiting the return of her husband in Macé de Villebresme's translation of Fausto Andrelini's *Epistre . . . en laquelle Anne, tres vertueuse royne de France . . . exhorte de son retour . . . le roy de France.* Jean Lemaire de Belges too dedicated three works to Anne of Brittany, *Le Temple d'Honneur et de Vertus, La Plainte du Désiré,* and *Les Épîtres de l'amant vert,* that implicate the French queen in his texts of sorrow. But Lemaire, ever concerned about procuring long-term patronage, integrates into some of these same writings allusions to Margaret of Austria, who also figures as protagonist in works about her own grief. Analyses of this corpus of works associated with Anne and Margaret foregrounds a discussion of the extent to which the imagery of sorrow associated with the French queen and her contemporaries defined and often confined women at the dawn of the Renaissance.

Just as the contemporary fascination with illustrated stories about women of antiquity resulted in parallels drawn between females of power, such as Anne of Brittany, Louise of Savoy, and Claude of France, by French translators, authors, and illustrators examined in earlier chapters, so too comparisons between contemporary women of rank and Ovid's heroines inspired writers and artists. In one case, the French queen herself entered the realm of literary fiction. While these analogies obviously aimed to flatter the female dedicatee, with artists vying for her attention in order to obtain her patronage, oftentimes these ostensibly laudatory works also implicitly promoted long-held male-constructed images of women as vulnerable, powerless, and excessively emotional individuals.

## Octovien de Saint-Gelais's Translation of the *Heroides*: Court Activity Illuminated

A few years after Charles VIII received a copy of Vérard's 1493 edition of the anonymous translation of Boccaccio's *De mulieribus claris,* the *Nobles et cleres dames* (see Chapter 3), Octovien de Saint-Gelais presented him with the translation of another work about famous women, the *XXI Epistres d'Ovide.* According to Saint-Gelais in the prologue of this work, Charles VIII's request that he write something for him inspired the author to undertake the translation of Ovid's *Heroides:*[1]

En ensuyuant ma primeraine intencion a vous, non a autre, vouee
et desdiee, i'ay esté semons poursuiure par instigation de bonne
voulenté le premier labeur de ma plume. . . . apres auoir tournoyé
la petite librayrie de mon entendement et visité les angletz de mon
gazophile, ung iour entre les autres assez curieux et embesongné
de scauoir ne en quel endroit dresser mon euure, je trouuay
parmy le nombre des aultres volumes les *Epystres heroydes* par le
treseloquent et renommé poete Ouide, iadis compilees en forme
latine doulce et melliflue . . . la matiere et son art me sembla telle
que langue de detracteur ne peut ferir ou attaindre contre l'escu
de sa value. . . . Et pour ce vous ay voulu ce present volume diriger
par translation, faicte selon que pouoir de treshumble subiect se
montre. (fols. aiir–aiiv)


[Following my first intention, promised and dedicated to you and
no other, I was invited, at the urging of [your] good will, to follow
up on the first labor of my pen. . . . [A]fter having leafed through
the small library of my understanding and visited the angles of my
mind, one particular day among others, [as I was] very busy and
preoccupied with deciding in which place to direct my work, I
found, among a number of other volumes, the *Heroides* by the very
eloquent and renowned poet Ovid, compiled in the past in sweet
and mellifluous Latin form . . . the subject and his art seemed such
to me that the language of a detractor could not strike out against
or attack the shield of its value . . . And to you I wanted to dedicate
this present translated volume, made according to the potential of
(your) most humble subject.]

Saint-Gelais completed his popular translation of Ovid's work sometime
before 16 February 1497 (n. st.), when he dedicated it to King Charles VIII.[2] It
does not appear that the king actually commissioned a French version of the
*Heroides* as some critics have suggested,[3] but rather that Saint-Gelais decided
to translate this particular work to enlighten and please the king.

Did Saint-Gelais's initiative have the queen's pleasure or instruction in
mind? Did it relate in any way to the court debates over female virtues that
the *Nobles et cleres dames* translator and Dufour had invoked in their dedicatory prologues to Anne of Brittany? Whatever the answer, the *XXI Epistres d'Ovide* were so popular that aristocrats and bourgeois alike obtained

manuscript and printed copies of it. Ovid was, after all, the most esteemed
Latin poet in France at the time,[4] and his *Heroides*, both in contemporary
Latin versions and in Saint-Gelais's translation, counted among the most
prized of Ovid's works.[5] Coexisting throughout the late fifteenth and early
sixteenth centuries were reproductions of both manuscript and printed versions of the translation, most of which were elaborately illustrated. More than
15 editions appeared between 1500 and 1546[6] and at least 14 manuscripts of the
work dating from the same period have come down to us today.[7] Anne and
her second husband, Louis XII, are also associated with the manuscript copy
of the *XXI Epistres d'Ovide* that is housed today in the Huntington Library,
San Marino, California.

What is most striking about a large number of the manuscripts of the
completed versions of Saint-Gelais's translation of the *XXI Epistres d'Ovide*
and what doubtless made them precious art objects as well as valued literary
works, are the superb miniatures of Ovid's correspondents. Many illustrations
offer a detailed image of a grieving female (and sometimes of a male) correspondent, in dramatic and very varied settings. Some illustrations display a
principal scene in which the correspondent from antiquity is surrounded by
subsidiary miniatures depicting the history of her liaison with her addressee.
Others, such as those decorating a manuscript belong to Louise of Savoy that
I examine below, focus in an extraordinary manner on the face of the correspondent as she writes her epistle. As in many other works of the period, such
as Boccaccio's *Nobles et cleres dames*, published by Antoine Vérard in 1493, the
subject of the *Heroides* readily lent itself to a visual exploitation of the image
of women. The quantity, quality, and variety of these illustrations confirm
the artistic and literary intensity associated with the French translation of the
*Heroides* at the end of the fifteenth and beginning of the sixteenth centuries.
This family of illustrated manuscripts, whose "publication" dates from February 1497 to 1530 or 1540,[8] doubtless seduced a wealthy clientele of readers
at the same time that the first printed edition of the work (Paris: Michel Le
Noir, October 1500), strewn with numerous generic woodcuts, attracted another audience of more middle-class readers. The woodcuts decorating this
first edition of the *XXI Epistres d'Ovide* as well as most of the subsequent editions of Saint-Gelais's translation contributed directly to their great popularity. The extensive attention this single work of Ovid received at the beginning
of the fifteenth century is thus extraordinary.

But manuscript and printed evidence of a presumably earlier version of
Saint-Gelais's translation, containing only five of the 21 epistles, has survived

in a collection that includes three contemporary narratives related to the French court. One manuscript copy of this abbreviated version of the *Heroides* features a stunning miniature of Anne of Brittany surrounded by several women at her court, thereby suggesting that the book was made for her. That the French queen was involved in varying ways in the dissemination of Ovid's *Heroides* attests to the lively interest in the classical author's work and in the related subject of famous women by both erudite and popular audiences at the end of the fifteenth century. What is not entirely clear is the relationship between the completed translation of Ovid's *Heroides* that Saint-Gelais dedicated to Charles VIII and the abbreviated manuscript that appears to have been made for the French queen. Did Anne of Brittany herself commission this shortened version—no existing relevant documentation confirms this—before her husband received a copy of the completed translation? Did Saint-Gelais provide her with a test-run, abbreviated version of his translation, juxtaposed with works about contemporary court events, perhaps to obtain feedback before its completion? Did the death of one Madame de Balsac, eulogized in an *Epitaphe* that appears in the same manuscript as the abbreviated version of the *Heroides*, prompt someone else to compile a series of poems on women, death, and grief? How did contemporary readers negotiate the narrative differences between the five *Heroides* and the three subsequent texts, not to mention the apparent inconsistencies among the three French texts?[9] While it is difficult to answer these queries with any certitude, the fact that this same manuscript anthology subsequently appeared in print suggests that it too may have proved to be popular and a potentially sound commercial investment. A printed copy of the same compositions—the five *Heroides* of Oenone, Ariadne, Dido, Phyllis, and Hysiphile, the *Epitaphe* of Mme de Balsac, and an *Arrêt* and an *Appel* associated with Anne of Brittany's court—is currently housed at the BnF as Rés. P.Yc.1567.

Listed in the Catalogue La Vallière in 1783[10] and more recently described in greater detail in the Breslauer and Grieb Catalogue #109 (1988), the manuscript of the abbreviated Ovid translation, which I will refer to as the Breslauer manuscript, was apparently transcribed and decorated for Anne of Brittany herself around 1492, shortly after her marriage to Charles VIII.[11] Similar to and perhaps the source of an edition of the abridged translation published around 1500 by Jean Trepperel and Michel Le Noir,[12] this manuscript contains five of Saint-Gelais's translated 21 Heroides as well as an epitaph and two poems involving ladies at Anne of Brittany's court. Of the eight full-page miniatures in the manuscript, illuminated by the Master of the

*Chronique scandaleuse*[13] or the Master of Jean de Bilhères,[14] the first five illustrations present in a principal image and subsidiary scenes the mythological correspondents whose epistles are included in the *recueil,* namely Oenone, Ariadne, Dido, Phyllis, and Hysiphile. Of all of Ovid's 21 correspondents, these females, two of whom end up committing suicide, present the most desperate plaints.

While the order of these five bereaved female grievances differs from that adopted by Ovid and by Saint-Gelais in his completed translation, their arrangement in the Breslauer manuscript and printed edition offers a pattern of similarly and progressively tragic stories of desertion that lead to dramatic consequences: the suicides of Dido and Phyllis and the soon-to-be-realized curse that Hysiphile casts upon her arch-rival Medea. Although victims of abandonment rather than of their husband's death, these Ovidian correspondents are nonetheless depicted verbally and visually as marginalized widow-like figures dressed in black, with long, wild flowing hair in extreme states of mourning.[15]

The three remaining miniatures that figure in the Breslauer manuscript provide visual renditions of each of the additional poems included in the volume. The Madame de Balsac identified and mourned in the "Epitaphe de feue Madame de Balsac" appears to have been a certain Marie de Montberon, who married Geoffrey de Balsac, seigneur de Montmorillon and the king's *premier valet de chambre* on 4 January 1492,[16] just one month after fourteen-year-old Anne of Brittany herself had wed Charles VIII; but the young Madame de Balsac died shortly after her nuptials. Breslauer and Grieb argue that the juxtaposition of the two literary sequences, the five *Heroides,* and the three poems relating to ladies at Anne's court was meant to extol Madame de Balsac as "peer and modern successor" to Ovid's heroines (32). This suggested connection between the deceased lady and Ovid's heroines is not entirely analogous, however, since Madame de Balsac was not abandoned by her mate, like Oenone, Ariadne, Dido, Phyllis, and Hypsiphile, nor was she given voice, in contrast to Ovid's protagonists, who proclaim their despair at length in first-person monologues. Nevertheless, the association of grief, death, and a celebrated noble woman in this poem doubtless served as enough of a pretext to link the *Heroides* and *Epitaphe.*

The second and third contemporary French poems in the Breslauer manuscript, the "Arret de la louange de la dame sans sy" and the the "Appel des trois dames contre la belle sans sy" initially appear to diverge substantively from the five *Heroides* and the *Epitaphe* and their dominant theme of mourning. The legal judgment about the unique beauty of the so-called *Dame sans sy* [the

Lady without peer] and the subsequent appeal against this verdict by ladies in Anne of Brittany's entourage resonate with the famous Judgment of Paris and the literary trial associated with Alain Chartier's *Belle Dame sans mercy*.[17] In addition, they seem to offer a somewhat ambiguous image of women at the French queen's court, particularly in the context of Madame de Balsac's death.[18] It is nonetheless curious that two manuscripts and a printed edition reproduce these three works together.[19] Although the correlation is never explicitly spelled out, the use of similar terms in all three works to refer to Madame de Balsac's beauty suggests that she could be one and the same as the *Dame sans sy* and that the *Arret* and *Appel* could be understood to have been consciously designed as a posthumous sequence to the *Epitaphe*—or, at the very least, as an originally independent sequence used in another context that was later introduced into this collection. Indeed, the *Epitaphe* foreshadows the main point of the *Arret* by submitting that everyone judged Madame de Balsac to be the paragon of France (fol. 51r), that she was the best of the best beneath the heavens (fol. 50r), anticipating the refrain in the *Arret* that the *Dame sans sy* was "la plus belle des belles" (fol. 53v) [the most beautiful of the beautiful], and that she was deemed very beautiful and received much praised during her lifetime (fol. 52v).

The *Arret*, a ballad, presents an unidentified narrator's account of Parlement's judgment about the beauty of the *Dame sans sy*. He relates how an assembly of gods, relying on the "legal" research of their assistants, who turn out to be French poets—Pomnier (Pommer?), Cretin, Robertet, Saint-Gelais, and Bremont (fol. 53r)—arrive at the conclusion, which also serves as the ballad's refrain, that the lady in question is "Seulle sans per, la plus belle des belles" [Alone without peer the most beautiful of the beautiful]. Assuming the role of court recorder, the narrator then receives the order to transcribe the decision into the Parlement's register. The reader learns, perhaps in anticipation of the *Appel*, that no opposing female voice was considered during the deliberation process:

... En prohibant tout fait communatoire,
Sans recepuoir a opposition
Femme qui soit, car c'est l'oppinion
Des assistens, cessans toutes querelles. (fol. 54r)

[Prohibiting all communicative activity, without receiving in opposition any woman whosoever, since it is the opinion of the attendees, ending all disputes.]

Such a reference to court disputes involving women resonates with similar narrative remarks in earlier works about women discussed above. In the *Arret*'s envoy, the poet-narrator delivers the court's decision to the "Prince" for his public pronouncement (fol. 54r).

Questions that arise concerning the identity of the poet-narrator and prince in this ballad implicitly prompt queries about the relationship between fact and fiction in the narrative. Was the proclamation about this unidentified woman's beauty actually made, for example, in a real or mock-court scenario?[20] If so, who was involved? How should the reader understand the actual role of the living poets invoked as the lawmakers' assistants? Droz attributes the composition of the *Arret* and the *Appel* to François Robertet,[21] rebutting earlier suggestions by La Vallière and Molinier that Saint-Gelais authored the poems. However, it is unlikely that a poet would invoke himself in his own poem; the same reasoning pertains to Saint-Gelais's possible authorship as well. And yet, if the reference to poets in the *Arret* is historically based—perhaps the named writers collaborated to praise this woman[22]—then either attribution could be valid. While internal evidence implies that Saint-Gelais authored the *Epitaphe*, it is more difficult to identify who might have penned the *Arret* and *Appel*. Given the awkward relationship of these two interconnected verse narratives with the *Epitaphe*, it is quite possible that a different poet composed them.[23]

In the *Appel* the narrator, following the decision to proclaim the unidentified female as the lady without peer, arrives at the queen's court where he discovers the sovereign and her ladies in discussion, some secretly grieving. But the reasons for such behavior differ dramatically from the complaints of Ovid's heroines. Three ladies from Anne of Brittany's court, identified as Jeanne Chabot, Blanche de Montberon, and Françoise de Talaru,[24] berate the poet for creating discord through the *Arret*, because the "sentence . . . trop criminelle" (fol. 56v) that the *Dame sans sy* has no peer in beauty constitutes an affront to all other women. Invoking the memory of famous women of the past, Jeanne Chabot poses the following queries:

> Est elle plus prudente que Palas,
> En chasteté plus digne que Lucresse,
> De qui Tarquin tant ayma le soulas?
> Esse Iuno, la plaine de richesse?
> Esse Medee ou Helaine de Grece,
> Qui de beaulte portoit le paragon?

. . . Esse Dido, la royne de Cartage,
La plus belle qui fust point en quart age? (fol. 56r)

[Is she more prudent than Pallas, more worthy in chastity than
Lucretia, whose solace Tarquinio so loved? Is she Juno, full of
riches? Is she Medea, or Helen of Greece, who was the paragon of
beauty? Is she Dido, queen of Carthage, the most beautiful who
ever was in her fourth age?]

This series of queries seems at odds with many of the works examined thus
far, in which Anne of Brittany was often compared to other famous women
in superior terms. But perhaps that is the implicit message behind the protest
of these women at Anne's court: the queen herself has been slighted by the
judgment rendered on behalf of the *Dame sans sy*. That is, while the court
ladies appealing the judgment concerning the peerless lady's beauty might appear to be catty, they could also be seen as properly acknowledging the status
of famous women, including Ovid's correspondents in mourning, by contest-
ing the unjust decision by the male lawmakers and poets, thereby standing up
to male court figures against the implicit abasement of any women.

Each of the three ladies requests in turn that her protest be transcribed
and submitted to the lover who wears black (fol. 57r), also identified as the
royal lover dressed in black livery (fol. 57v). According to their wishes, the
narrator-poet stays up late at night to record the ladies' appeal and presents
it to his dedicatee:

Lors tant me peine et si tresfort labeure
Qu'en celle nuyt leur appel redigay,
Lequel enuers pour vous, sire, mis i'ay.
Voyez que c'est; la cause se renuoye
Par deuant vous. Faictes que l'on y voye. (fols. 57v)

[So I struggled greatly and labored so hard that I wrote down their
appeal that night, which I have put into verse for you, lord. Here it
is; the case is sent back to you. Have it examined.]

Is the dedicatee in the *Appel* the same person as the "Prince" of the *Arret*
or someone else? Is he the French king himself? Reference to an "amant royal"
would seem to suggest so.[25] Whether or not this poetic narrative reproduces

a real court event is uncertain, but given the inclusion of the names of ladies known to have lived at Anne of Brittany's court,[26] it is possible that the mysterious male figure designates the king[27] and that the *Arret* and *Appel* may in fact have recreated a real-life drama, one that also related to the continuing debate over female virtues that is raised in the prologue of the *Nobles et cleres dames*, the *Vies des femmes célèbres,* and the *Advocate des dames.* Such discussions at the court of Charles VIII and Anne of Brittany, although never explored in depth, thus figure as a heretofore unidentified stage of the *Querelle des femmes.*[28]

The miniature paired with the *Appel* in the Breslauer manuscript (Figure 31) features Anne of Brittany as the enthroned queen of France, accompanied by the three ladies from her entourage named in verse. It is Jeanne Chabot, dame de Montsoreau and the queen's Lady of Honor,[29] according to Breslauer and Grieb (36), who speaks to the queen, while Blanche de Montberon[30] and Françoise de Talaru,[31] the queen's maids of honor, converse in the background to the right. Although she is not depicted as a commissioner of the work—this is not a dedication scene—Anne of Brittany is portrayed here in the conventional role of a reigning court figure. Her visual prominence in this illustration doubtless prompted scholars to assume that the manuscript was made for her. The miniature in the lower margin features three ladies; wearing black veiled headdresses, they are presumably the same females featured in the principal illustration.[32] The three ladies appear with talking hands before a crowned male figure, who likely represents the "amant royal" to whom they submitted their appeal via the narrator. The latter intermediary figure, so central in the text, is absent from the miniature. If the man in mourning in this and the subsidiary images of the two other miniatures in the series is indeed to be identified as Charles VIII—these figures all wear crowns over their hats—the last lines of the poems, which refer to the addressee as "Prince" (*Arret,* v. 37) and "sire" (*Appel,* v. 105), imply as much—then the Breslauer manuscript may well have been destined for the French king as well as the queen.[33]

Whoever the *destinataire(s)* of this manuscript might have been, the scenes depicted in it resemble other poetic and artistic endeavors in which male poets and artists at the French court transcribed, illustrated, and transmitted in verse fictional and real court scenarios. Whether or not the Breslauer manuscript was specially made for or dedicated to Anne of Brittany, this poetic anthology about women in general is directly associated with the French queen and her female entourage in particular. It provides a substantially different set of readings and images than the complete version of the

31. [Octovien de Saint-Gelais], Poetic anthology, Breslauer-Grieb Catalogue #109
(1988), fol. 54r: The Appeal of Anne of Brittany's entourage

*XXI Epistres d'Ovide*. The three French poems, the *Epitaphe, Arret*, and *Appel* confer a distinct character on Ovid's five *Heroides* by associating them with the eulogy to the deceased Madame de Balsac, a male judgment glorifying the *Dame sans sy*, and a legal challenge of this decision on the part of three court ladies.

In the end, women are visually exalted in the Breslauer manuscript in stunning fashion from the five miniatures of Ovid's famous mythological correspondents, which depict their narratives of grief in images detailing their interactions with their lovers or husbands and subsequent "widowhood," to a dramatic illustration of Madame de Balsac's death at the hands of Atropos (fol. 50r), to an image of the judgment about the *Dame sans sy*'s incomparable beauty (fol. 53r). Punctuating this dazzling pictorial display of mythological and contemporary women is the splendid miniature of Anne of Brittany herself in an extraordinary red dress, with three of her female attendants at her side, all of whom nevertheless display sadness about the judgment. The visual promotion of Anne of Brittany in this final manuscript miniature offers a dramatic staging of the French queen that rivals that of the *Dame sans sy* herself and perhaps counteracts, at least visually if not textually, the insulting judgment made against women by male judges.

Men's roles in the miniatures relegated for the most part to subsidiary visual images, are more mysterious and blurred in meaning, even though as narrator, secretary, court recorder, and ultimately judge, they play critical roles in the three French narratives.[34] Although exalted and more prominently staged in the miniatures, women at Anne of Brittany's court appear in more clearly defined roles but may be viewed to be of more ambiguous character in the text of the *Appel* itself, because of their supposed jealous reaction to a male court decision. In a sense, then, the artistic rendition has gone further than the text to restore some dignity to the slighted women in question. Perhaps the prince's actual judgment regarding the ladies' appeal, set to take place following the completion of the narrative, directly or indirectly resulted in the actual confection of the Breslauer manuscript.

## Reconfiguring the *XXI Epistres d'Ovide*: The Superimposition of Royal and Classical Characters

Just like the Breslauer manuscript of the abbreviated version of the French translation of the *Heroides*, which some scholars believe was made shortly after the wedding of Anne and Charles VIII in December 1491 (and after the death of Madame de Balsac following her January 1492 marriage), Huntington Library, Ms. HM 60, a copy of Saint-Gelais's complete translation of the *XXI Epistres d'Ovide*, may have served to commemorate a royal union involving Anne of Brittany. Called the "Anne de Bretagne Ovid" in one sales catalogue,[35] HM 60 has been repeatedly described as likely belonging to or having been made for Anne of Brittany and Louis XII; if so, it was apparently prepared around the time of Anne's marriage to Louis in January 1499.[36] Indeed many consider that images of the royal couple appear in the manuscript: a portrait of Louis XII in place of that of Acontius (fol. 112) (Figure 32), and a portrait of Anne of Brittany in place of Dejanira's (fol. 46) (Figure 33). What precludes any confirmation of these attributions, however, is the unfortunate fact that the original miniatures of Dejanira and Acontius in HM 60, as well as almost all other illustrations in the manuscript, were apparently retouched or repainted some time after their original creation. We must therefore rely on the informed opinions of earlier scholars and bibliographers, who, nevertheless, seem to repeat each other, following O. A. Bierstadt's 1895 claim that "The portrait of the queen bears a very close resemblance to that painted in the renowned 'Hours of Anne of Brittany,' now preserved in the great library of Paris and justly regarded as the finest example of expiring French miniature art" (17).[37] C. W. Dutschke is less categorical, referring to "f. 46, Dejanira (has been suggested to represent Anne of Brittany)" and "f. 112, Acontius (has been suggested to represent Louis XII)."[38] Typed notes dating from late September 1981 from a certain J. Preston, which the Huntington Library graciously made available to me during my examination of the manuscript, offer useful artistic details:

> The faces and hands as they now stand are painted in a light-
> toned closely stippled technique, which gives an effect of
> great softness; some of the faces are characterized by a slightly
> simpering prettiness which is exceptional for early 16th century
> works. . . . Several faces and hands appear on close inspection to
> show signs of modification along the edges. . . . On fol. 46 the
> image has been suggested to represent Anne of Brittany. Although
> it does not particularly represent her as now seen, it is of interest
> to note that the outline of both nose and chin were once more
> extensive and have been modified. Possibly the figure on fol. 112
> does in fact represent a glorified version of Louis XII. . . . The

32. Octovien de Saint-Gelais, *Les XXI Epistres d'Ovide*, San Marino, Huntington Library ms. HM 60, fol. 112: Acontius/Louis XII. This item is reproduced by permission of the Huntington Library, San Marino, California.

33. Octovien de Saint-Gelais, *Les XXI Epistres d'Ovide*, San Marino, Huntington Library ms. HM 60, fol. 46: Dejanira/Anne of Brittany. This item is reproduced by permission of the Huntington Library, San Marino, California.

questions to be settled would be (1): Can these miniatures as they
now stand be shown to be characteristic of early 16th century
productions? (2) Or might they be refurbishings executed ca. 1860
when the manuscript was in Libri's hands? (3) Or may they not
rather represent a 17<sup>th</sup> century modification executed at the time
and for the collector who furnished the binding?[39]

A detail that seems to corroborate the association of Acontius's portrait
with that of Louis XII is the barely distinguishable crown of fleurs-de-lis on
top of his hat. By the same token, the figure of Dejanira is one of only two
crowned females visually portrayed in this manuscript version of the *XXI
Epistres d'Ovide*. Dido's depiction with a crown (fol. 35v) corresponds to her
rank as queen of Carthage, whereas the figure of Dejanira, who was not a
royal figure, would not normally be painted with a crown, a disjunction that
may have alerted an informed reader-viewer of the manuscript to the substi-
tuted portrait of the French queen. If we accept the assessment of scholars
about the correspondence between the images of Dejanira and Acontius and
contemporary renderings of the French queen and king, then the idea of replacing Ovid's heroine and hero with the royal portraits is a fascinating one.
Although significant correlations exist between Anne of Brittany and the famous women that people many of the books associated with her, as we have
ascertained in previous chapters, by far the most direct paratextual connection established between the queen and her celebrated predecessors appears in
the HM 60 manuscript of the *XXI Epistres d'Ovide*, where she visually stands
in for one of Ovid's heroines. The portrait on folio 46 displays Dejanira/Anne
of Brittany in silhouette form facing left (Figure 33). Although seated in a
thronelike chair and crowned, she does not assume the regal, straight-on pose
of the Breslauer manuscript, where the French queen reigns before her court.
Rather she appears as an isolated individual—which is unique to her portrayal in other book miniatures—in the process of writing and pondering the
words she pens. Her red square-necked dress recalls the color of the queen's
garb in the *Appel* illustration of the Breslauer manuscript—apparently one of
the queen's favorite colors—but here, covered as it is with a blue mantle, the
effect is more subdued.

Such a substitution was doubtless intended to honor the French queen,
for she is granted the exalted status of a famous mythological character
through this overlaying of persons and personalities. And yet, a decidedly
ambiguous correlation underpins this visual adulation of Anne of Brittany,

because the image accompanies Dejanira's story, not that of Penelope, for example, who, as a less traumatized figure, symbolized marital fidelity and, of all of Ovid's heroines, experienced the happiest outcome through the return of her husband. Perhaps a practical matter dictated the Dejanira-Anne of Brittany association. Had the artist already finished painting a number of miniatures in the cycle before a decision was made to venerate the queen and her new husband through their superimposed portraits? Or perhaps there was never meant to be any correspondence between text and image in these personalized portraits, all but confirming a greater interest in the manuscript miniatures than in the actual texts themselves of the *Heroides*.

Despite the narrative disconnections between Dejanira and Anne of Brittany and between Acontius and Louis XII, each coupling shares features that may explain, at least in part, their unexpected associations in the HM 60 manuscript. In her epistle, for example, Dejanira begins by praising Hercules for his efforts in effecting global peace through combat, equating him with the gods. But then her discourse veers dramatically away from a glowing admiration of her spouse, as she first laments his constant absence, which has resulted in a life of domestic widowhood, and then rues his propensity for amorous liaisons. Most desperate is her realization that she has unknowingly caused Hercules' death because of the poisonous tunic she had sent to him. Dejanira's final self-recriminations and farewells foreshadow her subsequent suicide.

The first part of this epistle anticipates in an uncanny manner the love, admiration, solitude, and fear that Anne of Brittany herself was to experience during the Italian campaigns of Louis XII just a few years after their marriage. In fact, this letter and visual association between queen and mythological figure may have inspired subsequent imitations, which I discuss below. And yet, Dejanira's anxiety about and denunciation of Hercules' infidelities, despite his miraculous feats of strength and courage, his death at her hands, and her ultimate suicide, do not represent admirable features that one would consciously choose as points of comparison with the queen of France. The infamous dimension of Boccaccio's famous women thus resurfaces in ambiguous fashion.

A similar pattern emerges from the Acontius letter and matching illustration. The miniature depicts a male figure who does bear a close resemblance to Louis XII (Figure 32). Seated in a throne-like chair covered with a green star-studded drape, with his right arm leaning on the top of what may well be a scepter and dressed in an ermine-lined sleeveless cloak, the Acontius/Louis XII figure faces the viewer's left in an authoritative pose more relevant to a reigning prince than to Acontius himself. In addition, he is not depicted in the act of writing as are nearly all other correspondents painted in this manuscript.[40] The text of Acontius correlates in some respects with the recent marriage of Anne of Brittany and Louis XII through the repeated expressions of his devoted and patient love, his passion and loyalty for Cydippa as he awaits the fulfillment of her promise to wed him. And yet the deviousness Acontius employed to obtain Cydippa's still unfulfilled agreement to marry him—she is tricked into making that vow—does not register as upstanding behavior worthy of comparison with that of the French king. Again, focus on the visual dominates the reader's experience.

Specialists have also suggested that the other miniatures of women in the HM 60 manuscript, painted by Robinet Testard,[41] are so individualized that they likely represent the queen's maids of honor at her court. Bierstadt notes:

> instead of attempting vainly to reproduce the men and women of classical antiquity, the artists have wisely chosen to represent their own contemporaries, so thoroughly individualized and true to life, that they cannot be mistaken for mere imaginary creations. Some of these lovely women were probably maids of honor at the French court. (17)[42]

What is striking about the Testard images in manuscript HM 60 is the focus on only half of the body, especially the face of the correspondent in the process of writing, rather than on the actions making up the epistolary autobiographies of Ovid's protagonists, as is the case with most other manuscript illuminations of the *XXI Epistres d'Ovide*, including the five in the Breslauer manuscript.[43] It is especially in these illustrations that the fascination and even obsession of contemporaries with the representation of the female figure become most evident.

As it turns out, Robinet Testard also painted the illustrations in a manuscript version of the same work belonging to Louise of Savoy, namely BnF ms. ffr. 875.[44] While one illustration of an Ovidian heroine has been thought to be a portrait of Louise of Savoy (see below), the artist of ms. ffr. 875 employed additional means to honor his patroness. Symbols associated with the duchess of Angoulême decorate several close-up portraits of Ovid's correspondents in a manner that confirms her possession, and perhaps commission, of the manuscript, without upstaging the mythological figures themselves. For example, in the miniature of Penelope (Figure 34), who faces the viewer as she

34. Octovien de Saint-Gelais, *Les XXI Epistres d'Ovide*, Paris, BnF ffr. 875, fol. 1r: Portrait of Penelope writing to Ulysses, with the arms of Louise of Savoy. Bibliothèque Nationale de France.

sits writing at her desk (fol. 1r), the window behind her bears the arms of Louise of Savoy in each of the two upper panes. In the subsequent miniature, a portrait of Phyllis who sits facing left as she composes her letter to Demophoon (fol. 5v), an encircled L initial decorates each of the two upper panes of the window at the left. The miniature of Acontius (fol. 117v), which depicts a male figure facing right as he composes his letter likewise features windows with Louise of Savoy's arms. François Avril, who dates this manuscript between 1496 and 1498 and ascribes the transcription of the text to Jean Michel, makes the following comments about the miniatures:

> The . . . illustrations are surprising in their monumental format, marking a break with what [Testard] had painted up until then. They consist of a series of large miniatures representing the heroines, plus a few masculine figures mentioned in the text, shown half-length. . . . As always with Testard, the execution is very sharp and graphic, yet the faces—too large in proportion to the rest of the body and very carefully modeled—denote a certain quest for individuality and give the appearance of being authentic portraits. Maulde La Clavière has even suggested that Laodamia of fol. 71v is a portrait of Louise of Savoy herself. . . . Dress is alternately exotic or inspired by the fashion of the day. Although in general all dramatic effect is avoided . . . Testard nevertheless occasionally succeeds in stirring emotion through the simple play of line and color.[45]

Another manuscript, BnF ffr. 873, confected at a slightly later date according to Avril,[46] bears another set of symbols related to Louise of Savoy (rather than Louis XII, as some earlier critics have suggested).[47] In the margins surrounding the miniatures of the twenty-one *heroides*, the viewer discerns the initial L accompanied by windmill blades or "ailes," the homophone in French for L. Thus, the use of decorative emblems clearly marks Louise of Savoy's identity with two of the *XXI Epistres d'Ovide* manuscripts, whereas the two manuscripts associated with Anne of Brittany, the Breslauer manuscript and HM 60, offer more prominent images of the French queen herself, without, however, providing confirmation of the exact sociopolitical networks related to the production of these works. That neither the Breslauer nor Huntington Library manuscripts made their way into the royal library implies that Anne of Brittany—or perhaps another noble—subsequently owned the book.

In the end, the portrayal of the king and queen in relationship to each other in manuscript HM 60, assuming they are Anne of Brittany and Louis XII, is less ambiguous than the hierarchical depiction of Anne and Charles VIII in the Breslauer manuscript, if indeed the French king is to be identified as the "amant royal." Admittedly Anne of Brittany and Louis XII are not painted together in ms. HM 60, but they nonetheless emerge visually in the same circumstances as individuals in an isolated inner space. In addition, the absence of the *Epitaphe*, *Arret*, and *Appel* from this version of the *XXI Epistres d'Ovide* essentially eliminates the contemporary narrative about court controversies between men and women at the French court included in the Breslauer manuscript. As in the specially made vellum copies of the *Nobles et cleres dames* for the French and English kings, this absence and perhaps conscious erasure of an early stage of the *Querelle des femmes* was associated with the reign of Charles VIII. Could it be that such tensions actually diminished during the reign of Anne and Louis XII? Is there any significance to the fact that the popularity of the Boccaccio translation, *Nobles et cleres dames*, and its attendant ambiguities are associated more with Anne of Brittany's first reign than with the translation of the *Heroides*, more narrowly focused on grieving women, whose popularity coincides more with Anne of Brittany's second reign?[48] For it is not the wide range of empowered famous or infamous women, whether models of virtue or negative *exempla* of malice, that seems to have attracted the eye of book collectors during the French queen's marriage to Louis XII as much as the first-person autobiographies of vulnerable women in mourning, once empowered but who are now weakened through abandonment by their mates.[49] With this new focus in the *XXI Epistres d'Ovide*, many of the ambiguities of the *Nobles et cleres dames* message have been averted— although Saint-Gelais is often as moralistic as Boccaccio—and the interest of male and presumably female readers has, consciously or unconsciously, shifted to women who merit their unreserved sympathy in face of the male perpetrators of grief. And yet, these are women who have been rendered powerless, except for their very last action, that of suicide. Despite a more intense verbal and, in several cases, visual insistence on the individual female in the *XXI Epistres d'Ovide* manuscripts, ambiguity nonetheless surfaces in a different configuration, for the book purchaser and reading public are seemingly more attracted to defenseless women who are nevertheless more virtuous than their male counterparts.

Whatever the exact history behind the production and dissemination of the Breslauer and HM 60 manuscripts, whatever the French queen's exact association with them, they both visually and verbally dramatize women at Anne of Brittany's court who are directly or indirectly associated with females from antiquity. These manuscript books thereby set the stage for Anne of Brittany's actual appearance as a literary heroine in her own right. On the one hand, the *Dame sans sy* narrative sequence, which appears to be based on a certain historic reality, offers a semibiographical account of court events in which Anne figured centrally, without, however, playing a major role in the appeal, other than as an implicit support of her court ladies. On the other hand, if the association in HM 60 with the queen is valid, the image of Anne of Brittany has been assimilated visually and perhaps even textually with that of one of Ovid's heroines, thereby conferring a semiliterary status on the queen in an effort to honor and ennoble her. The portraits of the ladies-in-waiting may have also stood in for those of Ovid's heroines. In the next stage, it is Anne of Brittany herself who appears not only visually as a female mourning the absence of her husband as she pens him a letter urging his return from war, but her voice achieves literary and textual prominence as well. In other words, Anne was to figure visually and verbally as an Ovidian heroine in the three letters in her voice composed by Fausto Andrelini and translated by Macé de Villebresme. It is Ovid's "safe" model of a vulnerable, powerless female that Anne's court writers and artist adopt in recreating in poetic language the queen's own grief during the Italian Wars, what was likely an event based on reality.

## The French Queen Enters the Literary Text: The Saint-Petersburg Manuscript of *Epistres*

Whereas famous women were staged by the moralizing Boccaccio in his *De mulieribus claris* and its French translations and sometimes given voice by Antoine Dufour in his *Vies des femmes céblèbres*, as we saw in Chapter 3; whereas the personified enemy *Gênes* took center stage as a female griever in Jean Marot's *Voyage de Gênes*, as we learned in Chapter 2; whereas 18 female figures from antiquity were given voice by Ovid—and then French expression by Octovien de Saint-Gelais—to convey grief over their "widowhood" in the *XXI Epistres d'Ovide*; it is the male-created voice of the historic figure of Anne of Brittany herself who appears as the female mourner in the *Epistre . . . en laquelle Anne tresvertueuse royne de France, duchesse de Bretaigne, exhorte de son retour le trespuissant et invincible roy de France Loys dousiesme, son mary estant en Italie* [Letter in which Anne most virtuous queen of France, duchess of Brittany, exhorts the return of the most powerful and invincible king of France, Louis XII, her husband being in Italy]. Composed originally in Latin by the French queen's secretary Fausto Andrelini, this verse epistle represents the poet's attempt to create a contemporary version of Ovid's *Heroides*. One of the most popular works of the time, the *Heroides* circulated widely in both Latin and French manuscripts and editions at the end of the fifteenth and beginning of the sixteenth centuries. Subsequently translated by Macé de Ville-bresme, Andrelini's pseudoautobiographical letter introduces a manuscript collection of 11 fictional verse epistles composed by various French court poets around 1509–12.[50] The stunningly illustrated *recueil*, which is housed today at the National Library of Russia, Saint Petersburg, as Ms. Fr. F. v. XIV. 8,[51] contains several miniatures of Anne of Brittany and Louis XII.

There is no direct evidence, such as a dedicatory prologue or miniature, confirming that the Saint Petersburg *recueil* of 11 poems and 11 accompanying miniatures was dedicated to or transcribed uniquely for Anne of Brittany herself, although several critics appear to make this assumption,[52] based no doubt on the facts that Andrelini was the queen's secretary and the illustrator, Jean Bourdichon, was her preferred court painter.[53] Indeed, the exquisite illustrations of the king and queen,[54] among other figures, painted by Bourdichon, the same artist who had illustrated the queen's manuscript of the *Voyage de Gênes* and the famous *Heures d'Anne de Bretagne*, all but confirm that this was a royal copy. Whether it was made specifically for the queen, for the king, or for both the king and the queen is difficult to determine,[55] but, because the queen herself figures centrally in several pieces in the anthology as both a textual and pictorial character, I consider it to be particularly appropriate for analysis here. That this manuscript, like the Breslauer and HM 60 manuscripts and other works belonging to Anne of Brittany, did not end up in the royal library underscores a different distribution history than many of the manuscript books known to have belonged to the French king.

What distinguishes this manuscript from the other books in Anne of Brittany's library is the verbal and visual depiction of the queen not as the commissioner or recipient of the volume, but rather as the (pseudofictional) protagonist—or at least first-person voice—in three of its 11 compositions.[56] Anne addresses her husband, King Louis XII, in all three of "her" *épîtres*, but their focus and tone differ significantly. The queen's distress at her husband's prolonged absence, joy at the news of his victory over the Venetians, and urging of his return dominate the first letter (313 verses), which I will discuss at length below. In her second letter (431 verses), however, focus shifts entirely away from the queen to Louis XII's political world, with the queen lauding his military achievements, decrying the betrayal of French allies, and even counseling further action, like a military advisor. In addition, she urges the king to stand up to his (new) enemies. "Her" language in this second epistle strongly resembles that of a chronicler. Although she expresses great disappointment at the betrayal of French allies, no mention is made of Louis XII's absence or of Anne's own emotions about that situation, as in the first letter to her husband. Louis XII's response to the queen, in which he urges that she remain patient, follows the second epistle, although it appears to be a more fitting response to the first. Traces of Anne's grief punctuate her third letter to the king (301 verses),[57] which calumniates her husband's "new" enemy, Pope Julius II, whom she directly addresses in a letter within the epistle to Louis XII (see fols. 64r–66r). After providing justification for France's challenge to the head of the Church (a strategy presumably aimed more at the court reader than her husband), Anne strongly encourages Louis to attack the pontiff. The voice of the French queen in these two letters is that of a political advisor. Anne of Brittany may well have offered such counsel to her husband, although it is difficult to ascertain how historically accurate the verses composed by the Andrelini/Villebrême team actually were. To borrow a term from Jane Couchman and Ann Crabb, all of these letters use, in the end, "man-made language."[58]

The appearance elsewhere of the letters written in Anne's voice suggests that they must have been popular outside of the court. Andrelini's original Latin version of the first letter in this anthology was published around 1509 by Josse Bade, doubtless for Latin specialists or students. Another French translation of the same letter by Guillaume Cretin, in addition to that of Villebresme, appeared in two editions during this period. A contemporary manuscript contains the Latin version of the second and third letters written in Anne's voice by Andrelini.[59] The original Latin of these four epistles appears in the margins of the Saint Petersburg manuscript. Thus, these letters in their original and translated forms must have appealed to several different audiences at once.

Of the 11 miniatures in the Saint Petersburg anthology, many of which depict seemingly realistic scenes of court life, three portray the French queen herself. The initial illustration, accompanying the first letter (Figure 35), stages the queen in her windowless bed chambers, as she tearfully pens a letter to her husband. I will return to discuss this illustration at greater length below.

35. Fausto Andrelini/Macé de Villebresme, First letter from Anne of Brittany to Louis XII, Saint Petersburg, National Library of Russia, Ms. Fr. F. v. XIV.8, fol. IV: A weeping Anne of Brittany pens a letter to her husband.

In the miniature appearing with the second epistle (Figure 36), we discover a more public palace setting with Anne's royal emblems on the window in the background. The French queen, seated beneath a canopy in a thronelike chair on a slightly raised dais, offers a letter to a messenger (?) kneeling before her. A cleric stands close by looking on, while the queen's entourage of some 20 ladies-in-waiting are seated against the wall witnessing the action. The cleric may well represent the author of the Latin version of the letter, Fausto Andrelini, in which case the kneeling figure may be its French translator, Villebresme, rather than a messenger. In the illustration that accompanies the third letter (Figure 37), the queen sits beneath a canopy at her writing table on a raised dais in a more public space, for the open door in the background reveals a rider on horseback and a messenger who waits for the letter the queen has just finished writing and is folding. Ten ladies-in-waiting are seated in the background against walls filled with the queen's *cordelière* symbol and a window bearing Anne's royal arms and other symbols. With attention placed on the correspondent as she pens or folds her letter, these three illustrations obviously echo the miniatures that decorate the many *XXI Epistres d'Ovide* manuscripts discussed above. They also borrow from the pictorial system of emblems deployed to announce Louise of Savoy's ownership of BnF mss. ffr. 873 and 875.

Focus in the three Saint Petersburg miniatures of Anne of Brittany thus progresses from the queen located in her private quarters, an appropriate site for her weeping, to a more public room with windows that includes male witnesses along with her female entourage, to a space literally opened to the outside world. The locations associated with the queen in the miniatures thus gradually open up to the public. In each case, Anne of Brittany's female entourage figures prominently in the portrait of the queen. However, as the subject of each letter shifts from Anne (first letter) to her husband (second letter) and his enemies (second and third letters), so too visual focus expands from interior to exterior spaces. As Anne's words assume a traditionally more male-like rhetoric and defiant tone, the pictorial space broadens. Indeed, the third miniature of Anne folding her letter destined for Louis XII (Figure 37) very closely resembles the preceding illustration of Louis XII writing to Anne (fol. 51v).[60] Although he is in the process of penning his letter (rather than folding it after completion), the king, like the queen, is seated in the right foreground below a canopy at his writing table facing left. At the open door, also positioned in the background, three horsemen await the king and six of Louis' men stand (rather than sit) against the wall, next to a table filled with armor and swords that evoke battle.[61]

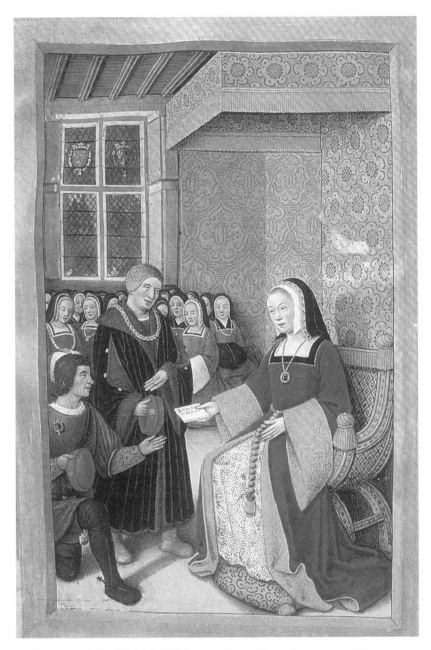

36. Fausto Andrelini/Macé de Villebresme, Second letter from Anne of Brittany to Louis XII, Saint Petersburg, National Library of Russia, Ms. Fr. F. v. XIV.8, fol. 40v: Anne offers a letter to a kneeling messenger.

37. Fausto Andrelini/Macé de Villebresme, Third letter from Anne of Brittany to Louis XII, Saint Petersburg, National Library of Russia, Ms. Fr. F. v. XIV.8, fol. 58v: Anne prepares to hand a letter to her husband to a waiting messenger.

Let us turn to the first letter in the Saint-Petersburg collection, a work ostensibly sent by Anne to Louis XII, in which the author Andrelini writing in Latin, his French translator Villebresme, and the artist Bourdichon all collaborate in a verbal and visual portrayal of the French queen as a woman in mourning. Just like the grieving *Gênes* in the two dramatic manuscript miniatures examined in Chapter 2 (Figures 15 and 16), Anne of Brittany appears in the illustration accompanying the first Saint-Petersburg *recueil* epistle in black mourning clothes, seated writing at her desk within the enclosed space of her windowless bed chambers, where six ladies-in-waiting sit in attendance; the queen holds a handkerchief in her left hand to wipe away tears from her red eyes as she pens a letter with her right hand (Figure 35).[62] Complementing the queen's visual portrayal here are her verbal lamentations about her absent husband, whose departure for his military campaign against the Venetians has left her alone in France. As in Marot's account in the *Voyage de Gênes* and in a number of the *Heroides*, such as Penelope's letter to Ulysses and Dejanira's epistle to Hercules, the opening lines of Andrelini's translated work juxtapose masculine triumph in the external world with female grief and isolation in interior spaces, with the third-person introductory voice (Andrelini's?) concentrating on the queen's anguish and ever-changing emotions:

> La chere espouse ayant le cueur marry
> Pour le destour de son loyal mary,
> Joyeuse aussi pource que conquerir
> Va ses pars et triumphe acquerir,
> En contemplant neantmoingtz l'advanture
> De guerre extresme et doubteuse rupture
> Aussi qu'il est en estrangere voye,
> Ce triste escript luy transmet et envoye;
> Pource que tant une loyalle amante
> Penser doubteux fort opprime et tourmente,
> Quant en grief dueil de tristesse saisie
> De plaisirs deubz est toute dessaisie. (fol. 2r)

[The cherished wife with heart saddened over her faithful husband's delay; joyous too because he sets out to conquer and gain victory, concerned nonetheless by the prospect of extreme war and worrisome separation while he is abroad, transmits and sends to him this sad letter; for fearful thoughts so strongly oppress

and torment this loyal lover, when in grievous mourning [she is]
gripped by sadness and completely deprived of expected pleasures.]

The juxtaposition of the king's victorious stance on the one hand and
Anne's mourning on the other highlights the dramatic contrast between male
and female activity in this passage. It is noteworthy that both author and
artist have constructed the queen's sadness upon the extended absence of her
husband in terms of mourning and that the text repeatedly invokes these
moments of "such grievous melancholy" (fol. 5r),[63] punctuating them with
the conventional stance of a woman praying on bended knee before Notre
Dame:[64]

Or en temples je me suys transportee
Ou de bon cueur j'ay offerte portee
Aussi priay le plus devotement
Que j'ai peu faire en mon entendement.   (fol. 5r)

[And so I went to temples, where, with good heart, I made
offerings and also prayed with the most devotion I could, according
to my understanding.]

This portrait not only brings to mind the famous illumination of Anne of
Brittany in prayer from Bourdichon's *Heures d'Anne de Bretagne* but also
echoes *Gênes*' own psychological trajectory in Marot's *Voyage de Gênes*. It
is almost as if this extreme rhetorical and pictorial discourse was the only
one that authors and artists knew how to deploy in depicting female emotion. Even though the verse account of Andrelini's *Epistre* actually places the
queen's grief in the past tense—Anne's fictional voice reveals the news of her
husband's Venetian victory as early as folio 8r and reiterates her joy at this
news in the final lines—Bourdichon and the other manuscript bookmakers
nonetheless chose to depict the French queen visually in this past state of
mourning, rather than in her more optimistic posture that looks forward to
Louis' return, now that victory is in hand. The verbal and visual images of
a bereaved woman had, especially in the context of her separation from—or
abandonment by—her lover or spouse, become a conventional pose, given
the extraordinary popularity of the *XXI Epistres d'Ovide*. The male-generated
image of the French queen and her thoughts in the opening letter of the Saint
Petersburg anthology projects the carefully controlled behavior of a woman

and wife of complete devotion to her husband, coupled with her frequent depiction in interior spaces, often in prayer, and her willingness to sacrifice (sometimes her very life) to maintain that honor and faithfulness. The reader ultimately learns as much about male cultural expectations concerning the queen in particular and women in general as Anne of Brittany's own perceptions about contemporary political and personal events. We know she was aggrieved at her husband's departure for war, and she was doubtless flattered by this portrayal. However, it is difficult to determine how direct a role she might have played in the construction of this representation, thereby preserving, consciously or unconsciously, its underlying cultural tensions.

Anne of Brittany's mourning for her absent husband in this *Epistre* sets the stage for a network of classical references to the loyal wife. For Andrelini's third-person invocation of the figure of the faithful Penelope in the opening lines of the poem places Anne's literary complaint squarely in the tradition of Ovid's *Heroides*.[65] In both works, the male author gives (his) voice to a female character, although Andrelini goes further than Ovid, who never intervenes as a third-person narrator in his *Heroides*, by ostensibly empowering a living historical figure through literary invention. Honoring Anne of Brittany by equating her with the example *par excellence* of fidelity was the author's obvious goal, corroborated by the presence of a dog at her side in the matching illustration. Although Andrelini and his translator were presumably unconscious about it, the portrait of the queen is nonetheless ambiguous:

Combien qu'escripz Penelope transmist
Souventes foiz et son estude mist
A s'enquerir d'Ulixes a toute heure,
Encor pleuroit sa trop longue demeure . . .
Mais que proffite ung grant royaulme avoir
Quant on ne peult du mary recepvoir
Les doulx baisers a son gré et loysir
Et qu'on ne peult avecques luy gesir ? (fol. 2r–2v)

[Although Penelope sent letters often and continuously devoted herself to seeking information about Ulysses, she still wept over his lengthy absence . . . But what benefit does a great kingdom have, when one cannot receive from her husband sweet kisses at her leisure and desire and cannot lie with him?]

It was not by chance that Andrelini made this overt association between Anne and Penelope and that Bourdichon painted the accompanying miniature of the bereaved correspondent. For Ovid's *Heroides*, especially through Saint-Gelais's 1497 translation, the *XXI Epistres d'Ovide*, had, as we learned above, become one of the most popular books during the reign of Anne de Bretagne,[66] appearing in both manuscript and printed form throughout much of the sixteenth century, often with an elaborate series of illustrations.

Like her Ovidian counterpart, then, Anne of Brittany is placed on the literary stage as a literate female and figured verbally and visually as a letter-writing character, one with a physical relationship to the letter she is in the process of writing and to those she receives:[67]

> Ha! cher espoux, quant ta lectre receu
> Dont ta victoire et triumphe je sceu,
> Tost je l'a leu sans faire aulcune attente
> Pour tost avoir de ton beau fait l'entente.
> La mille foiz, ce croyre, la baisay,
> Puys replyee en mon seing la pousay.
> Vray Dieu, combien furent mes sens ravis
> De joye extresme, alors que je la vis.
> A dire vray, langue tant fort diserte
> A l'exprimer ce trouveroit deserte. (fol. 8r)

> [Ah, dear husband, when I received your letter and learned of your victory and triumph, I read it immediately without delay, in order to learn right away about your great deed. Then I kissed it 1000 times, believe me, [and] I placed it folded in my breast. Good God, how revived my senses were with extreme joy, when I saw it. In truth, the most eloquent tongue would find it impossible to express (the feeling).]

Unlike Penelope, however, whose cold and empty bed and icy heart symbolize a complete absence of communication with her husband (for twenty years, no less),[68] Anne's receipt of word from her spouse inspires the literary incarnation of the queen to experience true joy as she responds in loving and even erotic terms to the object conveying her husband's very words; the letter from Louis XII essentially becomes the physical replacement of the man himself.[69] According to Andrelini's depiction, Anne, like anyone so elated, lacks words

to express completely her feelings of joy. Such communication between husband and wife underscores the fact that the French king has not abandoned
his spouse in the same way Ulysses had left Penelope, thereby implicitly promoting Louis XII's image as much as, if not more than, that of Anne in this
mythological comparison.[70] In addition, the more fiery and sexual emotions
elicited by this moment of communication contrast decidedly with the repeated metaphor of coldness articulated by Penelope.

Nonetheless, Anne's "plaincte feminine" (v. 54)[71] clearly echoes "my plaint"
(*mea . . . querela*) of Penelope (v. 70). Like Penelope, Anne is a devoted wife,
who is exultant to learn of her husband's military victory, but fearful and even
anguished about his extended absence[72] and impatient that he return home.[73]
Anne, of course, did not have to wait twenty years before the return of Louis
XII, as did her mythological counterpart, so her loyalty was not as sorely tried
as Penelope's. In the end, the Andrelini/Villebresme team concentrates less on
Anne as a model example of the loyal spouse—she is not, for example, tested
by suitors like Penelope, nor is she suspicious that her husband might have
other lovers—than as a bereaved wife.[74] The author insists on Anne's mourning,
exhibiting her grief over the king's absence even more than Ovid does in his
depiction of Penelope, who, especially concerned about the reasons for her husband's continued absence (since she knows he survived the Trojan War), does
not actually shed tears, like Anne,[75] and is at times even accusatory and harshly
critical of Ulysses.[76] Andrelini, on the other hand, following his portrayal of the
grieving queen, and long before actually giving his patroness voice, paints a picture of the entire country in mourning in almost allegorical-like terms. Villebresme employs richly rhetorical language in his translation of these lines:[77]

Icy en France on fait soupirs segretz,
Pleurs doloreux et ung tas de regretz,
Doubtes de dueil, ennuyeuses pensees,
Et jours et nuytz sont sans respoux passees.
Icy voit on faces toutes pallies,
Toutes de taingct naturel deffaillies;
Icy n'a cours qu'absince tresamere,
Herbe qui est d'amertume la mere.
Sans cesse icy sont les yeulx lermoyans,
Qui de pleurer ont tresjustes moyens.
Las ! pourquoy est ainsi seulle laissee
Espouse triste et d'attente lasse . . . ?    (fol. 2v)

[Here in France everyone makes secret sighs, dolorous tears and
a lot of regrets, doubts of mourning, painful thoughts, and night
and day are spent without sleep. Here one sees very pale faces, all
lacking natural color; here you only find very bitter absinthe, the
herb which is the mother of bitterness. Here endlessly filled with
tears are eyes that have very justifiable means for crying. Alas, why
is the sad wife left alone tired of waiting?]

Once Andrelini accords first-person status to the queen's pseudoautobiographical voice (from fol. 3r on), her "plainte feminine" (fol. 3r) resembles that
of Penelope and many of Ovid's other heroines, such as Oenone, Dejanira,
and Ariadne. Penelope's "chaste amour" (fol. 3r) is doubtless the source of
Anne's self-characterization as a "bonne et chaste femme" (v. 63) who dutifully foregoes the pleasure associated with her husband's presence for the
renown acquired through his military feats (fols. 3r–3v).[78]

In the letter composed in Louis XII's voice as a response to Anne's epistle,
Jean Francisque Suard and his translator Jean d'Auton also draw a clear par-
allel between the French royal couple and the mythological pair of Penelope
and Ulysses, for the king ends his epistle by urging the queen to be patient
about his delayed returned, just like Penelope:

Si Penelope eut parfaicte bonté
Vers Ulixes et chaste volunté,
Sans varier continance abstinee,
Ta foy loyalle et amour obstinee,
Que as envers moy, sera lors par raison
Plus a louer et sans comparaison.
Dont plus heureux seray et par excés
En cest endroit que ne fut Ulixes. (fol. 58r)

[If Penelope maintained perfect goodness and chaste will towards
Ulysses, without wavering in her continence, the loyal faith and
stubborn love that you have towards me will thus logically be more
praiseworthy and without comparison. Therefore I will be more
happy and ecstatic in this place than ever was Ulysses.]

We see here more obviously than in Anne's letter to Louis how the comparison between the French king and his epic counterpart constitutes a major

thrust of this association, with Louis XII emerging again as more heroic
and praiseworthy than Ulysses, albeit through his wife's expected loyalty.[79]
Both Penelope's and Anne's behavior ends up enhancing the image of their
spouses.

Ovid lends to Penelope a dimension entirely lacking in Andrelini's more
reverent portrait of Anne of Brittany, however. Penelope is self-conscious
about her lack of culture (vv. 77–78), her lack of power at court (vv. 97–
98, 109), and her twenty-year evolution into an aged woman (vv. 115–16).
These concerns never enter the mind of the literary queen of France, for she
is strongly supported on the home front, both by her female entourage and
her subjects at large, and she never worries about other women. Nevertheless,
describing him in the end as her anchor, Anne's ultimate appeal to Louis is
as dramatically expressive as Penelope's proclamation of undying devotion to
her husband (fol. 9r).[80]

Anne's terror and grief at the thought of Louis' possible death in military
combat, poignantly translated into French by Villebresme, elicits comparison
with another *Heroide*, namely the epistle of Laodamia, whose legendary grief
at the death of her husband Protesilaus in the Trojan War eventually leads to
her own suicide:[81]

[J]e craingnoye en poictrine royalle
Que glaisve feist execution malle,
Ou qu'ennemys par faulce traison
Ne t'eussent mys en horrible prison,
Ou que feusses par quelque grosse piece
De leurs canons desmembré piece a piece.
Et tant d'aultres perilleuses fortunes
Menoient mes sens par voyes importunes
Que moyns n'estoye espleuree et blesmye
Que fut jadis povre Laodomye,
Quand son mary pour Troyens assaillir
De son manoir veit en armes saillir . . . (fols. 3v–4r)

[I feared that a sword in the royal breast had made an evil
execution, or that enemies through false treason had placed you
in some horrible prison, or that you had, by some huge piece
from their cannons, been dismembered limb by limb. And many
other [potentially] dangerous outcomes led my senses down such

anguishing paths that I was no less full of tears and wan than poor
Laodomeia was in the past when she saw her husband in arms leave
home to carry out an assault on the Trojans.]

Making note too of "my faithful heart" (v. 30) and "faithful . . . embrace" (v.
78), Ovid's heroine grieves and weeps, anticipating her new role as a widow.[82]
Like Anne's, Laodamia's experience is more erotically charged than Penelope's[83] and, although critical of others,[84] she never disparages her departed
husband as Penelope does.

Laodamia is, in the end, more dramatic in her reactions than Anne as she
swoons upon her husband's departure,[85] an action foreshadowing her eventual suicide (only hinted at in her letter), as she alludes to her delirium.[86] In
fact, the uncharacteristic association of Laodamia with exterior space, unlike
most females, may owe to her unusual state of near madness. Her description
of the disorder around her, symbolized through her unkempt clothes and
disheveled hair,[87] may well have inspired Andrelini's verbal portrait of Anne's
elation upon learning of her husband's victory through his letter. However,
Anne's literary creator converts the disarray and dishevelment associated with
Laodamia's grief into a contained, positive image, doubtless deemed more appropriate for the queen. Indeed, one of the most dramatic passages in this first
Saint Petersburg manuscript letter is the queen's swift transformation from
widow-like mourning into celebration:

> Lors tout a coup de dueil mes vestmens
> Je espouillay et pris mes ornemens.
> Sur estoumac mys airain precieux,
> Et dedans doitz anneaulx solacieux,
> Après avoir mes cheveux preparez,
> Qui de long temps n'avoient esté parez.
> La tost survint en la mienne maison
> De toutes gens une grande foyson . . .
> Puys aulx temples aller je n'actendy
> Esquelz graces a mon Dieu je rendy . . . (fol. 8v)

[And so, all at once I got rid of my mourning clothes and took up
my ornaments. On my breast I placed my precious brass and on my
fingers delightful rings, after having coiffed my hair, which had not
been tended to for a long time. Then, immediately there came to

my home a great crowd of people. . . . Then I did not wait to go to
the temples, where I gave thanks to God.]

As noted above, the miniaturist Bourdichon opts not to depict this upbeat
moment in Anne's letter. The figure of the grieving female was perhaps more
familiar, more popular, more appropriate, and more compelling than a portrait of an elated queen.

Although avoiding any association between Anne's literary recreation
and the disarray of female grief often staged by Ovid, Andrelini appears to
have fused the hints of Laodamia's suicide in her *Heroide* with the story of
Semiramis in Anne's first letter, thereby creating a second theatrical moment.
Veering momentarily, but dramatically, away from the image of the mourning female, the author adopts the language of an offensive military mode,
perhaps in anticipation of Anne's second epistle, mixed with the image of
lovers conjoined in death. It is the female-warrior image of Semiramis, queen
of Babylon, that inspires the French queen, as she articulates her strong desire
to join her husband in battle and thereby hasten his return to France:

Par maintesfoiz me suys deliberee
D'icy partyr en armes preparee,
Pour tost aller ton fier ost rancontrer
Et de carcas et fleches m'acoustrer
Et porter arc comme Samiramys,
Affin que fust par mes propres mains mys
En dur estour quelque vng de tes aduers,
  Auec les corps sanglants tout à l'enuers.
Aussi affin meue d'enhortemens
Que vraye amour faict aux loyaulx amans
Qu'eussions peu lors demeurer la nous deux
Aprés l'exploict en champ victorieux,
Ou que vaincuz sur la terre estanduz
Noz esperits eussions a Dieu renduz. (fols. 4v–5r)

[Many times I have been determined to leave here in arms in
order to go meet your proud army and to equip myself with quiver
and arrows and carry a bow like Semiramis, so that by my own
hands one of your adversaries would be put into a difficult fight,
with bloody bodies strewn on the ground. And so that, moved by

exhortations that true love makes to its loyal lovers, we two would
be able to remain there after the victorious feat on the battlefield,
or that, vanquished, stretched on the ground, we could render our
spirits to God.]

But this self-empowering vision of a female behaving in male-like fashion
well outside a woman's traditionally enclosed space, clearly drawn from the
same tradition as Boccaccio's and Dufour's famous women, is short-lived.[88]
This striking image remains just that: a metaphor, whose aggressiveness and
violence is eventually undermined by the author's conventional image of
Anne of Brittany to which he returns. Indeed, this momentary explosion of
wishful action contrasts all the more with the "reality" of the queen's static
mode of waiting. Anticipated by the desire of her simultaneous death with
that of her husband, should there be defeat, Anne's subsequent words draw
the portrait of an ever-devoted wife, who, in an almost paralyzed, grieving
state, awaits the delayed return of her husband. Andrelini's shift in focus
from a militant female back to the grieving Ovidian-like correspondent is
reinforced by Bourdichon's accompanying miniature, which depicts Anne
of Brittany in her private quarters penning her missive to Louis through her
tears (Figure 35). The absence of any visual depiction of a female warrior, or
of the queen in a position of strength rather than weakness, points to the
underlying male-engendered tradition of a contemporary woman's place in
an interior space, either in prayer or in sorrow, rather than a person of action
in an exterior setting. As Anne's "own" words suggest, she is often depicted as
a female in prayer. Her Christian-inspired prayers echo Laodamia's repeated
pagan prayers:[89]

J'ay tant aussi d'aultres veuz acomply
Aultez d'encens et de mirrhe remply
Pour Dieu mouvoir par mes longues prieres,
Genoulz flexiz en devotes manieres . . . (fol. 7r)

[I have also made so many other vows, filled altars with incense
and myrrh, to move God by my long prayers, knees bent in a
devotional manner.]

Direct and indirect allusions to Penelope's marital fidelity and Laodamia's particularly intense devotion to her husband, punctuated by a brief but

dramatic invocation of Semiramis, thus shape the verbal and visual representation of Anne of Brittany as mourner in the first letter to Louis XII authored by Andrelini. In addition, the queen's vision of death, presumably through a similar suicide, should her husband perish in battle, inspires analogies with other past examples of loyalty and sacrifice, such as the tragic, self-imposed deaths of *Yphias* and Portia (fol. 5v).[90] The flip side of these classic images of a wife's undying loyalty and devotion is the disturbing suggestion—at least to postmodern readers—that female suicide was an expected natural extension of a woman's devotion and loyalty to her husband, and an implicitly admirable one at that.

The positive image of women as faithful to the point of suicide marks not only Andrelini's first epistle in Anne's voice but also pervades much late medieval, male-generated literature about famous women, more often than not through the classical examples of Lucretia or Dido. Andrelini somewhat surprisingly puts suicidal ideas in the head of a Catholic queen in this first *Epistre*, creating a close analogy between her and the two examples of devoted wives and ultimately suicide victims. Unlike Andrelini, Antoine Dufour, author of the *Vies des femmes célèbres* analyzed in Chapter 3, had repeatedly reminded his dedicatee of the objectionable nature of suicide, while endorsing women's extreme loyalty toward their husbands during their lives and as widows following their deaths.[91]

In the Saint Petersburg royal *recueil* at least two other letters are "penned" by allegorical characters whose relationship to Louis XII closely resembles that of the queen: *Eglise* in Jean d'Auton's first letter and *Eglise Militante* in his last epistle. The accompanying illustrations of these allegorical figures remind us not only of the miniature that accompanies the second letter in Anne of Brittany's voice in the same manuscript collection, but also of the various poses of the French queen in the dedication miniature of the queen's copy of the *Voyage de Gênes* and even the depiction of *Gênes* herself. They also recall the interchangeability of historical and personified figures discussed in Chapter 2.

It is in his *Espitres envoyees au Roy trescrestien Loys xiie dela les montz par les estatz de France, l'Eglise, Noblesse et Labeur* [Letters sent to the most Christian King Louis from beyond the mountains by the estates of France, Church, Nobility and Labor], Letters 2–4 in the Saint Petersburg manuscript collection, that the chronicler Jean d'Auton consciously aligns himself with the tradition of Ovid's *Heroides* by announcing his epistles in praise of Louis XII's 1509 Agnadello victory by each estate (my emphasis):

Je . . . ay voulu ci composer et faire
Ung petit brief en vulgaire commun
Sur le propos et dire de chascun
De noz estatz selon leurs faitz et tiltres
*Par maniere d'eroyques epistres*
Redigees en abregez sermons
Et transmises au roy de la les mons. (fols. 10v–11r)

[I wanted to compose and write a short letter in the vernacular
about the action and statement of each of our estates according to
their deeds and titles, *in imitation of the heroic letters* composed in
shortened sermons and transmitted to the king on the other side of
the mountains.]

A miniature of *Eglise* penning a letter, surrounded by *Foy* and *Devocion* (fol.
11v) prefaces this epistle. The words of *Eglise* recall in many respects those
of the Anne of Brittany figure in Andrelini's letters. Although the relationship between *Eglise* and her addressee, Louis XII, is that of mother and son,
rather than wife and husband, similarities nonetheless surface in her statements to the king. As in the *Heroides* and Anne's first letter, *Eglise*, begging
for the king's swift return, acknowledges the grief related to his absence—
although she emphasizes that of others rather than her own (fols. 19r–19v).[92]
And like Anne of Brittany's words in Andrelini's third letter, in which the
French queen attacks the pope, *Eglise* is a staunch supporter of Christianity. But for the most part, the letter Auton composes in the voice of *Eglise*
promotes historical precedence not only regarding Louis' recent military
successes in Italy but also regarding the traditionally strong and unique relationship between French kings and the Church. She thereby sets the stage
for the implicit argument that the French king should be supported in his
confrontation against the pope. In this sense, both Anne of Brittany in her
second and third letters and the allegorical figure *Eglise* serve as mouthpieces
for proroyal political and military policy, a literary device that decidedly
contrasts with the tenor of Ovid's *Heroides*. This mixture of allegory and
political reality, this overlapping of personification and biography, finds particularly relevant expression in the following passage, which clearly defines
the association between the static female allegorical figure and the male historical character in action:

[L]a France est nommee,
Seulle dame de haulte renommee,
Par les bienfaictz et oeuvres meritoires
De ses bons Roys qui d'heureuses victoires,
Et triumphes sceurent ourdir et tistre
Nom si treshault et tant excellent tiltre,
Desquelz tu es yssu par droicte ligne
Et les ensuyvis par louange condigne. (fols. 14r–14v)

[She is called France, the only lady of great renown, by the
meritorious good deeds and works of her good kings who knew
how to weave from happy victories and triumphs such a very noble
name and such an excellent title, from which you issued through
direct lineage and followed them through worthy praise.]

Anne of Brittany has often been described in the same terms as Lady France—
as a "dame de haulte renommee"—while her husband is often flattered by
repeated praise for his military victories.

In the subsequent letter that Auton has *Noblesse* send to the king, the
protagonist adopts a military tone from the opening lines, which are accompanied visually by a miniature of *Noblesse*, who wears a dress similar to that
of Anne of Brittany during her coronation (Figure 38), with *Prouesse* at her
side. *Noblesse*, who addresses Louis as "[my] leader and my chief" (fol. 21),
concentrates on the military victories of French nobility, particularly in its
support of the Church, and offers a lengthy description of the king's success
against the Venetians at Agnadello. It is therefore less a *Heroide* in the Ovidian style than a verse chronicle more typical of Auton's other work as royal
historiographer. The reader discovers only hints of *heroide*-like concerns as
*Noblesse*, described as "the one truly loved by noble hearts whose nobility is
renowned" (fol. 21r), regrets the lengthy absence of the king and his men,
along with others (fol. 25v) and offers a portrait of the grief of women at
the absence of their husbands, with special reference to Anne of Brittany
herself:

Maintes femmes pleurent la leurs maris
A triste face, ayans les cueurs marris,
Voire explorer parolle desolable,

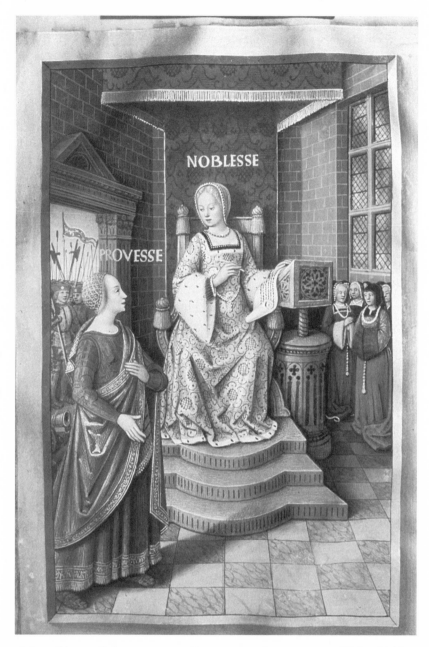

38. Jean d'Auton, *Espitres envoyees au Roy trescrestien Loys xiie . . . par l'Eglise, Noblesse et Labeur*, Saint Petersburg, National Library of Russia, Ms. Fr. F. v. XIV.8, fol. 20v: With Prouesse at her side, Noblesse pens a letter to the king.

Piteux maintien et dueil inconsolable ;
A ce depart chascun plus deult celuy
Que amour a faict plus approcher de luy,
Dont la Royne qui se plaint a bon droit
Et qui tousjours pres d'elle te vouldroit,
Voyant que c'est a tout et qu'il est force
De t'en aller, son dueil croist et efforce,
Sachant pour vray qu'en pays estrangiers
Veulx voyager ou sont mille dangiers,
Et que tu metz toy ta gent et ta terre
Soubz le hazard de perilleuse guerre. (fols. 25v–26r)

[Many women lament their husbands with sad faces and grieving
hearts, trying to find in truth an [adequate] sorrowful word,
pitiful bearing and inconsolable grief; upon this departure each
one mourns the one that Love made closer to him. Thus, the grief
of the queen who rightfully worries and who would always like
you near her, seeing that it is nevertheless necessary for you to
leave, her sorrow increases and weakens [her], knowing in truth
that in foreign lands where you wish to travel there are a thousand
dangers, and that you put yourself, your men and your territory
under the hazard of perilous war.]

*Noblesse*'s third-person assessment of female grief complements that of Andrelini and Anne of Brittany in the first letter of the Saint Petersburg collection.
Unlike Anne, however, *Noblesse* describes the grief of others, not her own. In
keeping with cultural norms, only women are associated with mourning.

Like these letters sent to Louis XII by his personified estates (as well as
Anne's second and third letters), the "petite elegiaque epistre" (v. 18, fol. 101v)
that Auton has *Eglise Militante* address to the French king, the final letter
in the Saint Petersburg manuscript collection, represents a pro-government
chronicler's promotion of the king's policy against the pope. And yet, traces
of the Ovidian tradition surface as *Eglise Militante* refers repeatedly to "my
sad situation" (fol. 101v) and "my extreme sorrow" (fol. 102r) in launching her
complaint about being assaulted by Turks and by her own allies.[93] Most reminiscent of the *Heroides*, however, are the tear-stained sheets *Eglise Militante*
sends the king, an echo of Anne's own physical reaction to Louis' epistle, as
detailed in Andrelini's first letter:

Ne lesse pas pourtant si l'escripture
Semble tachee, en ouyr la lecture,
Car tu veoirras au moings si la deffermes
Que les ruisseaulx et torrens de mes lermes,
Dont ma face est arrosee et moillee,
Ont mon epistre ainsi taincte et soilee,
Ce qui te doit (si tu as amytié
Aucune a moy) esmouvoir a pitié. (fol. 101v)

[Don't forget, however, to listen to its reading, even if the writing
seems stained, because you will see at least if you open it that the
streams and torrents of my tears, with which my face is wet and
damp, have thus stained and soiled my letter, which should move
you to pity, if you have any attachment to me.]

Although a personified figure, *Eglise Militante* nevertheless expresses herself
like a living female, confirming the verbal (but not visual) exploitation of the
*topos* of the bereaved lady in the most poignant and literal manner. References
are made to the grief of other women as well (fol. 109r), and, in the end, *Eglise
Militante*, like Anne in the opening epistle of the *recueil*, pleads that the king
end her sadness by returning (fols. 110v–111r). In these passages, differences
between the allegorical figure *Eglise Militante* and the pseudoautobiographical Anne of Brittany are all but erased, as personification is highly feminized
and the complaint closely resembles the words attributed to the French queen
by Andrelini. The two literary females, Anne of Brittany and *Eglise Militante*,
have thus been assimilated through their grief. Whether compared to famous
women of the past or to contemporary allegorical figures, the staged persona
of the French queen resurfaces in several guises as a female in mourning in
the Saint Petersburg manuscript collection.

## Jean Lemaire Inserts Mourning Women into His Texts

Anne of Brittany's role as mourner in the Saint Petersburg anthology as depicted in "her" letter to Louis XII and more indirectly through her alter ego
in *Eglise Militante's* epistle to the king finds similar expression in three of Jean
Lemaire de Belges's works about death: the *Temple d'Honneur*, *Plainte du
Désiré*, and *Epîtres de l'amant vert*. However, the author depicts Anne in her

more typical role as potential benefactor or literary audience rather than as a
grieving figure in the text itself, as he generally introduces the French queen
into the paratext of his writings. It is nonetheless noteworthy that Lemaire
repeatedly associates Anne with grieving and involves her in his works of sorrow more than any other person of the times.

Anne's profile in Lemaire's first work, *Le Temple d'Honneur et de Vertus*,
a eulogy of Anne of France's husband, Pierre II, duke of Bourbon who died
in October 1503, lies somewhere between a textual and paratextual presence.
The author's allegorical reconstruction of his patron's death, the resultant
mourning of France and his widow, and the duke's funeral are portrayed in
the second part of the celebratory poem. *Entendement* encourages Aurora,
homologue of the duchess of Bourbon, to cease her excessive grief,[94] since her
husband (under the guise of Pan) will live on forever in the Temple of Honor
and Virtues (vv. 791–982):

> Tu, o tresclere princesse, fille et seur de roy! as par pitié feminine
> et compassion muliebre plaingt le decez de ton feu seigneur
> & espoux, plouré son trespas et lamenté la separation de vous
> deux par une grande effusion de larmes et de regretz, partans
> de la source de ton amoureuse poictrine. . . . Mais aussi ne fault
> desormais que passes oultre, car autrement tu feroyes injure à
> ton bien amé et sembleroyes estre envyeuse de sa gloire. Ainçoys
> d'ung couraige eslevé en magnanimité, te fault, à l'exemple de la
> royne de Carle, la trescaste Arthemise, femme du roy Mausolus,
> excogiter quelque hault chief d'oeuvre miraculeux en nature.
> (ll. 887–903)

> [You, oh very renowned princess, daughter and sister of a king!
> You have through feminine pity and womanly compassion grieved
> the death of your deceased lord and husband, cried over his death
> and lamented the separation of you two by a great profusion
> of tears and regrets, separating from the source of your loving
> heart. . . . But also you must not go beyond [custom], for otherwise
> you would bring injury to your loved one and you would seem to
> be envious of his glory. Thus, with courage raised to magnanimity,
> you must, following the example of the queen of Caria, the very
> chaste Artemesia, wife of King Mausolus, imagine some noble
> masterpiece that is miraculous in nature.]

*Entendement*'s invocation of one of Boccaccio's and Dufour's famous women, Artemesia, as an inspirational model for Anne of France aims to rechannel the energies of the duchess from excessive lamentation to celebration. Social propriety regarding female grief thus surfaces in a text that echoes those examined throughout this discussion.

The figure of *Entendement* deploys a similar tactic in announcing to the French royal couple the architectural glorification of the duke in the Temple of Honor and Virtues:

> [L]e noble paranymphe Entendement s'estoit transporté devant les majestez et presences du trescretien roy Loys, douziesme de ce nom, tresaffectueux deplorateur du trespassé, et de treshaulte princesse, ma dame Anne, royne de France et duchesse de Bretaigne, sa tresamée compaigne, pour les advertir tous deux de la glorieuse inthronisation et celeste exaltacion du tresbon duc, et pour leur persuader de donner fin desormais à leur regret et doleance. Mesmement ladicte tresillustre dame, laquelle meue d'une amour tresbenivolente de long temps enracinée en son cueur, le plouroit par grant effusion de larmes, non autrement que s'il eust esté son propre geniteur. . . . Et pareillement . . . ma dame Marguerite d'Autriche . . . piteusement contristée pour le decez du tresbon prince. (ll. 1285–1309)[95]

> [The noble paranymph *Entendement* was transported before the majesties and nobles of the most Christian king, Louis XII, a most compassionate mourner of the deceased, and the very noble princess, Madame Anne, queen of France and duchess of Brittany, his beloved companion, to alert them both to the glorious enthronement and celestial exaltation of the very good duke, and to persuade them to bring to an end their regrets and grief. Even the very renowned lady, who, moved by a very benevolent love rooted for a long time in her heart, mourned him through a great effusion of tears, as if he had been her own relative. . . . And similarly . . . my lady Margaret of Austria . . . piteously sad on account of the death of the good prince.]

Although Anne of Brittany's grief, like that of the widowed Anne of France, was doubtless expected, it is more dramatically portrayed than that of

Margaret of Austria and more extensive than Louis XII's. This textual in-scription of the grieving Anne of Brittany as historical figure—alongside that of two other mourning females and a grievous king—into Lemaire's allegori-cal dream scenario about the death and glorification of the duke of Bourbon modulates to an extratextual function in the author's two other works of lamentation.

Lemaire's *Plainte du Désiré*, an allegorical eulogy of Louis de Luxem-bourg, count of Ligny, who died on 31 December 1503, juxtaposes Anne of Brittany and Margaret of Austria in a setting of greater tension. Their politi-cal and ultimately literary rivalry defined Lemaire's search for patronage fol-lowing the death of his second benefactor within three months after entering into his service. Two manuscripts of the *Plainte*, BnF ffr. 1683 and 23988, both bearing a dedication to the French queen, were followed by printed versions containing a dedication reworked for Margaret of Austria, who, by the time the *Plainte du Désiré* first appeared in print in 1509, had become Lemaire's official patroness.[96] As in the *Temple d'Honneur et de Vertus*, the French queen is associated with a text of sorrow, but Lemaire places her grief on stage in a brief dedication to Anne at the end of the literary text, following the alle-gorical speeches of *Paincture* and *Rhetoricque*. That Anne appears as addressee only in the extant manuscripts of the work suggests that she was Lemaire's first dedicatee, although she did not hire him on as court poet at the time:

> Et pour ce que vous, treshaulte et tresexcellente princesse, Madame
> Anne, royne de France et duchesse de Bretaigne, par l'instainct de
> vostre bonté naturelle avez tenu en estime les vertus du deffunct
> en son vivant, et icelluy maintesfois visité et consolé benignement
> durant le temps de sa langueur, et en prenant grant sollicitude de sa
> santé, et encores apres son trespas l'avez vous bien daigné honnorer
> de grant planté de lermes, et vous monstrer refuge a ses tresdesolez
> serviteurs: pour ces raisons il m'a semblé que je ne pourroye
> intituler ne dedier cette petite oevre a plus digne princesse, ne qui
> mieulx l'aymast que vous. (91)

> [And because you, most noble and most excellent princess,
> Madame Anne, Queen of France and Duchess of Brittany, through
> the instinct of your natural goodness have held in esteem the
> virtues of the deceased during his life, and visited and benignly
> consoled him many times while he languished and, in taking great

care of his health and again after his death, you deigned to honor
him with a great quantity of tears and showed refuge to his very
sad servants: for these reasons it seemed to me that I could not
entitle or dedicate this small work to a more worthy princess, one
who would love it more than you.]

In his address to the French queen, Lemaire calls attention to her caring
for Ligny during the illness leading up to his death, her tears upon his death,
and the hospitality she offered his servants. Such praise of Anne of Brittany's
attentions for a dying court noble eventually warranted the queen's patronage, but not until 1512. It was rather Margaret of Austria who stepped into
the fray by hiring Lemaire at this critical juncture in his literary career and it
is to her that the author turned in his rearticulated dedication that punctuated the 1509 edition of the *Plainte du Désiré*. Anne's personal attention to
the deceased count of Ligny in the manuscript dedication stands out all the
more in comparison with the later dedication, in which Lemaire seems to pay
lip service to Margaret's esteem for Louis de Luxembourg, who had, after all,
been dead some six years: "Pour ce que par l'instinct de vostre bonté naturelle
avez tenu en estime les vertus du deffunct en son vivant" [Because through
the instinct of your natural goodness, you greatly esteemed the virtues of the
deceased during his lifetime] (92). Of note in this rededication is Lemaire's
focus on his own career, as the poet underscores the fact that Margaret had
hired him as her court poet as a kind of consolation in light of the demise of
his patron:

> [I]l vous plaist en me recueillant restaurer la dure perte que j'ay
> fait a son trespas: je, vostre plus que treshumble et tresobeissant
> serviteur, de ce mien labeur, tel qu'il est, vous faiz ung petit
> present, ainsi que par maniere de primices en vostre tressouhaicté
> et tresvoluntaire service. (92)

> [It pleases you, in taking me in, to restore the difficult loss that I
> experienced upon his death: I, your most humble and obedient
> servant, offer you a small gift of my labor, just as it is, like the first
> fruits of the year, to your most desired and most voluntary service.]

Lemaire's concentration on Anne as a mourner in the manuscript dedications, a form of flattery doubtless aimed at obtaining a position at the French

court, gives way some six years later to a focus on the poet's (rather than his benefactor's) own "dure perte" following Ligny's demise and on his consolation through a post in Margaret's service.

The richly colored miniature that opens ms. 1683 (fol. 1r) of the *Plainte du Désiré* features the count on his death bed surrounded by the allegorical figures created by Lemaire: *Nature, Paincture*, and *Rhetoricque* (Figure 39). They in fact resemble ladies of the court, depicted as they are with "talking hands."[97] The three miniatures decorating ms. 23988,[98] the other extant manuscript of the *Plainte*, offer illustrations of Lemaire's allegorical tribute to Ligny.[99] However, neither of these manuscripts bears signs that suggest they were specially made for Anne of Brittany.

Similar codicological dynamics, although in reverse fashion, characterize the dedication and distribution of Jean Lemaire's *Epîtres de l'Amant Vert*, another work about death that bears the influence of Ovid's *Heroides*.[100] Dating from before 1506, the manuscript versions of the work—ÖNB Cod. palat. 2612 and BnF ffr. 24038 (fols. 105r–124r)—bear a dedication to Margaret of Austria, whereas the 1509 printed version, dedicated to Anne of Brittany, reflects Lemaire's gradual transition from Margaret's to Anne's court. Thus, the French queen is this time associated with the printed version rather than the manuscript version of the *Epîtres*, as had more often been the case in the past.[101]

It is in both the dedication to the 1511 edition and the conclusion to the *Seconde Epistre* in the subsequent editions that Anne's new presence as the author's (imminent) patroness is made manifest. Anne is again associated with a work of mourning that echoes the *Heroides* and its imitations, because of its first-person epistolary form and poetry of sorrow. But given that the subjects are animals, a parrot and dog, the tone is much more playful. In the *Lettre dédicatoire*, Lemaire beseeches Jean Perréal, who serves as a "cover" dedicatee, to act as an intermediary between himself and the queen by dedicating the work he has received from Lemaire to her:[102]

[J]'ay veu et entendu comment nostre premiere epistre de l'Amant Vert a despieça trouvé grace devant les yeulx de la Royne, voir tant qu'elle la ramentoit encoires quelque fois, à la tresgrand felicité et bonne aventure de celui mien si petit (mais tresjoyeux) labeur. Dont, comme je feusse prouchain de mettre fin à l'impression du premier livre des Illustrations et Singularitéz, je me suis advisé que ce ne seroit point chose malsëant ne desagrëable aux lecteurs

934
7665.

39. Jean Lemaire de Belges, *Plainte du Désiré*, Paris, BnF ffr. 1683, fol. 1r: *Nature, Paincture* and *Rhetoricque* mourn the death of the Count of Ligny. Bibliothèque Nationale de France.

de aussi faire imprimer ladicte epistre, attendu qu'elle est favorisée
par l'approbation de ladicte tressouveraine princesse, et encoires
y adjouster la seconde, pour estre ensemble publiées soubz la
tresheureuse guide et decoration du nom de sa haultesse et majesté
tresclere. (ll. 5–18)

[I have seen and heard how our first *Green Lover's Epistle* a while
ago found grace in the eyes of the queen, such that she remembered
it several times, to the great felicity and good fortune of my joyous,
little work. Therefore, as I was about to finish the printing of the
first book of the *Illustrations and Singularitez*, I thought that it
wouldn't be a bad or disagreeable thing for readers to have the
said *Epistle* printed as well, given that it was so favored with the
aforementioned most sovereign princess's endorsement and also to
add the *Second Epistle*, so that they might be published together
under the most fortunate aegis and decorated name of her highness
and most renowned majesty.]

As in the anonymous prologue of the *Nobles et cleres dames*, Anne of Brittany's
fame—note the use of "tresclere," now a more "loaded" term—is seen to
authorize the ultimate success of Lemaire's work (which now includes three
texts). Protocol may have prohibited the author from directly addressing
Anne of Brittany, but Lemaire cleverly appeals to the French queen for her
patronage by flattering Perreal as well (ll. 18–23).

In revising his conclusion of the *Seconde Epistre* for publication with his
other works, Lemaire deploys a different literary strategy vis-à-vis Anne of
Brittany. The author places in the mouth of his protagonist flattering third-
person references to the French queen herself as a griever and a sympathetic
reader of his first *Epistre de l'Amant Vert*:

Tesmoing en est . . .
La noble ermine, en richesse oultrepasse,
La dame illustre et portant sceptre en France,
Laquelle eust dueil de ma griefve souffrance:
Anne est son nom, des Bretons grand duchesse,
Anne, aux François bienheureuse princesse.
Certes, mon cueur à l'honnourer se tire,
Veu qu'elle eust dueil de mon doulent martire

Et scet encore . . .
Comme par cueur, mon doulent epitaphe. (vv. 557–66)

[A witness of this is . . . the noble ermine, surpassing others in
richness, the illustrious lady holding the scepter of France, who
mourned my great suffering: Anne is her name, great duchess
of the Bretons, Anne, most felicitous princess of the French.
Certainly, my heart strives to honor her, given that she grieved my
sad martyrdom and . . . she still knows by heart my sad epitaph.]

The parrot's insistence on Anne's grief through his repetition of the *dueil* she
has experienced for his suffering and martyrdom recalls Lemaire's description
of Anne as a sympathetic mourner for Pierre de Bourbon and Louis de Luxembourg. But in reiterating his dedicatory remarks that focused on his literary
success, he also draws attention to the queen's reception of his first works,
the *Temple d'Honneur et de Vertus* and the *Plainte du Désiré* respectively. The
speaker modestly ascribes the French queen's interest in him to her affection
for his current patroness, Margaret, whom he addresses alone (my emphasis):

Non que pour moy ne que pour ma value
(Ce sçay je bien) la mienne epistre ayt leue,
Mais en faveur de *toy*, en *ton* amour,
Pitié l'a meu d'estimer ma clamour. (vv. 567–70)

[Not because for me or for my worth (this I know well), she read
my epistle, but out of favor and love for *you*, pity moved her to
esteem my cries.]

But, as Deborah McGrady points out, Margaret must now share with the
French queen the final dedicatory space in the printed version of the *Seconde
Epistre* (my emphasis):

Or *vous* doint Dieu *toutes les deux* longz sejours
En heur prospere, et en fine de voz jours
*Montez* lassus au paradis celeste,
Comme ou terrestre, icy, suis sans moleste!
Icy prent fin le mien joyeux escripre
Dont on verra plusieurs gens assez rire. (vv. 571–76)

[Now may God grant *you both* long prosperous lives in fortune and at the end of your days may *you both ascend* to the celestial paradise above, as on earth, here, I am without burden. Here ends my joyous writing over which one will see several people laugh greatly.]

This grammatical ploy none too subtly underscores Lemaire's transition from Margaret's to Anne's court, as the printed book becomes a means to his procurement of patronage at the French court.[103] It was not by chance that through the exploitation of Anne of Brittany as the figure of a female mourner in this and his previous works, the author finally succeeded in attracting the queen's interest. Once under her aegis, Lemaire would, along with several of his colleagues, write a poem mourning the queen's near-death illness, which I will examine in Chapter 5.

## Margaret of Austria: Female Mourner

Many of Anne of Brittany's female contemporaries figure with the French queen in the numerous texts of sorrow that we have examined in this chapter. To a great extent, the verbal and visual images of sorrow defined the female sex at the end of the Middle Ages, especially in their public projection. Indeed, one of the most common and expected associations was between women and the act of mourning during this period.[104] In some cases, such correspondences were confining, for women were repeatedly portrayed as bereaved, lamenting, crying, disempowered figures. In other cases, given that widowhood often accorded women their greatest independence, associations with widowhood were not necessarily disapproving or judgmental.

Anne of France wielded considerable power as manager of the House of Bourbon's fortune during Anne of Brittany's reign.[105] However, unlike any other of her female contemporaries, Louise of Savoy cultivated the image of widowhood in the many books she commissioned. One of the most assiduous bibliophiles of the day, she appears time and again dressed in black in the many miniatures that decorate her books.[106] Indeed her image as a widow appeared to have been consciously exploited, perhaps to underscore her association with independent decision-making, especially in the context of her son and future king, Francis I. This was a bolder and more self-determined use of the image of a widow than that typified by Bourdichon's portrayal of Anne of Brittany as the weeping widow-like figure awaiting the return of her husband from Italy in the Saint Petersburg manuscript or of Lemaire's textual depictions of the grief-stricken Anne of France and Anne of Brittany.

Margaret of Austria's experience as a widow was even more frequent and perhaps more grievous than that of her female counterparts, with her loss of two husbands (Juan of Castille [1497] and Philibert of Savoy [1505]) and abandonment by her fiancé, Charles VIII. In addition, she lost her brother, Philip Archduke of Austria, in 1506, who left her with the care of his children, including the future Charles V, who would succeed Maximilian as emperor in 1519.[107]

As a result of her repeated misfortunes, Margaret earned the device *Fortune infortune fort une* [Fortune greatly importunes a certain lady], which she consciously promoted throughout much of her life in a willing appropriation of the image of an unfortunate victim of fate in mourning.[108] Reconfiguring the tragedies that repeatedly left her a young widow into subjects worthy of literary and artistic development, Margaret's court poets and artists dedicated to her works that depicted and analyzed the events surrounding her adversities. Three of the works that figured in her library, the *Complainte de Marguerite,* the *Malheur de France,* and Jean Lemaire's *Couronne margaritique,* offer representative constructions of Margaret as a mourner. Verbal and visual images of the grief-stricken princess translate Margaret's repudiation by Charles VIII and her grief following the death of her third husband, Philibert of Savoy.[109]

The *Complainte de dame Marguerite d'Autriche, fille de Maximilian Roy des Romains* was printed by Gheraert Leeu in Antwerp within a year of Charles VIII's marriage to Anne of Brittany.[110] Written in Margaret's own first-person voice,[111] the plaint, adopting the flower metaphor so commonly associated with her in order to dramatize for public consumption the French king's repudiation of Margaret and the shock and indignity it brought to her and the House of Austria,[112] poignantly expresses the forsaken eleven-year-old girl's wish to return to her native land. She directly beseeches her grandfather, Emperor Frederick III, to take pity on her; she implores her father, Maximilian, to urge his subjects to draw his disinherited, joyless "little girl, Margaret" quickly away from "those inhumain snares" of the French court; and she informs her brother, Philip, archduke of Austria, that "mon deul te doit doloir" [my grief should make you grieve]. In the *Complainte,* Margaret also asks her people to avenge the wrongs done to herself and her father. To the Flemish she reveals her fear of wasting away her youth in sadness. For the Burgundians, she describes the shame of her French imprisonment. A woodcut specially made for this publication[113] (Figure 40) depicts Margaret

¶ **La Complainte de dame Marguerite Daultrice /**
**fille de Maximilian Roy des Romains.**

Quant vne fleur:pssant daitre dhonneur
est entre:en vergier dun seigneur
noble puissant:z riche gouuernent
Et quelle croist en toute souffissance
en force.en bruit.en beaulte en verdeur
en fruit:en grace:en louenge.en grandeur
en purite.en substance:en odeur
Cest mal de lui ostre force z puissance
pour mop chascun en a eu cognoissance

Mop marguerite: de toutes fleurs le chois
ap este mpse ou grand vergier franchois
pour demourer.croistre: z hanter ainchois
que seusse grande:empres la fleur de lis
La ap receu tous biens z tous esbanois
la ap veu joustes danses z tournois.
Et maintenant je vois, z sp cognois
que ces grandz biens me sont prins z sallis
pas nen doiuent les miens estre iolis

Je p ap este noblement arousee
plus de dix ans:de tresnoble rosee
cuidant estre Riopne:et espousee
au Rop Charle:z corone portee
Mais bien parchop que me suis abusee
par quop dop estre:en mon cuer doloze
car de par lui:ap este refusee
et sp nia fait hors.du vergier ostee
pour vne aultre en nom lieu bouter

Cest espace Royne ap este nomee
mais maintenant suis la renommee
O Rop Charles.peu de top amee
puis q pour vne aultre.mauez volu chagee
mais non obstant pas nen sup diffamee
amoind:ie soulee ne blamee
se en ton paps.je ne suis confermee
dame z Royne:cause ap de mop plaintre
en aultre vergier:pour mop de top veger

O Empereur de rome redoubte
mon grand pere:de vertu illustre
qui cha ius porte:z as tousiours porte
le monde.aussi lespee de iustice
Je te prie:que tu prende ppte
de Marguerite:a qui on a oste
plaisir.solas.puissance z maieste
sans regarder a quelque preindice
cest peu prpse ton noble hostel Daultrice

Mon noble Pere aussi rop des Romains
tousiours auguste entre les corps humais.
Je te requier z pie a iointes mains
pour acquerir de Jhesu le merite
que tu veulles tant prier tes germains
et tes subgettz quen brief sans nulz demais
Ilz tirent hors de ces las inhumains
ta petite fillette Marguerite:
qui de solas z iope ou desherite.

40. [Margaret of Austria], *Complainte de dame Marguerite d'Autriche, fille de Maximilian Roy des Romains*, Bibliothèque royale, ms. 10926 (Antwerp: Gheraert Leeu, 1491–92), fol. 1r: Margaret kneels before her grandfather, father, brother and native representatives, whom she entreats to allow her return from France.

kneeling before the male relatives and native representatives she entreats in the text. This portrayal of a single female pleading to two crowned men and their court entourage dramatically conveys Margaret's vulnerability as a female pawn in the hands of male political rulers: she cannot find any comfort until the men in her life decide upon her future.

Terms of bereavement surface every few stanzas of the poem, as Margaret speaks of her "dolorous heart" [mon cuer doloree] and describes her humiliating predicament:

> Je y ay este noblement arousee
> plus de dix ans: de tresnoble rosee
> cuidant estre Royne: et espousee
> au Roy Charle : & corone portee
> Mais bien parchoy que me suis abusee . . .
> Royne ay esté nommee
> mais maintenant suis la renommee
> O Roy Charles, peu de toy amee
> puis que pour une aultre m'avez voulu changee. (314)

> [I was nobly sprinkled for more than 10 years with a most noble dew, believing myself to be queen and wife of King Charles, and wearing a crown. But now I see that I have been abused . . . I was once called queen but now I am renamed/renowned, O King Charles, little loved by you, since you decided to exchange me for another.]

In an implicit reference to famous women of the past, Margaret contrasts her mistreatment at the hands of Charles VIII, deemed as worse than any ancient transgressions, with Homer's characters: "en nulz livres d'Homere / home ne fist de telz fais la lecture" [not even in any books of Homer has any one ever read about such misdeeds] (316).

In a real-life adoption of the literary trope found in Christine de Pizan's writing a century earlier, Margaret holds up her experience as a warning to all women, noble and bourgeois alike, to carefully choose a respectable husband:

> O vous, dames, demoiselles and pucelles,
> Vous, bourgeoises, gentiles damoiselles,
> Vous, marchandes riches et toutes celles

A marier: prenez cy exemplaire,
Mirez vous y, et lisez mes libelles.
N'alliez pas vos faces qui sont belles
A hommes nulz qui vous soient rebelles,
Comme de moy est fait . . . (316)

[Oh you ladies, maidens and young girls, you bourgeois women,
noble maidens, you rich merchant women and all you women
planning to marry. Take me as an example, look carefully at my
situation and read my writing. Do not attach your beautiful selves
to any men who are rebellious, as I did.]

The irony, of course, is that most of the women she addresses, like herself,
were not in a position to determine their marital partners.

As Margaret bids adieu to all pleasure and acknowledges her pain, torment, and grief, she adopts a funeral literary trope by calling on Nature to
mourn what she labels "le fait Marguerite:" trees should lose their color,
flowers their aroma, fruits their taste, birds their song, the sun its ardor.
While such invocations are usually voiced in the third person over the death
of a beloved,[114] Margaret, the living victim, has cleverly manipulated the
elements of a funeral lament into an urgent plea by the living victim for
sympathy, revenge, and return to the land of her birth. The decision to print
and distribute the poem in the Netherlands may have been a form of revenge
embraced by Maximilian and his entourage to publicize the great affront by
the French king.

In the anonymous but more vituperative *Malheur de France*, dating from
a few years after the *Complainte*,[115] the allegorical figure Reason takes center
stage in Margaret's stead—visually and verbally—to lament the grief and
distress of her situation, forcefully accuse Charles VIII of betrayal and cruel
vengeance, and predict the French king's downfall.[116] Reason, in fact, enjoins
the French king to mourn his loss of "the most renown of all women:"

Donques doeul porter
Doibs et lamenter
D'avoir fait la debte
Quant tu voulz laisser
Et habandonner
Sy noble flourette.

Se tu le as quittee
L'Eglise abusee
Tu as et toy mesmes,
Car Dieu t'a ostee
La plus renommee
De toutes les femmes. (fol. 12v)

[Therefore, you should mourn and lament the debt that you
incurred when you decided to leave and abandon such a noble little
flower. In leaving her, you abused the Church and yourself as well.
For God took from you the most renowned of all women.]

Although Margaret is repeatedly depicted as a forsaken victim (fol. 10v), and
more often than not alluded to metaphorically as a betrayed, tender little
flower in the same pun on her name that was exploited earlier in the *Complainte*,[117] the anonymous author of the *Malheur de France* distinguishes his
work from the earlier poem by praising the future governess of the Netherlands in the middle of his attacks on Margaret's betrayer:

Car c'est la plus doulce
Qu'on sauoit de bouche
Jamais proferer
Bonnes meurs embouce
Et les vertus touce
Pour admenistrer.

Et se est la plus saige
Et humble en langaige
Dont on puist se enguerre
Et sy est bien say je
Du plus grant lignage
Qui soit sus la terre. (fol. 12r)

[She is the kindest lady ever described in words; she embraces good
manners, and embodies the virtues in governing. And she is the
wisest and most humble in language of anyone about whom one
might inquire. She also is, I know full well, of the greatest lineage
that has ever been on earth.]

In her prediction that Fortune will bring bad luck and a loss of renown to France as a result of the king's action (fol. 15v), suggesting as well that Anne of Brittany, who has just given birth, be sent back to Brittany, Reason unknowingly anticipates a series of misfortunes that would beset the French court well before the projected date of 1503: the tragic death of the dauphin in 1495, Charles VIII's demise in 1498, and the failure of Anne to produce a son during either of her marriages. Thus, the *Malheur de France* couples the conventional sorrow of and for a mourning female figure with praise of her. But instead of assailing the figure of Death for Margaret's grievous state, Reason launches a direct assault on the French king and his character. The poignant intensity of Margaret's first-person anguish in the *Complainte* has thus been replaced by Reason's accusatory speech. It is unlikely, however, that this work, which remained in manuscript form, ever reached an audience beyond Margaret's court circle.

Likewise evoking Margaret's grief from a third-person perspective, Jean Lemaire's *Couronne margaritique* stands out from the other works about female mourning written for (or by) the princess. For the author transforms the initial lament over the death of Margaret's third husband in 1504 midstream in the work by metamorphosing into a lengthy poem in her own honor that involves the complex allegorical construction of a crown of Margaret's virtues. It is Margaret's strength in reacting to yet another sling and arrow of outrageous fortune, along with the author's admiration of her fortitude, that provides the mechanism for this shift. An illustration from the one known version of the work, ÖNB ms. 3441 (Figure 41),[118] represents simultaneously several scenes that closely follow Lemaire's text. In the background Philibert of Savoy lies near death with a grieving Margaret nearby surrounded by her female entourage.[119] More striking is the scene in the foreground that portrays Margaret as an imminent widow displaying her enormous grief, while other court ladies attend to her. Lemaire's text offers the following description:

Adonques fut ce pitié trop miserable de voir la tresdesconfortee
Princesse acertainee de sa crainte, entamer un dueil desesperé,
et non appaisable, violer sa clere face, traire ses beaux cheueux
de couleur aureine, jetter vne grand impetuosité de cris et
vociferations de son tresamoureux estomach. Et qui plus est,
par la furieuse ardeur de vraye amour coniugale, se vouloir
irreuocablement precipiter en vn cas mortifere, comme feirent iadis
la noble dame Iulia, fille de Iulius Cesar, et femme de Pompee: et

41. Jean Lemaire de Belges, *La Couronne margariticque*, Vienna, ÖNB ms. 3441, fol. 14v: Margaret of Austria mourns her dying husband, Philibert of Savoy. Copyright: ONB, Bildarchiv+Signatures.

Portia fille de Caton et femme de Brutus. . . . Mais de ce motif
estrange et pitoyable fut preseruee nostre tresdesolee Princesse par
la prompte solicitude de ses feaux gentilz-hommes et seruiteurs,
et soudainement reduite en sa chambre, loing de la presence à elle
intolerable de son seigneur et amy trauaillant aux extremitez de la
mort. (30–31)

[It was such a miserable pity to see the most discomfited Princess,
filled with fear, begin to mourn desperately and disturbingly,
violate her lovely face, tear out her beautiful golden hair, throw a
great fit of cries and screams from her beloved heart. And what's
more, by the intense ardor of true conjugal love, she wished to
throw herself precipitously into death, as did before her the noble
Julia, daughter of Julius Caesar and wife of Pompey, and Portia,
daughter of Cato and wife of Brutus. . . . But our very disconsolate
princess was saved from such a strange and pitiful action through
the prompt solicitude of her faithful servants, and suddenly
retreated to her chamber, far from the intolerable presence of her
husband and friend struggling with death.]

Like Anne of Brittany as well as the famous grieving women staged by
Ovid, Boccaccio and their French translators with whom she is explicitly
compared, Margaret's excessive sorrow, depicted in dramatic terms both visually and textually, all but leads to her suicide. But this female excess is brought
under control by Prudence and Fortitude, two virtues who figure centrally in
Margaret's recovery, as depicted visually (Figure 42) and textually:

[D]ame Fortitude lenhorta de reprendre sa ferme animosité
accoustumee, de restaurer sa constance, et de remettre en auant
sa patience treslouable. Et à brief dire, tant de belles allegations et
remonstrances luy amenerent deuant les yeux ces deux habitudes
spirituelles [Prudence et Fortitude], que la tresillustre Princesse,
coulourant sa face pasle et verecunde dune couleur rosaïque, confessa
tacitement auoir honte de son glisser . . . chassa promptement la plus
grand partie des tenebres qui tenoient son cœur triste et nebuleux:
Puis esclarcit sa face, au mieux quelle peut, et luy donna serenité,
selon que le cas et le temps le pouuoient souffrir. (43)

[Lady Fortitude exhorted her to take up her habitual firm
resolution [courage], to restore her countenance and to find her
laudable patience once again. In brief, these two spirits [Prudence
and Fortitude] brought before her such compelling evidence and
warnings that the very illustrious princess, coloring her pale and
modest face with rose color, confessed tacitly to being ashamed of
her misstep. . . . promptly chased away most of the darkness that
imprisoned her sad and misty heart. Then she lit up her face as best
she could and brought to it serenity as much as the situation and
timing could bear.]

No longer dressed as a widow, Margaret appears in nun-like apparel in
an allegorical staging that features the two Theological Virtues bringing her
aid and solace. This modification in the widow's attitude prepares the reader
for the transformation of Lemaire's narrative about Margaret's despair into an
allegorical mise-en-scène that reenacts her disembodied victory over the evil
forces of Death and Misfortune.

The placement of Margaret rather than Philibert in the foreground of
these images visually translates Lemaire's textual focus not on the deceased,
as had been the case in his *Temple d'Honneur et de Vertus* and *Plainte du
Désiré*, but rather on how the "codification of grief" was usually "the special
preserve of women," as Binski maintains (51–52). Yet, the deemphasis on Margaret's late husband in the *Couronne margaritique*[120] and insistence on Margaret's grief is even less remarkable than Lemaire's allegoric construction and
presentation of her crown of virtues, the *Couronne margaritique* itself. Instead
of glorifying the deceased (male) figure or maintaining focus on the female
mourner, the author ends up exalting in elaborate fashion the widow herself.

Margaret's persona as mourner in life thus gave rise to a series of vignettes
about a woman's grief. Although Margaret of Austria remained a widow the
rest of her life, like Anne of France and Louise of Savoy, once she rose to political power in her own right—which, ironically, resulted from the death of
yet another male relative, her brother, in 1506—her ubiquitous depiction as a
mourner was replaced by the more stately public image of a woman as ruler.
The image of woman as mourner had become less appropriate for a woman
of state.

Thus, Margaret did not cultivate the image of a widow throughout her
life like Louise of Savoy. The reality was, however, that as a widow, Margaret

42. Jean Lemaire de Belges, *La Couronne margariticque*, Vienna, ÖNB ms. 3441, fol. 27v: Prudence and Fortitude bring aid to Margaret of Austria in her grief. Copyright: ONB, Bildarchiv+Signatures.

played a more powerful political role than she might have, had her husbands not died.[121] For example, she served as regent of the Netherlands on two separate occasions, wielding political power as a regent, like Anne of France during the minority of her brother Charles VIII, and Louise of Savoy during the absence of her son, King Francis I. It was through her widowhood that she attained such a stature. While we must differentiate between images of women and/or widows in mourning, a grieving that transmits the sense of a vulnerable female, and images of widows that can transmit the sense of independence and even power, the balance decidedly tilts toward a preponderance of images of mourning women in more vulnerable and even dependent postures.

In proceeding to a discussion of visual and verbal images of mourning *for*, rather than *by*, women, in particular for Anne of Brittany, in Chapter 5, we would do well to keep in mind the epitaph of Madame de Balsac that figured so centrally in the Breslauer manuscript examined above. This collection serves as a useful transition since it looks back to grieving classical females, Ovid's heroines, and integrates Anne of Brittany's persona and those of her female entourage into a contemporary court scenario that involves female protest and the death of a prominent lady at court.

# Women Mourned

As a counterpoint to the focus in Chapter 1 on entries and as an expansion of the discussion of women in mourning in Chapter 4, Chapter 5 treats departures from this world through a study of the rituals of grief and the related transmission of images about deceased women of rank. An examination of texts dealing with the near death of Anne of Brittany in January 1512 launches this discussion of funereal imagery created in memory of women of power, with a subsequent focus on the multiple illuminated manuscript copies of Pierre Choque's account of the elaborate ceremonies surrounding Anne of Brittany's death in 1514, in particular those dedicated to the queen's female relatives. Lacking the guarantee of real political power that sustained the ceremonial images of deceased male monarchs, for whom the transference of that power was a critical issue, the symbolic representations of queens such as Anne of Brittany in these pageants constituted flattering tributes but also figured as centerpieces of the royal propaganda machine. Indeed, the portrayal of the queen after death by her protégés does not change substantially from those images displayed during her lifetime. Generally speaking they continue to be similarly idealized portraits that often involve the allegorical mode and recall depictions of female figures during royal entries. That the very verses dedicated by André de la Vigne to the memory of his patroness, Anne of Brittany, in 1514 were recycled some ten years later to commemorate her deceased daughter, Queen Claude of France, all but confirms the characteristically predictable and interchangeable image of women during this time period. In addition, implicit rivalries for renewed court status among Anne's protégés, whose careers were threatened by the death of their patroness,[1] and publishers' unsanctioned appropriation of their works reveal that the demise of a woman of power could greatly affect the emotional psyche of her subjects as well as the economic livelihood of her court artists.

On 12 January 1512, Anne of Brittany gave birth to a stillborn son.[2] The intense fever that resulted from this delivery reappeared two months later leaving the queen near death for two critical days. Miraculously, Anne regained her health, an event that occasioned poetic compositions by her court protégés, Jean Marot and Jean Lemaire de Belges. They retraced the drama of Anne's near death and recovery in allegorical form.

However, two years later, on 9 January 1514, just a few weeks before her thirty-seventh birthday, Anne of Brittany died in the Château of Blois. The commemorating events in honor of the queen were the longest and most lavish funeral ceremonies ever known in France up to that time.[3] Anne of Brittany's legacy to posterity was defined not only through the sumptuous obsequies staged in her honor following her death, but also through the funeral account by Pierre Choque, Anne's herald, that Louis XII apparently commissioned. Just like the festivities associated with Anne's entry into Paris in 1492 and 1504 following her coronation, Choque's chronicle commemorated the repeated public displays of the royal corteges and religious ceremonies paying tribute to the queen.[4] Several of Choque's contemporaries, Jean Lemaire de Belges, Jean Marot, André de la Vigne, and Jean Bouchet, among others,[5] commemorated the queen in a variety of poetic lamentations.

Before analyzing the image of Anne of Brittany that Pierre Choque draws in his account of the extraordinary funeral proceedings that commemorated her life and death, I first examine the culture of mourning as revealed in the works under examination. Attention is then placed on poems written at the time of the queen's illness in 1512 and her death in 1514, with a focus on the masculine and feminine expression of grief and its relationship with the portrayal of Anne of Brittany. Lemaire, Marot, La Vigne, and Bouchet adopted multiple voices to describe Anne's imminent demise or death, with female characters generally embodying and/or expressing the grief surrounding the queen's death. These female voices often assume allegorical forms, such as those representing political institutions in Lemaire's *XXIV Coupletz de la valitude et convalescence de la Royne*, or sociopolitical or religious abstractions as in Jean Marot's *Prières sur la restauration de la sancté de Madame Anne de Bretaigne*. Nevertheless, we also hear the voice of the queen herself in Bouchet's *Épitaphe de madame Anne de Bretaigne* and *Épigramme d'Anne, deux foys Royne de France, et Duchesse de Bretaigne*. Although it is difficult to ascertain whether this staging of female voices was a conscious literary strategy on the part of these poets, related to the fact that the most noble lady of France had died and that grief was more commonly associated with females, the proliferation in these works of female personifications who pray for the life or salvation of the queen is striking.[6] By employing a variety of poetic forms and fictionalized allegorical voices, our poets created what may have been deemed a reassuring distance between the queen's death and the deep anguish of their readers, at the same time that they provided a form of comfort and consolation. However, while adopting personified forms like his colleagues, La Vigne chose to address these female abstractions directly rather than have them speak (*Épitaphes en Rondeaux de la Royne*), except in one dramatic case in which the poet created a dialogue between masculine voices, the Heart and the Mind of the king (*Rondeau de l'Esprit et du Cueur*).

In a world in which public reactions to such tragic deaths were closely observed,[7] it is logical that Anne of Brittany's protégés adopted poetic strategies that conformed to protocol's controlled expression of emotions. Several writers offering theoretical comments about such behavior often distinguished between male and female reactions. Indeed, an underlying tension between the dominance of feminine voices in the expression of grief and the implicit criticism of their excessive mourning tended to result in the ambiguous image of women. Thus, corroborating in yet another way the conflicting portraits of females that I have uncovered in previous chapters, an equally ambiguous staging of female discourse and comportment characterizes the males mourning the death or near death of the queen.

## The Cultural Codification of Grief in Early Sixteenth-Century Literature

Pierre Choque's chronicle of the obsequies of Anne of Brittany testifies to the existence of a cultural codification of grief at the beginning of the sixteenth century. Action taking place in the most private spaces coincides with the most poignant descriptions of sorrow associated with Anne of Brittany's demise, whereas moderation in behavior and narration characterizes more public mourning. For example, the following passage presents a scene in which a small group of intimates in the Château of Blois' Hall of Honor, including Choque (identified as Bretaigne) and La Vigne, witnessed the transferal of the queen's body from deathbed to bier.[8] The profound grief of several of the witnesses was so extreme that they were almost sent from the room:

> Lors fut la grant pitié et les grans regrectz, force pleurs et
> lamentacions et à hault cris, quant vint à luy couvrir la face. Car
> l'un cryoit: "Ha! noble dame!" autres: "Ha! souveraine et notable
> princesse, fault-il pour jamais perdre la veue de vostre noble face!"
> Plusieurs lui touchoient, les ungs au corps, les autres à la face; les
> ungs baisoient le cercueyl, les autres le suayre. Et par plusieurs foys
> fut celle noble face descouverte, et moult longuement durèrent
> les pleurs et crys, tellement qu'il faillit envoyer partie d'iceulx
> plaignans, leur disant: "Congnoissez que c'est nostre royne et
> maistresse; prions Dieu pour elle." (32)

> [Then, when it came to covering her face, great were the sorrow
> and regrets; there were many tears and lamentations and loud
> cries. For one person cried out: "Ha, noble lady!" And others "Ha!
> Sovereign and renowned princess, must we forever lose sight of
> your noble face!" Several touched her, some her body, others her
> face; some kissed the coffin, others the shroud. And on several
> occasions her noble face was uncovered, and the tears and cries
> lasted a long time, so much so that a group of the mourners were
> almost sent away with the words: "Remember that this is our queen
> and mistress; pray to God for her."]

The deep sadness of witnesses, or at least Choque's description of them, was significantly more moderate and controlled once the queen's body had been placed in a coffin and transferred to more public sites outside the château (my emphasis):

> Grant nombre de people s'i trouva; car ils venoient de Tours
> et d'Amboise, *pleurant et lamentant* la perte de la noble royne
> (53). . . . Il vint à une lieue hors la ville grant nombre d'officiers, tant
> de justice que autres, tous vestuz de deul, lesquelz, après avoir fait la
> révérence au corps, *pleurant moult tendrement*. . . . (62)[9]

[There was a large number of people there; for they came from
Tours and Amboise, *weeping and lamenting* the loss of the noble
queen. . . . A large number of legal and other officials, all dressed
in mourning apparel, came to a place outside the city, who, after
having paid reverence to the body, *crying very tenderly*. . . .]

In portraying the burial of the queen's body in Saint-Denis, Choque emphasizes the traumatic nature of the moment. However, instead of underscoring the intense emotion of individual participants, as he had done earlier in
narrating the placement of Anne's body in the coffin before a small intimate
audience, the chronicler describes how the general reaction of witnesses of all
classes to the queen's burial created solidarity among those present, a strategy
that tends to diminish the impact of emotion on the reader (my emphasis):

*Mains grans pleurs, cris, soupirs et lamentations* ce firent à ces piteulx
apeaulx; chascun joignoit des mains disant prierres et oraisons: et
croy que de mémoyre d'homme l'on ne vit pour ung jour plus grant
pitié. Car non seullement les princes et princesses, mais les gens de
tous les étatz qui là estoient, sembloit que autre mestier n'eussent
aprins que de *plourer, tortre les mains et cryer*. (87)

[*Many great tears, cries, sighs and lamentations* were made during
these piteous appeals; everyone held hands saying prayers and
orisons. And I believe that never in man's memory has one seen
such pity as on this day. For it seemed that not only princes and
princesses, but people of all estates who were there knew only how
to *weep, wring their hands and cry out*.]

This literary strategy employed by Choque implicitly imitates the codes of
conduct observed during the long funeral procession from Blois to Paris: the
chronicler gives freer reign to the expression of grief in private places, detailing the anguish of specific individuals, whereas mourning at public events
involving the collective, including the burial itself, is shaped in more general
and less traumatic terms.

Although Choque describes men and women alike in the grips of grief
in his account,[10] other authors differentiate more clearly between the sorrow
manifested by each sex. Philippe de Commynes, for example, made such a

distinction between the reactions of Anne of Brittany and Charles VIII to the death of their son, Charles-Orland, in 1495, as we learned above in Chapter 2. The "reasoned" behavior of the French king, whose grief lasted a short time, contrasted markedly with the queen's extreme emotion, described as even greater than one might normally expect of a woman or mother. This emphasis on a female's uncontrolled anguish was a topos in many writings of the time,[11] which I investigated in Chapter 4. Indeed, in one passage of his chronicle, Pierre Choque focuses on Anne of Brittany's desolation at the time of Charles VIII's death in 1498:

Mais par sur tous la royne ne cessoit
De grans doulleurs et piteuses complainctes:
La noble dame estoit si très dollante,
Tant marrye et tant desconfortée
Pour celle mort qui luy sembloit nuysante;
Aussi estoit moult fort désolée. (24)

[But more than everyone else the queen did not cease greatly lamenting and piteously mourning: the noble lady was grieving so very much, she was very sad and discomfited over this death that appeared so debilitating to her; she was also most disconsolate.]

The repetition of adverbs expressing extreme behavior in this passage—*par sur tous, si très dollante, tant marrye et tant desconfortée, moult fort désolée*—effectively translates into dramatic verse the queen's profound sorrow at the loss of her husband.

The distinctions introduced in these works between male and female conduct, as well as the implicit criticism of female or female-like behavior in certain cases, underscore the attention that questions about self-control held in the culture of the times. Just as the fascination of artists, readers, and viewers for the written and visual portrayals of famous women was accompanied by a concern for maintaining the proper moralistic assessment of them, as we learned in previous chapters, so too their curiosity about the emotional behavior of females, particularly at dramatic life junctures, was counterbalanced by issues of protocol. Jean Lemaire likewise treats this ambiguity about male and female expression of sorrow in his *XXIV Coupletz de la valitude et convalescence de la Royne*.[12] However, whereas Choque and Commynes presented literal details about Anne of Brittany's reaction to death in their chronicles, Lemaire employs poetico-rhetoric means to express the grief surrounding her near-death illness in 1512.

## Lemaire's *XXIV Coupletz*:
## Female and Male Mourners in Allegorical Fiction

In the *XXIV Coupletz* Lemaire gives voice to two female personified figures, *France* and *Bretaigne*, who hark back to the allegorical characters *Franc Vouloir* and *Seure Alliance* that were staged during Anne of Brittany's 1492 Parisian entry (see Chapter 1), although they appear in less politicized form here. As mother and daughter,[13] they express their anguish at the queen's imminent death. The narrator contrasts the initial excessive emotion of these "two very distinguished and noble princesses" (55) at the court of Blois,[14] which he implicitly criticizes, with the more moderate form of behavior that they eventually adopt (my emphasis):

[A]près avoir *femininement* gecté plusieurs exclamations piteuses avec interjections confuses, toutesvoyes en bruit taciturne, finablement reaffermerent leurs voix et rassirent leurs habitudes par plaincte moderée et facile à entendre. (55)[15]

[After having cried out *in a feminine manner* several piteous exclamations with a confusion of interjections, in the end they nevertheless reaffirmed their voices in a taciturn sound, and calmed down their behavior through a plaint that was moderated and easy to listen to.]

Thus, Lemaire does not place his female protagonists on stage without reassuring his readership, which included Margaret of Austria, most likely Anne of Brittany, and a broader public, that their grief will be expressed according to male dictates—with moderation, calm, and control—similar to the more reasoned conduct of Charles VIII following his son's death in 1495. Indeed, it is only after a decided transformation that entails a diminution of outcries, the reestablishment of a firm voice, and control of their behavior that the poet allows *France* and *Bretaigne*, each in turn, to implore God, the Virgin Mary, all heavenly saints and spirits, the French and Breton people,[16] the king, the heir apparent, and Nature[17] to protect the queen from death and pray for her life. The male poet thereby tames the excessive nature of his female characters by lending them more sober and discreet speech. In addition, he controls the poetic form of their words so that they speak in an ordered and coordinated versified fashion. As Jodogne points out (441), there are three series of eight stanzas, with each group displaying a different stanzaic form: in the first eight stanzas (vv. 1–64), all the rhymes are feminine, whereas there is an alternation of masculine and feminine rhymes every two stanzas in the second series of eight stanzas (vv. 64–128); in the third series of stanzas (vv. 129–92), masculine and feminine rhymes alternate within each stanza.[18] Moreover, the versification closely links the female protagonists, since the rhyme scheme of the stanza of the first speaker, *France*, is simply reversed in the lines pronounced by *Bretaigne*. It is as if the elaborate poetic structure embodies, in controlled form, the profound general anguish associated with the imminent demise of the queen. Thanks to their "sweet and lamentable feminine vociferations that penetrated the heavens" (62), the well-moderated appeals of *France* and *Bretaigne* replace their earlier excessive exclamations.

Curiously little focus is placed on Anne of Brittany's own qualities in this series of invocations to others to pray for the queen's recovery. Anne's religious faith is briefly invoked (vv. 29, 39–40, 44–45) as well as her support of others (v. 121). *Bretaigne* recalls the impact of the queen's visual presence in dramatic terms that recall her royal entry "performances" (vv. 125–28) and in the end bemoans what the loss of Anne of Brittany and her many virtues, the *valitude* of the poem's title, would mean:

> Se la royne ist de ce val transitoire
> Honneur et gloire
> Autant que on en peut croire
> Adieu vous diz, pour mon dueil exprimer;
> Adieu clemence et vertu donatoire,
> Pitié notoire,
> Aumosne meritoire,
> Et tous les biens qui font estimer. (vv. 169–76)

> [If the queen leaves this transitory world, honor and glory, as
> much as one can believe, I bid you adieu, in expressing my grief;
> farewell clemency and generous virtue, well-known compassion,
> meritorious alms-giving, and all the most respected qualities.]

Of all those addressed by *France* and *Bretaigne*, it is fitting that the only male character of this *dramatis personae*, Louis XII, is the one who responds with a prayer. Although Lemaire does not hesitate to express the king's great sorrow, he never gives him voice, thereby limiting the public's direct access to royal male emotion. Moreover, the fact that the king's lamentation appears in metaphoric form reveals how the subject of male grief was apparently best "described" in veiled form:

[L]e roy tresdebonnaire Loys xiie fut navré jusques au cueur d'une flesche empenée de pure et caste affection maritalle et plus que paternelle. Mais de la playe n'yssit autre liqueur fors eaue clere et vifve qu'on dit lachrymale en grand habundance, laquelle chose est trop plus difficille à tirer d'un cueur d'homme, et mesmement d'un prince tel qu'il est, que ne seroit traire du sang à force hors du corpz d'un vaillant homme d'armes, car ce ne se peut faire sans grand violence. (62)

[The very debonair Louis XII was wounded deep into his heart by a feathered arrow of pure and chaste marital and more-than-paternal affection. But from the great wound there issued forth only a clear and lively liquid that one calls lachrymal in great quantity, which is as difficult to draw from a man's heart, and especially from the prince that he is, as it would be to draw blood by force from the body of a valiant man of arms, for this cannot be done without great violence.]

Lemaire's decision to render masculine emotion in metaphoric terms by adopting the classical image of the arrow of love reinforces the idea that there existed a certain cultural malaise when dealing with masculine grief. In addition, the comparison the poet-narrator draws between royal tears and a warrior's blood effectively justifies in the most masculine of terms the king's profound sadness before Anne's grave illness. In fact, the prayer that the king offers is answered (63).[19] The success of the king's prayer—Anne of Brittany's life is in fact miraculously saved—emphasizes the important links between the moderate rhetoric ultimately adopted by the two female personifications, the metaphoric expression used to express the king's sadness, and the efficaciousness of his entreaty in preventing Anne of Brittany's death.

In his work, then, Lemaire successfully negotiates the complications associated with the expression of grief by males and females in the face of imminent death. It is probable that the poet, who had identified himself as the queen's historiographer since January 1512, offered a copy of the work to Anne of Brittany herself, for in what appears to have been the author's personal manuscript, Bibliothèque publique et universitaire de Genève, ms. fr. 74,[20] Lemaire indicates, at the end of the *XXIV Coupletz*, that he finished composing the work in Blois on 2 April 1512 [n. st.] in the month after the queen's recovery (fol. 199r).[21] In fact, Lemaire also added the *Double virelay de nouvelle taille et de l'invention de Jan le Maire* (fols. 199r–199v), in which he addresses not the queen, but an unidentified public at the French court as "Noble spirits of the great royal garden" (v. 1),[22] beseeching them to support his writing. In the first stanza Lemaire refers to his motivation to serve the queen well (vv. 2–3) and appears to allude again to Anne in the second strophe: "J'ay ma déesse, et l'ayme, honneure et crains" (v. 8) [I have my goddess, and I love, honor and fear her]. But these constitute third-person references. Of greater concern in these verses is Lemaire's fear that he will not be properly rewarded for his literary labors, which he advertises as potential celebrations of his addressees:

> Tendez voz mains à mes povres escriptz.
> Se je faiz bien, vous aurez honneurs maintz. . . .
> Se j'ay du bien, vous y serez compris;
> Se autrement va, tous mes biens sont restrains. (vv. 14–15, 21–22)

> [Reach out and take my poor writings. If I do well, you will receive many honors. . . . If I am compensated, you will benefit from it; if it goes otherwise, all my goods are limited.]

Lemaire's repeated appeal for aid that ends each strophe of his *virelai*— "Secourez-moy" [Come to my aid] (v. 12), "Aidez-moy doncq" [Help me then] (v. 24)—suggests that the queen's near death has, as in the past,[23] made him extremely vulnerable as a court poet to the vagaries of fortune and that his success in obtaining a post as the queen's chronicler did not assure him a long-term position. Indeed, just two years later, following Anne's death, Lemaire disappeared from the literary stage.[24]

It was perhaps out of concern for his livelihood that four months after the completion of the *XXIV Coupletz*, Lemaire offered a manuscript copy of the work to his former patroness, Margaret of Austria.[25] This was a somewhat ironic "gift," however, given that Anne of Brittany had displaced Margaret as queen of France with her marriage to Charles VIII (who had abandoned Margaret as his fiancée), and as Lemaire's patron. Besides its presumed reproduction in at least three manuscript books, those of Anne of Brittany, Margaret of Austria, and the poet, the *XXIV Coupletz* also reached a broader public in printed form when the work was published just one year later in August 1513 in Paris for Geoffrey de Marnef in a collection that contained other works by Lemaire, most of which also treated the theme of death.[26] According to the colophon, Lemaire, identified in this edition as the queen's "chronicler and historiographer," ordered its printing.[27] The poet's promotion of his association with the French queen was enhanced all the more so by a woodcut of Anne of Brittany appearing as the figure of Juno on the verso folio of the title page of the 1513 edition. The coincidence of the French queen with the queen of mythology obviously constituted a tribute to Lemaire's patroness, one that dovetailed with the fascination of contemporary readers, including Anne of Brittany herself, with the famous woman *topos*. In fact, this woodcut scene was based on a manuscript miniature that accompanied Lemaire's dedication to Anne of Brittany of his *Troisième livre des illustrations et singularitez de France orientalle et occidentalle* in December 1512.[28]

Through his involvement in the publication of his works, including the *XXIV Coupletz*, Lemaire was doubtless actively addressing the concern he had expressed in his *virelai* to the court in 1512 about his future livelihood, but in another arena, that of printing. The appearance of other editions of the *XXIV Coupletz* in similar collections as well as in the same volume as the *Regrets du Château de Blois*, a revision of La Vigne's quatrains written for Anne of Brittany, some time after January 1514 (see below), confirms the popularity of Lemaire's work about the queen's illness beyond court circles.

## La Vigne: The King's Heart and Mind in Mourning

Like Lemaire at the end of his *XXIV Coupletz*, La Vigne staged the problems surrounding masculine grief in his *Rondeau de l'Esprit et du Coeur du Roy*,[29] a poem that treats Louis XII's sorrow in 1514 following Anne of Brittany's death, by personifying two abstract dimensions of the king's nature: his Mind (*L'esprit*) tries to console and even control the excessive emotion of his Heart (*Le coeur*) through dramatic dialogue. Without explicitly invoking sexual oppositions, La Vigne's choice of personified characters here, although each a masculine word, makes obvious reference to the traditional opposition between male-associated reason and excessive female-associated emotion. In a sense, La Vigne's scenario recalls that of Charles VIII's attempts to comfort Anne of Brittany upon the death of their son in 1495. The 18-verse poem is a double rondeau with the refrain "Pour la royne."

While offering his readers intimate insight into the king's great sadness over the death of Anne of Brittany through the personification of a private experience, La Vigne, like his contemporaries, indirectly expresses the king's anguish by having abstractions speak, as if the allegorical process created an effective distance between the public and the monarch. Moreover, although the poet recognizes and even pardons the king's emotional mourning, he has The Mind play the role of a moralizer who wants The Heart's torment and profound sadness to be brought under control. Like the king in Lemaire's *XXIV Coupletz*, The Mind reacts to The Heart's desire to wallow in his grief—"Je veulx bien lamenter / Et pour jamais d'elle le dueil porter" [I want to fully mourn and forever lament her] (vv. 14–15)—by encouraging less emotional behavior and insisting that The Heart make a concerted effort to beseech God for the queen's salvation. The repeated fragmentation of a single verse into two and even three alternating line-segment responses between each personified figure in rapid-fire succession imitates the unruly aspect of The Heart, whereas the fixed rondeau form represents control over the situation by The Mind, who utters the last enduring words about proper decorum to ensure the queen's place in Paradise:

L'esprit
Erre tu?
Le cueur
        Non.
L'esprit
             Or entens mes édictz;
Puisqu'au Dieu plaist, lermes, criz, contredictz
N'y serviront.
Le cueur
          Je veulx bien lamenter
Et pour jamais d'elle le duel porter.
L'esprit
—Conclusion.—Il te faut depporter

Et désormais procurer paradis
    Pour la royne.[30]

[*The Mind*: Do you wander?—*The Heart*: No.—*The Mind*: Now
listen to my edicts; since it pleases God, tears, cries, objections will
not help.—*The Heart*: I want to fully mourn and forever lament
her.—*The Mind*: Conclusion.—You must be calm and from now on
seek Paradise for the queen.]

La Vigne's message that praying for the queen is better than lamenting excessively over her death thus embodies the same cultural criteria governing the
works of Commynes and Lemaire, examined above.

## The Glorification of Anne of Brittany in (Near) Death: Jean Marot and Jean Bouchet

Jean Marot's *Prières sur la restauration de la sancté de Madame Anne de Bretaigne* offer a similar protocol as La Vigne and Lemaire but one that is more
subtly expressed.[31] Less interested in publishing his work beyond court circles,
Marot does not focus as much on himself as the impoverished poet as Lemaire
does, or on the king's emotions, like La Vigne. While the female personifications in Marot's work behave according to the formula proposed by The Mind
in La Vigne's *Rondeau de l'Esprit et du Coeur* and their prayers lead to the
queen's recovery, the poet also expresses his own profound grief at the queen's
illness and, in a dream allegory that so often typifies the production of the
Rhétoriqueurs, provides repeated praise of Anne of Brittany's multiple virtues.
More than most other works written for or about the French queen, Marot's
*Prières sur la restauration* offers an elaborately constructed tribute to Anne.

However, in directly addressing the queen in his prefatory dedication,
Marot, unlike the authors heretofore examined, draws attention to his own
personal agitation during Anne of Brittany's illness and elation at her recovery in the metaphoric terms of a violent storm that is thankfully supplanted
by sunlight.[32]

Like Lemaire, Marot writes about his own poetic creation, mentioning
his desire to continue working for the queen, although he couches his words
in more self-deprecating language than Lemaire in his personal appeal for

financial support,[33] in the following manner, echoing his apologetic tone in earlier writings:

> Plaise vous sçavoir que je, Iehan des Marestz, alias Marot, de tous
> facteurs le moindre disciple et loingtain imitateur des meilleurs
> rethoriciens, vostre treshumble et tresobeissant et tresadvoué
> subject, serviteur et esclave, vous voullant monstrer et faire
> tesmoignage de l'affectueux vouloir et intencion tresdesireuse
> que j'ay de continuer le propos obstiné et non jamais variable de
> tousjours faire et exploicter quelque petite oeuvre à la recreation et
> delectation de vostre bieneurée noblesse, ay mys et employé la force
> et totalle vigueur de ma tresrude et imbecille capacité à construire,
> ediffier et composer ung oeuvre de la ressource et quasi nouvelle
> instauration de vostre santé. (120)

> [May it please you to know that I, John of Marestz, alias Marot,
> of all writers the lowliest disciple and distant imitator of the best
> poets, your most humble and most obedient and most devoted
> subject, servant and slave, wishing to show you and bear witness
> to the affectionate will and very desirous intention that I have
> of continuing the persistent and never variable proposition of
> always making and exploiting some small work for the recreation
> and enjoyment of your most fortunate highness, have used and
> employed the force and total energy of my very ignorant and feeble
> capacity to construct, erect and compose a work about the source
> and nearly complete restoration of your health.]

As in his *Voyage de Gênes* dedication to Anne of Brittany, the poet promotes the fact that he was eyewitness to the events, which presumably enhances the authority of his allegorical vision, and reminds the queen in rather witty terms that his other works, which include the *Voyage de Gênes* and *Vraye Advocate des dames* discussed above in Chapters 2 and 3, figure already in her library:

> [J]'ay experimenté vostre treshumaine benignité estre de profundité
> si immense que les petitz labeurs partans de ma rude capacité ont
> trouvé grace devant voz yeulx, ont esté honnorez de la conversation
> de voz aultres livres, ont esté plus par heur que par merite
> leuz en vostre tresnoble presence. Plaise vous dont, treshaulte,

tresexcellente, & tresmagnanime dame, recueillir et prendre en
gré ce mien humble petit present, et en icelluy veoir la forme et
maniere de vostre convallescence, attributable selon mon jugement
en la seulle main salutiffere du createur. (121)

[I have experienced your most humane goodness being of such
immense depth that the little labors resulting from my very
unskilled capacity have found grace before your eyes, have been
honored by conversation with your other books, [and] have been
read in your very noble presence more out of chance than merit.
Therefore, may it please you, my most noble, most excellent and
most magnanimous lady, to receive and willingly accept this
humble little gift of mine, and [may you] see in it the form and
manner of your recovery, attributable alone, according to my
judgment, to the salutary hand of the Creator.]

Yet, following earlier literary patterns, Marot belittles his own talents,
referring to his work as "of little value as far as its structure, fabrication [and]
composition are concerned" (120) in order to glorify all the more his subject,
which he does in decidedly more dramatic terms than Lemaire, by implying
that the story of Anne's recovery is of epic-like character.[34] In fact, when he
calls the near tragedy that he transposes into an allegorical scenario a "mis-
tere" and a "spectacle" (121), thereby confirming the close alliance between
royal ceremonies and imagined literary visions and theatrical stagings, Marot
adopts terms used by La Vigne to described Anne of Brittany's 1504 royal
entry. That is, once Marot's narrative introduces his audience into his dream
state, he verbally casts the queen's recuperation from her near-death affliction
in terms of a dramatic performance. That performance involves the appearance on the oniric literary stage of a procession of mourners:

Ainsi marchans, portoyent torches et cierges,
Hommes, enfans, femmes, filles et vierges.
Là n'y eut bruit, fors qu'on oyoit par coups
Des desolez les souspirs et sangloutz.    (vv. 63–66)

[Thus processing, they carried torches and candles, men, children,
women, girls and virgins. There was no sound, except that one
heard periodically the sighs and sobs of the desolate.]

These are followed by a cast of sociopolitical and theological personified figures, whose praise of Anne of Brittany's multiple qualities in prayers pleading for her life bring consolation and relief to the narrator and other mourners. This poetic staging of the queen's merits recalls the depiction of Anne of Brittany in association with a host of personified virtues in the liminal miniature of the *Toison d'Or* manuscript (see Chapter 1). In both portraits, the three Theological Virtues figure centrally as well as the Cardinal Virtues, here two of them, Fortitude (vv. 864–74) and Justice (vv. 875–98).[35]

The procession of mourners from all social classes takes center stage in the early phases of the nightmare of the narrator, who, as the poet's alter ego, provides a *prosimetrum* account of Anne of Brittany's recovery. But his bad dream gradually metamorphoses into an inspiring vision in which he witnesses a series of prayers proffered on behalf of the ailing French queen by the three Estates (*Noblesse, Eglise,* and *Labour*) and the three Theological Virtues (Hope, Faith, and Charity). These invocations to God pave the way for an epiphany-like apotheosis of Paradise. Thanks to divine intervention, the arrival of Forgiveness (*Miséricorde*) and Pity (*Pitié*) at the dying queen's side with a celestial ointment precipitates Anne's recovery. Marot expresses grief through his first-person narrator, whose sorrow, sobbing, and trembling derail literary inspiration:[36]

> Attaint au vif de regretz importables,
> Gorgogité de souspirs lamentables
> Par griefz ennuys dont je fuz agitté
> N'a pas long temps: sur mon lit me jetté,
> Rendant sangloutz et desteurtant mes mains,
> Comme celluy qui seuffre des maulx maintz,
> Craintif, paoureux, par infortune aperte
> D'ung cas doubteux, d'inrecouvrable perte. (vv. 1–8)[37]

> [Struck to the core with unbearable sorrow, chest sounds of lamentable sighs in dolorous pain with which I was agitated not long ago, I threw myself on my bed, sobbing and wringing my hands, like someone suffering from many evils, afraid, fearful, vunerable through misfortune with a doubtful case, with irrecoverable loss.]

However, these sentiments are mitigated through the prayers of his multiple female speakers,[38] who are consciously "avoiding the tumult of those lamenting" (vv. 94–95).[39] Their language, described as moderate and appropriate to the occasion,[40] brings about the queen's recovery to the great consolation of the poet-narrator and public alike.[41] Thus, the poet's original, female-like grief, although expressed in the privacy of his room, is realigned with a more acceptable public protocol.

In an ascending rhetorical trajectory that recalls other Rhétoriqueur poems inspired by the actual death of a patron, such as Jean Molinet's *Trosne d'Honneur* or Lemaire's *Temple d'Honneur et de Vertus*, the allegorical figures in the *Prières sur la restauration*, more than any previous literary characters yet examined, furnish, one after the other, a detailed, laudatory account of the queen's many qualities. Much adulation entails very general terminology, all but confirming the existence of an expected set of female traits associated with all women of power paraded in public.[42] For example, Anne is repeatedly extolled as the paragon of all virtues.[43] Because she actually held the title countess of Vertuz, poets may have consciously played on this association as well.[44] In addition, Anne is frequently praised as the bearer of peace,[45] the embodiment of all good,[46] a model of religious devotion,[47] and support to others, including nobles, but especially commoners.[48] However, it is Anne of Brittany's generosity that stands out as one of the attributes so frequently cited by the personified figures in Marot's *Prières sur la restauration*[49] that such praise must have been inspired by real-life examples.

The more specific qualities possessed by the queen that those praying for her mention must also have been drawn from historical reality. Besides her acknowledged support of men of knowledge (v. 276), Anne's devotion to women is emphasized:

> C'est des gentilz la resource et fiance
> La soustenance aux povres damoiselles.
> C'est d'orphenins la mere et la substance,
> Support des clercs, des veufves l'asseurance,
> Et l'esperance aux vierges et pucelles.
> C'est l'ardant feu rendant les estincelles
> De charité, et de vertus l'enseigne,
> L'honneur de France et gloire de Bretaigne. (vv. 129–36)

> [She is the refuge and security of nobles, the sustenance of poor
> young girls, she is the mother and livelihood of orphans, the
> support of clerics, the security for widows, and the hope of virgins

and maidens. She is the ardent fire emitting sparks of charity,
and the standard of virtues, the honor of France and the glory of
Brittany.]

This support involved her role as an arranger of marriages for young and
poor girls:

> Car nous estans es terrestres monarches,
> Voullut ouvrir le tresor de ses arches
> Pour marier nous aultres jouvencelles,
> Nous preservant des ardans estincelles
> Dame Venus, aussi de povreté,
> Souvent contraire à toute loyaulté. (vv. 671–76)

[For when we were living in earthly monarchies, she willingly
opened her treasure chests to marry us other young girls, protecting
us from the burning sparks of Lady Venus, and also from poverty,
which is often contrary to all loyalty.]

No queen in history has, according to *Eglise*, known such glory (vv. 283–84).
Like the *Dame sans sy* in the *Heroides* manuscript in the queen's library, examined above in Chapter 4, Anne of Brittany is described as a perfect lady without faults (vv. 218–19). Anne too ranks among Boccaccio's "famous woman,"
for *Labour* describes her as "Our Dido, Hester and Lucretia" (v. 496), while
*Foy* considers her to be "another Dido, the second Minerva, rich Juno" (vv.
771–72). The French queen's double comparison with Dido may derive from
the fact that both were examples of spousal loyalty and women of power, although Dido's political authority was considerably greater than Anne's. Association with Minerva is the highest form of mythological flattery as is Anne's
analogy with Juno, queen of the mythological realm.

*Faith* provides similar comparisons in her prayers seeking the recovery
of the queen, so devoted to God, just like that of the Canaanite whose faith
Christ recognized and the son of the centurion who was healed by the faith
of his master or father (see vv. 759–62).[50] In fact, Marot's tribute to the queen
is a form of canonization,[51] since *Labour* himself requests that Anne be first
restored to good health and then in a hundred years be made a saint (vv.
364–68), Hope refers to her saintliness (v. 896), and the narrator implicitly

equates Anne with the Virgin Mary, as angels beckon the French queen to leave earth and be crowned in heaven (vv. 533–46).

In the end, *Eglise*'s appeal for the restoration of Anne's health offers the most impressive and emphatic recapitulation of her many virtues:

> C'est de vertuz la closture royale,
> Le chef d'honneur, volunté cordiale,
> Cueur magnanime, et pensée integrale,
> Parfaicte en biens, si jamais en fut une.
> C'est le corps pur d'amour franche et loyale
> Langue en parler, au cueur juste et egale,
> Oeil de pitié et main tres liberale,
> Bras pacific brisant toute rancune.
> C'est l'aceré estoc contre infortune,
> Nef navigante en mer soubz seur hune
> Qu'onques fortune aux ventz ambicieux
> Ne sceut mouvoir moins que le pole es cieulx. (vv. 259–70)

[She is the royal enclosure of virtues, the head of honor, heart-strengthening will, a magnanimous heart, and complete thought, perfect in goodness, if ever there was one. Hers is the pure body of sincere and loyal love, the language of discourse, just and equal in affection, the eye of pity and a very generous hand, the arm of peace breaking through all rancor. She is the steely trunk against misfortune, the ship navigating through the sea supported by a strong mast that Fortune with its ambitious winds never knew how to move any [more] than the celestial pole.]

These last verses reveal how Marot, through the allegorical figure *Eglise*, returns to the image of storms he employed in his dedication to Anne of Brittany to describe the widespread turmoil and grief surrounding the queen's illness and embroiders upon it by describing his patroness as a forceful, steady ship safely navigating through the winds of potential misfortune (vv. 939–45). The poet's other allegorical characters also adopt a variety of metaphors in their glorification of Anne of Brittany as well. Horticultural images dominate, with the French queen depicted as the lady in whom God has planted grace and honor (vv. 743–44), but also as a pure rose (v. 125),[52] the lily (v. 293), the graft that nourishes the Third Estate with her fruit (vv. 341–43), the body linking lily and ermine (vv. 811–12), and the lilied ermine (v. 1054). These symbolic verbal images of the union of Brittany and France through Anne of Brittany's marriages appear frequently as visual emblems in books confirming Anne's ownership of them, as we have learned in earlier chapters.

Other analogies in the *Prières sur la restauration* describe, on the one hand, Anne as the sun (vv. 162, 754) and, on the other, in military or Minerva-like terms as the shield of Nobility's children (v. 176) and the Church (v. 256). In accordance with her repeated praise as the model of all virtues, *Labour* considers Anne of Brittany to be the mirror of virtue worthy of imitation by all (vv. 432–36), a conventional image earlier adopted by Antoine Dufour in his dedicatory prologue in the *Vies des femmes célèbres* (see Chapter 3). But the most original and memorable portrait, one that Marot places in the mouth of *Foy* and that predates his son's similar characterization of Margaret of Navarre, is the description of Anne of Brittany as a virile woman, or manly spirit in a lady's body ("cueur viril en corps de dame") (vv. 750–51).[53] Even though Marot found reason to employ this evocative image, which successfully and concisely translates the moral, cultural, and political strength that doubtless underpinned Anne of Brittany's actions, one that offsets accounts of her excessively emotional reactions, other poets were not as bold in their tributes to the queen.

As in his *Prières sur la restauration*, the principal aim of Jean Marot's epitaph composed upon the death of Anne of Brittany, was to glorify the queen. While the poet conforms to the formal expression of the epitaph in his forty alexandrine verses,[54] he offers the most original and most personal image of Anne of Brittany in his *Épitaphe Anne de Bretaigne*. Even though he adopts the most distant grammatical perspective here by writing in the third person, unlike Bouchet, who has Anne speak in the first person, as we will learn below, it is ironically Marot's funeral poem that provides the most intimate and illustrious portrait of the deceased queen. For example, the poet transforms the marriage between Anne and Charles into a love story, choosing to minimize the political exigencies that actually forced Anne to submit to Charles VIII in 1491:[55]

Ayant dans le treziesme, estant sans pere et mere,
De par Charles huitiesme eut guerre trop amere.

Neantmoings ne vainquit; amour fut seul vainqueur
Quant deux corps il conquit, ou il ne laissa que ung cueur.
D'amour tant le combla que la fleur lyliale
A l'hermine assembla en couche nuptiale.
Ainsi la belle et bonne, oultre chappeau ducal,
De France eut la coronne et le tiltre royal. (vv. 5–12)[56]

[Having had at age thirteen, being without father or mother, a
most bitter war with Charles VIII. Nevertheless he didn't vanquish
her; love was the only victor when he conquered two bodies, where
he left only one heart. She overwhelmed him with so much love
that the fleur-de-lis joined with the ermine in the nuptial bed.
In this way, the beautiful and good lady, in addition to the ducal
crown, received the crown and the royal title of France.]

As in his *Prières sur la restauration*, Marot praises Anne of Brittany in the
most generous manner of any (male) writer of the time. Borrowing the striking image from his *Prières*, Jean Marot once again attributes masculine qualities to Anne of Brittany: "C'estoit ung corps viril posé en corps de dame"
[Hers was a virile body placed in a lady's body] (v. 23).[57] In fact, the poet
reemploys several other verses from the earlier work in defining the queen's
heritage,[58] emphasizing Anne's considerable influence on women of all categories (vv. 23–32)—"She was the sustenance of poor young ladies and the
sole hope of virgins and maidens" (vv. 29–30)[59]—and reviewing the generous
nature of the queen who often gave before any requests were made (v. 28).[60]
Marot revisits other qualities of the queen he had previously exposed, describing her in the following terms:

Le plus hault et gentil que onques receut ame.
Les nobles mal content(s), doulcement conten[t]oit[61]
Et le plus, en tous temps de ses biens confortoit.
. . . liberale estoit et de cueur si tres grande . . .
Briefs, de toutes vertus et de graces de hault pris
Enrichiz et vestuz furent les siens esperits. (vv. 24–32)[62]

[The most lofty and noble of any soul, she sweetly satisfied
discontented nobles, and in all times she comforted the most with

her goods. She had a very big heart . . . In short, her spirits were
enriched and clothed in all virtues and the most esteemed graces.]

The poet invokes the same images, including the mirror of virtue (v. 3),
the seizure of Anne by Death, and the resultant grief (vv. 33–38). In the
end, the Rhétoriqueur insists less on his and others' present grief in his
*Épitaphe* than on Anne of Brittany's past glory, reminding his audience
that no other queen ever received such accolades (vv. 13–14)[63] and, like the
personified figures in his *Prières sur la restauration*, appealing to the subjects of his deceased patroness, Bretons and French, for prayers of salvation
(vv. 39–40).

It is the deceased queen herself who directly addresses the reader in
Jean Bouchet's *Épitaphe de madame Anne de Bretaigne, espouse du Roy Louis
XII de ce nom*. Alone among the Rhétoriqueurs, Bouchet gives voice to the
queen—or at least to her person beyond the grave—in both his epitaph
and epigram. Since the victim herself speaks out, all expression of grief
is absent from these verses. In contrast to Marot, the poet does not focus
on glorifying the queen, although the same themes as those in Marot's
poem reappear here—Anne's husbands, her specific qualities, and an invocation to the Bretons and French to pray for Anne's soul. Functioning like
the personified figures in the previously examined works, the first-person
voice in these funeral poems thus creates a certain distance between the
public and its anguish before the queen's death. First identifying herself
as the duchess of Brittany and loyal wife and companion of Kings Charles
VIII and Louis XII (vv. 1–4), without mentioning her position as queen
of France, Anne notes the disappearance of worldly goods at the time of
her death, despite her wealth, adding simply that she was also prudent and
good (vv. 5–8):[64]

Anne je suis, Duchesse de Bretaigne,
Qui fuz jadis de Charles, et Loÿs,
Roys des François, vraye espouse et compaigne,
Dont tant d'honneurs sont encores ouÿs.          4
Tous biens mondains se sont esvanouÿs
De moy qui fuz riche, prudente, et bonne,
L'am mil cinq cens et trez[e], qu'a la bonne
Conduicte fuz de la fiere Atropos.[65]          8

Priez a Dieu qu'a mon ame pardonne,
Et qu'il luy donne en Paradis repos.

[I am Anne, duchess of Brittany, who was formerly the faithful
wife and companion of Charles and Louis, kings of France, whose
many honors are still heard about. All earthly goods vanished from
me, who was rich, prudent and good, in the year 1513, for I was led
to the end by the fierce Atropos. Pray God that he pardon my soul
and grant me peace in Paradise.]

While Bouchet's concise poetic form of ten decasyllabic verses enhances the
perfunctory tone of this deceased female's voice, Anne's appeal to the reader
in the last two verses, reminiscent of Villon's "Ballade des pendus," is nevertheless quite poignant. In a sense, her directness here establishes a closer
bond with Bouchet's sixteenth-century readership than the implorations
declaimed by allegorical figures in the works by Marot and Lemaire examined above.

The same psychological and poetic dynamics characterize the *Épigramme d'Anne, deux foys Royne de France, et Duchesse de Bretaigne*, which
Bouchet composed on behalf of Anne of Brittany.[66] Although the poet has
Anne mention that she was twice queen of France as well as duchess of Brittany (v. 2), she emphasizes at greater length her two husbands rather than
her own piety and economic prudence, mentioned only briefly at the end
of the poem:

Anne je suys de Bretaigne Duchesse,
Royne deux foys, car en mon premier lict
Charles du nom huytiesme, en sa jeunesse
Roy des Francoys, j'espousay en liesse,                          4
Ou neuf ans fuz soubz son doulx hannelict.[67]
Mais la mort vint qui lors l'ensevelyt,
Et espousay le Roy Loys douziesme,
Desdictz François portant le diadesme,                          8
Duquel j'ay eu deux filles seullement.
J'aymay bien Dieu, semblablement mon presme,
Me retirant de despence moy mesme
Pour contenter les subgectz prudemment.                        12

[I am Anne, duchess of Brittany, twice queen, for in my first bed
I married in happiness Charles VIII, king of France, in his youth;
nine years I lived under his sweet protection. But death came and
buried him, and I married King Louis XIII, wearing the crown
of the French, with whom I had only two daughters. I loved God
well, likewise my kin, refraining from spending myself to satisfy
my subjects with prudence.]

In explaining in verse 9 that she had only two daughters—*seullement*
falls dramatically at the rhyme—the literary voice of the deceased queen emphasizes Anne of Brittany's failure as the wife of two kings to produce a male
heir. Of course, this admission arises from the literary consciousness of a male
writer, although neither Marot nor La Vigne brings up this subject.[68] While
the enumeration of some of Anne's qualities—her devotion to God, loyalty
to family, financial conservatism, and concern for her subjects—somewhat
neutralizes the stigma that marked Anne of Brittany's reigns as queen, the
portrait that Bouchet presents is still ambiguous. Where one would expect
to find praise of the queen, this epigram offers instead a rather paradoxical
image of Anne, doubtless a reflection of contemporary attitudes, since Anne's
remarks relate above all to her husbands and to her failure as a royal wife
to produce an heir. Bouchet, the only writer examined here who was not
an officially named court poet,[69] furnishes the least personalized and most
conventional portrait of Anne of Brittany. This likely explains the fact that he
redacted these verses for publication in anthologies containing similar poems,
perhaps many years after the queen's death. The epitaph appeared in the *Annales d'Acquitaine* of 1524, some ten years after Anne of Brittany had died, and
in the *Généalogies, effigies, et épitaphes des Roys de France* of 1545.[70] The epigram
that Bouchet composed in the queen's voice appeared in his *Jugement poetic
de l'honneur féminin* in 1538.[71]

Thus, unlike Marot, who never published his *Épitaphe* about the French
queen, Bouchet did not compose his funeral poems uniquely to celebrate
Anne of Brittany, but also—and perhaps primarily—to complement other
similar homages that were to appear in the books he intended to publish.
Although his epigram about Anne of Brittany comprises part of a printed
work entirely devoted to the praise and even the defense of women in general,
the traditional—or masculine—perspective prevails in Bouchet's emphasis
on the queen's association with Charles VIII and Louis XII and inability
to produce a male heir. Bouchet's epitaph about Anne of Brittany can be

similarly characterized, although its inclusion among poems treating other famous men and women in the *Généalogies, effigies, et épitaphes des Roys de France* somewhat enhances the conventional image of the queen contained therein.

## La Vigne's *Épitaphes en rondeaux de la royne*: Dramatic Stagings of Grief

Like Bouchet, André de la Vigne composed his *Épitaphes en rondeaux de la royne* in the first person, but the voice he adopted resembled that of the poet himself. Instead of writing poems from the tomb in which the deceased person or Death herself speaks directly to the audience, La Vigne penned appeals to his readers to mourn Anne's demise ("En ce monde," "De mort, d'envie," "Povres humains," "Aprés la mort"), a prayer to God asking for the queen's salvation ("Pere eternal"), invectives against Death's murder of the queen ("Cruelle mort," "Traistresse Mort," "Mort inhumaine"), and invocations to several towns along the 1514 funeral route from Blois to Saint-Denis ("Cueurs desolees," "Plorez humains").[72] These latter two rondeaux, coupled with a series of quatrains, played a dramatic role in the funeral ceremonies, for, according to Pierre Choque's account in which many of La Vigne's other funereal verses appeared, they were posted in highly visible places, such as on church doors or city walls.[73] Like his allegorical counterparts in Marot's and Lemaire's works, the narrator in this poem calls on the citizens of Orleans to mourn the death of their queen:[74]

> Cueurs désollez, en qui douleur habite,
> Espritz dollants que malheur débilite,
> Corps opressez de souffrance mortelle,
> Pour cette mort dont ne fut onc mort telle,
> De pleurer fault qu'un chascun s'abilite.
> Afin d'avoir perpétuel mérite,
> Et pour montrer que en vous tristesse hérite,
> Larmoyez tous, sans fainctisse et cautelle,
>     Cueurs désolez.
>
> Puys qu'Atropos, dépiteuse et mauldite,
> Tant et si fort vous point et précipite,

Qu'elle a surquis et mys en sa tutelle
Celle de qui la gloire est immortelle,
Monstrez qu'en vous liesse est interdite,
    Cueurs désolez. (60)

[Desolate hearts, in whom sadness lives, grieving souls whom evil
weakens, bodies oppressed by mortal suffering, for this death of
which there was never one like it, each one (of you) must be ready
to weep so that she has eternal glory, and to show that you have
inherited sadness. Weep everyone, without false pretense or deceit,
desolate hearts. Since Atropos, spiteful and cursed, pricks you so
much and throws you down so greatly that she has overcome and
put in her power the one whose glory is immortal, show that joy
has no place in you, desolate hearts.]

By inciting the personified city and its citizens to mourn the queen, the poet
explicitly emphasizes the necessity of manifesting grief. However, these are
rhetorically moderate words that are embodied and even constrained by the
fixed rondeau form. In fact, in two of his other rondeaux, "Povres servants"
and "Aprés la mort," La Vigne emphasizes the role reason must play in public
grieving.

In a more charming series of verses, the *Déploracion au Chasteau de Bloys
des lyeux ou la royne frequentoit plus souvent*, La Vigne's personification of the
spaces that the queen inhabited before her death bring a smile to the reader.[75]
The narrator of this poem, who, like the poet, knew certain personal traits of
the queen well, addresses the rooms and places in the Château of Blois that
had an intimate connection with Anne of Brittany.[76] La Vigne thereby transforms the queen's domicile—her bedchamber, her wardrobe, her garden,[77]
and *gallerie*,[78] her terrace,[79] her chapels[80] and the chateau itself—into public
areas. By metamorphosing each architectural space into a grieving person
and by converting the literal emptiness associated with each space into an
emotional emptiness, La Vigne imaginatively humanizes the queen's favorite
places, as we learn in the following examples:

        A la garde-robe
    Trop piteuse et povre garde-robe,
    Pleure ton deul, regrette ta maistresse.

Puisqu'à présent n'a plus en garde-robe
Habillement de la royne et duchesse. (41)

A la terrasse
Terrasse, hélas! tu n'auras plus l'honneur
De soustenir et porter la princesse
Qui t'avoit mys en nature et valleur,
Dont depuis fus fréquentée sans cesse. (41–42)

[To the Wardrobe: Most piteous and poor wardrobe, weep
and grieve, mourn your mistress, since at present there is no
longer in her wardrobe any clothing belonging to the queen and
duchess. . . . To the Terrace: Alas, terrace! you will no longer have
the honor of supporting and bearing the princess, who had you
created and greatly valued you, such that from then on you were
repeatedly frequented.]

While the poet cannot help but laud his patroness in these various
poems,[81] La Vigne seems less focused on staging the qualities of Anne of Brittany than on the sadness of an entire collective shocked by the queen's death.
Indeed, in abandoning the allegorical dimension of the literary speakers of
his peers, La Vigne appropriates the tone of the female voice of the complaint
in the funeral poems examined above and redirects his remarks to appeal
directly to the wider mourning public. Whereas Marot's grieving is indirectly
manifest through his *Prières* narrator, La Vigne dares to display overtly and
publicly his own sadness in a more direct and more authoritative fashion than
his contemporaries. It is the poet who attacks death and offers prayers; it is La
Vigne who describes his own grief in well-measured verses, but associates his
sorrow with the "nous" of the collective:

Traistresse mort, de nature ennemye,
Je congnois bien ta cruelle infamye . . .
Quant bien je pense a sa grant preudommie
Incessamment cueur et corps me fremye.
Je pers le sens, le taint et la couleur,
Car procuré nous as trop grant malheur
D'auoir si tost sa personne endormye. (fols. 2r–2v)[82]

[Traitorous Death, Nature's enemy, I know your cruel infamy
well . . . When I think about her great integrity, my heart and body
tremble incessantly; I lose all feeling, tincture, and color, for you
have brought upon us the greatest misfortune by having so early
killed her person.]

It is perhaps the poem La Vigne actually placed on Anne of Brittany's
grave that most poignantly expresses grief surrounding the queen's death, for
here the poet addresses her most faithful servants:

> Poures seruans, plus qu'autres tormentez,
> Au cry de pleurs, venez et vous hastez,
> Assemblez vous, les iours en sont venuz.
> Par les malheurs qui vous sont suruenuz,
> Raison entend que grant deuil en portez.

> Allez, venez, saillez, de tous costez
> Pour vous pourueoir desormais, et notez
> Que voz regretz seront par tous congneuz,
>     Poures seruans.

> De la royne qui vous a supportez,
> Tant bien traictez, nourriz et substantez,
> Traitresse mort a ses iours preuenuz.
> Et si du roy n'estes entretenuz,
> A l'opital fauldra que vous trottez,
>     Poures seruans. (fols. 4r–4v)[83]

[Poor servants, tormented more than others, hurry and come at
the sound of tears; assemble together, the days have come to this
through the grief that you have experienced; reason wishes that you
show great mourning. Go, come, issue forth from all sides, to offer
yourselves from now on, and note that your regrets will be heard by
all, poor servants. From the queen who supported you, treated you
so well, nourished and fed you, Traitorous Death forestalled her
days, and, if you are not sustained by the king, you will have to go
to the hospital, poor servants.]

Although the refrain, "Povres servans," may well allude in general terms to all those who knew Anne and were her subjects, one could interpret this appeal on a more literal level as La Vigne's sympathy for and effort to publicize the plight of Anne's very servants, who were in danger of losing their positions as a result of her death. This concern may have consciously or unconsciously embodied an equally compelling message about the poet himself, whose secretarial post was threatened with the French queen's demise. In fact, La Vigne's presumed initiation of at least one edition of his funeral poems may be related to this looming career change.

Thus, whereas Lemaire in his *XXIV Coupletz* had worried about the expression of excessive female emotion, even in allegorized form, and discovered the way to control it; whereas Marot had staged an allegorical vision in which all characters, in addition to his alter ego, inspired and interacted with each other, in an effort to bring about Anne of Brittany's recovery in his *Prières sur la restauration*, André de la Vigne sought to bring out the sadness and grief of his readers and to associate his own sorrow with theirs through a transparent masculine voice. Lemaire and Marot invented personified female figures to calm the suffering of court nobles, while La Vigne chose to emphasize the poet-narrator's authoritative voice and his relationship with the public, perhaps because he already envisaged bringing his work into print for a larger and broader readership. Marot praised the queen more enthusiastically in his writings than any other writers, but his works never circulated beyond the restricted circle of the royal court during his lifetime. La Vigne and Lemaire, on the other hand, whose work appeared in manuscript and printed form, simultaneously targeted a court and wider bourgeois public with their funeral poems. They both thereby created the possibility of profiting from the tragic situation by reaching out to readers within and beyond royal circles.

In the end, Marot's personified female voices, which offered the most intimate and detailed portrait of Anne of Brittany, enhanced by his personal grief expressed in the dedication, reached a court readership alone. Bouchet's fictionalized and rather conventionalized voice of the deceased queen in his *Épitaphe* and *Épigramme* remained more or less silent for a decade, addressing a different generation of readers some ten to twenty years after Anne of Brittany's death. Lemaire's allegorized female voices appealing for Anne of Brittany's recovery in 1512 targeted a court readership, to whom he pleaded extratextually for support in his own voice. But a year later he ushered the *XXIV Coupletz* into print.[84] The transparent masculine voice of La Vigne ended up authorizing public grief over the queen's death in moderate terms in both manuscript and printed form, while simultaneously promoting his own image as court poet. All these various literary reactions, an understandable exploitation of the death of the queen for one's continued artistic livelihood, reflect the dynamic of the poet-patroness relationship, which lost all definition upon the queen's death. Both La Vigne's and Lemaire's ties with Anne of Brittany were so important that their careers all but faded with her disappearance from the scene.[85] La Vigne's poems in the queen's memory, however, remained alive through print, even after his death, thanks to shrewd publishers who reused his work upon the death of Anne's own daughter twenty years later.

## Mourning Poems for Anne of Brittany Recycled for Claude of France

Sometime after Anne of Brittany's funeral, 11 funeral rondeaux by La Vigne appeared along with a quatrain in a 4-folio imprint under the title *Epitaphes en rondeaux de la royne. Avec celle qui fut posee sur le corps a Saint Denys en France apres le cry fait par le herault de Bretaigne & la deploration du Chasteau de Bloys composees par maistre Andre de la Vigne son secretaire.*[86] Seven poems printed in this volume also appeared, presumably simultaneously, in Choque's manuscript account: "Cruelle mort" (fols. 1r–1v), "En ce monde" (fol. 1v), and "Rondeau [double] de l'Esprit et du Coeur du roy" (fols. 1v–2r)[87] as well as "Le rondeau que mist ledit de La Vigne a Saint Saulveur de Bloys" [The rondeau that La Vigne placed at Saint Saulveur in Blois] (fols. 2v–3r) with the refrain "Pere eternal,"[88] "Cueurs desolez" (fol. 3v) and "Plorez humains" (fol. 3v).[89] The last poem in the *Épitaphes en rondeaux*, a quatrain announced as "S'ensuyt le jour et l'an qu'on l'amena du chasteau de Bloys a Sainct Denys" [Here follows the day and year that she was led from the Château of Blois to Saint-Denis] (fol. 4v), also figures in Choque's account in anonymous fashion:

> Au Chasteau de Bloys.[90]
> Chasteau de Bloys, plus n'a[s] cause d'estre aise
> Puys que la royne en tristesse et doulleur
> Le vendredi d'aprés la Chandelleur,
> Mort la ravit l'an mil cinq cens [et] treze. (52)

[Château of Blois, you can no longer rest easy, since Death ravished the queen, in sadness and grief, Friday after the Chandeler, 1513.]

As for the series of 7 quatrains entitled "La Déploracion au Chasteau de Bloys," this anthology was published in revised form under a slightly modified title in the same 8-folio edition with Lemaire's *XXIV Coupletz* in *Les vingt et quatre coupletz de la valitude et convalescence de la feue royne trescrestienne. Avec les regretz du chasteau de Bloys Et des lieux ou ladicte dame frequentoit le plus.*[91] Neither Lemaire nor La Vigne is identified as author of these verses. In addition, Anne of Brittany has been written out of Lemaire's work,[92] even though reference to Louis XII remains (fol. 6r). The "Regretz du Chasteau de Bloys" are even more substantively revised from the original "Déploracion." La Vigne's 7 original quatrains have evolved into 6 ten-verse stanzas, with the original verses describing the sorrow of the Chateau of Blois having been eliminated.[93] These alterations suggest that the edition was published at a later time, perhaps following the death of Claude of France in 1524, who could have still been identified as the queen who frequented sites at the Château of Blois. If this was the case, the two deceased poets would not have been alive to make (or challenge) these modifications.

Even more curious was the recycling of La Vigne's *Épitaphes en rondeaux* ten years after Anne of Brittany's and likely the poet's death[94] in *Les epitaphes et rondeaulx. Composez sur le trespas de feue, tresexcellente et tresdebonnaire princesse Claude par la grace de Dieu Royne de France et duchesse de Bretaigne,* published sometime after 20 July 1524 to commemorate the death of Anne of Brittany's daughter, Queen Claude of France.[95] La Vigne's identity as poet goes unacknowledged even though this publication includes at least three of his poems.[96] Two other poems ("Au hault climat" and "Au departir") appear in this volume and although Montaiglon and Rothschild included them in their nineteenth-century edition of La Vigne's funeral poetry of Anne,[97] no document in this anonymous edition or elsewhere confirms that La Vigne authored them.

Another more substantial edition bearing a similar but more ambiguous title, since it identifies neither Anne of Brittany nor Claude of France— *Epitaphes en Rondeaulx de la feue Royne Duchesse de Bretaigne. Et plusieurs aultres choses dignes de voir* (although several verses refer to Claude's death)— provides a greater number of La Vigne's poems, for it is an 8-folio rather than a 4-folio imprint.[98] Twelve of the poetic compositions La Vigne had originally composed for Claude's mother figure in this version.[99] While the

original form of La Vigne's "Déploration au Chasteau de Blois" quatrains
was essentially maintained in this edition, they were updated for the later
event.[100] In a sense, both poet and patroness experienced a common fate at
the hands of a savvy, exploitative publisher, for La Vigne's authorship of
these works goes unacknowledged as does the subject of his personal words.
Claude of France's replacement of her mother as both duchess of Brittany
and, a year after Anne's death, as queen of France through her marriage to
Francis I, crowned king in January 1515, greatly facilitated the publisher's
task of recycling the rondeaux originally written by La Vigne about Anne
of Brittany. On the one hand, La Vigne's personalized words for and about
the French queen are reemployed to mourn Claude's death in a gesture of
reappropriation that implicitly depersonalizes both mother and daughter
through a lack of individualized distinction. It is possible that economic
imperatives overrode literary propriety and the respect due the two queens,
especially Claude of France—although many of the readers would never
have known about this reappropriation. On the other hand, the integration
of Anne of Brittany's specially crafted verses with those celebrating Claude
had the effect of "keeping it all in the family."

Thus, through a posthumous reincarnation of La Vigne's poems,
sixteenth-century publishers, ever-ready to exploit existing material to trim
production costs, recycled several of La Vigne's rondeaux-epitaphs for Anne
of Brittany to commemorate the death of her daughter, Queen Claude of
France, in 1524. As disembodied cultural artifacts detached once again from
their original mode of presentation—this time without the sanction of their
now deceased author—revised, and reused, they had come to acquire their
own destiny. That the death of two maternally related queens twenty years
apart could be eulogized in nearly identical terms suggests that, in the minds
of certain editors at least, these women too had become interchangeable to-
kens; their prestige as queens derived less from function than from symbolic
representation.

But Claude does get her due, at least to a limited degree. For, along
with the two rondeaux printed in the 4-folio edition (BnF Rés. Ye 1432)
that do not appear to have been written by La Vigne, "Au hault climat"
(fol. 2r) and "Au departir" (fol. 5r), three other unanimous works, "Cyté de
Blays" (fol. 2v), "Devotion" (fols. 2v–3r), and "O royne Claude" (fol. 3r),
are also included in the Versailles collection and were doubtless redacted
after Claude's death in 1524. This is clearly the case for the rondeau "O

royne Claude."[101] Nevertheless, these more generic-type poems offer less intimate portraits of Claude than those La Vigne had provided of Anne of Brittany.

However, the anonymous poet or poets of the verses written on the occasion of Claude's death also composed a series of more personalized quatrains entitled "Salmandre, plore ta doulce hermine" (fol. 4r), which appeal in turn to Francis I, Esther, "Michol," Abigail, the Virgin Mary, and Judith to mourn Claude's death. The famous-women *topos* thus reappears to commemorate the loss of France's queen, although the females invoked here hail uniquely from the biblical rather than classical tradition. In a gesture that recalls the miniature illustrating Claude's earlier analogy with many of these women at the time of her 1517 Parisian entry (see Chapter 1), these verses associate her with Esther's wisdom, Abigail's justice and pursuit of the three Theological Virtues, and Judith's chastity; the grief surrounding Claude's death is impressively likened to the sorrow felt upon the Virgin's death.

Two additional tributes to Claude of France merit mention. One of Bouchet's first "épigrammes," was an epitaph dedicated to Claude of France, described by Britnell as "indistinguishable from a whole series that Bouchet had previously called *épitaphes* (54–55):

Cy dessoubz gist dame Claude de France
Fille de roy, de roy femme et espouse,
Qui surmonta de tous vices l'oultrance
Et triumpha par vertuz, où se expouse
L'ame est en ciel, le corps icy repouse;
On n'a poinct sceu que offense fist mortelle,
Et deceda, laissant lignée belle,
On moys juillet mil cinq cens vingt et quatre.
Prions tous Dieu que la sienne sequelle
Puisse tousjours ses ennemys combatre.


[Here lies Lady Claude of France, daughter of a king, wife and
spouse of a king, who overcame the violence of all vices and
triumphed through virtues wherever she was exposed. Her soul
is in heaven, her body lies here in state. No one knew any mortal
offense she made, and she died, leaving a beautiful lineage, in the

month of July 1524. Let us pray to God that her surviving heirs
might always fight her enemies.]

He also wrote the following epigram in Claude's memory:[102]

Fille je suys de Loÿs Roy Francique,
Qui espousay Françoys son successeur:
Claude est mon nom, qui par don deifique
Eu de ce Roy de France magnifique
Trois filz vivans, de noblesse la fleur.
Qui est en France ung tresbon, et grand heur
Fort desiré, dont je suis honnorée:
D'humilité je mouruz decorée:
Mon coeur n'avoys aux honneurs temporelz:
Secours donnoys quand j'estoys implorée:
Pour ma doulceur fuz à ma mort plorée:
Maintenant suis ès plaisirs eternelz.

[I am the daughter of the French king Louis, who married his
successor, Francis: Claude is my name, and, by divine gift, I had
with this magnificent French king three living sons, the flower of
nobility, which in France is a very good, great and much desired
happiness, for which I am honored. I died decorated with humility.
I did not have my heart in temporal honors; I gave help when I
was asked to do so. Because of my sweetness, I was mourned at my
death. Now I am resting among eternal pleasures.]

Thus, although Claude's cultural and political impact as queen of France
proved to be substantially less than her mother's, her considerable success as
a child-bearer coupled with her mother-in-law's dominance at court keeping
her out of the public limelight,[103] she benefited after her death from what
had become conventional modes of mourning royal women. In fact, praise
of Claude's progeny contrasts sharply with Bouchet's depiction of Anne's offspring. However, these printed testimonials to Claude of France offered far
less powerful eulogies of the French queen than those written by Anne of
Brittany's court protégés, in particular, Pierre Choque's eyewitness narrative
of the five-week commemoration of Anne of Brittany following her death in

January 1514, the *Commémoration de la mort de madame Anne . . . Royne de France*, to which I now return.

## Pierre Choque's *Commémoration de la mort de madame Anne . . . Royne de France*: Images of the Queen in Death

Besides financing and presumably playing some role in the organization of the elaborate funeral ceremonies in Anne of Brittany's honor, Louis XII apparently commissioned Pierre Choque to pen an account of the obsequies in which the latter participated. That he commissioned multiple copies of the work is especially noteworthy.[104] Such an action on the king's part is not surprising, given his own savvy exploitation of the public relations machine by this point in time for his own political ends. Nonetheless, it was a pioneering decision by Louis. Indeed, the hybrid system of reproduction and dissemination adopted for Anne of Brittany's funeral records brilliantly imitated and rivaled the new print technology.

As was the case during Anne of Brittany's Parisian entries following her coronation, court females figured centrally in the processional that wended its way from Blois to Saint-Denis and then back to Nantes for the deposition of Anne of Brittany's heart in her native duchy. That is, women were specially associated with the court's mourning protocol. For example, Choque comments on the order and rank of court ladies around Anne's bier (30), and in the procession from the chateau to the church in Blois (47–48), and through Paris (75–76). Mention is likewise made of the continued presence of women, along with the religious figures, holding vigil day and night over the queen's body (35). And in a rondeau posted in the Church of the Carmelites in Nantes at the time of the ceremony of the burial of Anne's heart, Choque calls on noble women to mourn the French queen: "notables gentilz femmes, / Dedans vos cueurs, pour gloire, laz et fames, / Portez ce mot que en pleurant vous assigne, / Deul à jamais" [notable noble women, bear in your hearts this word for glory, praise, and fame that in weeping I assign to you perpetual mourning].

What is more unusual, however, is the fact that some thirty "relatives, nobles and major court dignitaries,"[105] many of them women, received an illustrated manuscript copy of Choque's account of the queen's funeral.[106] Nearly all extant copies contain a personalized dedication, followed by an illustrated version of Choque's record of the ceremonies surrounding the queen's death. Just as the manuscript of Anne of Brittany's 1504 coronation documented and embodied performances associated with the queen's coronation and entry into Paris, so too these various copies of Choque's *Commémoration* transpose the public mourning of Anne of Brittany's death into a multilayered political and codicological drama with a personal touch. Of particular interest in this study of books for and about women is the number of Anne's female cousins and relatives who received dedication copies of this funeral commemoration of the most famous French woman of the times. As dedicatees they at once witnessed and participated in the propagation of Anne of Brittany's image after death in a decidedly French reappropriation of the famous-women *topos*.

At least ten dedications address Anne of Brittany's female relatives, including her daughter Claude of France; her cousins Philippa of Guelders, queen of Sicily;[107] Louise of Coëtivy, countess of Taillebourg; Renée of Bourbon, abbess of Fontevrault; Françoise of Albret, countess of Nevers;[108] Marie of Luxembourg, countess of Vendôme;[109] an unidentified lady from the House of Bourbon, and Catherine of Aragon, queen of England and wife of Henry VIII (or Margaret of Scotland);[110] and her royal *parentes*, Louise of Savoy, and Catherine of Foix, queen of Navarre.[111] These names doubtless figured among the famous women of Anne's time, and some may have comprised part of her entourage who often appeared by her side in dedication miniatures. Pierre Choque repeatedly recycles verses in these poems to the extent that every dedication—except that for Claude of France—shares at least two lines with one or more other dedicatory poems. For example, the dedications to Louise of Savoy and Catherine of Foix differ only in their first few verses (vv. 1–4 for Louise, vv. 1–2 for Catherine), which, by virtue of their individualized salutations, are strategically designed as personalized addresses.

Offering insight into the various modes of audience reception of his book, Choque also introduces into his dedications comments about the reading, hearing, and/or viewing of the individual manuscript books, each of which bears up to 11 miniatures that depict the staging of Anne's body and processions through France.[112] In three instances, the author alludes to his expectation that his female dedicatee will *read* his prose account (my emphasis):

*Prestés voz yeulx a faire ysy lecture,*
Ou veoir pourrés, soubz piteuse figure,

Comme la mort en tristesse et doulleur
Print et rauit la grant royne d'honneur.[113]

[*Prepare your eyes to make this reading*, where you will be able to see,
by way of piteous representation, how death in sadness and grief
took and ravished the great queen of honor.]

*Ouurez voz yeulx, faictez sy lecture,*
Ou veoir pourrez soubz piteuse figure
Comme celle mort en tristesse et doulleur
Prinst et rauyt la grant royne d'honneur.[114]

[*Open your eyes, read here*, where you will see, through piteous
image, how this death in sadness and grief took and ravished the
great queen of honor.]

However, in most other verses, Choque urges his female dedicatee to *listen to*
(*ouez*) the details of Anne's funeral, while he suggests, without making reference to the activity of reading, that they will be able to "see" how death took
their queen (my emphasis):

*Ouez* le grant pitié, fraieur et piteuse journee,
Et comme la mort dangereuse
A de ce monde la grant royne duchesse ostee.
Ycy dedans *verrés* la grant dolleance
Et le[s] regrectz de la grant royne de France.[115]

[*Hear [about]* the great pity, fear and piteous day, and how
dangerous death removed from this world the great queen-duchess.
Here *you will see* the great grief and mourning for the great queen
of France.]

While the absence of any mention of reading in most of these verses may be
related more to the exigencies of versification than to an individual's level of
literacy, we are nevertheless provided insight here into the multidimensional
reading practices of noble women and men at this time.[116] That is, Choque's
references to "seeing" doubtless refer to the expectation that some dedicatees
will view the miniatures as they read or hear the work read to them.[117] These

implicit analogies with the real-time viewing of events reinforce the idea that these are truly "books in performance." In fact, in his actual account Choque mentions three times how his audience will "hear" his text, while only once, in the appended description of the burial of Anne of Brittany's heart in Nantes, does he mention readers (91).[118] Reference is repeatedly made to the "seeing," or "viewing," of the miniatures portraying the events he describes.

Whereas all dedications include references either to Death's ignoble abduction of the queen and/or the grievous mourning over the queen's demise, Choque also takes the opportunity to comment on Anne of Brittany's renown, both before and after death.[119] In this sense, the queen's herald adopts the literary conventions of his contemporaries:

> Mais si la mort a deffaict
> Son noble corps, qui tant fut honnorable,
> La renommee en sera parmanable
> A tousiours mais entre seigneurs et dames. (BnF ffr. 23936, Arsenal
>    5224)[120]

[But if death defeated her noble body, which was so honorable, her renown will remain forever permanent among lords and ladies.]

While Choque launches each dedication with a personalized address to his dedicatee, identifying her relationship to the deceased queen, he closes each stanza in symmetric fashion by announcing his own association with the queen—naming himself on at least three occasions.[121] The chronicler thereby ensures that his identity as Anne of Brittany's herald will be forever remembered and linked to the queen's memory.

Thus, all the dedicatory verses feature essentially the same details, even though each stanza has a different rhyme scheme and number of verses.[122] However, Claude of France's commemoration book stands apart from the others in a number of ways. Although the shortest dedication, hers is the most elaborately arranged on the page: it is transcribed in two columns, with an illustrated capital letter initiating every verse. As the daughter of a king, queen, and duchess, her prestigious position is thus highlighted visually and verbally, unlike that of the other dedicatees:

> Fille de roy, de royne et de duchesse,
> Ce piteulx liure en ceste heure presente,

Comme a ma dame et ma seulle princesse,
Treshumblement de bon cueur vous presente.
Voir y pourrez soubz figure aparente,
L'obseque, helas, le gros train, l'ordre amere,
L'enterrement et la mort trop dolente,
De la royne duchesse, vostre mere. (BnF ffr. 25158)

[Daughter of a king, queen and duchess, this piteous book in
this present hour I very humbly, with good heart, present to you,
as to my lady and my only princess. You will see in it through
remarkable representations the obseques, alas, the enormous
procession, the sorrowful organization (of mourners), the burial
and the most grievous death of the queen duchess, your mother.]

Unlike all the other dedications, it is in the first half, rather than at the end, of the stanza that Choque underscores his relationship with his dedicatee. His allusions to Claude as "my lady and my only princess," without mention of his own position as Anne's (former) herald, may constitute a subtle appeal to Claude for support. The second part of the stanza focuses uniquely on Choque's reconstitution in verbal terms of all the stages of Anne of Brittany's funeral that Claude will "see." Most poignant is the last deferred verse that finally mentions the dedicatee's own relationship to the deceased; the word "mere," rhyming with "amere" [bitter] in verse 6, dramatically punctuates the poem as the last word.

Also unique to Claude's book is the appearance on the same folio (3v) of a dedication miniature, positioned above Choque's verse dedication. This illustration replaces the image of the queen's arms and insignia that decorates the first folio of all other commemoration books, at least those with dedicatory verses.[123] In the dedication scene (Figure 43), Claude sits at the left in a gold decorated throne-like chair that is quite large, such that it accentuates her small size as does the fact that her feet rest on a gold and black brocade pillow, instead of the floor. Such a disproportionate display is likely meant to depict the relative youth of Claude, who was thirteen years old at the time of her mother's death. That Claude is not crowned in this illustration suggests that it was completed before she became queen of France in January 1515.[124] Claude's black, nun-like apparel, like that of other women featured in the miniature, is appropriate attire for the mourning of her mother's death. With her left hand, Claude reaches out

R ille de roy de royne et de duchesse          V oir pourtez fonds figure apte
C e piteulx liure en ceste heure pnte         obseq lxl as legros tant lord e amere
E ôme amadame a ma seulle pncesse             eterement et lamort trop dolete
T reshublemêt de bon cueur vo' pnte           e la royne duchesse vre mere

43. Pierre Choque, *Commémoration de la mort madame Anne . . . Royne de France*, Paris, BnF ffr. 25158, fol. 3v: Dedication of the book by Choque to Claude of France. Bibliothèque Nationale de France.

to take from Choque the black-covered book, which figures at the center of the image.[125]

In the center background of the miniature stand five other women, likely from Anne of Brittany's (or Claude's) court entourage, dressed exactly like Claude, and, displaying "talking hands," appear to be in conversation. Two men in black also stand behind these women. Kneeling before Claude, Choque is dressed in black and folded over his left forearm is a shift, or "cotte," bearing the coat of arms of Anne of Brittany. Behind Choque stand two other herald figures similarly dressed.[126] As in the subsequent miniatures, we are offered a visual testimonial to the mourning customs of the day.

To Claude's right, in the left foreground, sits another female dressed in exactly the same attire. It is unclear who this person represents. Louise of Savoy? Anne of France? Claude's tutor? Most mysterious is the identification of the young girl to Claude's left, seated in a smaller chair facing her. She stands out in the illustration as the only figure not dressed in mourning clothes, which would presumably be inappropriate even for Claude's three-and-a-half-year-old sister Renée. Indeed, this girl wears a more colorful outfit: a red Breton cap with white trim, a blue dress with black square collar, black fur cuffs, and a gold belt. This unusual figure may represent "Anne of Brittany in life," whose virtues will be passed down to her daughter Claude.[127]

The dynamics of Claude's *Commémoration* book are decidedly different than those of other dedicatees, in particular that of Louise of Savoy. Even more than Claude's version, Louise's manuscript book served both as a memorial to the queen and as a testimonial to court politics. As in the other copies of Choque's account, the verbal and visual performances embodied in Louise of Savoy's manuscript book move beyond the glorification of a venerated female royal figure to an affirmation of prescriptive court behavior and its symbols. However, the dedication of BnF ms. ffr. 5094 to Louise of Savoy, Anne of Brittany's rival during the last years of her queenship, adds a unique level of tension to the dynamics of this volume that complicates what I refer to as the politics of the page.[128]

On the opening folio of ms. 5094 Louise would have discovered individualized verses Pierre Choque had addressed to her as "Dame royalle, tresexcellente princesse / D'Angoumays et d'Anjou, noble duchesse, / Mere du roy. . . . [Royal French lady, very excellent princess of Angoulême and Anjou, noble duchess, mother of the king].[129] And yet, Louise's personalized dedication appears below the arms and symbols of Anne of Brittany (Figure 44)—which figure in all other dedicatory copies—rather than those of the dedicatee herself, as one

On the banderoles: ROGO PRO TE ANNA · LIBERA EAM DEO REI LEONIS · AMAVIE

A me Royalle tresexcellente princesse
Dangoumays et danIou noble duchesse
Mere du Roy entre aultres le plus grant
Du monde entier par filtre le maieur
Prestes voz yeulx a faire ysy lecture
Ou voir povres soubz piteuse figure

44. Pierre Choque, *Commémoration de la mort madame Anne . . . Royne de France,*
Paris, BnF ffr. 5094, fol. iv: Opening folio of Louise of Savoy's copy. Bibliothèque
Nationale de France.

might have expected. This visual juxtaposition of Anne's arms, exactly as they appeared in the entrance of the Church of the Carmelites in Nantes, where Anne's heart was buried,[130] and a dedication to Louise explicitly define the relationship between the deceased subject and living recipient of the book, but implicitly invokes the notorious rivalry over royal succession between the duchess of Angoulême and the queen of France, whose death facilitated the rise to power of Louise's son, Francis I. Had Anne succeeded in giving birth to a male, he would have displaced Francis as heir to the throne. Furthermore, in an effort to ensure the independence of her duchy of Brittany, whose ermine symbols figure prominently both within and below the queen's arms displayed on the opening folio, Anne had repeatedly sought to wed her daughter, Claude, to a non-French noble, such as the future Holy Roman Emperor, Charles of Austria. However, as discussed above in greater detail (see Chapter 2), the king's desire for a domestic union prevailed, and shortly after Anne's demise, Claude and Francis were joined in marriage, leading to the eventual assimilation of Brittany into the French kingdom. The interdependence of Louise's political future and Anne's life and death are thus figuratively invoked on this first leaf of ms. 5094. In fact, echoes of the underlying tensions on the opening folio resurface throughout the commemoration book, since Louise was prominently featured in the public ceremonies commemorating Anne.

Turning from his private dedication to Louise of Savoy, Choque offers, in an opening verse *Complainte*, a theatrical prelude to his account, which figures in all the other versions of his *Commémoration* as well. Here he stages the collective mourning of the French through personified sociopolitical entities familiar to contemporaries—Nobility, Commoner ("le povre commun"), and The Church Militant, whom he calls on to mourn the deceased queen (5–6). Like his contemporaries, and like Lemaire's invented character *Rhetoricque* in the *Plainte du Désiré*, Choque recognizes the inadequacy of his words to render faithfully such a tragic event in a modesty *topos* (5). Nonetheless, he writes his account under the sign of reason:

> . . . raison m'amoneste
> D'en pourgecter quelque récit honneste,
> Non pour plaisir, mais en grant dolléance
> Pour ceste mort. . . .

> Elle nous a prins celle royne et duchesse
> Que l'on tenoit soubz vertuz singulière,

Au monde entier des dames la première,
Seulle sans per et sans compariaison,
Qu'on doibt pleurer et plaindre par raison. (5–6)

[Reason admonishes me to pour out some honest narrative, not
out of pleasure, but in great sorrow, for this death. . . . She [Death]
has taken this queen and duchess that one held to be singular in
all virtues, first of all ladies in the world, the only one without
peer and without comparisons, whom one must cry for and mourn
through reason.]

From the outset, then, Choque's verbal reconstruction of Anne of Brittany's funeral takes on the aura of an allegorical drama, reminiscent, on one
hand, of Anne of Brittany's 1492 and 1504 Parisian entry theaters and, on
the other, of the allegorical funeral poems by Lemaire, Marot and La Vigne,
examined earlier in this chapter. The real-life sociopolitical performance of
the queen's funeral ceremonies is thus rearticulated into performances at the
poetic level. This opening allegorical staging resurfaces during Choque's account of two sermons offered in Anne's name. In Blois at the Saint Saulveur
Church, the lord of Parvy, the king's confessor, preached about the carriage
of Honor surrounded by 37 virtues, one for each year of the queen's life, that
carried the queen to Paradise (51). At Notre Dame in Paris, in a gesture that
anticipated Choque's own allegorical staging, the same orator divided the
cathedral into four parts to represent the Church, Justice, the University, and
the People (80–81), upon which he elaborated.

A rather lengthy verse genealogy of Anne of Brittany (8–25), in which
Choque recalls her male and female ancestors,[131] follows Choque's allegorical
drama, and is punctuated by yet another invocation of the famous-women
*topos* that serves to confirm that in fact Anne surpassed all classical and biblical models of female virtue:

Es histoires escriptes anciennes,
Y a mencion de Judic et Hélaine,
De plusieurs dames de beaulté plaines,
De Hester, Lucresse et aussi Policyne :
Mais à parler de la royne souveraine,
Elle a passé toutes et chascune

Qui ont esté ne qui en présent règnent
Car sa pareille il n'en est nulle. (25)

[In ancient histories written down, there was mention of Judith and
Helen, of many ladies filled with beauty, of Esther, Lucretia and
also Polixena: but as far as the sovereign queen is concerned, she
has surpassed all and every single one who has been or is presently
living because no one is her equal.]

Thus, by drawing on literary tradition in multiple ways, the preliminary material in the *Commémoration* dramatically sets the stage for Choque's eyewitness account of the extraordinary funeral ceremonies surrounding Anne of
Brittany's death.

In his narrative of these mourning rituals that moved from the private
space of the queen's bedroom to increasingly larger public spaces within the
Château of Blois and beyond en route to Saint-Denis, Choque's vigilance
about court decorum surrounding how one mourns, which we examined
above, is complemented by a concern, if not downright obsession, about two
other dimensions of the public rituals: rank and order. Details concerning
the care, movement, and presentation of the body of the deceased queen are
balanced by an equal emphasis on the naming of major participants and
their exact positions in the dramatically staged performance of court officials.
Repeated expressions about the orderly fashion of the procession (46, 48, 68)
build up to a crescendo like that in the following passage (my emphasis):

Aussi *ordonna* le cappitaine messire Gabriel de la Châtre[132] nombre
d'archers de sa charge, qui estoient venuz à la conduicte et garde de
la dicte dame, tellement qu'*il n'y eut point de désordre; et celluy ordre
a esté bien gardé.*
Pour tant que l'église de Paris est moult grant et plantureuse,
*l'ordre y fut moult belle,* et chacun personnage, digne d'estre assis et
avoir *lieu et ranc,* fut mys au lieu *où il devoit estre.* (75)

[Captain Gabriel de la Châtre thereby *ordered* a number of archers
under his charge, who had come to conduct and guard the
aforementioned lady, to such a degree that *there was no disorder
whatsoever*; and *this order was well maintained.* In as much as the

church of Paris is so great and expansive, the *order* maintained
there was a sight to behold, and each person, worthy of being
seated and having his *place and rank* there, was placed *in the seat he
was supposed to occupy.*]

Choque's preoccupation with *rank* and his establishment of various meanings
of *order*—doubtless a product of his official function as the queen's herald—
all but confirm the underlying concerns in Marot's and Lemaire's works examined above that there existed a general anxiety about the court's ability
to display and control decorum in public at a time of "national" grief. But it
also reflects the real-life disorder and chaos that marked French royal funerals
since at least the time of Charles VIII's obsequies in 1498.[133] Rank in Choque's
account was marked not only through the hierarchical placement of nobles in
the various processions, but through fashion as well, with progressively longer trains distinguishing more highly ranked ladies, such as Anne of France
and Louise of Savoy, from others (36). Just like La Vigne in his manuscript
account of Anne's 1504 Parisian entry (see Chapter 1), Choque devotes folio
after folio to the identification of high-ranking court and church officials,
while listing lesser-ranked participants according to their function alone.

Thus, although the queen figured at the center of the original ceremonial
drama, the numbers and names of prominent nobles and ecclesiastics dominate the written record. Details abound about who carried the queen's body
from site to site, who held the four corners of her mourning drape or funeral
canopy, who stood to her right, left, at her feet, and nearest her, who led and
who brought up the rear of the procession, who bore the symbols of her royalty, in what configuration the procession advanced from chateau to church
in Blois, in what order the church officials presided at mass, how participants
in the Parisian entry were arranged and in what places they were seated at
Notre-Dame Cathedral. The illuminations in Louise of Savoy's copy of the
official account, and in most other copies, feature the queen surrounded by
these same nobles and royal officers, which included Louise of Savoy herself
whose presence in the Mourning Hall (36), the procession from the chateau to
the church in Blois (48), and the Paris procession (74) is duly noted.[134] Other
dedicatees, such as Mary of Luxembourg, William of Loyon, and Charles of
Bourbon, are featured in Choque's narrative and may even have been recog-
nizable in the book's miniatures.

While one miniature depicts the queen's body lying before a small assembly of household officials and religious figures in the Hall of Honor at

Blois (Figure 45), subsequent illustrations feature the substitution of her royal symbols—crown, scepter and rod of justice—for her body, as it was placed in the coffin (Figure 46). In the visual depiction of the funeral mass at Notre-Dame Cathedral in Paris (72), the public views Anne's effigy, a recreation of the queen in full regalia that Jean Perréal had painted on a gold drape covering her coffin (72–73) (Figure 47).[135] The queen's persona was thus gradually reduced to symbol and image.

The remarkable correspondence between depictions of Anne at the center of her entry into Paris and departure from the world is reinforced by a certain depersonalisation and abstraction of her image. Surrounded as she was during her funeral rites by processions of diplomats and urban officials called upon to offer homage, just as she had been during her entry ceremonials, referred to by the same titles in each account, and, reduced finally to symbols and a painted image, Anne of Brittany came to assume the role of one of the allegorical figures on the stage of her entry theaters and in the literary accounts associated with her. In contrast to the strikingly similar forms of pageantry and imagery exhibited during the entries and funerals of French kings, the symbolic representations of Queen Anne of Brittany were decidedly less momentous, for they lacked the guarantee of the real political power that sustained the ceremonial images of male monarchs,[136] for whom the transference of power was a critical issue. Whereas the ceremonial of a deceased French king had its particular vested anxieties and related rituals, given that the problem of where power was located in the period between the death of one monarch and the inauguration of the next was absolutely critical,[137] the death of a French queen did not raise the same concerns about a political power vacuum. A king could remain ruler without a queen, but a queen could not retain her position without a king. Indeed, France could not survive without a king.

Nonetheless, in making reference to the deceased monarch, Choque repeatedly speaks of "the noble queen," "the royal princess," "the noble queen and duchess, our sovereign lady and mistress"[138] to such an extent that Anne of Brittany is given a "life" that all but resembles descriptions of her person in the 1504 royal entry.[139] The ambiguity of the following description is a case in point: "Le lendemain, qui fut le vendredi, ariva la royale princesse en sa conté et ville d'Estampes, où moult estoit aymée, et bien le monstrèrent à sa réception" [The next day, which was Friday, the royal princess arrived in her county and city of Étampes, where she was well beloved, and [the townspeople] demonstrated this clearly through their reception of her] (62).[140] The queen's lifelike presence

45. Pierre Choque, *Commémoration de la mort madame Anne . . . Royne de France*, Paris, BnF ffr. 5094, fol. 12v: The queen's body lying in state before a small assembly of household officials and religious figures in the Hall of Honor in the Château of Blois. Bibliothèque Nationale de France. ·

46. Pierre Choque, *Commémoration de la mort madame Anne . . . Royne de France*,
Paris, BnF ffr. 5094, 16v: Substitution of the queen's royal symbols—crown, scepter,
and rod of justice—for her body, after its placement into coffin. Bibliothèque
Nationale de France.

47. Pierre Choque, *Commémoration de la mort madame Anne. . . Royne de France*, Paris, BnF ffr. 5094, 42v: The funeral mass at Notre Dame Cathedral in Paris, with Anne of Brittany's effigy. Bibliothèque Nationale de France.

after death is intensified through a detailed description of the clothing she wore when displayed in the Hall of Honor (29), reminiscent of assessments of her attire during her entries into Paris, mention of the fact that she was served all meals until her burial (65–66),[141] and Choque's own personal comments that "it seemed as if she had only fainted or was just sleeping" (29).

How does Choque stage himself in his dramatic recreation of Anne of Brittany's funeral *spectacle*? On the one hand, he briefly adopts a first-person stance in his introductory material when, in a mode similar to La Vigne's, he calls upon all classes to mourn Anne's death and invokes the prayers of his own compatriots, the heralds, to whom he offers special tribute (7), before placing himself and his own suicidal grief on stage:

Moy avec vous n'ay cause de me taire,
Mais tout ainsi comme homme solitaire,
N'ayant de vivre au monde plus d'envye,
En gémissant veulx consommer ma vye. (7)[142]

[I too, like yourselves, have no reason to remain silent, but just like a lonely man, without desire to live any longer, groaning, I wish to end my life.]

On the other hand, Choque employs the more distant third person in describing all those events in which he directly participated. That is, he plays not only an eye-witness function, for as the queen's principal herald, he is positioned nearest the queen's body during processions (71). In addition, it is he who, after pronouncing the queen dead three times, places the hand of justice, scepter, and crown on Anne of Brittany's grave at Saint-Denis (85–86) (Figure 48); it is Bretagne who, tossing his coat of arms into her grave, most piteously cries out a versified prayer for the salvation of the queen's soul (87); and it is Bretagne's announcement in the banquet hall following her burial that ends the funeral ceremonies (89). As herald, Choque/Bretagne plays a similar role during the burial of Anne's heart in Nantes in March 1514.

Whereas the location and actions of Choque himself as well as high-ranking aristocrats and church officials are duly memorialized in the written record and often reproduced in the miniatures, middle-class French spectators are treated more abstractly both in the written and illustrated account. The principal towns and cities through which the funeral procession passed as it

48. *Le Trespas de l'Hermine Regretee*, Paris, Musée du Petit Palais, Collection Dutuit ms. 665, fol. 36v: Pierre Choque about to place Anne of Brittany's crown in her grave at Saint-Denis. Stéphane Piera / Petit Palais / Roger-Viollet.

advanced to Paris and then Saint-Denis essentially functioned as emblems or allegories. Municipal coats of arms visually displayed on city streets during the funeral find their way into the margins of the books of Louise of Savoy and other dedicatees.[143] Furthermore, 4-line poems displayed as public notices at prominent locations along the funeral route, either at municipal gates or on church doors, were also inserted in distinctive fashion in the various manuscript copies of Choque's record.[144] These quatrains called upon the town or city to mourn collectively for the queen. It was as if the funeral procession, upon entering the city gates or church portals, spoke in one voice, inviting the municipality, usually by addressing it in the familiar "tu" form,[145] to grieve publicly. Examples such as the following illustrate this theatrical dynamic:

O Artenay, pauvre petit village,
Viens en grand deul auec nous déplourer
La grant royne que tu verras plourer
Plus de mille ans au moins, si tu viz l'aage. (60–61)

Estampes, las! sans à jamais te faindre,
La magnanime et royalle duchesse,
De ton enclos souveraine contesse,
En grand doulleur tu doibz pleurer et plaindre. (64–65)

A ceste foyz, Nostre-Dame-des-Champs,
Prenez pitié de vostre humble servante,
Dont tout le monde en pensée fervante,
Par mort cruelle escript de piteulx chantz. (67)

[Oh Arthenay, poor little village, come mourn with us in deep grief the great queen who will be lamented for more than a thousand years, if you live until then. . . . Estampes, alas, with great sadness you must cry and mourn, without ever feigning, the magnanimous and royal duchess, sovereign countess of your town. . . . In this faith, Nostre-Dame-des-Champs, take pity on your humble servant for whom the entire world in fervant thought composes piteous songs about cruel death.]

The real-life verbal and visual urban drama of the original events thus retains its performative character in Louise of Savoy's manuscript book, as it does in the copies of other book recipients:[146] towns are personified in verse as protagonists, manuscript margins are decorated with municipal coats of arms, and miniatures, marking the transition from royal body to royal symbol to royal effigy, reflect the role of court nobles, such as Louise herself, and trace the evolving political iconography of the queen and of controlled court behavior in this cultural rite of passage. The interplay of text and image both on city streets during the funeral ceremonies and in the funeral book copies is strikingly similar, suggesting that the real-life rituals were themselves "books in performance."

The insertion into Choque's work of other poetic epitaphs composed by La Vigne is yet another example of the transposition of city dramas from the original to the recorded obsequies of the queen and the personification of space and object. In the *Déploration au Chasteau de Blois* (41–42), as we learned above, the poet transforms the queen's living quarters into more publicly accessible spaces for the reader as he creatively humanizes the queen's favorite *lieux* by converting them into spatial abstractions that mourn their emptiness. In the *Rondeau de l'Esprit et du Cueur du Roy sur le Trespas de la Royne* (39–40), La Vigne gives utterance to a private experience through personification of the king's emotional devastation upon the death of Anne, expounding the moral lesson that grief must come under the sway of Reason (see above). La Vigne's rondeau thus dovetails well with the underlying didacticism of Choque's prose account, with both authors emphasizing controlled courtly conduct. As publicly posted invocations and a final funeral offering interred with his deceased patron,[147] La Vigne's poems played an integral part in the theatrical dynamic surrounding the public mourning of Anne's death, which embraced the use of texts and images much like personalized funeral books, such as Louise of Savoy's. In their reincarnation in ms. 5094 and other commemoration books, however, La Vigne's epitaphs came to serve a more private function as individual prayers of mourning for all the dedicatees, whose singular voices would presumably have replaced the personified "I" of the funeral procession. Thanks in no small part to the incorporation of La Vigne's verses into the official account, Choque's *Commémoration* shifts back and forth between the private and public domains, perhaps in a deliberate mimetic effort to reproduce the tensions at work during the funeral rites themselves.

As recipient and reader of ms. 5094, Louise of Savoy was probably positively reminded of her prominent role in French royal dramatics as well, although, always figured in relationship to Anne of Brittany, she never quite took center stage, as had her rival in life and death. Nevertheless, through her son's ascension to the throne and her direct engagement in French internal affairs as regent and advisor, Louise of Savoy succeeded in reconstructing a role for herself in the royal spotlight. Even as the memory of the complex links and tensions that tied her with Anne of Brittany was kept alive in manuscript 5094, Louise found ways to reshape that image both in her own commissioned works and on France's political stage, as many scholars have shown.[148]

## Court Competition and Rivalry After Anne of Brittany's Death

While printed accounts of the queen's royal entries and funeral rites did not result in the same level of performance that we find in the illustrated manuscripts dedicated to Claude of France, Louise of Savoy and other court figures, these alternate versions nevertheless embody signs of other kinds of textual tensions. The poems La Vigne had composed upon Anne of Brittany's death are a case in point. Besides figuring publicly in the queen's funeral rituals and textually in Pierre Choque's manuscript accounts, La Vigne's poems were, as I noted above, also published separately for more popular consumption in the *Épitaphes en rondeaux*. The advertisement of the author's name on the title page, along with his professional association with the deceased queen, assured that La Vigne would be properly identified with his works. Given the heightened defensiveness of writers of his day about issues of authorship, this announcement—and the publication itself—may well have been a conscious reaction on the part of La Vigne to Choque's failure to carefully identify all his verses that had been inserted into his *Commémoration*, including Choque's failure to mention or include the poem La Vigne had dramatically placed in the queen's coffin.[149]

In fact there may have been a conflict of interest, that is, a tension between La Vigne and Choque as competing court officials. For at the very moment that La Vigne likely placed his poem on Anne's tombstone, the herald Bretagne himself took center stage—as his account and at least one miniature suggest (Figure 48). Taking off his coat of arms, Bretagne publicly pronounced his own versified prayer before placing it in the grave (86–87):

Veoiés cy la cotte d'armes triumphante,
Les armes et intersigne de noblesse

De la très crestienne royne et duchesse,
Nostre souveraine dame et maistresse,
Que je porte soubz cette lame :
Priez Dieu qu'il ait mercy de son ame. (87)

[See here the triumphant coat of arms, the arms and sign of
nobility of the most Christian queen and duchess, our sovereign
lady and mistress, that I place beneath this gravestone: pray that
God have mercy on her soul].

Throughout the account, we have witnessed Choque's ability as eye-witness and chronicler, recounting events in prose, as a participant describing his own prominent actions and also as a poet who versified sections of his narrative as well. Moreover, at the ceremonies surrounding the burial of Anne's heart in Nantes, we learn of the staging of rondeaux and epitaphs, reminiscent of those posted along the funeral route from Blois to Saint-Denis, for Choque recounts that poems were posted on the four pillars of the royal "chappelle ardant" inside the Church of the Carmelites (102). While these are announced in anonymous fashion, one rondeau suggests that Choque may have authored the verses, and thus the other poems as well, as he once again places the arms of Brittany he has been wearing into the grave:

                              Rondeau
     Deul à jamais pour la royne des dames,
     L'honneur des bons, le confort des gendarmes,
     Des vertueulx le trésor et la myne,
     De tous avoir; et puys que mort la myne
     Plaindre on doit, de corps, de cueurs et d'ames.
     Pareillement, notables gentilz femmes,
     Dedans vos cueurs, pour gloire, laz et fames,
     Portez ce mot que en pleurant vous assigne,
                    Deul à jamais.

     Et moy, voyant ces douloureulx vacarmes,
     En sa fosse gecte ma cothe d'armes,
     Des fleur[s] de lys le royal intersigne
     Et le blason[150] de la tant noble hermyne,

Dont porteray pendant aux yeulx les larmes:
        Deul à jamais. (103–4)

[Eternal grief for the queen of ladies, the honor of the good, the
support of the police, the treasure and mine of the virtuous, the
richness of everyone; and since death undermines her we must
lament, with body, heart and soul. The same must be done, notable
noble women, in your hearts, for glory, posterity and fame, carry
these works that I assign to you in weeping, eternal grief. And I,
seeing this dolorous commotion, into the grave I toss my coat of
arms, the royal symbol of the fleurs de lys, and the arms/poem in
praise of the most noble ermine, for whom I will carry with tears
flowing from my eyes, eternal grief.]

Thus, Choque's officiating role at the burial of Anne of Brittany's body
at Saint-Denis had the effect, at least in his own account, of eclipsing La
Vigne's moving poetic tribute that he placed in the queen's grave at the time
of her burial. In the same way, Choque's presence and actions must have
upstaged the absent La Vigne at Nantes, for the burial of the French queen's
heart. These and other measures taken by Anne's herald were also visually
and verbally highlighted in the many copies of the *Commémoration*, whose
organization and presentation were doubtless supervised by Choque himself.
La Vigne was, therefore, likely forced to choose an alternative mode of advertising his work. The separate publication of his epitaphs in Anne's name,
reproduced in a less elaborate, less expensive format, certainly set the record
straight about his contributions to Anne's life and death for a broader, more
anonymous public. In the end, the context and presentation of the manuscript and printed versions of André de la Vigne's poetry functioned to maintain a separation between ranks in the French kingdom.

In his final act concerning Anne of Brittany's death, Pierre Choque perpetuated the implicit poetic competition running throughout his *Commémoration* by ending his work with an epitaph in the voice of Anne of Brittany.
Curiously, he himself did not author these verses, but rather, as controlling
organizer of his manuscript account, selected it to place on her tomb through
an informal poetic competition six months after the queen's death. The reader
learns the identity of the "judge"—Choque himself—but not that of the
prize-winning poet:

Le jeudi, premier jour de juing l'an mil cinq cens quatorze, moy
estant à Sainct-Denys en France, avec mes compaignons d'office,
sur la tumbe et représentation de ma souveraine dame, après avoir
veu et leu plusieurs épitaphes, en latin et en françoys, fait en haulx
et subtilz termes, coppie et escrips celle qui s'ensuit. (113–14)

[On Thursday, the first day of June 1514, being at Saint-Denis
in France with my fellow heralds, on the tomb and statue of my
sovereign lady, after having seen and read several epitaphs, in Latin
and in French, written in noble and subtle language, I copied and
wrote down the one that follows].

Anne, qui fuz de Bloiz transmise morte ici,
De Françoys, duc dernier de Bretaigne je issy;
Après la mort duquel, en mon unziesme année,
Par Charles, roy gaulloys, me fut guerre menée,                    4
Que aucuns mes subgectz et hardis estrangers
Soustindrent soubs mon nom par périleux dangers.
Mais quant eusmes troys ans l'exploit d'elle senty,
Il me requist à femme et je m'y consenty.                          8
Combien que l'Empereur me fist dire et savoir
Que pour chère compaigne il désiroit m'avoir.
Avecques Charles eut troys enffans que mort print,
Puys à vingt et huit ans luy mesmes le surprint.                   12
De France regrectée après je départy,
Ayant vingt et ung ans. Lors de second party
Loys, son successeur, me pria par instance,
Dont fuz, grâces à Dieu, deux foys royne de France,                16
Juste et loyal me fut, et telle je luy fus;
Et ou temps de seize ans, quatre beaulx enfans eus,
Des quelz moururent deux, et deux filles resta,
Quant le benoit Sauveur de ce monde m'osta,                        20
Qui fut mil cinq cenz treze, en janvier, le neufiesme,
N'ayant encore actaint mon an trente-septieseme;
Dont Françoys et Bretons receurent perte égalle,
Car ma main à tous deux fut tousjours libéralle,                   24
Et à eulx et à tous fus cordialle tant
Qu'onques homme de moy ne partit malcontant.

Aussi de mon douaire de duché joissoye,
Par quoy biens à plante je leur eslargissoye.                    28
Si les prye et requiers de faire à Dieu prière
Qu'il mecte ma pauvre âme en céleste lumyère. (113–14)

[I, Anne, who was transferred dead from Blois to this place, from
Francis, the last duke of Brittany issued forth; after whose death, in
my eleventh year, by Charles, French king, I was led to war, which
many of my subjects and bold foreigners sustained in my name
through perilous dangers. But when we had felt its abuse for three
years, he asked me to be his wife and I agreed to that, even though
the Emperor had me say and acknowledge that he wished to have
me as his dear companion. With Charles there were three children
that death took, then at the age of 28 [death] surprised him
himself. Afterward I left France with regret, at 21 years old. Then
in a second stage Louis, his successor, urged me to marry him,
with whom, thanks to God, I was twice queen of France. He was
just and loyal to me, and I to him. And over the period of 16 years,
I had four beautiful children, two of whom died, and two girls
survived. When the blessed Savior took me from this world, which
occurred on January 9th 1513 [o. st.], before I had yet reached the
age of 37, both French and Bretons experienced the same loss, for
my hand had always been generous to both and to them and to all
I was so cordial that never did anyone leave me discontented. I also
enjoyed my dowry as duchess, through which I greatly increased
my support to them. And so I pray and request them to pray to
God that he place my poor soul in heavenly light.]

Presumably given voice by a male author, Anne identifies herself in the epitaph first and foremost through the men in her life, her father and (three)
husbands. Unlike Bouchet's and Marot's epitaphs examined above, mention
is made of her marriage by proxy to Maximilian and the war with Charles
VIII preceding his marriage to Anne merits three lines. It is not surprising
that Anne's function as a child-bearer is what ultimately defines her here, as
elsewhere. Although she focuses on the death of three children with Charles
and two with Louis XII (vv. 18–19) as in Bouchet's epitaph, the queen is grammatically portrayed as less responsible for their deaths in this epitaph: Death
took two of them, two others died. The survival of two of her offspring and

the mutual loyalty with her second husband counterbalanced the tragic loss of her children (vv. 17, 19). But what is notable and contrasts with the funeral poems discussed above, is the fact that Anne expounds at length at the end of this epitaph about how her economic independence, thanks to her duchess dowry, allowed her to offer equally generous treatment and support of both Bretons and French, who, in turn, supported her (vv. 24–28). Choque, then, wisely selected this epitaph, written perhaps from a Breton perspective, since the deceased queen invokes the people of Brittany and France and seeks out their prayers for her salvation. In addition, this succinct portrayal depicts in the most positive manner the dependent and independent profiles of the queen of France and duchess of Brittany.

In the end, Anne—and by proxy her daughter Claude of France—earned extensive praise and glorification in (near)death as much as she had during her lifetime in both live "performances" and textual and pictorial souvenirs of those performances. These final tributes to the queen essentially provide a microcosm of the various textual and visual accolades of her that inspired the books that she and her female contemporaries commissioned and received. Indeed, the *spectacle* of the queen's funeral ceremonials as recaptured by Pierre Choque distinctly echoes the *spectacle* of her royal entries, especially the 1504 ceremonies encapsulated by André de la Vigne and the Master of the *Chronique scandaleuse* on the manuscript folios of Waddesdon Manor ms. 22, as we learned in Chapter 1. The poems written upon Anne of Brittany's (near) death, the funeral processions and their illuminated accounts remind us as well of the inextricable connection between female personification allegory, Cardinal and Theological Virtues, and the praise (but also critique) of women that figured at the center of my investigation in Chapter 2. Likewise, the acclaim Anne repeatedly received in death continued to integrate comparative images of famous women—that is, virtuous ones—with tributes to the French queen, just as earlier acquired books featured Anne and her female cohorts in equally honorable standing, as Chapters 3 and 4 explored. Absent in the distinction accorded Anne in death, however, doubtless out of respect for the gravity of the moment, were the overt and less overt tensions associated with the "famous women" debates at court between males and females. Although appearing as almost incidental comments in the prologues addressed to her and other women of rank, these allusions confirm that the *Querelle des femmes* was still a lively topic of discussion, at least at the French court, in the late fifteenth and early sixteenth centuries. The mourning that characterized many of the famous and infamous ladies who figured in these debates, in particular Ovid's *heroides*, and that attracted the interest of Anne and her entourage, resulted in the literary and artistic depiction of the French queen (and of Louise of Savoy) as an Ovidian heroine, as Chapter 4 confirmed. But these women in mourning developed all too soon into the literary and visual expression of the deep-felt grief occasioned by the French queen's unexpected death in 1514. Offered up by nearly all of her court protégés in more or less obvious states of competition, these commemorative pieces not only shed light on the fascinating attempts to control the culture of male and female mourning but also set the stage for a recycled salute to a subsequent French queen, Anne's daughter Claude of France.

In these multiple ways, the books associated with Anne of Brittany and many of her female contemporaries that I have discussed throughout this investigation have proved to be extremely valuable sociopolitical, literary, and cultural documents for assessing the dynamics of the power of females of rank in late fifteenth- and early sixteenth-century France. Clearly wielding authority through the financial muscle of her duchess dowry, Anne of Brittany, one of the most generous patrons of her time, was in a position to exploit her role as artistic benefactor, as were other women of rank such as Anne of France, Louise of Savoy, and Margaret of Austria. But just as those male writers and artists that they supported depended on their female patrons for their very livelihood, so too these noble women implicitly depended on their court poets for the more or less successful fashioning and dissemination of their image, both during their lifetime and after death. In numerous instances, the textual and visual representations of Anne and her female cohorts examined above are revealing images, because they bear witness to underlying cultural contradictions at work in the design and propagation of female power, contradictions that these women of power themselves doubtless promulgated, consciously or unconsciously. The woman of rank, her writers and artists, and her entourage at court—in the roles of commissioner, bookmaker, disseminator and audience—thus collaborated in the creation of "books in performance" that provided contemporary and future generations with a deeper understanding of how the "politics of the page" played out in France in the late fifteenth and early sixteenth centuries.

# APPENDIX. MANUSCRIPT AND PRINTED BOOKS ASSOCIATED WITH ANNE OF BRITTANY

Titles in bold are printed editions; all others are manuscripts. Asterisks indicate works I have examined. Abbreviations refer to the following authors: EQB = E. Quentin-Bauchart, *Les Femmes bibliophiles de France*, II, 374–82; LD = L. Delisle, *Le Cabinet des manuscrits de la Bibliothèque Impériale*, I, 124–25; MJ = M. Jones, "Les Manuscrits d'Anne de Bretagne"; MBW = M. B. Winn, *Anthoine Vérard*; PT = P. Thibault, *Les Manuscrits de la collection d'Anne de Bretagne*.

## Religious and Moralistic Works

*\*Tres petites heures* (c. 1498)[1]—Paris, BnF, nouv. acq. latin 3120 (MJ1, PT 12)

\*Robert du Herlin, *L'Acort des mesdisans et bien disans*—Paris, Arsenal, ms. 3658 (13 December 1493) (MJ3, PT 18–20): Dedication to Anne of Brittany

\*Prayerbook for Anne of Brittany/Charles-Orland (1492–95)—New York, Pierpont Morgan Library, M 50 (LD1?, MJ6? PT 14–15)

Lamentation (single leaf) (1492–98)—Philadelphia, Free Library, Lewis E M 11:15A (MJ33)[2]

**\*Robert de Saint Martin, *Le Trésor de l'âme*—Paris: for Vérard, c. 1497 (EQB 380, PT 9, MBW 134–37)**

*\*Heures d'Anne de Bretagne* (c. 1498)—Nantes, Médiathèque, Ms. 18 (EQB 375–77, MJ2, PT 10)

Book of Hours (Latin) (after 1499)—Edinburgh University Library, Ms. Laing 15[3]

Prayerbook for Anne of Brittany (after 1499)—Chicago, Newberry Library, Ms. 83

\*Olivier Le Rouyer, *Traité de l'Eglise, de ses ministres et de la messe* (before 17 July 1505)—Chantilly, Musée Condé, ms. 159 (MJ11, PT 20–21)

Primer of Claude of France (ca. 1505–10)—Cambridge, Fitzwilliam Museum, ms. 159

*\*Grandes Heures* (c. 1508)—Paris, BnF, ms. f. lat. 9474 (EQB 374, MJ 7, PT 17–18)

*\*Petites Heures* (c. 1499–c. 1514)—Paris, BnF ms. nouv. acq. latin 3027 (MJ8, PT 16)

Antoine Dufour, *Ancien testament* (1505–9) (LD3, MJ28, PT 20)[4]

Antoine Dufour, *Epistres de St. Jérôme* (1505–9)—SP, MS. fr. F.v. I. 3: Dedication to Anne of Brittany (LD4, MJ32, PT 20)[5]

*Maximien, *La Vie de Sainte Anne* (beg. 16th c.)—Nantes, Médiathèque, ms. fr. 652: Dedication to Anne of Brittany (MJ19, T20)

*Heures à l'usage de Rome*—Paris: Gillet Hardouin (Bibliothèque de Bordeaux) (EQB 4)

*Horae ad usum Rothomagensem*—Paris, BnF n.a.i.3027 (EQB 377–78)[6]

*Heures* (formerly in Lyon, Bibliothèque des Cordeliers) (MJ27)[7]

Antiphonary (dispersed fragments) (LD2, MJ31, PT 17–18)[8]

# Literary and Historical Works

*Christine de Pizan, *L'Instruction des princesses, des dames de court et d'aultres femmes* [*Le Livre des trois vertus*]—Paris, BnF 1180[9]

*Boccaccio, Giovanni. *De la louenge des nobles et cleres dames*—Paris: for Vérard, 1493 (BnF, Rés. G. 365 [BnF Rés. Vélins 1223; London, BL C.22.c.2; Manchester, University of Manchester, John Rylands Collection, Inc. 15.E.2]): Anonymous dedication to Anne of Brittany (MBW 114–15)

*Christine de Pizan, *Le Tresor de la cité des dames*—Paris: for Vérard, 8 July 1497 (Vienna, ÖNB Ink.3.D.19): Dedication by Vérard to Anne of Brittany (MBW 132–33, 362–69)

*Alberto Cattaneo de Piacenza, [History of the Kings of France from Francion to Charles VIII] in Latin (Italy, c. 1497)—Paris, Arsenal, ms. fr. 1096: Dedication to Anne of Brittany (MJ4, PT 23–24)

[Octovien de Saint-Gelais], *Cinq Epistres d'Ovide et poésies anonymes (L'Epitaphe de Mme Balsac, L'Arrêt, L'Appel)* (ca. 1497)—*Breslauer and Grieb Catalogue* #109 (1988) (EQB 380–82, MJ29?)

*Guillaume Fillastre, *Histoire de la Toison d'Or* (c. 1492–c. 1498)—Paris, BnF, ms. fr. 138 (MJ 5, PT 24–25)

Plutarque, *Le Discours sur le mariage de Pollion et Eurydice* (1499)—SP, Ms. fr. Q. v. III. 3 (LD5, EQB 379, MJ9, PT 26)

*Pierre Choque, *Relation du voyage et du sacre de la reine de Hongroie* (1502)—Paris, BnF ffr. 90 (LD14) and BL,Stowe Ms, fols. 69–78: Dedications to Anne of Brittany (MJ10, PT 28)

*Jean Lemaire de Belges, *La Plainte du Désiré* (1504)—Paris, BnF ffr. 1683 (MJ36) and 23988[10]

*André de la Vigne, *Comment la Royne a Sainct Denys sacree . . . a Paris elle fit son entree* (ca. 1505)—Buckinghamshire, Waddesdon Manor, James A. Rothschild Collection, Ms. 22 (MJ13, PT 30)

*Pierre Le Baud, *Le livre des cronicques des roys, ducs et princes de Bretaigne armoricane aultrement nommee la moindre Bretaigne* (before 19 September 1505)[11]—BL ms. Harleian 4371: Dedication to Anne of Brittany (LD8, EQB 380, MJ12, PT 22)

*Antoine Dufour, *Les Vies des femmes célèbres* (1506)—Nantes, Musée Dobrée, ms. XVII: Dedication to Anne of Brittany (LD6, MJ14, PT 25–26, 30–32)

*Jean Marot, *La vray edisant advocate des dames* (1506)—Paris, BnF, ffr. 1704:[12] Dedication to Anne of Brittany (MJ34)

*Jean Marot, *Le Voyage de Gênes* (after May 1507)—Paris, BnF ffr. 5091: Dedication to Anne of Brittany (LD11, MJ15, PT 30)

***Claude de Seyssel, *Les Louenges du roy Louis XIIe*—Paris: for Vérard, 1508 (Paris, BnF, Rés. Vélins 2780) (EQB 379, MBW, 97–99)

**Fausto Andrelini, *Epistolae Annae Reginae* [Letter 1, Saint-Petersburg Collection]— Paris: Josse Bade, c. 1508

Jean Marot, *Le Voyage de Venise* (after May 1509). Published posthumously in *Deux heureux voyages de Genes et Venise*, Paris: G. Tory, 22 January 1532 (BnF Rés. Y 4482): Dedication to Anne of Brittany

Fausto Andrelini, *Epistolae Annae Reginae* [Letters 2–3, Saint-Petersburg Collection] (c. 1509–10)—Chantilly, Musée Condé, ms. 890 [XIV 3.19] (MJ25, PT 34)

*Disarvouez Penguern, *La Genealogie de treshaulte, trespuissante . . . royne de France et duchesse de Bretaigne* (1510)—Paris, BnF, ffr. 24043 (MJ 41, PT 22)

Fausto Andrelini/Macé de Villebresme, Jean Francisque Suard/Jean d'Auton, Jean Lemaire de Belges, M. Mailly, *Collection of Versified Royal Epistles*—SP, Ms. Fr. F.v. XIV.8 (1510–11) (LD10, MJ16, PT 21, 37, 42)

***Jean Lemaire, *Les Epîtres de l'Amant Vert* (published with the *Illustrations de Gaule et Singularitez de Troye)*—Lyon: Étienne Baland, 1511.

*Jean Lemaire de Belges, *Le Dyalogue de Vertu Militaire et de Jeunesse Françoise . . .* (1511)— Paris, BnF, ffr. 25295: Dedication to Anne of Brittany (LD15, EQB 378–79, MJ17, PT 21)

*Jean Marot, *Prières sur la restauration et la sancté de madame Anne de Bretagne* (ca. 1512)—Paris, BnF ffr. 1539: Dedication to Anne of Brittany (LD12, MJ35)

*Jean Lemaire de Belges, *Les XXIIII Coupletz de la valitude de la Royne* (1512)—Geneva, Bibliothèque publique et universitaire, Ms. fr. 74 (MJ37)

*Jean Lemaire de Belges, *Troisième livre des illustrations et singularitez de France orientalle et occidentalle* (December 1512)—Bern, Burgerbibliothek, Ms. 241: Dedication to Anne of Brittany (LD7, EQB 380, MJ38)

***Germain de Brie, *Chordigerae nauis conflagratio.* Paris: Josse Bade, 15 January 1513 (Paris, BnF, Rés. m. Ye. 68): Dedication to Anne of Brittany dated 10 November 1512

*Pierre Choque, *L'Incendie de la Cordelière* (translation of Germain de Brie) (ca. 1512–14)—Société des Manuscrits des Assureurs français, ms. 85.1: Dedication and poems to Anne of Brittany and Claude of France[13]

*Robertet, François, "Trois rondeaulx faictz sur la deuise de la feue Royne Anne de Bretaigne" (sixteenth century)—Paris, BnF, ffr. 1717, fols. 12v–13v (MJ40)

# Books for Charles VIII or Louis XII, with Arms, Symbols, or Portrait of Anne of Brittany

**Jacobus de Voragine,** *Legende doree*—Paris: for Vérard, 1493 (Paris, BnF, Rés. Vélins 689) (MBW 237–45)

Robert du Herlin, *Les Heures de la Croix* (1493)—Paris, BnF ffr. 5661 (LD, p. 343)[14]

**Aesopus,** *Apologues L. Valle*—Paris: for Vérard, c. 1493 (Paris, BnF, Rés. Vélins 611) (MBW 97)

*André de la Vigne, *La Ressource de la Chrestienté* (ca. 1495)—Paris, BnF, ffr. 1687 (MJ20, PT 26–27)

*Ravigneau, *La Ressource de la Monarchie Chrestienne* (ca. 1495) (MJ21)—Paris, BnF, ffr. 20055

Guilloche de Bordeaux, *La Prophécie du roy Charles VIII* (ca. 1495)—Paris, BnF, ffr. 1713 (MJ22, PT 27)

*Octovien de Saint-Gelais, *XXI Epistres d'Ovide* (ca. 1497)—San Marino, Huntington Library, Ms. HM 60[15]

Fausto Andrelini, *Chant royal pour le mariage de Louis XII et Anne of Brittany* (ca. 1499)—Paris, BnF lat. 8132 (PT 34)

*Les Quatre Etats de la Société* (1500)—Paris, Bibl. de l'École Nationale des Beaux-Arts, Collection Masson (MJ39)

Robert Frescher, Translation of Darès le Phrygien's *De excidio Troiae* (ca. 1500)—Paris, BnF, ffr. 9735 (MJ23)

*Pontificale ad usum Gallicanum* (end 15th c.)—Camarillo CA, Edward Laruence, Doheny Memorial Library, St. John's Seminary, ms. 3929 (MJ24)

Clément V, *Constitutiones cum commento Johannis Andreae* (end 15th c.)—Philadelphia, Free Library, John Frederick Lewis Collection, ms. 65 (MJ26)

*Petrarca, Francesco, *Remedes de l'une et l'autre Fortune* (translation) (1503)—Paris, BnF, ffr. 1225

**\*Henri de Ferrières,** *Modus et Ratio*—Paris: for Vérard, 1505/6 (BnF, Rés. Vélins 1763) (MBW 124–25)

Fausto Andrelini, *Ecloga de patienti ac laboriosa industria ad Ludovicum XII Francorum regem* (1509–10)—Paris, BnF lat. 8395 (LD9, MJ30?, PT 34)

Jean de Saint Gelais, *Histoire de Louis XII* (1510)—Vienna, ÖNB codex 2588 (PT 34)

Paul Riccio *Contra Judeos* (PT 36)

| | |
|---|---|
| Arsenal | Paris, Bibliothèque de l'Arsenal |
| *AV* | Winn, Mary Beth. *Anthoine Vérard: Parisian Publisher (1485– 1512): Prologues, Poems and Presentations.* Geneva: Droz, 1997. |
| BBR | Brussels, Bibliothèque Royale |
| BL | London, British Library |
| BnF | Paris, Bibliothèque Nationale de France |
| *ER* | Gringore, Pierre. *Les Entrées royales à Paris de Marie d'Angleterre (1514) et Claude de France (1517).* Ed. Cynthia J. Brown. Geneva: Droz, 2005. |
| ÖNB | Vienna, Österreichische Nationalbibliothek |
| SP | Saint Petersburg, National Library of Russia |

# NOTES

## INTRODUCTION

1. Avril and Reynaud, *Les Manuscrits à peintures*, 414–15, state that this book was offered to King Louis XII around 1503; the liminal miniature featuring the dedication of the book to the French king (fol. Av) confirms this. The French queen may well appear in two other miniatures in the book. On fol. 55r a miniature of a woman in a brocade dress wearing a black veil, identified as a noble married woman, is holding a girl in blue identified as a chaste girl. In the center of a subsequent miniature (fol. 66v), which illustrates the chapter on second marriages, "The man" ["L'ome"] points to a female in a red dress with a cordelière-like belt and black veil-like headdress, identified as the second wife. This image may well refer to Anne of Brittany, whom Louis XII took as his second wife in 1499, after divorcing Jeanne de France. In the accompanying text, Reason states that human and divine law support the idea of second and third marriages if there has not been any abuse in the first marriage.

2. For further discussion of this topic, see C. Brown, "Like Mother, like Daughter."

3. Book I offers remedies for prosperity ("Fortune prospere"), whereas Book II offers remedies for adversity or "Fortune aduerse."

4. Rawski uses this title in his translation, *Remedies for Fortune Fair and Foul*, III: 177.

5. François was born on 21 January 1503 and died in mid February 1503. See E. Brown, "The Children of Anne de Bretagne." See the citation in note 7 below in which *Rayson* mentions Fortune's "having taken away or never having given you a son."

6. This anxiety was no doubt fueled by Anne's failure to produce an heir during her marriage to Charles VIII in 1491–98. Charles-Orland was born in October 1492 but died in 1495. According to E. Brown, "The Children of Anne de Bretagne," a son, Charles, lived less than a month in 1496; François was born and died in 1497. A daughter Anne was born and died on 20 March 1498.

7. This exchange provides a rather complicated assessment of the issue. Whereas *Douleur* complains that she has no male heir, *Rayson* suggests this is not so bad, since sons can bring difficulty and uneasiness, not to mention distraction to a king, whose responsibility of a kingdom requires great care: "You must understand that there is no public burden more weighty than a kingdom nor private burden heavier than a son" (for the

French text, see fol. 165v). *Rayson* adds that a king's subjects are freer as a result: "If you have no heir to your kingdom, you will not have a destroyer of your works. But you will have the people who will love you after your death in praising your name. And they will always pray for you. Know that Fortune has done better in having taken away or never having given you a son than in having given you a kingdom" (for the French text, see fol. 165v). All translations are my own unless otherwise noted.

8. "Can't you understand that he has not forgotten to provide for great kingdoms and empires, which he has established to dominate, rule and govern all the things subject to them, each one in his way? Know for certain that he has not forgotten to do this, but has arranged through his divine prescience all things to come. Allow, allow, therefore, the one who does nothing without reason to manage your kingdom and all things and study virtue. And strive to do good works so that after you have reigned temporally you may reign eternally in Paradise. And through virtuous, lofty and magnificent deeds you might perpetuate your name and its glory as have done many good and virtuous kings and emperors, whose renown and memory will last until the end of the world" (for the French text, see fol. 165v).

9. According to Carraud, recent editor of Pétrarque, *Les Remèdes aux Deux Fortunes/ De Remediis utriusque fortune (1354–1366)*, II, 43–45, the *Remèdes* were translated into French in 1378 by Jean Daudin for Charles V. The translation made for Louis XII, completed on 6 May 1503, was anonymous. Without having actually examined BnF ms. ffr. 625, Carraud suggests that the Daudin translation was likely a better translation. For a discussion of the Daudin translation in the context of Christine de Pizan's *Cité des dames*, see Lori Walters, "Translating Petrarch." Editions of Petrarch's work in Latin appeared in 1468, 1490, 1492, 1496, and 1501 (Rawski, II, xxiii–xxiv).

10. Anne would give birth seven years later (1510) to another daughter, Renée, but the queen nearly died in childbirth in January 1512, when a son was stillborn. Following Anne's death in 1514, Louis XII married the very young Mary Tudor in the hope of producing a male heir as well, but he died without a son some three months after their wedding.

11. Chapter 77 in Book I does deal with "The Marriage of One's Children," in particular a daughter given away in marriage. No discussion about the future of the kingdom surfaces, and Reason's cynical words anticipate the different situations in which Anne of Brittany and Claude of France would find themselves: "If she is a good daughter, you have lost a sweet and gentle child and have given it to another's house. If she is bad you have rid yourself of a grave burden and imposed it on another man. . . . You must not rejoice too much. . . . If children are born into her home, they will be a wellspring of worries. If she has no children, then that will be wretched and grievous. Thus fruitfulness will make her burdensome; and barrenness, hated" (Rawski, trans., I, 216).

12. The one known extant copy of the work, BnF ms. ffr. 24043, contains no illustrations of the queen and was probably not the copy he offered her, although the queen did commission Penguern to write the *Genealogie*. All citations are taken from this version. Capital letters and modern punctuation have been added.

13. The BnF copy ends with a colophon indicating that the book was "made and completed" in 1510.

14. This image may have inspired an entry theater created by Pierre Gringore on the occasion of Claude of France's 1517 coronation. See *ER*, 170–71, and fig. 1.7.

15. The author does note the death of the short-lived sons to whom Anne gave birth during her first marriage, but this occurs in the context of the sorrow she experienced rather than in reference to her failure to bear a son: "Et elle conceupt trois filz de sa semence / Qu'ilz moururent ieunes par mort greuaine: / Ce fust dommaige en Bretaigne et en France" [And she bore three sons with her seed, who died young through grievous death: this was a great loss in Brittany and in France] (fol. 40v).

16. See the discussion of Bruster, "New Materialism in Renaissance Studies," 231, who states that "Cultural materialism can be defined as a critical practice concerned with the cultural embeddedness of aesthetic objects . . . and the inescapably political nature of all cultural production and interpretation." His reference to English Renaissance scholarship applies equally to those of other cultures: "studying the English Renaissance no longer means reading its books alone. It means, instead, reading a variety of objects and people's relation to these objects" (324). See also the relevant comments of Starn, "Seeing Culture," 206, who posits that "cultural historians must be concerned as much with form as with content, and, further, that the formal properties of cultural performances or productions *have* content as representations of structures of authority." Starn calls on scholars "to see art as a form of power while at the same time charting the traces of power represented in the forms of art."

17. See "Reassessing Women's Libraries," "Livres et lectures de la reine Jeanne de Laval," "Charlotte de Savoie's Library and Illuminators," "Le *Pèlerinage de Vie humaine* en prose," and "Les Bibliothèques des deux princesses."

18. See other studies, such as the major volumes edited by Jane Taylor and Lesley Smith: *Women, the Book, and the Godly*; *Women and the Book: Assessing the Visual Evidence*; *The Book and the Worldly*. See also Bell, "Medieval Women Book Owners" and Huot, "A Book Made for a Queen."

19. See especially Jeannot, "Les Bibliothèques de princesses en France," 192–93.

20. See Legaré's discussion of Margaret of Austria's library, which she acquired through gifts, inheritance and especially huge purchases ("Les Bibliothèques de deux princesses," 257–62) and Buettner's study about the role of gifts in females' library collections in "Women and the Circulation of Books."

21. Claerr, 107, claims in "Que ma mémoire 'là demeure' en mes livres," that "la dame de Magné acquit des livres parce qu'il était de bon ton d'en posséder, à l'instar des reines et des princesses."

22. Jeannot, 191.

23. "Images de maternité," 35.

24. See Hemptinne, in "Lire et écrire, c'est prier un peu," 156: "Pour les bourgeoises, nobles dames et leurs soeurs dans les couvents, les livres étaient en premier lieu des instruments de prière et de dévotion, qu'elles étaient heureuses de recevoir en cadeau de leur directeur de conscience ou d'autres hommes de leur entourage, mais qu'elle aimaient particulièrement s'offrir ou se léguer l'une à l'autre. C'étaient parfois des objets ostentatoirement précieux plus fait pour être montrés que pour être lus, mais souvent aussi des

instruments d'usage quotidien pour les dévotions privées, les offices ou l'enseignement religieux des enfants. Ces livres donnaient aux femmes qui les utilisaient l'opportunité de conserver des liens d'amitié et de solidarité malgré leur confinement réciproque."

25. "Les Livres de la 'damoiselle de Dreux'," 74.

26. "Le Coffre aux livres de Marie de Bretagne," 89.

27. See Jeannot, 195–96, and Korteweg, 221. In "La femme au livre dans la littérature médiévale," 33, Cerquiglini-Toulet explains that medieval women were counseled to read the Bible, Psalter or a Book of Hours continuously without looking up. She claims that the Psalter, through its close association with the Virgin herself, was the emblem of the virtuous and chaste woman, whereas the association of women and romances led to more dangerous alliances with love.

28. "Les bibliothèques de deux princesses," 254, 261.

29. One such library was doubtless that of Charles V; another was that of Philip the Good, duke of Burgundy. In her article entitled "On the Epistemology of Images," 419, Liepe claims that Philip "established and confirmed his political power and status, not least with the help of illuminated manuscripts. The collection of art and literature was a political and social means of influence among the highest levels of the Burgundian society: 'art functioned as a passport to the ruling elite.'" Liepe also reminds us how "Charles V . . . made strategic use of words and images to strengthen the position of the French monarchy, by commissioning translations of carefully chosen texts on royal power, furnished with illuminations showing himself in different contexts, but primarily as 'le roi sage'."

30. See, for example, Fradenburg's "Introduction: Rethinking Queenship"; Parsons, ed., *Medieval Queenship*; Duggan, ed., *Queens and Queenship*; Cosandey, *La Reine de France*; Stirnemann, "Women and Books in France"; Walters, "Jeanne and Marguerite de Flandre as Female Patrons;" McCash, ed., *The Cultural Patronage of Medieval Women*; Kettering, *Patronage in Sixteenth- and Seventeenth-Century France*; Wilson-Chevalier, ed., *Patronnes et mécènes en France à la Renaissance*; Müller, "Marguerite d'Autriche (1480–1530);" and Eichberger, ed., *Women of Distinction*, in particular, her article "Margaret of Austria's Portrait Collection."

31. In *Livres et lectures de femmes*, 49–65.

32. Past scholars, such as Leroux de Lincy, in *Vie de la reine Anne de Bretagne*, II, 34, who claims she had 1300–1500 books in her library, have often assumed that Anne of Brittany acquired all the books that Charles VIII brought back from the Italian wars. While she likely had access to this number of books, her own library was apparently smaller, as Thibault, *Les Manuscrits de la collection d'Anne de Bretagne*, 7–9, 37–40, points out. See also Baurmeister and Laffitte, *Des livres et des rois*, 163: "Le sort des manuscrits personnels d'Anne de Bretagne est différent. Après sa mort en 1514, ni les livres hérités de son père le duc François II de Bretagne, ni ceux qu'elle a reçus ou commandés ne sont intégrés dans la Librairie royale de Blois. Les *Grandes Heures* peintes par Jean Bourdichon (latin 9474) et parmi les écrits du poète Jean Marot, *Le Voyage de Gênes* daté de 1507 (français 5091), passeront plus tard dans le Cabinet du roi à Versailles. *L'Histoire de Bretagne* de Pierre Lebaud, les œuvres de Jean Lemaire de Belges (français 25295), du confesseur

de la reine Antoine Dufour ou de son héraut d'armes Pierre Choque connaîtront d'autres destins." See also Delisle, *Le Cabinet des manuscrits*, I, 121–25, and Jones, "Les manuscrits d'Anne de Bretagne."

33. See Jones, 153–54, and Thibault, 10–21.

34. See among others, Leroux de Lincy, II, 46–86; Delisle, *Les Grandes Heures de la Reine Anne de Bretagne*; and Mâle, *Les Heures d'Anne de Bretagne*. Other beautifully illuminated books of hours owned by Anne include the *Petites Heures* (BnF ms. nouv. acq. lat. 3027), the *Très Petites Heures* (BnF ms. nouv. acq. lat. 3120), and the Prayerbook in the Pierpont Morgan Library (ms. 50). See L'Estrange's study of the prayerbooks of Breton duchesses, including Anne of Brittany, in *Holy Motherhood*, 199–247. She states: "It is likely that they saw the textual and visual representations of successful, comfortable, and holy maternity in their manuscripts as a way to manage, if not to gain some control over, those duties, especially concerning the difficulties of conceptions and the risk of maternal and infant mortality that they expected to, and did, face" (241). See also L'Estrange, "Penitence, Motherhood, and Passion Devotion," Kamerick, "Patronage and Devotion" and Wieck and Hearne, eds., *The Prayer Book of Anne de Bretagne*.

35. Jones, 68, states: "Le nombre croissant de poésies originales, d'allégories politiques et spirituelles et d'ouvrages commémoratifs, même éphémères, rassemblés par la reine après 1500, de même qu'un intérêt grandissant pour l'histoire écrite de la manière la plus moderne et authentique qui soit, sont un trait caractéristique." Besides the bibliographical descriptions of the works offered by Jones and Thibault (see note 32), Le Fur, in *Anne de Bretagne* has most recently assessed many of the books associated with Anne de Bretagne. In subsequent chapters, I contest or support a number of his analyses. Recent important studies dealing partially with Anne of Brittany's books include L'Estrange, *Holy Motherhood*; Hochner, *Louis XII*; and Swift, *Gender, Writing and Performance*.

36. See also Quentin-Bauchart, *Les Femmes bibliophiles de France*, II, 374–82; Booton, *Manuscripts, Market and the Transition to Print*; and C. Brown, ed., *The Cultural and Political Legacy of Anne de Bretagne*.

37. See "Some Portraits of Women in Their Books."

38. Cerquiglini-Toulet, 33, points out that medieval women were commonly depicted visually in only one book—the Bible, Psalter, or Book of Hours.

39. *Women and the Book: Assessing the Visual Evidence*, 16. See also Driver, "Mirrors of a Collective Past," and Penketh, "Women and Books of Hours."

40. "On the Epistemology of Images," 424–25. See also Sears, "'Reading' Images," 2.

41. "The Book of Signs," 138.

## CHAPTER I. RITUALS OF ENTRY: WOMEN AND BOOKS IN PERFORMANCE

1. The volume was copied around 1490–1500 and the images were painted by the Master of the *Chronique scandaleuse*, according to Hablot, "Pour en finir . . . avec l'ordre de la Cordelière," 56. Brejon de Lavergnée, "L'Emblématique d'Anne de Bretagne," 93–95, persuasively maintains that this was a manuscript made for Anne of Brittany. Le Fur's

contention in *Anne de Bretagne*, 44, that the volume dates from Anne's second marriage is not compelling. Based on the depiction of the female in the miniature, Hablot, 56, convincingly argues that it is Anne who is represented here.

2. Complementing the stunning initial miniature of manuscript 138 is a series of exquisite illustrations throughout both volumes, painted by another hand (Brejon de Lavergnée, 94).

3. Le Fur's claims (*Anne de Bretagne*, 44) that the Ss appearing in conjunction with As on nearly every folio of the manuscript do not refer to Charles VIII, as most specialists contend, are not convincingly argued. His statement that the letter S appears regularly in the emblems of Anne of Brittany during her second marriage and was used to indicate the *Salvator* is based on the mistaken claim that they appear in the 1504 manuscript account of her second coronation, which they do not, and on a folio of a now missing manuscript. Brejon de Lavergnée, 93–94, offers a more cogently argued discussion of the difficulties interpreting the S in this manuscript. See also Baurmeister and Laffitte, 91, whose explanation of the S in another context might be relevant: "Charles VIII a plusieurs devises . . . Son emblème, un S gothique fermé, orne le texte des *Vigiles de Charles de VII* de Martial d'Auvergne, composé en 1484 pour l'éducation du jeune roi (français 5054), les *Commentaires de César* . . . , offerts en 1485 par Robert Gaguin, et un *Pèlerinage de vie humaine*. Le même motif figurait sur de l'argenterie, un cor de chasse et une tapisserie transférée d'Amboise à Blois en décembre 1501, dont le damas gris et jaune était semé de S de velours noir brodés. Un semé de S et de C ornait aussi la reliure perdue d'un livre d'Heures de la collection Gaignières peint par Jean Bourdichon (latin 1370)." In fact, if one looks closely at the letters, the S's appear to be formed by a forward-facing C on top and a backward-facing (or upside-down) C below. During Anne's 1492 Parisian entry, the interweaving of K (for Karolus) and A decorated the horses drawing the queen's litter (*ER*, ll. 294–97).

4. See Brejon de Lavergnée, 86–88, for a discussion of the origins of the *cordelière* as Anne's emblem. He notes, 87, n. 4, the following: "la cordelière n'a pas seulement une signifiance religieuse; elle est le symbole des liens qui unissent les amants et s'identifie alors aux lacs d'amour, de symbolique traditionnelle." See also Jones, "Les signes du pouvoir." Hablot, 47–70, offers the most comprehensive discussion of the history of this emblem, scrutinizing evidence about its association with Brittany in general and with Anne of Brittany in particular.

5. For further details on the symbols associated with each virtue, see the description of this miniature by Santrot, *Entre France et Angleterre*, 253–54, and Le Fur, *Anne de Bretagne*, 42–44.

6. The first part of this phrase recurs in conjunction with other words on folios 167v (left margin: "A SE ME RENS FAIS SE QVE TV VOVDERAS AVOIR FAIT QVANT") and 168r (right margin: "A SE ME RENS FAIS SE"; lower margin: "QVE TV VOVDERAS"; left margin: "AVOIR FAIT QVANT TV"). See the interpretation of Brejon de Lavergnée, 95: "Il ne s'agit pas d'une devise d'Anne de Bretagne mais l'enlumineur, associant cette phrase aux autres devises de la miniature, a voulu sans doute signifier que seule pouvait se rendre à jamais à Dieu celle qui pratiquant les vertus qui

devaient la mener à la bonne mort trouvait dans la parole divine la garantie de son salut." See also Santrot, 254.

7. Santrot, 266.

8. Brejon de Lavergnée, 93–94, suggests that, given the fact that Fillastre had died before Anne of Brittany was born, she may have had the work copied, illuminated with the opening miniature and decorated throughout with her and her husband's insignia.

9. See Appendix.

10. Le Fur, *Anne de Bretagne*, 20, suggests that "ces entrées entretenaient mieux que des cérémonies exceptionnelles, comme celle du sacre ou des funérailles, le sentiment monarchique et national."

11. Colette Beaune reminds us that no other French queen before Anne of Brittany had been the object of such massive propaganda programs. See her "Préface" in Le Fur, *Anne de Bretagne*, 3,

12. For details on the Parisian entries of medieval French queens, see *ER*, 11–106. All subsequent citations are taken from this edition. For general details about Parisian royal entries, see Guenée and Lehoux, *Les Entrées royales françaises*; and Bryant, *The King and the City* and "The Medieval Entry Ceremony at Paris."

13. "The Early Modern Festival Book," 3–17.

14. Watanabe-O'Kelly, 5, states: "This instability and conflict provided not just the background, but the raison d'être for many court and civic festivals, and it was frequently in times of change, instability and insecurity that rules and cities staged festivals." Although this article and the others in the collection focus uniquely on male rulers as protagonists of these festivals, many insights hold true for festivities associated with queens.

15. See Fradenburg's discussion of this and related issues in "Introduction: Rethinking Queenship."

16. Prior to her marriage to Charles, Anne had made at least one entry. On 10 February 1489, at the age of twelve, she entered Rennes to be crowned duchess at the Cathedral of St. Pierre, where she received a ducal circlet and sword of justice; a seal circulated marking this event (see Le Fur, *Anne de Bretagne*, 14ff). After her first marriage, Anne made an entry into Lyon on 15 March 1494, an event commemorated by a medal apparently offered the queen at the time (see the Musée Dobrée catalogue titled *Anne de Bretagne et son temps*, #85). See also Labande-Mailfert, *Charles VIII et son milieu*, 152–53, and Gabory, *L'Union de la Bretagne à la France*, 85–91. Le Fur, *Anne de Bretagne*, 29 also mentions Anne's entry into Nantes on 8 November 1498 and two entries that Anne made into Tours in December 1491 and November 1500, at which time "le mystère de madame Anne," presumably an entry theater created by the municipality, was presented in her honor (106). For details on Anne's September 1505 entry into Morlaix, in Brittany, see Cassard, "Du passage historique à l'invite touristique," 125–30.

17. For details on the wedding of Anne and Charles at Langeais in December 1491, which, like most medieval marriages, did not involve an extravagant ceremony, see Le Fur, *Anne de Bretagne*, 18. For further details concerning Anne of Brittany's life, see the following studies from which I borrow for subsequent comments: Labande-Mailfert;

Markale, *Anne de Bretagne*; Minois, *Anne de Bretagne*; Tourault, *Anne de Bretagne*; Matarasso, *Queen's Mate*.

18. Le Fur, *Anne de Bretagne*, 89, claims that Isabeau de Bavière was the first French queen whose coronation in 1389 was linked to her subsequent Parisian entry. However, she was crowned at the Sainte Chapelle, not at Saint-Denis. It is uncertain whether Marie d'Anjou or Charlotte de Savoie were crowned before their entries into Paris in 1437 and 1467 respectively. Anne of Brittany's 1492 coronation and entry into Paris appear to have inaugurated a trend linking both events, a trend that continued until 1610.

19. See *ER*, 20–58, for a general history of queens' entries into Paris and a discussion of the seven entry theater sites during the entries in 1514 and 1517, inspired by the organization of Anne of Brittany's 1504 entry.

20. For an edition of the anonymous text, which includes variants from Nicolaï, see *ER*, App. I. All references are taken from this edition. Unlike Anne's second coronation, no royal copy of this spectacle has come down to us today, suggesting that Charles VIII did not take steps to have Anne's coronation rendered into a specially made manuscript. For an edition of the entries of French kings from the fourteenth to the sixteenth century, see Guenée and Lehoux.

21. For details, see Pradel, *Anne de France*, 160.

22. Following the coronation mass, prelates replaced the original crown with a smaller one to facilitate movement the next day during the queen's entry into Paris. Earlier in the account, Louis, as the king's cousin, had supported the queen's arm while leading her into the church at Saint-Denis (ll. 18–20).

23. See Chapter 2 for further discussion of this subject.

24. Octavian, ruler of a peaceful world was associated with Paris, love with *Amour*, security with Reason, the court of Parlement with Justice, and the University with Knowledge. For an analysis of this linguistic phenomenon in later poetic texts, see Rigolot, *Poétique et onomastique*.

25. I adopted this analogy earlier in "From Stage to Page," 52.

26. The *tableau vivant* at the Trinity, organized by the Confraternity of the Passion, presented a purely religious scenario: the Transfiguration at the time of the ascension of Mont-Thabor by Christ and his disciples (ll. 203–7).

27. A similar staging at the Trinity punctuated Mary Tudor's Paris entry in 1514, confirming the popularity of this theme.

28. *Enter the King*, 311.

29. Solomon's famous judgment about the true mother of a child was presented near the Châtelet, the site where justice itself was rendered, with the famous biblical figure's integrity thus serving again as a model for the French kingdom.

30. Le Fur, *Anne de Bretagne*, 22, offers a similar interpretation.

31. See C. Brown, "From Stage to Page," 49–72, for a discussion of the use of texts on stage by Pierre Gringore during Mary Tudor's 1514 entry into Paris.

32. This account can be found in a late copy of the work in BnF ms. Dupuy 542 on folios 29r–64v.

33. According to Minois, 431, Anne played a major role in this event. Following

Anne de Foix's marriage to the king of Hungary by procuration, she lived in a royal state with Anne of Brittany until her departure for Hungary in May 1502 (Auton, *Chroniques,* II, 217).

34. See Chapter 2 for a discussion of Anne's unsuccessful attempts to select a non-French spouse for her daughter Claude of France.

35. It may well be the first such coronation book since the famous manuscript account commissioned by Charles V. See Dewick, ed., *The Coronation Book of Charles V of France,* and O'Meara, *Monarchy and Consent,* for an analysis of this earlier work.

36. For an edition of this work, see Leroux de Lincy, "Cérémonies du mariage d'Anne de Foix." All subsequent references are taken from this edition.

37. See the BnF *Catalogue des manuscrits français,* I, 6, for a brief description of this manuscript.

38. I am grateful to Elizabeth A. R. Brown for providing this information.

39. See also Auton, *Chroniques,* II, 212–17, for a description of the marriage treaty negotiated with Ladislaus and 241–42 for general details about the first stage of Anne de Foix's travels to Hungary.

40. See Leroux de Lincy, 164: "Ce volume est entièrement l'oeuvre du roi d'armes de la reine Anne, *Pierre Choque* dit *Bretagne.* . . . Non-seulement il en a composé le texte, mais il l'a écrit de sa main; il a peint aussi les blasons nombreux qui décorent plusieurs feuillets." Leroux de Lincy implicitly refers to Choque's caveat that as a new officer and "rather poor painter" he asks the queen's forgiveness for anything badly written or portrayed (185).

41. This may be the manuscript (or a copy of the manuscript) that Leroux de Lincy mentions in his article, when he states: "La copie qui se trouve dans le fonds des Blancs-Manteaux (n° 46) se termine en cet endroit" (435, n. 2). The BL version also ends after Choque's description of the "feste royalle" held on 6 October 1502 following the coronation and marriage of Anne de Foix to Ladislaus and omits Choque's general overview of the area around Buda and general comments about the Hungarian kingdom. For this missing section, see Leroux de Lincy, "Cérémonies," 435–39. Also lacking in the truncated version of BL ms. Stowe 584 is Choque's final address to Anne of Brittany. The relevant entry in the *Catalogue of the Stowe Manuscripts in the British Museum,* I, fol. 469–70, #584, identifies the signature and monogram of one Stowe 384 owner, Claude d'Argentré, and the fact that it was presented by the Princesse de Rohan to Charles de Rohan, Prince de Soubise on 14 February 1774. The *Discours des ceremonies du sacre et mariage d'Anne de Foix* is collated with Pierre Choque's *Commemoracion* of Anne of Brittany's death, discussed below in Chapter 5.

42. "May it please you, Madame, to know that I, cognizant of the fact that your pastime involves virtuous activities and that after service to God, you hear and willingly listen to noble and solemn things when they derive from virtuous deeds" (423).

43. The artistry of Stowe 584 resembles miniatures of the destruction of the battleship in BnF ffr. ms. 1672, *L'Incendie de la Cordelière,* a translation by Pierre Choque of Germain Brice's Latin account of the 1512 defeat of Anne of Brittany's ship, *La Cordelière,* at the hands of the English. Did Choque also paint these images? See Provini's recent edition of the work and C. Brown, "Like Mother, like Daughter."

44. See also 167 and 185 for similar descriptions of ceremonies in Crema and Venice.

45. See the following, for example: "The aforementioned lady was accompanied by Hungarian ambassadors . . . and representing our lord the king and yourself there remained ambassadors Mr. Claude d'Est, bishop of Laude, the lord of La Guierche and Mr. Galliace Ficonte, and several other good personages, as much the king's noble men as yours."

46. For example, Choque describes the royal "presence" at events in Crema ("around the canopy were the arms of the king and of yourself and those of the king of Hungary and of the aforementioned lady and those of Saint Mark"; 168); see also 172, 182.

47. He deems the palace of Saint Mark one of the most sumptuous and most costly edifices he has ever seen (180) and the banquet room in Venice the largest and most ornate he has seen (181). He later alludes to the king's gifts of three chariots as the best made and gilded in the most gold that he has ever seen (425). See also his superlative description of the river in "Orvasie" (435–36).

48. "So the time came when Madame Anne de Foix, queen of Hungary, left Blois to travel to her country. Despite the royal titles that had been bestowed upon her, in seeing that she had to leave her parents, distance herself from her friends and estrange herself from her birthplace, she made such piteous lament and excessive grief upon leaving, that all those who saw her depart felt bitter grief and dolorous pain, so much so that there were some French who, on account of her rich value and praiseworthy goodness, mourned her by breaking down into a torrent of hot tears" (*Chroniques*, II, 241). According to Minois, 431–32, Anne of Brittany, who assumed control in finding appropriate husbands for her maids of honor with a view to familial political and financial interests rather than the desires of her ladies-in-waiting, played a key role in forcing Anne de Foix to comply with the decision to wed her to Ladislaus.

49. The only times Anne de Foix chose not have the canopy held over her by urban officers was when she was accompanied by the king of Hungary himself, as, for example, in Alba Regia (430). As in other works of this nature, Choque frequently remarks on the hierarchical order of the processions and the fact that all was carried out according to protocol, using the following expressions such as "chascun en son degré" (171, 434) [each according to his rank], "chascun selon son degré" (172, 173) [each according to his rank], "marchèrent en ordre" (174, 175) [they walked in order], "laquelle les regarda passer en ordre" (175) [she watched them pass by in order], "en bon ordre" (425) [in good order].

50. Charlotte of Savoy appears to have been one of the only French queens to have made her Paris entry by boat in 1467. For details, see *ER*, 34–35.

51. Upon Anne's arrival in Venice, some 80 covered boats accompanied her as she moved from "barque" [little ship] to "plus grans basteaulx" [larger boats] to "ung grant basteau" [a large boat] (176) and finally the royal boat (177) in her processions from island to island.

52. In one boat, a god of love appeared on a pillar (178); in another, a noble dressed in Turkish fashion had oliphant and arrow in hand, while eight Moorish ladies held banners displaying a variety of coats of arms (179).

53. These scenes are reminiscent of those at the famous Feast of the Pheasant (*Banquet*

*du Voeu*) in Lille in Burgundy in 1454. For a description, see Beaune and d'Arbaumont, *Mémoires d'Olivier de la Marche*, II, 340–79.

54. See the display of inscriptions upon her entry into the harbor of Veglia (423–24) and banners bearing the coats of arms of the Hungarian territories. Choque describes many celebrations and paintings in the queen's honor as well as the numerous gold-lettered inscriptions in Latin that read "Welcome anticipated one" (424).

55. Of interest too is Choque's description of the castle's beautiful library containing some 300 to 400 books in Latin, Greek, and Hungarian, most of which were illuminated masterpieces (438).

56. A third miniature depicts the landscape of *Cirvasie* and includes the marvelous river filled with tons of fish, mentioned by Choque himself in his account (72r). In addition, a miniature of the multitiered fountain flowing with wine, which so amazed Choque at Buda (435), fills the lower half of folio 77r (see his description, 435]). In his edition of BnF ms. ffr. 90, Leroux de Lincy notes that this image does not appear as indicated (435, n. 1), suggesting that this may not have been the manuscript Choque offered Anne of Brittany. That this and other announced illustrations appear in the BL but not the BnF manuscript suggests that the fragment constituting Stowe 584 may have figured as part of the original manuscript. Three other miniatures depict four Hungarian musicians (73r), a display of the very royal instruments given to Anne de Foix during her coronation—a crown, orb, and scepter (75v)—a joust between two knights following the coronation and wedding (77v), a dragon and a dragon's mouth (78r), and an unfinished illustration of four women dressed in the red attire of the bourgeois and lower classes (78v).

57. Such direct contact during a royal entry was somewhat unusual.

58. Positioned in a temple erected on a chariot, the god of love entered the banquet hall holding an orb, royal scepter, papal hat, and a two-headed wild ox (183).

59. See Labande-Mailfert, 55–80.

60. Even though Anne's marriage to Charles's successor had been dictated by the marriage treaty with her first husband, a situation complicated by Louis XII's marriage to Jeanne de France whom he divorced, the French queen succeeded in maintaining more control over her duchy throughout Louis' reign. For details about negotiations surrounding the marriage contract, see Bridge, III, 17–21, Le Fur, *Louis XII*, 48–49, and Nassiet, "Les traités de mariage d'Anne de Bretagne." In his "Introduction" to *Pour en finir avec Anne de Bretagne?*, Le Page, 9, offers details about Anne of Brittany's control over her duchy following Charles VIII's death.

61. For a description of this manuscript, see Laborde, *Les Principaux manuscrits à peintures,* 132–33. See also Delisle, *Le Cabinet des manuscrits,* I, 124. There are no apparent signs that Anne commissioned the book.

62. For a discussion and an edition of a Latin marriage poem offered to Louis XII by the Italian author Gianmichele Nagonio at the time of his marriage to Anne of Brittany, see Tournoy-Thoen, "Les premiers épithalames humanistes en France," 199–204, 207–11.

63. The full title reads "Le Discours de Plutarque sur le mariage de Pollion et d'Eurydice, briefvement recueilly et dirigé par petiz chapitres et testes par aulchunes

similitudes" (Laborde, 132). For details on Laudet and the different owners of this manuscript, see Aulotte, "Études sur l'influence de Plutarque au seizième siècle," 610–11.

64. For a reproduction of these arms, see Voronova and Stergligov, *Western European Illuminated Manuscripts*, 189.

65. See Zöhl, *Jean Pichore*.

66. For a reproduction, see Voronova and Stergligov, 190 (Fig. 231).

67. See Laborde, 133, for a more extensive description of this miniature.

68. My translation. See Aulotte, 611, for Laudet's text. A modern English translation reads: "The ancients set Hermes at Aphrodite's side, knowing that the pleasure of marriage needed his word more than anything, and with them they set Persuasion and the Graces, that married couples might gratify their desire with each other by persuasion, not in conflict or quarrelsomeness" (Donald Russell, "Advice to the Bride and Groom," 5).

69. For a reproduction of this miniature, see Hochner, *Louis XII*, 254.

70. As I have not been able to examine the manuscript in St. Petersburg, I quote here from a modern English translation of Plutarch's *Marriage Precepts* (Russell, 12).

71. This includes advice to obey "men of sense" (#6), to avoid extramarital pleasures (#7), "to be seen most when she is with her husband, and stay at home and be hidden when he is away" (#9), to display modesty (#10), to perform household actions through agreement which "displays the leadership and decision of the husband" (#11), to behave moderately, laying aside luxuries and extravagances (#12), to keep quarrels private (#13), to "have no feelings of her own, but share her husband's seriousness and sport, his anxiety and laughter" (#14), "not to have friends of her own, but use her husband's as their common stock" (#19), "to cultivate the art of handling her husband by charms of character and daily life" (#29), to be modest in speech, especially in public (#31), to "speak only to her husband or through her husband" (#32), Russell, 6–13. Among his precepts Plutarch mentions examples of famous women, including Helen, Penelope, Olympias, Hera, Hermione, Claudia, Cornelia, and Sappho (#40), who appear in many collections of famous women discussed in Chapters 3–4.

72. Following the death of Charles VIII and before her marriage to Louis XII, Anne made an entry into Nantes on 8 November 1498, to reestablish her authority as duchess of the duchy (Le Fur, *Anne de Bretagne*, 29). Preparations for an earlier entry into Paris in 1502 had been cancelled. See Bonnardot, *Registres des délibérations*, I, 93–102, for the City Hall account about preparations for the 1504 entry and a description of the entry itself. For a discussion of the theoretical and juridical importance of this second coronation, see McCartney, "Ceremonies and Privileges of Office." Sherman studies the political function of this and other such ceremonials in "'Pomp and Circumstance,'" 20–23. Scheller examines the political symbolism of this ritual in "Ensigns of Authority," as does Le Fur, *Anne de Bretagne*, 89–93. See also Oulmont, "Pierre Gringore et l'entrée de la reine Anne." Some of the following details were presented in an earlier form in "Books in Performance" and "Le Mécénat d'Anne de Bretagne et la politique du livre."

73. Cosandey, 177, underscores this dimension of ceremonials involving the queen in general terms: "A travers l'exaltation de la reine, c'est la magnificence du roi, et donc de la monarchie, qui est révélée." Anne made other entries during her marriage to Louis XII,

including one into Lyon in 1499 (*Anne de Bretagne et son temps*, #88, p. 45) and another into Rouen in 1508 (Le Verdier, "L'Entrée du roi Louis XII et de la reine à Rouen [1508]"), both with the king, and two into Nantes, one with Louis XII in 1500 and another alone in 1505 (Lelièvre, "Entrées royales à Nantes," 81). In his *Genealogie . . . d'Anne tresillustre royne de France et duchesse de Bretagne* of 1510 (BnF ms. ffr. 24043), Disarouez Penguern describes Anne's 1505 entry into Nantes in the following manner (fol. 42): "L'an mil cinq cens et cinq alla tout droit / En Bretaigne ceste haulte princesse / Pour visiter son pais et a Folgouet, / Acompaignie d'une grande noblesse. / Comme dame, souueraine duchesse / Fust receue en grande reuerance / De ses subgectz en ioye et liesse, Et par apres s'en retourna en France" [In 1505 this high-ranking princess went directly to Brittany to visit her country and Folgouet, accompanied by a large retinue of nobles. Like a sovereign lady-duchess, she was received with great reverence by her subjects, with joy and delight [as well], and then afterward she returned to France.]

74. Scheller, 138–39; Sherman, 22–23.

75. Auton, III, 350–51, n. 2; Scheller, 139; Sherman, 21–22; McCartney, 210. See also Chapter 2.

76. Bryant, *The King and the City*, 95; Kipling, 333, n. 68.

77. As this was La Vigne's first known work on behalf of the queen, he likely became her secretary around the time of her coronation in November 1504 or perhaps as a result of his account of the coronation and entry festivities. For other records of these events, see Bonnardot, I, 93–97, and Godefroy, I, 690–95, who bases part of his account on Bonnardot's record. Sherman, 22, analyzes the documents concerning the preparations for this event.

78. For a description of this manuscript, see Delaissé, Marrow, and de Wit, *Illuminated Manuscripts*, 484. They claim that this festival book was "made for the Queen." For details about the miniaturist, see Avril and Reynaud, 276. An edition of La Vigne's account appears in *ER*, 215–56. All subsequent references are taken from this edition.

79. Unlike the 1492 account, La Vigne's record focuses first on the court entourage (ll. 55–247) before the procession of ecclesiastics (ll. 248–86).

80. La Vigne registers the queen's words at this time, albeit in indirect discourse: "the most virtuous lady, like someone very happy to see them and pleased with their humble and generous offerings, very wisely made a response, saying that she thanked the named lords of the city very much, found their good will most pleasing, and would do everything possible for the best outcome" (see ll. 1151–52 for the French text). Only one other reference is made to the queen's words, when, during the banquet, she thanked the city for its gift (ll. 1151–52).

81. See, for example, the comments of a contemporary, Jean Molinet, in his *Chroniques*, 101.

82. See Sherman, 20–22, for a discussion of the 1502 preparations for the postponed royal entry of the queen into Paris. Scheller, 135, n. 260, suggests that the cancellation of the 1502 entry may have been due to the queen's pregnancy.

83. Sherman, 20–22; Scheller, 135, n. 260. La Vigne nonetheless mentions the great effort they expended (ll. 593–96).

84. Pierre Gringore was commissioned to organize all of the entry theaters for the two subsequent entries of French queens in 1514 and 1517, an action that was apparently without precedent in Paris.

85. The limitations of this particular study do not permit here a fuller examination of Anne's affiliation by name with Saint Anne, mother of the Virgin. Several scholars have carried out research on this saint, including Ashley and Sheingorn, eds., *Interpreting Cultural Symbols*.

86. But see my discussion in the Introduction about the more direct treatment in BnF ms. 225 of the lack of a male heir in a work dedicated to the king, rather than the queen.

87. The second miniature in ms. 22 (Fig. 1.5a) provides a view of some of these details. See our discussion below of this illustration.

88. The City Hall accounts specify that there were other "mystères" as well, all organized by the secondhand clothes dealers (*fripiers*) (Bonnardot, 97).

89. The *tableau vivant* created by Gringore at the Châtelet, seat of royal justice, presented singing shepherds and shepherdesses joined in peace and union inside the Garden of France (ll. 971–75). See Kipling, 101, and Le Fur, *Anne de Bretagne*, 27–34, on the subject of symbolic gardens. This staging apparently included "several other things of great consequence" (ll. 974–75), according to La Vigne, but he offers no further details.

90. La Vigne refers repeatedly to the orderly nature of the procession and related events throughout his account (see ll. 78–81, 453–57, 467–76, 699–702, etc.).

91. La Vigne mentions only that "a very beautiful mystery play of great meaning" (l. 979) was presented at the Palais Royal, but he provides no further details. The City Hall's accounts offer no additional information either (Bonnardot, 97)

92. Georges d'Amboise also placed "a wedding band" on the finger of the queen (l. 316). McCartney, 202, n. 7, points out that the coronation rite of queens differed from that of kings by its absence of the anointing ritual, reduction of prayers, and abbreviated ceremony. The liturgical rite and queen's regalia essentially reflected her inability to ascend to the crown or assume authentic power in her own right (182). See also Scheller, 134–36.

93. Particularly prominent in the illustration because of their kneeling position in front of the other participants and their black garb are two court widows, usually mentioned early in the royal hierarchy by La Vigne, Anne of France, the former regent and sister-in-law of the queen, and Margaret of Lorraine, duchess of Alençon (ll. 124–34). Their prominent placement is mentioned again as part of the queen's entry entourage (ll. 855–67). Two other court ladies dressed in black are singled out: Charlotte d'Albret, duchess of Valentinois, whose husband was a prisoner in Spain at the time (ll. 141–45, 868–71) and the widow Mary of Luxembourg, countess of Vendôme (ll. 152–54, 877–79). Widows are centrally featured in Claude of France's coronation and Parisian entry as well (see below).

94. Every other horizontal row features a blue letter A on a gold background in each of the attached diamonds across the folio, echoing the golden panel that distinguishes the crowned queen in the banquet scene on the facing folio. The emblems from

the queen's arms appear in the alternate rows, with gold fleurs-de-lis painted on a blue diamond-shaped background, echoing the blue draping and partially blue columns in the facing miniature; these alternate with black ermine symbols on a silver diamond-shaped background.

95. The verbal portrait of the queen at the time of her entry is similar (see ll. 806–14).

96. Other authorial remarks include references to shortening descriptions so as to avoid prolixity (ll. 421–26).

97. For a discussion of authors' signatures, see C. Brown, *Poets, Patrons, and Printers*, 153–95.

98. See *ER*, 157–94, from which all subsequent references are taken. The unique copy of Gringore's version is currently housed in Nantes, Bibliothèque municipale, as ms. 1337. Although it contains the author's dedicatory verses to Claude of France, no evidence indicates that Claude commissioned Gringore to redact his version of events nor does this document appear to have been the copy he dedicated to her. An anonymous account of Claude's coronation and entry has come down to us today in seven contemporary manuscript copies, which provides more details about the coronation rituals and entry ceremonies than Gringore's record. While the copies of this anonymous version contain illuminations of the coronation and entry theaters, no document confirms that it was commissioned either. There also exists a printed edition of an account of the festivities, housed today in the BnF (Rés. Lb³⁰29). Editions of the anonymous manuscript account and the printed edition appear in Appendices V and VI of the *ER* respectively.

99. In the anonymous account of Claude of France's coronation ceremonies (see *ER*, App. IV, ll. 1–7 from which all subsequent references are taken), Claude's title is even longer. See also App. IV, ll. 29–30, 85–86, 529–30 for slightly different configurations of her title. She is only referred to as "la royne de France" in the printed version (App. V, 315).

100. Anne's earlier entry into Morlaix in 1505 had in fact featured a similar genealogical tree, but it seems unlikely that it served as a model for the organizer of Claude's Parisian entry in 1517. The theme of Anne of Brittany's genealogical tree figures centrally in Disarouez Penguern's *Genealogie* (see Introduction). See Cassard, 127, who cites the description of the genealogical tree by the anonymous continuator of Alain Bouchart's *Grandes croniques de Bretaigne*.

101. The printed account of Claude of France's coronation and Parisian entry (BnF Rés. Lb³⁰29), edited in Appendix V of *ER*, fails to mention that the ancestry figured in this scene was Breton. The theme of Anne of Brittany's genealogical tree figures centrally in Disarouez Penguern's *Genealogie . . . d'Anne tresillustre royne de France et duchesse de Bretagne* of 1510 (see BnF ms. ffr. 24043), in which the author describes his literary mission in the following terms, a passage which precedes the one cited above in the Introduction: "Et premier vueil vng arbre composer / Plain de branches et de chaires a choys / Pour ces princes tout en ordre poser / Comme celuy de Iesse aultreffoys. / Et tout en hault sera entre deux roys / Ladicte royne en grant magnificence, / Pour demonstrer que elle a esté par deux foys / Couronnee souueraine de France" [And first of all I wish to create a tree full of branches and numerous thrones to place these princes all in order, like [the tree] of Jesse in the past. And at the very top will be placed, between two kings, the

aforementioned queen in great splendor, to demonstrate that she has been twice crowned sovereign of France] (fol. 2).

102. When she died in 1524, Claude bequeathed the duchy of Brittany to her eldest son, not to her husband, although Francis I continued to administer it while Francis II was a minor. It was not until August 1532 that Brittany became a formal part of France, following the king's success in persuading Breton estate owners to agree to the annexation of Brittany to France. See Knecht, *Francis I*, 242–43.

103. For an edition of Gringore's account of the 1514 entry of Mary Tudor, see *ER*, 127–55. Similarities between Anne's 1492 and 1504 entries and that of Mary Tudor include the appearance of *Honneur* at the Saint-Denis Gate entry theater and the reappearance of the Solomon and Sheba couple at the Trinity site in 1514, reminiscent of the Painters' Gate stagings in 1492. In addition, the entry theater at the Saint Innocents in 1514 featured four virtues (Fortitude, Clemency, Mercy, and Truth) similar to, but not exactly the same as those represented in the *Toison d'Or* liminal miniature examined above. Generally speaking, the 1514 entry theaters, all organized by Pierre Gringore, appear to have been more personalized and complex than those staged for Anne in 1504.

104. App. IV, ll. 59–62.

105. ll. 23–24; App. IV, ll. 181–82. Three of the four who had figured in Anne of Brittany's ceremonials reappeared in Claude's: Anne of France, Margaret of Lorraine, duchess of Alençon, and Mary of Luxembourg, countess of Vendôme.

106. For Claude's apparel, see ll. 112–17; App. IV, ll. 145–64, 508–17; for the crown, see ll. 106–7; App. IV, 96–103, 337–38, 460–62, 511–15; for the scepter and hand of justice see ll. 45–46; App. IV, ll. 102–3, 225–26, 233–39; for the ring, see l. 49; App. IV, ll. 87, 233. Slight differences include mention of the queen's unction (App. IV, ll. 226–32, 238–39) and oblations (App. IV, l. 314), and a description of the jousts that took place following the banquet (App. IV, ll. 778–809).

107. ll. 50–51; App. IV, ll. 248–51, 259–60. Other male nobles held the scepter and hand of justice (App. IV, ll. 262–64).

108. App. IV, ll. 306–10, 537–42, 730–34.

109. See ll. 118–41 and App. IV, ll. 344–542; ll. 142–514, vv. 23–58 and App. IV, ll. 543–631, 673–89; App. IV, ll. 632–68; App. IV, ll. 690–765.

110. As was the case with Anne of Brittany herself, very little insight is provided in these festival books into Claude's personality and individual actions, besides her lamentations before her parents' tomb prior to her coronation (App. IV, ll. 43–46) and her ordering of the construction of her device for the Saint-Denis Gate staging (App. IV, ll. 76–78). For biographical details, see Castelain, *Au pays de Claude de France*, and C. Brown, "The Patron."

111. ll. 16–18, 35–36, 128–31; App. IV, ll. 37–38, 156, 186–87, 239–57, 518–21.

112. See *ER* for a description of the entry theaters at the Trinity (ll. 225–51), which invokes Francis I's recent victories and peace treaties, and at the Painters' Gate (ll. 252–308), which stages, among other things, the unification of religious and political figures. Most unconventional, however, was the king's very presence at Claude of France's coronation (App. IV, ll. 36–37).

113. See App. IV, ll. 624–25 and ll. 239–49. At the Trinity the queen was associated with *Liberalité* (Generosity), *Congnoissance* (Wisdom), and *Prudence* (Prudence).

114. See *ER* for a description of this entry theater at the Palais Royal (ll. 425–514, vv. 46–58).

115. In the anonymous account, *Temperance* replaces Gringore's *Continence*.

116. In the *Toison d'or* the seven virtues include the following four Cardinal Virtues: Temperance, Fortitude, Prudence, and Justice.

117. Given the failure of the two previous queens, Claude's mother and Mary Tudor, to produce a male heir, the stakes were particularly high and anxiety at many levels doubtless surrounded this issue.

118. Claude later bore Henry (1519), Madeleine (1520), Charles (1522), and Margaret (1523).

119. Knecht, 88. Claude apparently died of syphilis contracted from Francis I.

120. See McCartney's discussion of the juridical arguments of sixteenth-century jurist Barthélemy de Chasseneuz: "Whereas a king enjoyed full sovereign authority, the queen enjoyed a symbolic form of that power" (193). The French queen could not exercise temporal authority like the king, although she enjoyed privileges derived from her marital and maternal status (190).

## CHAPTER 2. FEMALE PATRONAGE
## AND THE POLITICS OF PERSONIFICATION ALLEGORY

1. According to extant documents, the French queen appears alone as dedicatee from 1491 to 1498 in some four instances. Robert du Herlin's *L'Acort des mesdisans et bien disans* (1493) (Arsenal ms. 3635) constitutes one of the few works commissioned by Anne of Brittany and dedicated to her during her first reign. See Chapter 3 for a discussion of the hybrid copy of Christine de Pizan's *Trésor de la cité des dames* (also known as the *Livre des trois vertus*) that Antoine Vérard offered Anne around 1497. According to Willard and Hicks, eds. *Le livre des trois vertus*, xxiii–xxiv, Anne owned a manuscript copy of Christine's *Livre des trois vertus*, which they identify as BnF ffr. 1180; it bears the arms of Brittany, not the joint arms of Brittany and France, suggesting that Anne may have acquired it before she married Charles VIII in 1491. The fact that it figured in the library at Blois (xxiv) implies that it eventually entered the royal collection through Anne. A manuscript copy of Cattaneo's history of the kings of France from Francion to Charles VIII in Latin (Arsenal ms. 1096), likely composed during Charles VIII's reign, contains a dedication to Anne alone. A copy of Guillaume Fillastre's *Histoire de la Toison d'Or* (BnF ffr. 138) features a miniature of Anne of Brittany facing personified virtues, discussed in Chapter 1; however, no written reference to the queen appears in the manuscript. While the *Catalogue des manuscrits*, 1, 10, dates ms. 138 from the sixteenth century, Deuffic, "Les Livres manuscrits d'Anne de Bretagne," 4, claims the copy was made for Anne between 1492 and 1498. A liminal miniature of Vérard offering Anne a volume decorates a copy of his edition of Robert de Saint Martin's *Trésor de l'âme* (ca. 1497), BnF Rés Vélins 350,

although the rest of the volume lacks any reference whatsoever to the French queen. See Chapter 3.

2. I borrow this useful term from Regalado, "Allegories of Power," 135.

3. Auton, *Chroniques de Louis XII*, IV, ii.

4. Born in October 1492, Charles-Orland died in December 1495.

5. The four emblems appear again below French arms in two shields supported by two angels prominently placed after the last verses of the work (fol. 46r). Scheller, "Imperial Themes," 57, calls attention to the rarity of this kind of decoration. For a discussion of the use of *prosimetrum* in this work, see Brown, "La mise en œuvre et la mise en page du prosimètre," 87–110. For an earlier version of some of these ideas, see Brown, "Le Mécénat d'Anne de Bretagne," 195–201.

6. It is only in the last stanza that the author dedicates his work to the king (vv. 1561–69). All references are taken from André de la Vigne, *La Ressource de la Chrestienté (1494)*.

7. While I examine the complicated implications of Anne's resolution to marry Charles VIII below in several different contexts, Labande-Mailfert, 101, points out too that marrying Anne of Brittany was not necessarily a happy decision for Charles: "si l'on cherche à connaître quelle fut la position personnelle du souverain en face du mariage breton, au moment de son acquiescement, l'on ne trouve pas trace de joie dans son attitude ou ses propos, et l'on peut se demander si celle qui détenait les secrets de pacification des terres conquises apaisa jamais la conscience et le coeur du roi."

8. As we learned in Chapter 1, there does not appear to have been an elaborate record made of Anne of Brittany's first coronation.

9. *Je ne sçay qui*'s depiction in a tripartite costume (fol. 31r) suggests that opposition to the king's foreign policy was located in all three different social classes (clergy, nobility, and bourgeoisie).

10. Fols. 2r, 2v (Figure 11), 10r, 44v.

11. In these illustrations, we observe *Dame Chrestienté* (fol. 2v), *Dame Chrestienté*, and *Dame Noblesse* in the Garden of France (fol. 10r) and *Magesté Royalle* before her entourage and guest speakers, *Chrestienté, Noblesse, Je ne sçay qui,* and *Bon Conseil* (fol. 15v, 23v [Figure 12], 25v, 31r, 37v). One final historiated initial (fol. 42v) portrays the departure from court of these speakers.

12. See the decoration and manipulation of CHARLES DE VALOIS in the pseudo-ballad found in vv. 678–719 and the vertical sentence honoring the king that is constructed from the first letter of vv. 1364–1445: "Charles hvitjesme et dernjer de ce nom par la grace de Djev roy de France a qvj Djev doint bonne vje et longve et paradis a la fin."

13. The king actually holds the scepter in his left hand in the opening miniature.

14. La Vigne, who composed this work as propaganda in support of the king's anticipated, albeit not fully supported, expedition to Italy in 1494, was subsequently hired as Charles VIII's secretary during the expedition, about which he wrote an account entitled *Le Voyage de Naples*. See Slerca's edition of this work. Anne of Brittany does not appear to have hired La Vigne as her secretary until 1504, around the time of her second coronation as Louis XII's queen.

15. She thus echoes the figure of *France* in Alain Chartier's *Quadrilog invectif* (1422). But she may also recall the historic situation of Anne of Brittany herself during the invasion of her duchy by French forces under Charles VIII in 1491. For details on the latter, see Labande-Mailfert, 55–115, and Minois, 273–307.

16. La Vigne speaks of quantities that cannot be counted (ll. 34–35) and the impossibility of finding language sufficient enough to describe a tenth of her mellifluous sweetness (ll. 32–33).

17. When he invokes her eyes that sparkle like the sun's rays, her lively, joyful heart, her mind rich in intelligence, her small powerful body, her good manners and other virtues, La Vigne relies on descriptions commonly associated with other women of renown, in particular the Virgin Mary.

18. It is possible that La Vigne or Anne of Brittany might have been influenced by Christine de Pizan's Minerva figure through the *City of Ladies* tapestries the queen supposedly owned (see Bell, *The Lost Tapestries*), or through access to the *Epître d'Othéa* or the *Cité des Dames* that apparently figured in the library of Charles VIII in 1490 (Baurmeister and Laffitte, 90).

19. For more details, see C. Brown, "Le Mécénat d'Anne de Bretagne," 199–201.

20. See also Seyssel's *Victoire du roy contre les Veniciens* (1510).

21. Louise of Savoy and Georges d'Amboise likewise received special copies of this work (BnF Rés. Vélins 2779 and 2781 respectively). To my knowledge, there is no extant copy of the version Louis XII might have received from Seyssel.

22. See "Le Proheme de l'acteur au Roy" (fols. 2r–3v), preceded by Seyssel's own arms and followed by a miniature of the king's porcupine emblem, which replaces the woodcut of French arms that appears in the printed version of the work.

23. No dedication miniature decorates the volumes offered to Louise of Savoy and Georges d'Amboise, which are nevertheless decorated with their coats of arms. According to Winn, *AV*, 97, Seyssel seems to have controlled the publication of this and other works he wrote that Vérard published.

24. In the woodcut featured in paper copies of the publication, the king's throne bearing fleurs-de-lis fills a similar space. See McFarlane, *Antoine Vérard*, frontispiece, for a reproduction of the original woodcut.

25. The insertion of a folio containing a rondeau specially composed for Anne of Brittany following the second flyleaf of Vélins 2780 is somewhat problematic. While it is difficult to determine if Seyssel himself or a subsequent owner of the book included these verses in Anne of Brittany's copy, or if Seyssel himself authored them, Poujol, editor of Seyssel's *La monarchie de France*, 28, claims that this handwritten rondeau "est sans doute de la main même de Claude de Seyssel." The rondeau appears to refer to a different work, a book of hours dedicated to the queen, which apparently emphasizes a particular male saint, although Poujol assumes these to be allusions to the *Louenges* and to Louis XII himself. Of additional interest is the poet's reference to the queen's "reading" of the work (my emphasis): "Quant de la veue du saint serés absente / J'ay fantaisie que jours ouuriers et festes / *Lisant* au liure ses tresmerueileux gestes / Ceste legende *trouuerés* moult plaisante / A vostre vsaige" [When you are absent from the view of the saint, I imagine on work days

and feast days that in reading in the book about his very marvelous actions you will find this legend very pleasing for your use].

26. A color reproduction of this image appears in Thibault, *Les manuscrits* (between 16 and 17).

27. A similar rendition figures prominently in the numerous manuscript copies of Anne of Brittany's funeral book (see Figure 44).

28. Munn, *A Contribution to the Study of Jean Lemaire de Belges*, 158–60, offers a description and analysis of ffr. 25295, and an edition of the *Dyalogue* appears on 160–66. A more recent edition of the work appears in Jean Lemaire de Belges, *Épistre du roy à Hector*, ed. Armstrong and Britnell, 1–9. Unless otherwise noted, all subsequent references are taken from this latter edition. For other analyses of this work, see Brown, *The Shaping of History and Poetry*, 101ff, and Jodogne, *Jean Lemaire de Belges*, 387–90.

29. Munn, 158, and Armstrong and Britnell, 1–5, make this suggestion.

30. See the analysis of "potenciallement" and of this passage in Armstrong and Britnell, 1–2, n. 1, who interpret the liberation of *Dame Vertu militaire* from her body as the ability to take action.

31. See Armstrong and Britnell, 11–12, for an edition of this work, from which all references are taken. Munn, 160–66, also edits the work. Louis' presence as a heroic example in the *Dyalogue* thus shifts into allegorical mode in the third work, entitled *Vim Ludovicus habet* by its most recent editors (V) (see their edition, 15–29), in which he appears in personified form as *Puissance Royalle* (although Armstrong-Britnell, XII, suggest this personification represents *Monarchie Française*), a figure who resembles *Magesté Royalle*. Three female figures in the work, *Ingratitude*, *Obstination*, and *Folle Esperance*, the so-called "filles d'enfer" (v. 44) are visually depicted as females in the accompanying miniature (see Armstrong-Britnell, XIV–XV, for an analysis of this illustration), as is the positive character, *Puissance Royalle*, the alter ego of the French king, who wears a crown on her head, armor on her upper body, and a fleur-de-lis skirt, while holding a banner with the Latin name of Louis. *Le Pape Julles* literally represents the pope, while *Le Sainct Siege Apostolicque*, representing the Church at Rome, appears as a cardinal in the miniature. A passage follows in which Louis XII's name is spelled out repeatedly in a play on words between *Lvdovicus*, *vim* and *vis*.

32. See Munn, 166, n. 23, and Armstrong-Britnell, 106, for details.

33. A subsequent stanza representing a dialogue between History and a potential patron reinforces this ballad's message (see Armstrong-Britnell, 13).

34. For historical details, see Auton, *Chroniques*, IV, 87–282, and his "Exil de Gennes la superbe," 376–78; Bridge, III, 252–94; Quilliet, *Louis XII*, 377–83; and Baumgartner, *Louis XII*, 183–97. For a discussion of the cultural and artistic context of this event, see Scheller, "Gallia Cisalpina." For a discussion of the *Voyage de Gênes*, see Sherman, "The Selling of Louis XII," 120–25; C. Brown, *The Shaping of History and Poetry*, 47–51; and Trisolini's edition of the *Voyage de Gênes* 25–33, from which all references are taken. Trisolini, 59, claims the work dates from 1507. Avril and Reynaud, 303, date the manuscript (BnF ffr. 5091) "vers 1508."

35. Although Coudrec, "Les Miniatures du *Voyage de Gênes*," 46–47, Scheller,

"Gallia Cisalpina," 37, Trisolini, Introduction, 58–59, and others were more tentative about this attribution, Avril, *La Passion des manuscrits enluminés*, 104, clearly names Jean Bourdichon as the artist of these miniatures. He was paid in 1508 for this work (Avril and Reynaud, 293 and 303).

36. Some of the ideas in this section appeared earlier in C. Brown, "Grief, Rape and Suicide."

37. This scene recalls the more complicated allegorical staging in Alain Chartier's *Traité de l'Espérance* (an unfinished work begun in 1428) in which *Foy, Esperance,* and *Charité* save the *acteur* from the depressive effects of *Melencolie, Defiance, Indignation,* and *Deseperance.*

38. The repeated association of women with grief and mourning is more fully examined in Chapters 4 and 5.

39. I borrow this term from Caviness, "Anchoress, Abbess, and Queen," 142, who discusses female owners of books of piety in the eleventh to fourteenth centuries.

40. See Minois, 429–33, who speaks of Anne's unusual role in bringing women into her entourage.

41. Aliverti mentions this miniature in "Visits to Genoa," 222. For black-and-white reproductions of these three scenes, see Coudrec, "Les miniatures," Plates V, VII, and VIII. See Avril and Reynaud, Plate 167 (p. 304) for a color reproduction of fol. 15v.

42. This supports Giordano's claims about Louis XII's entries into Milanese territory about this time: "Toutes les entrées en Milanais eurent pour but de faire remarquer de façon éclatante qui était, désormais, le nouveau seigneur du domaine, et de lui signifier l'hommage et la fidélité de son peuple. Il s'agissait d'un grand rituel qui était une mise en évidence de l'état politique du moment et qui se faisait dans l'intérêt du roi comme des villes dominées" ("Les entrées de Louis XII en Milanais," 141–42). See also pp. 144–48 for a discussion of the entry into Genoa.

43. In *Images of Rape*, 185–86, Wolfthal confirms the association of women with private, interior spaces in medieval art and literature, while men are associated with public, exterior spaces. See also Parsons, "Ritual and Symbol in the English Medieval Queenship," 60.

44. See Stafford, "The Portrayal of Royal Women in England," 157, who explains: "Gender definition that stressed the public, military man appeared to preclude female activity. The increased professionalization of church and state sharpened the public-private distinction which the dynastic kingdoms of the early Middle Ages had blurred. Authority was increasingly located inclusively in the public sphere."

45. In *Le Depucellage de la ville de Tournay*, which dates from ca. 1513, Laurens Desmoulins places similar words in the mouth of Tournay, who states "suis rompue et violee" "me laissay deflorer" [I was broken and raped . . . I let myself be deflowered] in describing the attack on her by the English (cited by Cowling, *Building the Text*, 52).

46. Scheller, "Gallia Cisalpino," 37, interprets the presence of women in this way: "the ladies of Genoa were expressly asked to show themselves at the windows lining the route, which was a useful ploy if one wanted to mollify a wrathful monarch. . . . the 'penitential choir' recalled the children who had greeted Cardinal d'Amboise at Milan in

1500. At Genoa it was girls and young women who, kneeling and waving olive branches, loudly cried out 'misericordia,' begging the king for compassion and forbearance."

47. See Avril, *Creating French Culture*, 179, for a color reproduction of this image (fol. 22v). See Auton, *Chroniques*, IV, 232, for a description of the armed monarch and his entourage. For a discussion of Louis in battle attire, see Giordano, 144–45. Scheller, "Gallia Cisalpina," 7–37, and Giordano, 139–46, offer details about the ceremonial nature of Louis XII's various entries into Italian cities during the first decade of the sixteenth century. Up until his entry into Genoa in 1507, Louis XII, like his predecessor Charles VIII during his campaign through Italy in 1494–95, had been willingly and cordially received at the time of his entries into Italian cities (Milan, 1499; Genoa, 1502). But the Genoa entry of 1507 marked a change in this tradition, for Louis entered as conqueror, as a martial albeit clement ruler entering a repentant city at the head of his army. This dynamic was symbolized by his armor and by the fact that, as Marot describes it, one of the French king's men followed the king carrying an unsheathed sword (vv. 720–50). See also Auton, *Chroniques*, IV, 235. According to *La Conqueste de Gennes*, it was Louis XII himself who held "his naked sword in his hand as a sign of victory," signaling his intention of humiliating the Genoese (cited by Mitchell, *The Majesty of the State*, 91). Quilliet, *Louis XII*, 382, alludes to this very humiliation in his description of the entry.

48. Marot's description of the women of Pavia extols their beauty as well in more venerable terms (vv. 806–12).

49. The narrator refers to Genoa's three sons (vv. 114–15).

50. By comparison, La Vigne conscientiously maintains grammatical gender identity in his *Ressource de la Chrestienté* of 1494, although, as we learned above in this chapter, the figure of *Magesté Royalle* is particularly complex, given that she is a female allegorical figure representing the French king himself. See also the discussion of Alain Chartier's *mise en question* of the feminine gender in his *Quadrilog invectif* in C. Brown, "Allegorical Design and Image-Making, 385–404.

51. Vv. 182–83, 190–95; ll. 40–72; vv. 993–1001, 1058, 1068–82.

52. *Medieval Death*, 520.

53. The kneeling black-robed male mourners, urban representatives seeking the French king's clemency, who are depicted in the visual renditions of Louis XII's recapture of Genoa (fol. 20v) and who subsequently had to carry his canopy, constitute the literal version of *Gênes*'s allegorized funeral portrait. In the chronicle section of his *Voyage de Gênes*, Marot includes women in his description of the city's representatives (vv. 696–702). But in his *Chroniques*, Auton does not specifically state that women figured in this group of urban representatives (IV, 233–34).

54. I am grateful to Myra Orth for calling my attention to this work. Claiming authorship of the work, Auton actually includes it in his *Chroniques*, IV, 13–25, explaining that after receiving the work from his chronicler and carefully reading it, Louis XII sent it to Genoa to be placed on Thomassine's tomb (26). In this narrative, Genoa delivers a lamentation about the death of one of her citizens, Thomassine Espinolle, followed by an epitaph delivered by the deceased herself. Four manuscripts of this work have come down to us today. The opening miniatures in BnF mss. ffr. 1684 (fol. 2) and 25419 (fol.

3v) appear to dramatize the literal version of Thomassine's despair upon the departure of Louis XII, although the principal female figure depicted in this illustration could also be interpreted to be that of *Gennes*. Nonetheless, the two subsequent miniatures provide literal interpretations of women mourning over Thomassine's coffin (fol. 7v in ms. 1684, fol. 8v in ms. 25419) and of Louis XII's supposed grief upon learning of her demise (fol. 9r in ms. 1684, fol. 10r in ms. 25419). Thus, unlike the illustrated ms. 5091 of the *Voyage de Gênes* offered to Anne of Brittany by Marot, a disconnect exists between the allegorical nature of the text of the *Complainte de Gennes* and its illustrations. See Thibault, *Louis XII*, 61–62, for a description of Montpellier, Bibliothèque de la faculté de Médecine, ms. H.439. The fourth manuscript, BnF fr. 6169 bears no illustrations (folios prepared for them remain blank).

55. The missing husband and father figure reinforces *Gênes*'s precarious and threatening position as an unattached female, until she submits to the rule of the victorious foreign invader, Louis XII, who may be seen as an ersatz husband or father figure.

56. She also appears as an image on the wall in the mourning scene on fol. 34v (Figure 17). Marot makes no mention whatsoever of the Virgin, although *Raison* makes an occasional reference to God in her speech—"Ne doubte pas que c'est Dieu qui te donne / Ces haultains biens [Do not doubt that it is God who gives you these worthy goods" (vv. 1172–73)]; "Retourne à Dieu, soyes humble desormais [Return to God, be henceforth humble" (v. 1197)]—as does *Gênes* (vv. 1215–19, 1302–6). For a discussion of the artistic tradition of the *Madonna Avocata*, see Baldwin and Marchand, "The Virgin Mary as Advocate." I am grateful to Pamela Sheingorn for this reference.

57. Although the French queen may not have read or even known about Auton's *Complainte de Gennes*, *Gennes* was created to attract the reader's pity as well.

58. Genoa confirms this when she proclaims in the *Voyage de Gênes*: "Dame, j'estoyes, maintenant suys esclave; / Du solier suys descendue en la cave; / Jadiz batiz, maintenant suys batue" (vv. 1102–4) [I was a lady; now I am a slave; / I have been kicked into the dungeon; / Once built up, I am now torn down]. See also vv. 959–61.

59. See, for example, the dedication miniature that introduces the manuscript copy of the *Vies des femmes célèbres*, offered by Antoine Dufour to Anne de Bretagne (Figure 26). For other similar examples of dedication scenes in which the queen's seat is at floor level, see the dedication miniature introducing *La Traduction des épistres de Saint Jérôme* by Antoine Dufour (SP, MS Fr. F. v. I. 3, fol. 1r) (Plate LVIII in Laborde, *Principaux Manuscrit*) and the miniature introducing the *Epistre composee . . . par . . . Fauste Andrelin en laquelle Anne tresvertueuse Royne de France est courroucee que le trespuissant et invincible Roy Loys douziesme, son mary, soit de rechief contraingct guerre mouvoir contre les desloyaulx et rebelles Veniciens* (SP, MS Fr. F. v. XIV. 8, fol. 40v) (Figure 36), which is discussed in Chapter 4.

60. Lowden adopts this term in "The Royal/Imperial Book," 215.

61. For a reproduction of this scene of Louis XII seated on a raised throne in SP, MS Fr. F. v. XIV. 8, fol. 81v, see Laborde, Plate LXI. Compare with the scene of Anne de Bretagne on fol. 1r.

62. Parsons, "Ritual and Symbol," 64.

63. Mitchell, 92, provides the following details about the French king's entry into Genoa in 1507: "Louis, who seems to have had a keen sense of the dramatic and of the power of public spectacle, decided to hold a *siège royal*, or royal court of justice, in public view. A large platform was erected in the courtyard of the doges' palace, and on top of that construction a smaller platform was built to hold a throne. Both were draped with a rich cloth that was woven with fleurs-de-lys, and there was a *baldacchino* over the throne. . . . When Louis had taken his place, a *roy d'armes*, or master of ceremonies, cried 'De par le roy!' . . . to impose silence."

64. See Huneycutt, "Female Succession," 191, who claims that medieval chroniclers accepted the idea of women as regents or transmitters of power, but did not often tolerate women exercising authority in their own name.

65. In this piece she calls for a broader reconsideration than scholars have traditionally provided of "the methods, places, forms and agents that historical writing has traditionally associated with sovereignty" (9). Fradenburg claims, for example: "If in fact sovereignty depends upon and exists through constructions of gender (and transgressions thereof), the kingly as well as queenly potencies must be reread in terms of gender, and kingly and queenly potencies must be re-read as always mutually implicated" (3).

66. Anne had become duchess of Brittany at age eleven, on the death of her father in 1488.

67. See Poulet, "Capetian Women and the Regency," 105–6, about the differences in coronations of kings and queens in Capetian France.

68. Fradenburg, 80.

69. Parsons, "Family, Sex, and Power," 4, speaks of "both the promise of alliance and the threat of division" involved in the choice of a queen. He adds: "Whatever their origins, queens as daughters and wives had to negotiate divided loyalties, an essential aspect of queens' understanding of themselves and others' understanding of them."

70. Parsons, "Mothers, Daughters, Marriage, Power," 77. See also Wood, "The First Two Queens Elizabeth," 127.

71. In fact, Anne had refused the hand of Alain d'Albret at an earlier date. Moreover, she had actually married *par procuration* Maximilian, a union undone by her alliance with Charles VIII. For details, see Minois, 244–78.

72. See Markale, 167–68, 189. See also Fradenburg, 80–81, who reflects that "queens usually both exemplify sovereignty *and* are subject to it; queens are simultaneously inside and outside 'structure.' Most queens come to an 'inside' from an 'outside' and bear something of the outside with them."

73. Markale, 172, 198 ff.

74. It is nonetheless a fact that Anne's marriage to Louis XII had been dictated by her marriage treaty with Charles VIII. See Nassiet, "Les traités de marriage."

75. Bridge, III, 27.

76. "Mothers, Daughters, Marriage, Power," 65.

77. For details, see Bridge, III, 242–51, and E. Brown, "Order and Disorder in the Life and Death of Anne de Bretagne."

78. Anne was so furious upon discovering Louis' reversal of their earlier decision that she stayed in Brittany for many months (Baumgartner, 145).

79. Upon her death in 1524, Queen Claude willed the duchy to her eldest son, not to her husband, although Francis I managed the duchy during his reign. It was eventually integrated into France in 1532.

80. McCartney, "The King's Mother," 119. Anne's daughter Claude was shunted aside even more so; her husband gave his mother, not Claude, regent authority over France during his absence. See Poulet, 111, who claims that dowager queens were often preferred as regents over wives, although it is noteworthy that Louise of Savoy had never been queen. See also McCartney, 117, 125, and Stafford, 145.

81. I also discuss this in the Introduction.

82. Maulde La Clavière confirms that this volume figured centrally in Louis XII's library along with the other volumes of Auton's *Chroniques* (IV, xxiii, xliii). See his description of the manuscript (Auton, IV, 40, n. 1), and of the miniature discussed here (IV, 42, n. 1). See Tournoy-Thoen, "Les premiers épithalames humanistes," 203–4, for a discussion of the Latin nuptial poem that Fausto Andrelini offered Louis XII in 1506 to commemorate Claude's engagement to Francis.

83. Auton, *Chroniques*, IV, 45.

84. See Minois, 477: "La reine retourne donc dans son duché, rappelant par là sa position de semi-indépendance. Son voyage ressemble à une longue bouderie. Car au lieu de se limiter à un pèlerinage aller-retour au Folgoët, elle entreprend un tour complet de la Bretagne, qui dure plus de trois mois. Cette volonté affirmée d'indépendance finit par devenir suspecte, et il faut que le roi se fâche pour la faire revenir."

85. Maulde La Clavière suggests that Anne was likely the person responsible for bringing Jean d'Auton to court, although he seems to have gradually lost favor with the queen as his chronicles became less influenced by Anne's perspective ("Notice sur Jean d'Auton," in Jean d'Auton, *Chroniques*, IV, xiii–xv)

86. At least one account, that of Brantôme, alleged that during one of Louis XII's illnesses, Anne of Brittany, having actually assembled boatloads of valuables for transport to Brittany, was stopped by Gié in the king's name. The absence of this story from trial records, however, puts into question the truth of the rumor, according to Bridge, III, 231.

87. *Mémoires*, 1418–19.

88. Minois, 363, claims that doctors also encouraged this form of "traitement 'psychothérapique' pour chaser la mélancolie" of the queen. See Minois, 374, for details of Anne's grief over the loss of five infants by age twenty-one.

89. Accounts of the queen's reaction in 1498 to Charles VIII's death point to an equally emotional display of grief, making reference to her death wish, a common *topos* in lamentation descriptions (Minois, 377). Minois's strong reaction to Anne's apparent change of mood just two days after the king's death is tinged with a misogynistic tone: "Mais ce qui est surprenant, c'est que dès le lendemain, 9 avril, cette femme brisée, qui se disait prêt à mourir, affirme sans faille son autorité de duchesse de Bretagne. Retrouvant brusquement son énergie, elle . . . affirme la plénitude de son pouvoir. . . . Sans aller

jusqu'à parler de simulation, il faut sans doute attribuer ses marques excessives de chagrin à l'imitation des modes espagnoles qu'elle apprécie tant. Car une telle présence d'esprit, une telle activité et une telle clairvoyance sont peu compatibles avec l'état d'effondrement qu'elle affecte alors" (378–79). Markale relates this moment in a much less judgmental way in his *Anne de Bretagne*, 198: "On a dit qu'elle avait pleuré, s'était lamentée de son triste sort, veuve après avoir perdu cinq enfants. Peut-être, mais on ne sait rien . . . Son chagrin, si chagrin il y eut, nous ne le connaissons pas."

90. Parsons, "Family, Sex, and Power," 9.

91. Stafford's discussion of how tensions of familial and dynastic politics were often suppressed behind images of harmony (145) resonates with this work.


CHAPTER 3. WOMEN FAMOUS AND INFAMOUS:
COURT CONTROVERSIES ABOUT FEMALE VIRTUES


1. Buettner, 21, attributes recent scholarly interest in Boccaccio's *De mulieribus claris* to the resurgence of research on Christine de Pizan over the last few decades.

2. *Le Champion des Dames* does not appear to have figured among Anne of Brittany's readings, although it influenced works in her library, such as Jean Marot's *La Vraye disant advocate des dames* (see below).

3. In *Virtue and Venom*, a study of catalogues as an expression or critique of cultural attitudes toward women, McLeod, 3, claims: "Catalogs can not only illuminate the stubborn persistence of Western misogyny but also reveal struggles and doubts about this line of thought."

4. *De mulieribus claris* was apparently translated several times into French (in addition to other languages), including the first and most famous 1401 translation (no longer attributed to Laurent de Premierfait), recently edited in two volumes by Baroin and Haffen, eds., *Des Cleres et Nobles Femmes*. See Franklin, 9, for references to works on the various translations of *De mulieribus claris*, some of which we will examine below. See Taylor, "Translation as Reception," for an insightful comparison between Boccaccio's Latin text and the 1401 French translation. Taylor demonstrates that "the careful equivocations of Boccaccio's *de Mulieribus claris*" are "rendered unequivocal" by the anonymous French translator (507). See also Sozzi, "Boccaccio in Francia nel Cinquecento," for a discussion of sixteenth-century French translations and imitations of the work. According to Bozzolo, *Manuscrits des traductions françaises d'oeuvres de Boccacce*, 23, the first to provide extensive bibliographic descriptions of the 16 known manuscripts of the French translations of Boccaccio's work, the author of the earliest known French translation of Boccaccio's *De mulieribus claris* remains anonymous.

5. Franklin, 1, notes that Boccaccio continued editing this work until his death in 1375.

6. Boccaccio, *Famous Women*, trans. V. Brown, xi. All subsequent English citations of this work are taken from Brown's translation. As Tomalin, *The Fortunes of the Warrior Heroine*, 20, reminds us, Boccaccio himself suggests that he was the first to discuss famous

women. However, as Franklin, 1, n. 2, points out, Boccaccio was unaware that Plutarch had included examples of 27 women in his *Moralia* of 120 B.C.E. For details on the nine .stages of the composition of Boccaccio's work, see V. Brown, ed., xii.

7. Jordan, "Boccaccio's In-Famous Women," 25–47; Tomalis, 13–31; Buettner; and Kolsky, *The Ghost of Boccaccio*. Kolsky, who claims that the *De mulieribus claris* "laid highly influential groundwork for a sociological analysis of women's inferiority" (225–26), states that the work "exemplifies male ambivalence towards women."

8. McLeod, 64, 78–79, discusses the possible influence of Jerome's *Adversus Jovinianam* on Boccaccio.

9. V. Brown, xix, claims: "In general he is much more expansive than his sources in praising women's intellectual powers or their literary accomplishments or their moral virtues or their artistic creations."

10. V. Brown, xix, xvi; Franklin, 18–19. Pamela Benson, *Renaissance Women*, goes so far as to claim that Boccaccio had a "profeminist voice," ascribing supposed "contradictory notions of women" in the work to conflicts between authorial ideas of feminine virtues and evidence from legal and historical accounts (cited by Franklin, 7).

11. See, for example, how Dufour explicitly places Boccaccio in the category of past misogynist writers whom he seeks to correct: "Pource ce que la plus commune partie des hommes se adonnent à blasmer les dames, tant de langue que de plume, et en ont composé des livres, comme Bocasse, Théophraste et ung tas d'aultres, j'ay bien voulu cercher par les anciennes librairies à celle fin de trouver aucun véritable acteur qui sagement, loyallement et véritablement parlast d'elles" [Since most men tend to blame women, both in speech and in writing, and have composed books about them, such as Boccaccio, Theophrastus and a lot of others, I wanted to search through old book collections with the goal of finding some truthful author who spoke wisely, loyally and truthfully about them] (1). Currently housed as MS XVII in the Musée Dobrée in Nantes, the manuscript of the *Vies des femmes célèbres* was edited by G. Jeanneau in 1970. This and all subsequent references are taken from this edition.

12. BnF ffr. mss. 133 and 590 contain an illustration of Boccaccio's dedication of his book to his patroness. In the dedication scene in BnF ffr. 598, the dedicatee, surrounded by numerous court ladies, receives an open book (a rather unusual occurrence) from the kneeling author. This miniature is followed by that of a single author alone in his study. BnF ffr. 12420 opens with an author miniature (fol. 3), although, in this case, the Boccaccio figure reads to an audience of three males, all but confirming his intention of reaching out to a male readership. A dedicatory image depicting the author kneeling before his patroness follows (fol. 4v). See Buettner for an insightful analysis of all the miniatures in this manuscript copy. The Spencer Collection Ms. 33 in the New York Public Library opens with an author image (fol. 1), but no dedication miniature is found in this version. The liminal illustration in Pierpont Morgan Library ms. M381 (fol. 1) offers two juxtaposed images (in somewhat poor condition): the author writing at the left and the author presenting his book to his dedicatee at the right. A smaller single author illustration on fol. 2v may well have been designed to depict the French translator at work. See my discussion of the BnF 599 miniatures below.

13. Curiously, the first printed vernacular translation of Boccaccio's *De mulieribus claris* in Italy appeared in 1506, almost a decade later than the publication of the first French translation of the work. In addition, all previous editions of the Latin text were published outside of Italy (Kolsky, 1–2).

14. Through their creation of a "lingua cortigiana," Kolsky continues, "The discourse on women acquired the status of a courtly discourse, suggestive of a particular elevated institution and lifestyle" (228).

15. In describing the miniatures in BnF ffr. ms. 12420 as "more monologically positive than the text," Buettner, 22, wonders if they reflect traces of the writing of Christine de Pizan, claiming that by "contracting and expanding the narrative flow, images have a powerful way with which to intervene in the textual diegesis" (55).

16. Ségemaud, *La bibliothèque de Charles d'Orléans*, 19.

17. "Louise de Savoie, ses enfants et ses livres," 254.

18. It's worth noting as well that Charles's library also included a paper copy of the work as entry #42 confirms (Ségemaud, 40). This copy, originally commissioned by Jean d'Angoulême, sometime before 1467, is today housed at the BnF as ffr. 1120. Both manuscripts figure in the same family (B), according to Bozzolo, 25.

19. See note 12.

20. Although the author miniature in manuscript 599 does not compete with the opening dedication miniature, as it does in at least two other manuscripts of the *Cleres et nobles femmes*, because of its placement at the end of the manuscript (fol. 94v), it is nevertheless the last image with which the reader is left. Curiously, Boccaccio (if indeed this portrait is designed to represent him) has aged since the dedication miniature, for, while wearing the same colored robe as the kneeling author in the dedication miniature his gray hair protrudes from beneath the red hat, suggesting the passage of time, not so much beginning with the dedication of his work to Countess Andrea, but rather from the period when Boccaccio wrote most of the *De mulieribus claris* (1460–61) to its completion around his death in 1475. His hand is placed on the closed book on the desk to his side, likely signifying that the work has been completed.

21. Scholars can consult the BnF website Mandragore for scanned images of these miniatures.

22. Vérard was, according to Winn, *AV*, 36, "the first publisher to make systematic use of vellum for at least a few copies of almost every edition." According to her, some 150 extant vellum copies made from his 280+ editions are still extant (31, n. 52).

23. See C. Brown, "Paratextual Performances," 255–64.

24. Some of the following remarks are found in an earlier form in "La Mise en oeuvre et la mise en page des recueils traitant des femmes célèbres."

25. BnF ffr. 133: *Cy commence le livre que fist Jehan Boccace de Certal des cleres et nobles femmes. Lequel il envoa* [sic] *a Andree des Alpes de Florence et contesse de Haulteville* (my emphasis). See Bozzolo, 91–100, 149–55, 180–82, for the titles of the other extant manuscripts: BnF ffr. mss. 598, 599, 1120, 5037, 12420; Ex Phillipps 3648, Musée Condé ms. 856, ÖNB ms. 2555, BBR, ms. 9509, BL mss. Royal 16 G V, Royal 20 C V; Lisbon, Fundação

Gulbenkain ms. L.A. 143, New York, Pierpont Morgan Library ms. M381, New York, Public Library, Spencer Collection ms. 33,

26. Except for BnF ffr. mss. 598 and 12420 and Musée Condé ms. 856.

27. See V. Brown, xiv–xv, for details. She suggests that the dedication may have been written in haste. "Or," she adds, "perhaps he did not expect that Andrea Acciaiuoli would actually spend much time reading the *Famous Women*" (xv–xvi). See Franklin, 23–29, for an insightful analysis of Boccaccio's dedication to Acciaiuoli.

28. Franklin, 9, 23–24, in arguing that Boccaccio's work was written for the moral edification of a predominantly male audience, refers to Andrea Acciaiuoli as "a screen dedicatee" (23). See Chapter 2 for a discussion of the abstraction of female figures into personified figures as a literary ploy to mediate between examples of powerful females and contemporary realities about women's roles.

29. By contrast, almost all the manuscript and printed imitations of Boccaccio's *De mulieribus claris* in late fifteenth- and early sixteenth-century Italy were dedicated to noble women by male authors (Kolsky, 2).

30. See Jeanneau's edition of Dufour's *Vies des femmes célèbres*, 174–77, for a transcription of the entire prologue.

31. Boccaccio's dedication makes it clear that he was interested in obtaining patronage, as he explicitly wonders "to whom I should first send this work so that it would not languish idly in my possession" (3). He admits that his first choice of dedicatee, Joanna, Queen of Sicily, seemed too dazzling for his "little book so small and weak" (3). Boccaccio then praises his chosen dedicatee as "a shining model of ancient virtue in our time" (5). The anonymous translator is not as daunted as Boccaccio before his first choice of a dedicatee, although the Italian author is much more direct in connecting his writing to her fame: "and so I should like to increase your well-deserved fame by dedicating this little book to you" (5).

32. See "Paratextual Performances," 267–68, for a discussion of the role of fame in the creation, translation, reproduction, and dissemination of this work, and for an earlier version of the ideas developed in this section.

33. See Boccaccio's praise of his dedicatee (3–4).

34. The italics indicate amplification of Boccaccio's words. Compare with his final request of his dedicatee: "If you judge it worthy, most excellent lady, give this book the boldness to appear in public. Under your auspices it will go forth, I believe, safe from malicious criticism" (7).

35. Compare with Boccaccio's final lines to his dedicatee: "and [this book] will make your name and the names of other illustrious women glorious on the lips of humankind" (7).

36. See Buettner, 29–31, for a discussion of the instruments and symbols of power in miniatures.

37. Vérard used 9 different woodcuts for 76 illustrations in his edition of the *Nobles et cleres dames*. Twenty-eight famous women have no accompanying illustration.

38. Compare with Boccaccio's last lines to his dedicatee: "As you cannot be physically

present everywhere, my book will make you and your merits known to those now alive" (7).

39. Compare with Boccaccio's words: "The book, I believe, will do as much to keep your name bright for posterity as (with Fortune's help) the county of Monteodorisio did formerly and as the county of Altavilla does now" (5). See also: "my book will . . . preserve you forever for posterity" (7).

40. Compare to Boccaccio's more imperious tone: "You will find, at times, that an appropriate recital of the facts has compelled me to mix the impure with the pure. Do not skip over these parts and do not shy away from them, but persevere in your reading. As on entering a garden you extend your ivory hands toward the flowers, leaving aside the thorns, so in this case relegate to one side offensive matters and gather what is praiseworthy. Whenever you, who profess the Christian religion, read that a pagan woman has some worthy quality which you feel you lack, blush and reproach yourself that, although marked with the baptism of Christ, you have let yourself by surpassed by a pagan in probity or chastity or resolution. Summon up the powers of your already strong character and do not allow yourself to be outdone, but strive to outdo all women in noble virtues" (5–7). In addition, unlike the French translator, Boccaccio goes so far as to warn his dedicatee about certain female vices: "Remember that you should not embellish your beauty with cosmetics, as do the majority of your sex, but increase its distinction through integrity, holiness, and the finest actions" (7).

41. By contrast, Boccaccio counsels his dedicatee in a more patronizing manner than the anonymous translator: "accept with favor this small gift from a scholar. If you will take some advice from me, I urge you to read it occasionally: its counsels will sweeten your leisure, and you will find delight in the virtues of your sex and in the charm of the stories. Nor will the perusal have been vain, I believe, if it spurs your noble spirit to emulation of the deeds of women in the past" (5).

42. See Boccaccio, 3: "Since women are the subject of the book, I saw that it ought to be dedicated, not to a prince, but to some distinguished lady. As I searched for a worthy recipient, the first woman who came to mind was that radiant splendor of Italy, that unique glory not only of women but of rules: Joanna, Most Serene Queen of Sicily and Jerusalem. . . . I was strongly tempted to place this humble and pious work before Her Majesty's throne. In the end, however, as her royal luster is so dazzling and the flickering flame of my little book so small and weak, I gradually changed my mind, fearing that the greater would altogether eclipse the lesser light" (3).

43. In addition, the author's name was announced in the rubric preceding the translator's prologue as well as in the rubric announcing Boccaccio's prologue.

44. In his edition of the *Nobles et cleres dames* prologue, Jeanneau suggests that the anonymous translator may have been associated with the Church, given the liturgical formulation of a passage near the end of the prologue. Is it possible, however, that the translator was Guillaume Tardif, who authored or translated several works for Charles VIII, which Vérard then printed, often without identifying him as author (*Grandes Heures royales* [1490–92], *Art de bien mourir* [1492])? See Winn, *AV*, 68, 86–87, who states: "Tardif's name is absent from works commissioned by the king, but very evident in both

the *Art de faulconnerie* and the *Apologues de Laurens Valle*. Presumably Tardif insisted on recognition for works which he had planned to offer to Charles VIII."

45. I note, however, that the dedication to Louis XII that opens Vérard's edition of Claude Seyssel's *Louenges du roy* (1508), discussed in Chapter 2, was not suppressed in the queen's copy of the work.

46. Winn, *AV*, 114, 148, discusses these details, pointing out that folios a1–a2 were actually excised from Charles VIII's copy, while the same two folios were left blank in Henry VII's copy. For information on Henry VII's patronage and connections with Vérard, see Winn, *AV*, 138–53, and Kipling, "Henry VII and the Origins of Tudor Patronage," 125–26.

47. It is not entirely clear why the BL copy has been deemed to be the original property of Henry VII, since there are no definitive signs of his ownership. Crown decorations on the inside covers, which postdate the sixteenth century, and the book's elaborate decoration do suggest royal ownership at some point in time. Moreover, the following remarks by Plomer,"Bibliographical Notes," 299, bear relevance: "the majority of printed books belonging to Henry VII now in the British Museum consist of Vérard's publications. They are sumptuous copies printed on vellum, with hand-painted illustrations, and are now bound in red velvet, which may indicate that the original covers were of the same material." Winn, *AV*, 141, n. 48, quotes Plomer's mention of a payment by Henry VII on 29 September 1499 "to a Frensheman for sertain bokes," which, she suggests, "amounted to an impressive £56 3s, a total indicating a large number of books." According to Winn, *AV*, 140, the first vellum copy of a Vérard edition in Henry VII's library dates from 1493, and was presumably the *Nobles et cleres dames*. Therefore, it is quite possible that this very copy figured among those bought by the English king in 1499, if indeed the "Frensheman" referred to Vérard.

48. For details on Robert de Saint-Martin, see the introduction to Brisson's *Critical Edition and Study of Frère Robert*, 72–80.

49. Frère Robert thus represented yet another deceased author whose work Vérard published.

50. Winn, *AV*, 134–35, poses similar questions.

51. I am grateful to Helen Swift, St. Hilda's College, Oxford University, for drawing my attention to this copy.

52. The English king's copy likewise contains the original woodcuts over which miniatures have been painted. Winn, *AV*, 141, discusses Henry VII's tendency to purchase "already-made books in lieu of custom orders."

53. A red caplike covering on top of the crown, absent in the original woodcut, has been added.

54. The earliest available information informs us that the book was in the hands of the Englishman Mr. Utterson by the early nineteenth century. See Dibdin, *Bibliotheca Spenceriana*, 4, 857. I am grateful to Julie Ramwell, assistant librarian (Printed Books) at the John Rylands University Library, for this reference.

55. Winn, *AV*, 48, confirms that "Many extant vellum copies destined presumably for presentation to other noblemen retain the original prologue addressed to the primary

patron," although, as noted above, the prologue is absent from the English king's copy of the *Nobles et cleres dames*.

56. The author-figure still wears a miter, as he does in the original woodcut, presumably to signal in generic terminology Boccaccio's status as a cleric. Of note is the fact that in the British Library copy, the author-figure's headdress has been transformed into red turban-like headwear.

57. In the BnF Rés. 1223 copy, an author-portrait fills the entire double space. At the right Boccaccio, depicted as a cleric figure, is seated at his work desk, which is covered with books. To the left stand four women in relatively modest dress. The hands of two of them signal their engagement in conversation with the author. Thus, unlike Boccaccio's prologue and text, which never give voice to women, the females here are depicted as speaking figures. In the English king's copy, the miniature closely follows the woodcut image.

58. But the final "word" is given to the author, who appears in the concluding miniature that accompanies the *Recapitulation* (fol. t v).

59. The same applies to the BnF Rés. 1223 copy.

60. I have not been able to ascertain where the *Nobles et cleres dames* woodcuts might have been used beforehand.

61. For example, modifications to the original woodcut of Ceres (fol. bvr) result in an illustration that more faithfully represents the narrative. Many of these miniatures completely alter the original woodcut, others feature some form of modification, while others merely offer a painted version of the woodcut. The miniatures in the two other luxury copies present similar kinds of modifications.

62. We learned above that Vérard offered Anne of Brittany a specially made luxury version of the *Trésor de l'âme* (ca. 1497). In 1508 he would prepare for her a special copy of his edition of Claude de Seyssel's *Louanges du roy* (see Chapter 2). Three other works contain visual references to Anne and Charles VIII or Louis XII (see Winn, *AV*, 478). Was there any competition between Anne of Brittany and her rival, Louise of Savoy, vis-à-vis Vérard, who, it turns out, dedicated many editions to the duchess of Savoy?

63. For a description of this dedication copy, see Pächt and Thoss, *Die illuminierten Handschriften*, I, 175–76, and Winn, "Treasures for the Queen," 669–76.

64. See Chapter 2, n. 1.

65. Because this is the only dedicatory prologue that Vérard addressed to Anne of Brittany, and because no evidence in the prologue or elsewhere suggests that the queen ever commissioned other works from Vérard, critics have concluded that Vérard never succeeded in procuring her patronage and that Anne probably never appreciated Vérard's specially prepared hybrid volumes as much as her first husband, Charles VIII (Winn, *AV*, 136) or even her rival Louise of Savoy. All references are taken from Winn's edition of this prologue (*AV*, 362).

66. See the connection Winn makes between the two *Trésors* (*AV*, 135).

67. Although Vérard does not exalt his dedicatee as forcefully as Christine did hers (see below), the publisher's remarks about the manner in which his edition would be read sheds light on the dissemination of literature at court. His comments confirm both

the queen's individual reading of this and presumably other literary works as well as the expectation that it (they) would reach her female entourage as the focus of a more public court event.

68. This and all subsequent references are taken from the Willard-Hicks edition.

69. For details, see C. Brown, "The Reconstruction of an Author in Print," 220–22; Winn, *AV*, 366.

70. Unlike the text, the image actually refers to "Doctrine" instead of "Rectitude." For a discussion of the substitution of the term "Doctrine," see Walters, "Anthoine Vérard's Reframing of Christine de Pizan's *Doctrine*."

71. For an image of Christine at her desk, see BL ms. Harley 4431, 4. For illustrations of Christine dedicating her work to her patrons, see BnF ms. ffr. 1177, fol. 114 (the original dedication of the *Trésor* to Margaret of Guyenne); BL ms. Harley 4431, fol. 1 (dedication of Christine's collected works to Isabeau de Bavière), fol. 95r (dedication of the *Epître d'Othéa* to Louis d'Orléans), and fol. 178r (dedication of the *Chemin de long estude* to Charles VI).

72. See Summit, *Lost Property*, 95–105, for a discussion of a similar posture adopted by Henry Pepwell, who published the *Cyte of Ladyes* in 1521. Summit's astute analysis of Pepwell's Prologue brings to light the manner in which the publisher reappropriates Christine's ideas for a masculine readership and displaces female control of literary production by marginalizing the original author through the image of Christine in religious confinement. See also Bradley's enlightening discussion of how the cloistering of Christine in English tradition moved the politically active writer out of the more threatening politico-military sphere of influence in *Women of God and Arms*, 58–86.

73. In fact, the French queen may have been familiar with Christine's *Cité des Dames*, a tribute to famous women that dramatically reconfigured Boccaccio's *De mulieribus claris*, even though it did not figure in her personal library. Documentation suggests that Charles VIII owned Christine's *Epître à Othéa*, *Epître à la reine de France*, and her *Cité des Dames* bound in velour in 1490, before his marriage to Anne (Baurmeister and Laffitte, 90).

74. *Thomas Dobrée 1810–1895*, 167. The *Vies des femmes célèbres* was therefore composed the same year that Anne of Brittany made her Parisian entry as queen of Louis XII. For further details about its dates of composition and decoration and the attribution of miniatures to Jean Pichore, see Avril and Reynaud, 415.

75. Whether or not Dufour was directly influenced by Champier's *Nef des dames vertueuses* of 1503, which the author dedicated to Anne of France and her daughter, is difficult to ascertain, although comparisons suggest that Champier's work was more closely affiliated with Christine de Pizan's *Cité des dames* than with Dufour's work, which bears stronger ties with Boccaccio's *De mulieribus claris*. For details, see C. Brown, "The 'Famous Women' Topos," 155–60.

76. See Jeanneau, xxxix–xliv, for a discussion of Dufour's other sources and his uncritical use of them. An additional source was apparently Jacopo Filippo Foresti's *De plurimis claris selectisque mulieribus* of 1497 (Jacques Santrot, ed., *Thomas Dobrée*, 168).

77. For details on Pichore and his output, see Zöhl and Cassagnes-Brouquet, 33–40.

78. See also Cassagnes-Brouquet, 16–18, 22–23, 229–37.

79. An earlier form of some of the subsequent comments appeared in C. Brown, "Textual and Iconographical Ambivalence." For a slightly different perspective, see Szkilnik's "Mentoring Noble Ladies." See also Swift, 202–22, for a discussion of this work.

80. I do not completely agree with Jeanneau's interpretation of the two scenes in this image (lvii–lix), which he bases on G. Durville's assessment. Le Fur's analysis of this miniature in *Anne de Bretagne*, 70, concurs with my own. He notes the pattern of crowned A's around this miniature as well (71). See also the description of Cassagnes-Brouquet, 16–18.

81. Whether or not Dufour actually authored or merely translated this work, as he claims in the prologue, is difficult to ascertain. If it is a translation of another work, that work has not been identified (Dufour, xxix–xxx). Like the early manuscript versions of the French translation of *De mulieribus claris*, Dufour used the term "femmes" rather than "dames" in his title, differentiating his work from Vérard's title (*Nobles et cleres dames*). For details, see Chapter 3.

82. This and all subsequent references are taken from Jeanneau's edition of the work.

83. Anne of Brittany also commissioned Dufour to translate the Old Testament and the letters of St. Jerome, the copies of which are now lost. The manuscript of the *Épîtres de S. Jérôme* that was offered the French queen, was illuminated by Bourdichon around 1505 (see Jones, nos. 28, 32); the prologue confirming this request on the French queen's part appears in a 1519 edition of the work (see BnF Rés. C5984 and Rés. D80287).

84. In the text, Dufour makes numerous references to a mirror, such as Dido's story, advertised as "a beautiful mirror for chaste Christian widows" (54), Amalasonte's life, described as the mirror of honesty (130), and Blesilla, seen as "the mirror and example of all virgins, married women and young widows" (130). Some women are included in the catalogue of ladies of honor (109) and others are catalogued among the number of virtuous women (117).

85. Leroux de Lincy, III, 93, quoting Charles de Sainte-Marthe, describes the books Anne's entourage read in the following manner: "Autant en faisoit-elle de la lecture de leurs livres, car comme elle ne lisoit qu'en la saincte Escripture, ou en quelque historiographe qui ne donnoit aucune mauvaise doctrine; aussi ne vouloit-elle que ses demoiselles s'occupassent à lire d'autres livres."

86. In 1492, 16 *dames* and 18 *demoiselles* were in the queen's charge, and by 1498 the numbers had increased to 59 ladies and 41 girls. See Leroux de Lincy, III, 90–98.

87. As we learned above in the case of Anne de Foix (Chapter 1), those for whom Anne of Brittany arranged marriages were not always delighted with the measures she took. See Walsby, "La famille de Laval et Anne de Bretagne 1488–1514," 117–18, for a discussion of the French queen's intervention in the marriage of her maid of honor, Charlotte d'Aragon.

88. Jeanneau, 174, n. 1, suggests that the author may have borrowed the ideas he presents in his prologue from the prologue that prefaces Anthoine Vérard's 1493 edition of the *Nobles et cleres dames*. It is just as likely that Dufour was influenced by the ideas in Champier's prologue to his *Nef des dames vertueuses* of 1503.

89. For details on Dufour, who was the official court preacher at the time of this commission and was subsequently named the official royal confessor (1506) and became bishop of Marseilles in 1507, see Dufour, xix–xxi, and Cassagnes-Brouquet, 25–31.

90. In his *Nef des Dames* preface, Champier enters contemporary debates in more dramatic fashion by overtly defending women, emphasizing that some, but not all, are corrupt; that the Bible offers evidence that men sin one thousand times more often than women; that wives' sweet nature and honest persuasions tame their spouses' fury and passion; and that a man who finds happiness with a good woman lives longer. Champier's work stands apart from others, except Christine de Pizan's, in his staging of a pseudoauto-biographical narrator alone in his study visited by Lady Prudence who urges him to write a work in defense of women. See Champier, ed. Kem, 55–64.

91. Jeanneau, xliv, lii, likewise interprets Dufour's praise of the political skill and culture of several famous women as indirect praise of Anne of Brittany.

92. At first celebrated for her political savvy, Niobe falls in the end due to her pride, a disgrace that destroys her family (34–35). Faustina embodies the worst possible female traits about which Dufour seems to rant in his lengthy denigration of her (112).

93. Boccaccio described Joanna as "more renowned than any other woman of our time for lineage, power and character" (467). Like Anne, Joanna became a ruler "of a mighty realm of the sort not usually ruled by women" (Calabria, Sicily, and Jerusalem) (Boccaccio, 471) and brought order to it at an early age (although Anne was unable to defend her territory against French invaders). Unlike the Boccaccio vignette, however, written during Joanna's lifetime, Dufour's biography provides the details of her betrayal and tragic death.

94. However, Theodolinda, described as queen of the Lombards, figures in Foresti's *De plurimis claris selectisque mulieribus* of 1497 (fols. CXXIXv–CXXX).

95. Anne of Brittany was not a foreign queen like others, as Cosandey, "Anne de Bretagne, reine de France," 83, confirms, pointing out that she was the last royal spouse chosen inside the kingdom. However, as the last royal spouse to bring land as her dowry to her two marriages, Anne functioned in many ways like a foreign queen, especially because of her interest in maintaining Brittany's independence.

96. Most of these females mentioned figure in Boccaccio's work. Five are absent from Boocaccio, although they appear in Foresti (Battista Malatesta, Albunea, Mammea, St. Helen and Blesilla). For color reproductions of the miniatures of the last two, see Cassagnes-Brouquet.

97. See Dufour, 122: "Elle ayma les livres et grandement hault louoit gens sçavans et lettrés, tant pour éviter oysiveté que pour entendre les ambassadeurs estranges, qui de jour en jour la venoyent visiter, conférant en elle-mesmes pour les contenir par parolles et dons différens" [She loved books and highly praised wise and lettered men, as much to avoid idleness as to listen to foreign ambassadors who came to visit her from day to day, devising ways to keep them with words and various gifts] (122).

98. All these religious figures do appear in Foresti's work. While Erythrea and Amalthea figure in Boccacio's work, Albunea, Saint Helen, Mammea, Blesilla, Battista Malatesta and Mathilda of Tuscany do not. However, all of them, except Mathilda,

figure in the work of Foresti, who includes a whole host of saints. See Dufour's remarks about Diana, who, he claims, deserved great praise, except for the fact that she was a pagan (34).

99. See the color reproduction of this miniature in Cassagnes-Brouquet.

100. Boccaccio's comments on Nicostrata are entirely positive as well.

101. Dufour thereby invokes a central idea of Jerome's *Adversus Jovinianum* that reappeared in medieval catalogues of women (see McLeod, 36, 64).

102. Like a good Catholic, however, Dufour denounces her suicide (unlike Boccaccio). Other suicides denounced include Diana's (34) and Lucretia's (64–66).

103. Anne of Brittany's decision to remarry only months after the death of her first husband, Charles VIII, does not fit, then, into Dufour's paradigm. Nevertheless, as Jeanneau points out (97, n. 205), Dufour implicitly justifies such actions if undertaken for the good of the state (97).

104. Jeanneau points this out as well (liii).

105. By comparison, the *Nobles et cleres dames* translator saw no need for his or anyone else's moral guidance of his dedicatee when it came to discerning between positive and negative models of behavior, at least according to his prologue comments. And yet, by rendering Boccaccio's words into French, he too perpetuated the Italian author's viewpoint, thereby contradicting the claims he made to the French queen about defending women.

106. There are, however, certain mismatches of word and image. For example, Penthesilea is portrayed with books in the miniature accompanying her biography, but this dimension of her interest is not mentioned at all in her biography. Sappho is portrayed among her books as if teaching other men, although most of Dufour's narrative, like Boccaccio's biography, focuses on her failure in love.

107. For a color reproduction, see Cassagnes-Brouquet. See Buettner, 39–40, for a discussion about the reluctance to depict rape visually in the late medieval period, and Franklin, 138–43, for a discussion about different Italian portrayals of Lucretia. It is worth noting that Pichore portrays Cleopatra, a negative exemplum, committing suicide (fol. 42r), while the suicide of Lucretia, who is promoted as a positive example of female virtue, is not depicted visually.

108. For a color reproduction, see Cassagnes-Brouquet.

109. See also the biographies of Albunea, Proba, Trianaria, Hypsicrathea, and Maria Putheolina.

110. See Cassagnes-Brouquet for a color reproduction.

111. The females painted with armor or arms include Semiramis, Minerva, Marpaisa, Deborah, Orithea, Argia, Penthesilea, Thamaris, Ipsicretha, Zenobia, Maria Putheolina, and Joan of Arc. Those celebrated for military prowess but not depicted pictorially as such include Camilla, Artemis, Urania of Milan, Amalasonta, and Triaria. For a discussion of images of female warriors in the earliest French translation of Boccaccio's *De mulieribus claris*, see Buettner, 34–36.

112. See Katzenellenbogen, *Allegories of the Virtues and Vices*.

113. "Women Warriors," 128–29.

114. The text reads: "Depuis, le roy Louis fist examiner son procès, là où fut trouvée véridique et innocent. Car seullement fut rapporté sa condampnation ne avoir esté faicte si non que elle, contre la coustume des dames, cheminoit armée" [Since that time, King Louis had her trial reexamined, and she was thereby found to be truthful and innocent. For it was reported only that she would not have been condemned if she had not, against the custom of ladies, ridden horseback and carried arms] (165). It's not entirely clear if Dufour mistakenly identifies "Louis" here instead of Charles VII in reference to Joan's rehabilitation trial, or if he means to refer to Louis XII's review of the records.

115. The well-known miniature of Anne in Jean Bourdichon's *Heures d'Anne de Bretagne* (BnF, ms. lat. 9474, fol. 3r provides a case in point.

116. The *Speculum dominarum* was addressed around 1300 to Queen Jeanne de Navarre by her confessor, Durand de Champagne. See Szkilnik's assessment of Dufour as a moral guide at the court of France and mentor for the queen and her entourage.

117. Smith, *The Power of Women*.

118. Jehan Marot, *Les Deux Recueils*, ed. Defaux et Mantovani, 364. All subsequent citations are taken from this edition. According to the editors, Marot borrowed the title either from "L'Advocat des dames" in Pierre Michault's *Procès d'honneur féminin* of ca. 1461 or from a work entitled "L'Advocat des Dames de Paris," which dates from ca. 1500 (363). Found in four existing manuscripts and in several sixteenth-century editions (358), the poem, according to Defaux and Mantovani, is a defense of the honor of Anne of Brittany against the Maréchal de Gié, who had criticized the queen (364), a hostility discussed in Chapter 2. For an earlier version of some of the ideas in this section, see Brown, "Le mécénat d'Anne de Bretagne et la politique du livre," 195–224. See Swift, 109–14, 188–94, for an excellent analysis of this work.

119. Like the *Nobles et cleres dames* translator (fol. aiv), it was for Anne of Brittany's pleasure that Marot wrote this work (95).

120. As Defaux and Mantovani, 363, suggest, Marot may have been inspired by Martin Le Franc's *Champion des dames* or Pierre Michault's *Procès d'Honneur féminin* in creating this character.

121. For an excellent study of female rhetoric of praise in Renaissance anthologies, see Breitenstein, "La rhétorique encomiastique dans les éloges collectifs de femmes."

122. Given that she does not appear in an allegorical setting that provides a detailed description of her physical being and that of other personifications, the *Advocate* appears in this work more as a voice than an embodied female figure, with focus placed on her words rather than on her physical appearance.

123. Christine de Pizan had formulated the same argument in her debate about the *Roman de la Rose*.

124. See her numerous juridical references throughout this poem (vv. 34–35, 68–69, 235–41, 349, 593–94). The very actions of the *Advocate* actually contradict Christine de Pizan's advice who suggested in her *Cité des Dames* (ed. Hicks and Moreau, 62) that it was inappropriate for women to practice law.

125. For details on acrostics in general and La Vigne's use of them, see Brown, *Poets, Patrons and Printers*, 153–95.

126. See Defaux and Mantovani, 357: "Le ms. BnFF fr. 1704 . . . est peut-être celui qui a été offert à la duchesse à la fin de l'automne 1506—sinon à elle directement, à tout le moins à une très grande dame de sa cour."

127. Jean Lemaire de Belges goes to even greater extremes in his deployment of the acrostic form in honor of a noble lady, Margaret of Austria, in his *Couronne margaritique* (Jodogne, 215–54).

128. Symphorien Champier's *Nef des dames* also featured Anne of France, a model of female virtues, in a verbally and visually prominent position. See C. Brown, "The 'Famous Women' *Topos*."


CHAPTER 4. FAMOUS WOMEN IN MOURNING: TRIALS AND TRIBULATIONS

1. All citations of this prologue come from Michel Le Noir's October 1500 edition of the work (Parma: Biblioteca Publica, 237). Saint-Gelais refers here to his first work for the French king, which may have been his translation of Aeneas Sylvius's *Euriale et Lucrece* or his recently completed *opus magnum*, *Le Séjour d'Honneur*, dated after August 1494 by J. Lemaire in "Note sur la datation du "Séjour d'Honneur,'" 74–78. For the difficulties Saint-Gelais had in undertaking the translation because of moralistic concerns, and his subsequent critics, see Molinier, 67–74. See also Dörrie, "Die Briefdichtung in Frankreich," 147–56, 347–452.

2. Although many scholars mistakenly cite the year of dedication as 1496, Thoss, editor of the Vienna manuscript of the *XXI Epistres d'Ovide* (see Publius Ovidius Naso, *Héroïdes traduites en vers français par Octovien de Saint-Gelais*, 9) and Breslauer and Grieb (*Catalogue One Hundred and Nine*, #9, 32) correctly refer to the year as 1497 (new style). It is in BnF ms. ffr. 873 that one finds the announcement of a dedication date on folio 1 (my emphasis): "Cy [com]mencent les espitres de ouide translatees de latin en // francois *le xvie iour de feurier mil CCCC. iiii.$^{xx}$ xvi.* // Par reuerend pere en dieu maistre octouien de saint // geles a present euesque dangoulesme." [Here begin the Letters of Ovid, translated from Latin into French the 16th day of February 1496 [old style] by Reverend Father in God, Master Octovien de Saint-Gelais, presently Bishop of Angoulême]. BnF ms. ffr. 25397 makes a similar announcement on fol. [a]. A colored drawing of a dedication scene of a tonsured cleric who kneels with a bound book before an enthroned French king follows on fol. 1 of this version.

3. The only allusion I have found that actually identifies the dedicatee, albeit in a mistaken reference to Charles VII instead of Charles VIII, opens BnF ms. ffr. 874: "Cy commence les epistres douide lesquelles ont este translatees par feu monsieur leuesque dangoulesme nomme octouien de saint gelais. Par le commandement du feu roy charles septiesme dont dieu ait lame lesquelles epistres ouide recueillit" [Here begins the Epistles of Ovid, which have been translated by the late bishop of Angoulême named Octovien de Saint-Gelais. By the order of the late King Charles VII [sic]—may God have his soul—which letters Ovid compiled]. But nothing in Saint-Gelais's dedication prologue indicates that the translation of the *XXI Epistres d'Ovide* was specifically requested by the French

king. For further analysis of this manuscript, see Brueckner, "Octovien de Saint-Gelais' Ovid Übersetzung."

4. Moss, *Ovid in Renaissance France*, 1.

5. White, "Ovid's *Heroides* in Early Modern French Translation," 165.

6. Scollen, *The Birth of the Elegy in France 1500–1550*, 157–59, presents an inventory of 26 éditions of Saint-Gelais's translation dating from c. 1500–1580.

7. The complete extant manuscripts of the *XXI Epistres d'Ovide* include Arsenal Rés. 5108, BnF ffr. 873, 874, 875, 876–877, 1641, 25397, ÖNB 2624, BL, Harley 4867, Oxford, Balliol 383, Chambre des Députés 1466, Huntington Library HM 60, and Dresden O 65.

8. Durrieu and Marquet de Vasselot, "Les Manuscrits à miniatures des Héroïdes d'Ovide, 17, date Dresden manuscript O65 c. 1530–40.

9. It is clear that the *Arret* and the *Appel* are strongly linked, but the *Epitaphe* does not necessarily relate to the two other works (see below).

10. See III, 293–94. See also the description of this manuscript by Quentin-Bauchart in *Les femmes bibliophiles de France*, II, 380–82, and Molinier, *Essai biographique et littéraire sur Octovien de Saint-Gelays*, 144–45.

11. Breslauer and Grieb, 32, 36, also speak of the "fair likeness" of Anne of Brittany, Charles VIII, and Marie de Monberon in the manuscript's miniatures. I am grateful to the owner of this manuscript for granting me permission to examine it. I wish to thank Roger Wieck, Curator of Medieval and Renaissance Manuscripts at the Pierpont Morgan Library, for graciously facilitating my access to this manuscript.

12. For details on the complex history of the manuscript and early printed versions of Saint-Gelais's translation, see C. Brown, "Du manuscrit à l'imprimé: *Les XXI Epistres d'Ovide* d'Octovien de Saint Gelais."

13. See Avril and Renouard, 276, who claim: "C'est sans doute pour la reine qu'il [le Maître de ls Chronique scandaleuse] peint vers 1493 un étrange et luxueux manuscrit des premières *Héroïdes* d'Ovide."

14. Breslauer and Grieb, 32. Zöhl recently attributed some miniatures to Pichore.

15. See Breslauer and Grieb, 33, for a color reproduction of the miniature of Hysiphile.

16. Breslauer and Grieb, 32. Droz, "Notice sur un manuscrit ignore de la Bibliothèque Nationale," 506–7, without ever designating Madame de Balsac, as Breslauer and Grieb do, convincingly contests the identification of Madame de Balsac as Anne de Graville or as Anne de Granville's mother, Marie de Balsac, as other scholars suggested.

17. See the recent edition of Alain Chartier, Baudet Herenc, and Achille Caulier, *Le Cycle de La belle dame sans mercy* by Hult and McRae.

18. Although compiled together with the *Epitaphe* of Madame de Balsac in this and at least one other manuscript and a printed edition, the *Dame sans sy* narratives and the *Epitaphe* do not obviously relate to each other. Droz argues that the *Dame sans sy* cannot be identified as Madame de Balsac and that the *Epitaphe* is unrelated to the *Arret* and the *Appel*, because no such appeal would have been submitted against a deceased woman (503–13). Another known manuscript of this series of works is bound at the end of an

edition on vellum of Olivier de la Marche's *Chevalier délibéré* (BnF Rés. Vélins 2231) and other poems by Saint-Gelais and La Marche's eulogy to Mary of Burgundy (for further details, see Droz, 504–5). The first 37 verses and the accompanying miniature have been excised from the *Epitaphe de la Dame de Balsac*, which now appears on folios 59r–50v, and the first 34 verses and accompanying miniature are missing from the *Appel*, which figures on folios 61r–62r. Only the miniature accompanying the *Arrest*, which appears in its entirety, survives in the manuscript (fols. 60r–61r).

19. Droz, 509, does point out that the *Arret* appears alone in BN ffr. Ms. 2206 (fol. 195v).

20. Breslauer and Grieb, 34, imply that the *Arret* and the *Appel* are based on real events that took place after the marriage of the French king and queen but before the marriage of Marie de Montberon to Balsac.

21. Her contention is based on the identification of the mysterious crowned figure in the miniature as the Duke of Bourbon (511–13). But see C. Brown, "Celebration and Controversy."

22. Or perhaps they actually eulogized Madame de Balsac, thereby linking the *Epitaphe* and the *Arret*. Is there possibly an Angoulême connection between Saint-Gelais, who eventually became the bishop of Angoulême, and the Montberon or Balsac family from the same region?

23. Breslauer and Grieb, 32, also attribute the *Epitaphe* to Saint-Gelais, but without explaining why. A unique prologue that Saint-Gelais appears to have written for the printed version all but confirms his involvement in this anthology of poems. See C. Brown, "Celebration and Controversy" for details and a complete edition of the Prologue, *Epitaphe*, *Appel*, and *Arret*.

24. All three women figure in Anne of Brittany's accounts of 1492–98, according to Breslauer and Grieb, 32. See notes 29–31.

25. Droz, however, makes a case that this figure represents Pierre de Bourbon, considered to be royal through his marriage to Charles VIII's sister, Anne of France (510–11), and in mourning following the death of his son Charles de Bourbon in 1498, the date she assigns to the story of the *Dame sans sy*. However, if the date of composition and decoration is that late, the figure could also represent Charles VIII, following the death of his son, Charles-Orland, in December 1495.

26. Molinier, 144, although incorrectly identifying Madame de Balsac as Anne de Graville, describes this scenario, albeit with a certain patronizing tone, as "un petit episode assez amusant . . . qui vint rappeler . . . qu'il est bien difficile de contenter tout le monde et surtout . . . les femmes."

27. But see the extended argument in C. Brown, "Celebration and Controversy."

28. For details on the *Querelle des femmes*, see, for example, Angenot, *Les Champions des femmes*; Blamires, *The Case for Women in Medieval Culture* and *Women Defamed and Women Defended*; Bock and Zimmermann, "Die *Querelle des femmes* in Europa;" Kelly, Early Feminist Theory and the *Querelle des femmes 1400–1789*"; Grieco, "*Querelle des femmes*" or "*guerre des sexes*"?; Catherine, *La Querelle des Femmes*; Engel et al. eds.,

*Geschlechterstreit am Beginn der europäischen Moderne: die Querelle des Femmes*; Swift; and Breitenstein.

29. See Droz, 510, who describes her as the "femme de Jean III, comte d'Astarac, premier chambellan et maistre d'hôtel de Louis XI," and adds that "elle est mention-née dans l'état des officiers de la maison de la reine Anne de Bretagne pour les années 1496–98, parmi les dames et demoiselles: 'Jeanne Chabot, dame de Montsoreau [arr. De Saumur, Maine-et-Loire] et du Petit Chasteau, mille livres'. Sa fille épousa Philippe de Commynes."

30. See Droz, 510: "Blanche de Montberon appartenant à une famille de l'Angoumois est citée parmi les filles d'honneur de la reine et reçoit cent livres." Is she related to Marie de Montberon?

31. See Droz, 510: "quant à Madame de Talaru elle est nommée dans un compte fourni par le receveur Hugues Pinelle à la duchesse Anne de Bourbon: 'Autre despence faite par ledit Pinelle à cause de plusieurs personnes, a Madame de Talaru, Françoyse du Boys, la somme de 240 l.t. pour sa pension a elle ordonnée par madite dame pour l'année de ce present compte (14 février 1497).' "

32. However, the colors of the dresses of the females in the lower-margin miniature (mauve, red, blue) do not exactly match those of the ladies in the principal miniature (mauve, blue, blue). The motif of women in black veils appears throughout the illustrations in the Breslauer manuscript.

33. The relationship between the king and queen is somewhat ambiguous here, as she visually dominates the manuscript folio in a reversal of at least one other book from the period during which Anne was married to Charles VIII. See the BnF Rés. Vélins 689 copy of Jacobus de Voragine's *La Legende doree*, edited by Vérard in 1493, in which the French king is figured in the primary miniature and the queen appears only in a subsidiary image. A copy of this miniature can be found in Winn, *AV*, 245. This focus on Anne strengthens that argument that she was the manuscript's dedicatee.

34. For further details, see C. Brown, "Celebration and Controversy."

35. Hoe sale catalogue (24 April 1911), #2168.

36. The Sotheby Catalogue of 25 July 1862, Libri Collection "Reserved and Most Valuable Portion," 113, states that this "is indeed a truly Royal Manuscript, and there cannot be the slightest doubt of its having been executed for the illustrious couple, Louis XII and Anne of Brittany, who did so much for advancing the progress of Art in France." See also Bierstadt, *The Library of Robert Hoe*, 17; Shipman, *A Catalogue of Manuscripts Forming a Portion of the Library of Robert Hoe*, 153; De Ricci and Wilson, *Census of Medieval and Renaissance Manuscripts in the U.S and Canada*, 47; and Saxl and Meier in *Handschriften in englischen Bibliotheken*, 191.

37. In his 1909 description of the portrait of the miniature coupled with Dejanira's letter, Shipman suggested, "This painting is supposed to be a portrait of Anne de Bretagne, as it resembles the one in her Livres d'Heures" (154). In reference to the presumed portrait of Louis XII, the Sotheby Catalogue of 25 July 1862 states: "Amongst all these portraits those of Louis XII and Anne of Brittany shine forth by their peculiarly truthful character.

The King, who, according to history, was in bad health, is here represented as suffering and feeble" (113). The Hoe sale catalogue of 1911 reiterated the same analysis, further suggesting that the portrait of Paris might represent Charles VIII (#2168).

38. *Guide to Medieval and Renaissance Manuscripts in the Huntington Library*, I, 123.

39. Avril claims the faces of Ovid's heroines were retouched in the eighteenth century (Avril and Reynaud, 408).

40. Sixteen of the 21 miniatures in HM 60 depict the correspondents in the act of writing or having written their letters, correcting, or reading them. The Louis XII/Acontius figure joins Ariadne, Hypermnestra, Leander, and Hero as the only other characters depicted without writing instruments.

41. Avril, *Creating French Culture*, 173–74. See also Avril and Reynaud, 175, and Dutschke, 123.

42. See also Shipman, 155; Sotheby Catalogue of 25 July 1862, 113; Sotheby Catalogue of 9 May 1892, #2168.

43. Other manuscripts containing miniatures of the 21 correspondents (or most of them) that focus on events in their lives, rather than on the correspondents' faces, include BnF mss. ffr. 873, 874, BL Harley ms. 4867, Bibliothèque de la Chambre des Députés ms. 1466, ÖNB ms. 2624, Oxford Balliol Ms. 383 and Dresden O 65. Several of these miniatures (such as BnF ms. ffr. 873, ÖNB ms. 2624, Oxford Balliol Ms. 383) include multiple scenes, either in the side or lower margins or in the background of the principal illustrations. Arsenal ms. Rés. 5108 contains 21 illustrations that appear *en grisaille* and BnF ms. fr. 25397 contains 22 colored drawings.

44. Avril and Reynaud, 498.

45. *Creating French Culture*, 173–75. Unfortunately, the miniatures of BnF ms. ffr. 875, in particular that of Laodamia (fol. 71v) do not appear on the BnF Mandragore website and access to the manuscript itself has become increasingly difficult.

46. Avril suggests that manuscript 873, along with BnF ffr. 874, Assemblée nationale 1455 and the ÖNB Cod. 2624, were illuminated by artists associated with Jean Pichore's circle (Avril and Reynaud, 408).

47. Durrieu and Marquet de Vasselot, 11, mistakenly claimed that the manuscript was made for Louis XII. See the BnF Mandragore website for this image.

48. Although Saint-Gelais dedicated the *Heroides* to Charles VIII in 1497, the French king died the following year.

49. Although Dufour's *Vies des femmes célèbres* represents a rewriting of the *De mulieribus claris*, it has survived in only one manuscript copy, suggesting that it was not as widely known as either the Boccaccio or Ovid translations.

50. For the dating of these letters, see Tournoy-Thoen, "Fausto Andrelini et la Cour de France," 70. See also Britnell, "L'Épître héroïque à la cour de Louis XII et d'Anne de Bretagne."

51. Tournoy-Thoen, 68–76, provides a description of the manuscript and brief analysis of its contents, as does Laborde in *Les Principaux manuscrits à peintures*, 147–49. See also the description by Avril and Reynaud, 303–5. The first epistle, which is of most

interest here, falls on fols. 1r–9v. Tournoy-Thoen, 74–75, also offers a history of this manuscript's peregrinations from France to Russia.

52. See Avril and Reynaud, 305.

53. Tournoy-Thoen, 68, states: "Fausto Andrelini, de même que Bourdichon, appartenaient à ce cercle exclusif d'artistes que la reine avait groupés autour d'elle à l'époque des expéditions de Louis XII en Italie et de la campagne anti-papale; il semble avoir été un des artistes préférés de la reine." See Tournoy-Thoen, 75–76, and Avril, *La Passion des manuscrits enluminés*, 104, for attribution of the miniatures in this manuscript to Bourdichon.

54. See Illustrations 1, 5, 6, 7, 9 in Britnell, "L'Épître héroïque," 473–81.

55. Britnell, 464, is equally equivocal.

56. The 11 items in this collection include a letter composed in Latin by Fausto Andrelini and translated by Macé de Villebresme in Anne's voice addressed to the king; three letters by Jean d'Auton in the voices of *Eglise*, *Noblesse*, and *Labeur* addressed to Louis XII; a second letter in the voice of the queen by Andrelini/Villebresme expressing Anne's anger that disloyal Venetians have prolonged the war in Italy and delayed her husband's return; a letter written by Jean Francisque Suard in Latin and translated by Jean d'Auton in which the king exhorts the queen to be patient; a third letter by Andrelini/Villebresme in which Anne of Brittany voices dissatisfaction with the pope's treatment of the king; a letter from Hector to Louis XII, composed by Jean d'Auton; a letter in Louis XII's voice to Hector, written by Jean Lemaire de Belges (dated 10 November 1510); a letter by Mars sent to the king, composed by M. de Mailly; an elegiac letter from the *Eglise Militante* to the king composed by Jean d'Auton. See Jean Lemaire de Belges and Jean d'Auton, *Épistres*, ed. Armstrong and Britnell, 77–103 and 31–54, for editions of the Auton and Lemaire epistles.

57. Andrelini has Anne blame the pope for her sorrow in the opening lines of this epistle (fols. 59r–59v).

58. See "Form and Persuasion in Women's Letters, 1400–1700," 7.

59. According to Tournoy-Thoen, 69, and Armstrong and Britnell, VI, n. 17, the first of these *Epistolae Annae Reginae* was published by Josse Bade in Paris ca. 1509. Guillaume Cretin's translation of the same work was also printed in two different editions as *Epistre de Fauste Andrelin de Forly* (BnF Rés. M.Yc.74 [1]) and Rés. Ye. 1302); it was edited by Chesney in *Oeuvres poétiques de Guillaume* Crétin, 317–38. The second and third letters composed in Anne of Brittany's voice were apparently never printed during the queen's lifetime, but appear in Chantilly, Musée Condé ms. 890 (1411) and were edited in 1969 by Tournoy-Thoen in "Deux épîtres inédites de Fausto Andrelin et l'auteur du *Iulius Exclusus*."

60. See Avril and Reynaud, 305, Plate 168, for a reproduction. See Britnell, "L'Épître héroïque," 474–76, 480–83, for reproductions of the other illustrations in the manuscript collection, which include images of *Eglise*, *Labeur*, Hector giving his letter to Louis XII to a Faun, Louis XII dictating his letter to Lemaire de Belges, Mars with Vulcan and Concord, and an enthroned *Eglise [militante]* flanked by *Charité* and *Dissolucion*.

61. Unlike the image of Louis XII, however, the comparable miniature of Anne of

Brittany contains a series of her emblems in the background: the red curtains in the back right corner and around the entryway bear a pattern of gold *cordelières*. In addition, reminiscent of the miniatures in the Waddesdon Manor manuscript account of Anne of Brittany's 1504 coronation and entry into Paris, the stain-glass windows located between the two sets of curtains in the background feature Anne's crowned coat of arms surrounded by her *cordelière* and by margins of alternating gold crowned initial A's on a brownish background and gold fleurs-de-lis on a blue background.

62. For a color reproduction of this miniature, see Avril and Reynaud, Plate 168.

63. See also fol. 3r.

64. The passage bears remarkably similar language to Marot's in the *Voyage de Venise*, vv. 1682–1705, suggesting it was drawn from reality.

65. Tournoy-Thoen, 69, claims that "Fausto Andrelini fut le premier en France à écrire de véritables épîtres héroïques à l'exemple d'Ovide et avec ces épîtres il introduisit le genre épistolaire dans la littérature de ce pays."

66. Britnell, 461, n. 14, reminds us that the queen's own secretary, Jean Marot, makes direct comparisons between Anne of Brittany and several of Ovid's correspondents in his *Voyage de Venise* (ed. Trisolini). See his analogies of Anne with Dido and Hysiphile (vv. 876–81), Hecuba and Andromache (vv. 896–901), and Penelope (vv. 1694–97).

67. Penelope claims the following: "Whoso turns to these shores of ours his stranger ship is plied with many a question ere he go away, and into his hand is given the sheet writ by these fingers of mine, to render up should he but see you anywhere" (vv. 59–63). All English translations of the *Heroides* are taken from Showerman's translation of Ovid, *Heroides and Amores*.

68. See vv. 7–10, 22.

69. In his *Voyage de Venise*, vv. 2632–51, Marot makes reference to a similar joy, all but confirming the historical truth of this event.

70. From the beginning lines, Louis is described as "son loyal mary" and Anne as "une loyalle amante" (fol. 2r).

71. Andrelini's Latin text underscores the male-female contrast described earlier (my emphasis): "Mascula *femineos* pensat victoria *questus*" (fol. 3r).

72. Compare with Penelope: "But now, what I am to fear I know not—yet none the less I fear all things, distraught, and wide is the field lies open for my cares. Whatever dangers the deep contains, whatever the land, suspicion tells me are cause of your long delay. While I live on in follies fear of things like these, you may be captive to a stranger love—such are the hearts of you men!" (71–76).

73. See fols. 7r, 9r. The queen exclaims: "Doncques affin que tes pays et moy / Ne delaisses en miserable esmoy / Revien acoup sans aulcune retarde / Car ton retour trop longuement me tarde" (fol. 9v) [Therefore, so that you do not abandon your country and me in miserable grief, return immediately without delay, for your return has made me wait too long]. Compare with Penelope: "These words your Penelope sends to you, O Ulysses, slow of return that you are: writing back is pointless: come yourself "(vv. 1–2); "Do you yourself make haste to come, haven and altar of safety for your own!" (v. 110).

74. Compare Anne's plaint (fol. 3r) with Penelope's (vv. 41–46).

75. Dufour (49), on the other hand, presents Penelope as a woman always weeping greatly for her husband.

76. See vv. 1, 41, 57–58, 76–80, 93–94.

77. The similarity between these lines and vv. 902–12 in Marot's *Voyage de Venise* underscores the reality of this general grief, although Marot focuses on female mourning. See also vv. 1706–24.

78. Verses 938–48 in Marot's *Voyage de Venise* evoke similar ideas.

79. Seyssel, *Louenges du roy Louys XIIe* contains a passage about Louis XII's loyalty to Anne (see Chapter 2).

80. See vv. 83–84, 110. Dufour's much shorter portrait of Penelope in his *Vies des femmes célèbres* is different than Ovid's. He describes her as very wise and patient and one who keeps herself like a chaste widow, one who put off suitors by unraveling her weaving each night (a detail hardly mentioned by Ovid's Penelope) (49).

81. Laodamia appears neither in Dufour's *Vies des femmes célèbres* nor in Boccaccio's *De claris mulieribus*.

82. See vv. 51–52, 107–8, 124, 149–50.

83. See vv. 83–84, 115–27, 152–54.

84. See vv. 43–44.

85. See vv. 23–24 and vv. 887–91 in Marot's *Voyage de Venise*.

86. See vv. 33–34. But see also Marot's description of Anne of Brittany's grief, which is more sobering and contained, but nonetheless like that of a widow in the *Voyage de Venise*, vv. 876–912, 1662–1724, etc.

87. See vv. 31–42. The image of disheveled hair is perhaps the most recurrent visual theme of despair in the manuscript illustrations of the *XXI Epistres d'Ovide*.

88. Boccaccio devotes much space to this "famous and very ancient queen of the Assyrians" (17), both praising and castigating her (21–23).

89. "I shake slumber from me, and pray to the apparitions of night; there is no Thessalian altar without smoke of mine; I offer incense, and let fall upon it my tears, and the flame brightens up again as when wine has been sprinkled o'er" (vv. 111–14). See also: "O ye sons of Dardanus, spare, I pray, from so many foes at least one, lest my blood flow from that body !" (vv. 79–80). " 'May this, I pray, be omen that my lord return!' " (v. 90).

90. Anne earlier invokes the figure of Lucretia, although not in the context of her rape and subsequent suicide, with which she was routinely associated, but rather in light of her fear at the impending danger faced by her husband (fol. 4r). This allusion would have doubtless awakened in the reader the image of Lucretia's virtuous suicide.

91. See, for example, Dufour's discussion of Dido as a good example for chaste, Christian widows, with the disclaimer that he would never advise them to kill themselves, but would counsel chastity and honesty to protect themselves (54). However, as in most *XXI Epistres d'Ovide* miniatures, Dido's expression of marital fidelity through suicide by stabbing and subsequent self-immolation is graphically translated in the miniature that accompanies her biography in this work (fol. 25r). Such visual rendering of a violent death is avoided in the case of Lucretia. In fact, Dufour invokes Saint Augustine's condemnation of Lucretia's suicide (66). While Pichore, the artist of the *Vies des femmes*

*célèbres* manuscript, chose to depict the scene leading to Lucretia's rape (fol. 31r) instead of her suicide, perhaps to avoid any Christian impropriety, it is nonetheless an ambiguous gesture that emphasized the violation of a naked woman in a book offered to the queen. For a discussion of medieval images of Lucretia's rape and suicide, see Wolfthal, 75–89.

92. She also prays, but here for the Church's rather than Louis' victory (fol. 12v).

93. Other works, such as La Vigne's *Ressource de la Chrestienté*, discussed in Chapter 2, feature the same characters and complaints.

94. Earlier in the work, reference is made to Aurora's/Anne of France's grief in the following passages: "Ce matin triste, on perceut Aurora / Prendre pasleur pour blancheur rubicunde, / Et si veit on que griefvement ploura" (vv. 526–28) [On this sad morning, one perceived Aurora take on a paleness for ruddy whiteness, And thus one sees that she grievously cried]. "Trop piteux fut de veoir lors les semblances / D'Aurora triste et de ses nymphes belles, / Qui sans cesser faisoient doleances, / Et tout ainsi qu'aux doulces coulombelles / Plaindre et gemir est leur naturel chant, / Ainsi le font ces nobles jouvencelles" (vv. 362–67) [It was too pitiful to see the faces of sad Aurora and her beautiful nymphs, who grieved endlessly and just like sweet doves, complaining and moaning is their natural song; in such a way these noble young girls behave]. Lemaire depicts the grief for Pierre de Bourbon in universal and collective terms as well. All references are taken from Hornik's critical edition of Lemaire's *Temple d'Honneur et de Vertus*.

95. The only other woman described in as much grief as Anne of Brittany during *Entendement*'s visit to royalty is Jeanne de France (l. 1327), whom she replaced as Louis XII's wife in 1499, although the narrator explicitly makes note of her recovery (ll. 1331–35).

96. For details, see Yabsley's introduction to her edition of the *Plainte du Désiré*, from which all citations are taken.

97. Dressed in a blue robe with a white ermine collar, the count lies on a raised bed, his crowned head on a green pillow. Nature, wearing a blue tunic over a gold skirt and an unusual red headdress stands at the foot of the count's bed pointing to him with her right hand. In the foreground stand *Paincture* and *Rhetoricque*. *Paincture* is likely the figure at the right, dressed in a white-lined red dress with large sleeves and a green underskirt and wearing a green pointed cap. In her left hand she holds what appears to be a paintbrush; her right hand is raised in conversation with *Rhetoricque*, wearing a blue dress with a blue underskirt, standing to the left with her right hand raised in the direction of *Paincture*. In stark contrast, two nun-like figures in black hooded attire sit in the lower left section of the painting. A coat of arms beneath the miniature on the first folio has not been identified.

98. Ms. 23988, transcribed on parchment and dating after May 1506, has, according to Yabsley, 61, a more accurate text than ms. 1683, one that more closely resembles the edited text. But its three miniatures are not as finely executed as the one in ms. 1683.

99. The first miniature (fol. 2v) features *Paincture* in the foreground before three seated figures in black robes and caps reading. A nun-like figure, who according to Yabsley represents *Nature*, holds several tomes. *Rhetoricque*, appearing in a flowered dress, stands by the bed on which Ligny lies. In the second miniature (fol. 17v), Ligny lies naked in his grave. Above this scenario the king is featured in the center, with two grieving

women and two sad men looking down at the left. In yet a higher section of the illustration, the Trinity appears in a circle. The third miniature (fol. 19r) features a tomb in a churchlike setting with the deceased count (or his effigy) and his coat of arms (a lion with white cross and crown) below.

100. See LeBlanc, *Va Lettre Va*, 193.

101. For an excellent discussion of the modifications made in the different versions, see McGrady, "Printing the Patron's Pleasure for Profit," 89–112.

102. All citations are taken from Frappier's edition of the *Épîtres de l'Amant Vert*.

103. In May 1512, Lemaire finally announced to Margaret that he had been taken on by Anne of Brittany to compile chronicles of Brittany. See Grand, "Anne de Bretagne et le premier humanisme," 51.

104. See Santinelli, *Des Femmes éplorées?*, for a discussion of why women rather than men are associated with grieving and a review of the common gestures and actions of women in mourning.

105. For details, see D'Orliac, *Anne de Beaujeu, roi de France*, and Chombart de Lauwe, *Anne de Beaujeu ou la passion du pouvoir*.

106. For studies of Louise of Savoy's book interests, see Winn's work, including "Louise de Savoie, ses enfants et ses livres," "Louise of Savoy, 'Bibliophile,'" *AV*, 168–82, and "Books for a Princess and her Son." See also Orth, "Louise de Savoie et le pouvoir du livre."

107. Margaret also lost a child at birth during her marriage to Juan of Castille.

108. The image of Fortune is brought center stage in Michele Riccio's *Changement de Fortune en toute Prosperité* (1504–5?) in which Margaret's many misfortunes are attributed not to the men in her life but, more abstractly, to the goddess Fortune, who is dramatically portrayed in the act of repeatedly uncrowning her. Although Margaret is again depicted as a victim of circumstances beginning with Charles VIII's repudiation of her in 1491 and including the deaths of her two subsequent husbands in the intervening fifteen years, her losses are textually and visually portrayed as political rather than emotional: the forfeiture of her French and Spanish queenships. Thus, in a didactic move that goes beyond the laments of other works and employs epideictic rhetoric as a central rather than a minor literary tool, Riccio's writing offers Margaret's responses to her many misfortunes as exempla of virtue to men and women alike. For a discussion of this work, see C. Brown, "Textual and Iconographical Ambivalence."

109. See Marvin, "'Regret' Chansons for Marguerite d'Autriche," 23–32, who examines other songs and poems of regret associated with Margaret of Austria.

110. A copy of this 148-verse poem is housed at BBR as ms. 10926 (although it is an imprint); it was transcribed by Bruchet in *Marguerite d'Autriche, Duchesse de Savoie*, 313–17. All citations are taken from this edition to which I have added punctuation and resolved abbreviations. The actual printed text is reproduced by Vandeweghe in *La Complainte de dame Marguerite*, 530, 532. Based on his identification of Gheraert Leeu as the work's printer, Vandeweghe claims the *Complainte* was printed between 6 December 1491, when Charles VIII broke off his relationship with Margaret by marrying Anne of Brittany, and December 1492, when Leeu died (531–33). Since Charles VIII and Maximilian

remained at odds for some time, Margaret actually had to wait two more years before safely returning to Flanders in 1493.

111. Winn, "Marguerite of Austria and her *Complaintes*," 157, claims that the *Complainte* was written by Margaret herself. She discusses three other *complaintes* and five lyric verses attributed to Margaret.

112. She speaks of how she "Moy marguerite: de toutes fleurs le chois" [me, Marguerite, the choice of all flowers]—was raised in the French orchard but whose force and power was stripped away: "Cest mal de lui oster force & puissance" [It is evil to seize from such a flower its force and power].

113. Vandeweghe, 533.

114. See Lemaire's *Les Regrets de la Dame Infortunee sur le trespas de son trescher frère unique* (in Stecher, ed., *Oeuvres de Jean Lemaire de Belges*, III, 187–95), in which the author has Margaret's voice invoke Nature to mourn the death of her brother. This conventional invocation also figures in the epitaph for Madame de Balsac, discussed in Chapter 3.

115. Textual allusions to the recent birth (but not the death) of the dauphin (October 1492) and to the Treaty of Senlis, signed on 23 May 1493, suggest that the poem was probably written shortly after the negotiations between Charles VIII and Maximilian that allowed Margaret to return to the Lowlands. Octovien de Saint-Gelais also wrote a poem lamenting Margaret's departure from France in 1493 (see Winn, "Marguerite of Austria and Her *Complaintes*," 153–54, for a discussion of this work in which the poet speaks of Charles's remorse), whereas Jean Molinet authored "Collaudation à Madame Marguerite" in praise of her return to the Netherlands (ed. Dupire, *Les Faictz et dictz*, I, 265–58).

116. BBR ms. 11182, contains miniatures on folios 2r (Maximilian, Margaret, and Philip) and 5r (Reason berates Charles VIII). All citations are taken from this manuscript.

117. Reason refers to her as "une fleur," "la fleur marguerite" against which the French king took "cruel vengeance." Reason elaborates by describing Margaret, the abandoned "noble fleur remplie d'honneur" [noble flower filled with honor] as "esbaye . . . presque transsie jusque a l'ame rendre" (9v) [astonished . . . almost dead to the point of rendering her soul]. Reason goes on to lament: "O en quelle oppresse / Quel doeul et distresse / As tu la fleur mise / quant par ta simplesse / Au lieu de noblesse / As l'ermine assise" (fol. 9v) [Oh, in what oppression, what grief and distress you have put the flower, when by your stupidity, instead of nobility, you seated the ermine]. Charles is accused of having wrongly betrayed "la flourette" [the flowerette] and having "done such injury" to the flower (fol. 10r)

118. According to Pächt, I, 87, this copy was not originally offered to Margaret, but rather to her brother.

119. Through the window to the left, the earlier onset of his illness is figured in allegorical terms.

120. One illustration (fol. 4v) features the story of Philibert's tragedy in multiple scenes. Another (fol. 21v) recreates an official-like scene of mourning of Philibert in a configuration that anticipates the funeral scenes of Anne of Brittany that we will examine

in Chapter 5. While Lemaire alludes to the "grand pompe funeralle" in Philibert's honor, he does not develop this event in any detail before changing narrative tracks.

121. Gelfand, in a discussion of the Brou memorial for Philibert of Savoy that Margaret of Austria supervised in "Margaret of Austria and the Encoding of Power in Patronage," 145–59, underscores Margaret's independence as a widow in the following way: "After 1509, the church was no longer a memorial to her Bourbon in-laws and husband; rather, it asserted the importance of Margaret herself and, after 1512, it also prominently featured her matrilineal family heritage. These are significant changes that are strongly correlated with the transitions that Margaret was experiencing in her own life, especially her widowhood and regency and the social and economic differences that resulted. Margaret's relative freedom from the fetters that encumbered most married noblewomen enabled her to commission the architectural monument with which she has best been remembered."

### CHAPTER 5. WOMEN MOURNED

1. Jones, 68–69, makes the following suggestive remarks: "Les lamentations générales provenant de tant de plumes à la mort d'Anne en 1514 peuvent être interprétées, non seulement comme un signe d'affection envers la reine disparue, mais elles peuvent aussi être comprises comme une campagne concertée d'écrivains individuels pour s'attirer l'attention des successeurs d'Anne entre les mains de qui l'avenir se trouvait désormais." I further develop this idea in the individual cases of the different authors in this chapter.

2. She gave birth some ten times during her lifetime. Only her two daughters with Louis XII, Claude, born in 1499, and Renée, born in 1510, survived. For a list of the children to which she gave birth, see E. Brown, "The Children of Anne de Bretagne."

3. See Leroux de Lincy, II, 200; McCartney, 191; Bloem, 148; and Pierre Choque, *Récit des Funérailles*, xxvi–xxvii. All subsequent references are taken from this edition unless otherwise noted. According to Giesey, *The Royal Funeral Ceremony in Renaissance France*, 47, Louis himself paid all the expenses for Anne of Brittany's funeral ceremonies. For reference to and a copy of the relevant documentation, see Chotard, ed., *Anne de Bretagne*, 102–3, 184 (#152).

4. Binski, *Medieval Death*, 30, makes comparisons between rituals of entry and departure in a different context. See also Cosandey, "Anne de Bretagne, reine de France," 88.

5. Fausto Andrelini, Germain de Brie, and Jean-François Quentin Stoam also composed Latin verses on Anne's death and Laurent Desmoulins published *La Déploration de la Royne de France* on 11 February 1514. Germaine de Brie's Latin epitaphs were published in *Diversa Epitaphia Anne Britannae Francorum reginae ae Britannie ducis* [Paris, 1514] (BnF Rés. M-YC 760) (Montaiglon and Rothschild, eds., *Recueil de poésies françoises des XVe et XVIe siècles*, XII, 109–10). Laurent Desmoulins translated them in *Les epytaphes de Anne de bretaigne royne de france & duchesse de bretaigne composees par maistre Germain de Brixi. Et translatees de latin en francoys Par L. D.* [BnF Lb.29[41] (1)*]. This same work also contains the Latin epitaphs of Jean-François-Quentin Stoam (BnF Lb[29] 45 [3]). A

certain Fonsomme apparently penned the *Doloreuse querimonie de Blès* (Montaiglon and Rothschild, *Recueil*, XII, 128).

6. See Binski, p. 51–52; Beaune, "Mourir noblement à la fin du Moyen Âge"; and Callahan, *Signs of Sorrow*, 287–377. See also Ariès, ed., *Essais sur l'histoire de la mort en Occident* and *L'homme devant la mort*. For a study of the material organization and management of death, see the various articles in Alexandre-Bidon and Treffort, eds., *A Réveiller les morts*. This revised discussion of the poetry about Anne's near death in 1512 is partially based on my earlier treatment of the subject in "Les louanges d'Anne de Bretagne."

7. See Binski and Beaune for discussions of these issues.

8. A list of those witnessing this event includes the ladies of Mailly, Anne's lady of honor, her wardrobe mistress; the lords of Menou, Porcon, Gilles d'Ogny; the squires La Guierche, Beton; the cup-bearers and pantlers Montaubon, Borne; the carver Piedouault; the king of arms and heralds, Bretagne, Vannes and Hennebont; the chaplain, Abbot de la Roue; André de la Vigne; the chamberlain of the king and queen and Jean de Paris, "who carefully oversaw the handling" of the queen (30–32). Some of the ideas in the following pages constitute a revised discussion of "Books in Performance."

9. See also 51, 81.

10. See, however, Choque's descriptions of a particular moment of grief shared by Anne's female entourage, in which Anne of France played a critical role (37).

11. See also Yabsley, in the introduction to her edition of Lemaire's *Plainte du Désiré*, 25–37, and Callahan, 26–78, 267–377.

12. In *Jean Lemaire de Belges et Jean d'Auton*, ed. Armstrong and Britnell, 55–65. All subsequent quotes are from this edition.

13. It is noteworthy that *France* is portrayed as the mother of *Bretaigne*.

14. Did the personification of *France* and *Bretaigne* as two princesses at the court recall in any way the queen's two daughters, Claude and Renée?

15. Compare these lines with those of the two allegorical figures in Lemaire's earlier work, the *Plainte du Désiré* (ed. Yabsley), examined in Chapter 4. In the *Plainte*, *Paincture* appeals to noble feminine hearts to join in the mourning for the count of Ligny. She also asks *Rhétorique* to "Cry out loudly and publicly the enormous grief that flows in Nature" (vv. 92–93). See also the description of the witnesses' "great force of impetuous sobbing" (76). But *Paincture*'s admittedly unsuccessful attempts to mourn the count of Ligny are replaced by those of *Rhétorique*, who seeks to diminish Nature's grief through her harmonious words (vv. 449–64).

16. Lemaire does have both *France* and *Bretaigne* encourage people to weep, as they pray for Anne's recovery (vv. 52–54, 60). They single out female virgins (vv. 65–72) and male religious figures (vv. 81–88) and more generally women (vv. 73–80) and men (vv. 89–96).

17. See vv. 145–60.

18. In this last series of rhymes, the first 8-versed stanza opens with 3 masculine rhymes followed by a feminine rhyme, a pattern repeated within the stanza. The second stanza reverses this configuration by opening with 3 feminine rhymes and 1 masculine

rhyme, a pattern repeated within the stanza. Each of the 6 subsequent stanzas adopts either the masculine dominating rhyme pattern or the feminine dominating rhyme pattern.

19. The words of the king's prayer are not, however, transcribed in Lemaire's text.

20. Armstrong and Britnell, VII, VIII, LVII. The manuscript contains a copy of the second book of Lemaire's *Illustrations* as well.

21. Armstrong and Britnell, LVII, confirm that this version predates the subsequently published version.

22. For other similar verses of address, see vv. 12, 13, 24. See Armstrong and Britnell, 67, XXVIII–XXIX, for an analysis of this poem's versification.

23. See Jodogne, 84–85, for biographical details about the deaths of two of Lemaire's earlier patrons, Pierre II, duke of Bourbon, and Louis of Luxembourg, count of Ligny.

24. Jodogne, 137–41.

25. In a letter edited by Stecher in *Œuvres de Jean Lemaire de Belges*, IV, 425, Lemaire reveals that he sent a copy of the poem to Margaret on 14 May 1512. For details about this work, see Jodogne, 440–42, Munn, 85, #1, and Armstrong and Britnell, VIII, XXII, and the edition (55–65). See also Stecher, *Notice sur la Vie et les Oeuvres de Jean Lemaire de Belges*, xcv; Stecher, *Œuvres*, III, 87–97; Becker, *Jean Lemaire*, 388, no. 7; Munn, 109, n.16; Brunet, *Manuel de Libraire*, III, 963; Chesney, ed., Guillaume Crétin, *Œuvres poétiques*, lxxxix–xc.

26. The *XXIV Coupletz* appear on fols. B2v–B5r of this edition. The other works in this collection include *L'Epistre du roy a Hector de Troie*, *L'Epitaphe de Gaston de Foix*, *La Concorde des deux langages*, *La Plainte du Désiré*, and a letter to François Le Rouge. The *XXIV Coupletz* appeared with these same works in numerous other editions until the mid-sixteenth century. For additional details, see Armstrong and Britnell, eds., Lemaire de Belges, *Épistre du roy à Hector*, LXI–LXXXV.

27. Armstrong and Britnell, eds., Lemaire de Belges, *Épistre du roy à Hector*, LXI–LXII.

28. The dedication manuscript is currently housed in Bern's Burgerbibliothek as ms. 241. For further details on this manuscript, see Grand, 45–70, and C. Brown, "Like Mother, like Daughter."

29. This double rondeau figures in Choque's *Récit*, from which all quotes are taken. This double rondeau is also found in several contemporary editions dating from ca. 1514 (BnF Rés. Ye 1371 and Rés. Y. 4457.2) and ca. 1524 (Versailles, Bibl. mun., E 472C). See below. For additional details, see Montaiglon and Rothschild, XII, 105–10.

30. Choque, *Récit*, 40.

31. The entire work appears in Jehan Marot, *Les Deux recueils*, ed. Defaux and Mantovani, 120–54, from which all citations are taken. For additional details, see, 382–401. For a study of this poem, see Guiffrey, *Poème inédit de Iehan Marot*, and Cornilliat, "Rhétorique, poésie, guérison de Jean à Clément Marot."

32. Apres, ma treshonnoree dame, que les tempestueux orages et nubileux tourbillons de vostre tresenuieuse maladie qui totallement troublee auoyent la transquilité de mon rustique et tresfragile esprit ont esté dechassez par la clarté et illumination de

conuallescence tresdesiree. Et que l'entendement agité par les flotz et vagues de perturbation a finablement trouué port salutaire de consolation opportune, et s'est en luy mesmes
recueilly, apres toute diuturne tempeste en la station de ioyeux repos, ainsi que les fleurs
decidues et ternissantes par intemperance pluuiale se ressourdent et recouurent la pristine dignité de leur dyapreure dyaphanee aux nouueaulx rays du cler Phebus [My most
honored Lady, after the tempestuous storms and raging whirlwinds of your very grievous
illness, which totally disturbed the tranquility of my ignorant and very fragile mind,
were chased away by the light and illumination of your much desired recovery, and after
apprehension, agitated by the surges and waves of perturbation, finally found a salutary
port of timely consolation and, after the long-lasting storm withdrew back into a place of
joyful repose, much like flowers fallen and discolored by rainy intemperance spring back
and recover the pristine dignity of their diaphanous bloom with the new rays of bright
Phebus]. The dedication to Anne of Brittany appears in BnF ms. f.fr. 1539, fols. 1r–2v.

33. At the end of his poem, however, Marot implicitly asks that the queen for continued support, by praising the hoped-for generosity of his patroness toward her subjects.
Perhaps Marot was celebrating both Anne's recovery and the continuation of his position,
which he had almost lost (vv. 1063–67).

34. "Mais quant au subiect de telle magnitude et excellence que vng aultre Virgille
ou Homere, poetes de immortelle renommee trauailleroyent beaucop a l'execution souf-
fisante d'icelle. . . . [qui] appartient plus a sublimite heroique ou resonance tragediale que
au petit et humble stille de bas maternel langage" (120–21) [But as for the subject, of
such magnitude and excellence that another Virgil or Homer, poets of immortal renown,
would work greatly in order to execute it properly. . . . [it] belongs more to the heroic
sublime or tragic expression than to the small and humble style of the lowly mother
tongue].

35. While the other two Cardinal Virtues, Prudence and Temperance, do not appear
in Marot's dream vision, other abstract virtues, including Generosity (*Liberalité*) (v. 900),
Pity, and Forgiveness (*Miséricorde*) (vv. 1830–34), do make their way onto Marot's literary
stage in the *Prières sur la restauration*.

36. See also vv. 13–22, 67–74.

37. See also vv. 87–90.

38. One of them is a male character because of the gender of the word *Labour*.

39. See also the words of *Noblesse* (v. 108).

40. "[E]n langage bien duit" (v. 111) [in a very commodious language] describes the
words of *Noblesse*, while the following describes those of *Foy*: "le beau propos a / Meu a
pitié toute la court divine . . . / ses doulx motz sa [Dieu] fureur appaisa" (vv. 791–92, 794)
[her beautiful discourse moved the entire celestial court to pity . . . her sweet words ap-
peased God's fury]. Marot promotes a concern for reasoned speech at a time of grief in his
*Doctrinal des princesses*, written around the same time (Marot, *Les Deux recueils*, 9).

41. See vv. 862, 1038–42, 1047–48.

42. For a detailed examination of many of these female virtues, see Martin-Ulrich,
*La Persona de la Princesse au XVIe siècle*.

43. See vv. 62, 135, 220, 232, 246, 428, 429, 635, 787.

44. Defaux and Mantovani, eds., 388, 389.

45. See vv. 164, 228, 302, 376, etc.

46. See vv. 218, 232, 417, 425, 725, 830, 611–16.

47. See vv. 765–66, 837–44, 845–52. Basing her comments on the Bible (Defaux and Montavani, eds., 390), *Eglise* grants Anne a political power involving the confrontation between the French monarch and Catholic pope, a particularly "hot" issue at the time, that may well have been a reflection of historical reality (299–302).

48. See vv. 129, 166–68, 277, 373–77, 453–55, 584–92, 646–48, 663–64, 677–80.

49. See vv. 163, 277–78, 441–44, 466–68, 772–79. *Libéralité* arrives on the scene bearing the standard of Anne of Brittany's father, Duke François II (vv. 899–916), ushering in a prayer in rondeau form by the duke himself (vv. 918–31). Other areas of praise include her love (vv. 165, 286, 746), her ability to make others live (188) and to win over the hearts of others through her willful work (vv. 239–42).

50. These stories are found in Matthew 15.21–28 and Luke 7.2–3 (Defaux and Mantovani, eds., 396).

51. Defaux and Mantovani, eds., 389, n. 32.

52. This is likewise a symbol relating to the Virgin Mary.

53. In his epigram entitled "De Ma Dame la Duchesse d'Alençon," written before 1527, Clément Marot refers to Margaret of Navarre as a "Corps femenin, cueur d'homme, & teste d'Ange" (*Oeuvres poétiques*, ed. Defaux, 205, 989). Did Clément consciously borrow from his father's earlier description of Anne of Brittany?

54. For details on the classical tradition of the epitaph de l'époque alexandrine à la fin de la Renaissance, see Laurens, *L'Abeille dans l'ambre.*

55. Marot also invokes *Amour* in discussing Anne's marriages in the *Prières sur la restauration* in relation to Charles VIII (vv. 289–90) and Louis XII (vv. 291–94), as in the *Epitaphe* (vv. 16–19).

56. The epitaph was first edited by Rutson in *The Life and Works of Jean Marot,* 250–51, from which all citations are taken.

57. Compare with *Prières*, vv. 750–51.

58. Compare *Prières*, v. 4, with the *Epitaphe*, v. 4.

59. Compare with *Prières*, vv. 130, 133.

60. Compare with *Prières*, v. 278.

61. Compare this verse with *Prières*, v. 168.

62. Compare this verse with *Prières*, vv. 440–41.

63. Compare these verses with *Prières*, vv. 283–84.

64. The text is taken from the *Généalogies, effigies, et epitaphes des Roys de France,* Poitiers, 1545, f. 72, col. 1.

65. The allusion to Atropos recalls her appearance in Marot's allegorical scenario in the *Prières* and in the narrative of Madame de Balsac's death.

66. The text is taken from *Le Jugement poetic de l'honneur femenin* (Poitiers, 1538), fol. lx[x].

67. Anne actually lived with Charles VIII for seven years, from 1491 until his death in 1498.

68. See the renewed hope that a male heir would be born in Marot's *Prières* (vv. 159–60).

69. It was through the intermediary of Gabrielle de Bourbon that Jean Bouchet established ties with Anne of Brittany, as Britnell points out in *Jean Bouchet*, 261–62, 265, 310.

70. However, Britnell, 313, suggests that Bouchet began what he entitled the "annales et epitaphes des roys de France" around 1514.

71. According to Britnell, 326, Bouchet mentioned his epigrams as early as 1532 in his *Annales*, eighteen years after Anne's death.

72. Like the *Rondeau de l'Esprit et du Cueur du Roy* examined above, many of these poems written by André de la Vigne appeared in Pierre Choque's chronicle of Anne of Brittany's funeral ceremonies, which I examine below, although Choque does not always identify their author.

73. See Choque, *Récit*, 52, 57, 60, 61, 62, 65, 67.

74. These cited poems are taken from Choque, *Récit*. A discussion of some of these funeral poems appears in a different context in "Like Mother, Like Daughter."

75. Like his epitaphs addressed to French towns along the funeral route, this poem of La Vigne figured in Choque's manuscript accounts. The *Déploration* was considerably revised and published anonymously around the same period with Lemaire's *XXIV Coupletz*.

76. Montaiglon and Rothschild, XII, 124, n. 1, claim that the very spaces La Vigne places on stage in the *Deploration* were those very sections of the Chateau de Blois that had been constructed during Louis XII's and Anne of Brittany's reign. See also Baurmeister and Laffitte, *Des livres et des rois*, 14–20.

77. See Baurmeister and Laffitte, 17–19, for a description of the gardens.

78. See Montaiglon and Rothschild, XII, 125, n. 4, for a description of the "galerie des Cerfs" and gardens.

79. See Montaiglon and Rothschild, XII, 125, n. 7, and Baurmeister and Laffitte, 16, for a description of the terrace.

80. One of the quatrains addresses "Saint Calaix," which may well be the chapel that was consecrated in November 1508 by Antoine Dufour (Baurmeister and Laffitte, 16).

81. Anne is praised in "Cruelle mort" as the mother and hope of nobility, the honor of good people, the consolation of the desolate; in "De mort, d'envie" she is praised for her gifts that eliminate sorrow; in "Mort inhumain," she is seen as firm, constant, sure in counsel, truthful, and extremely generous.

82. This rondeau does not appear in Choque's *Commémoration*, but was printed in *Epitaphes en rondeaux de la royne . . . par maistre Andre de la Vigne* (BnF Rés. Ye 1371).

83. This rondeau does not appear in Choque's *Commémoration*, but was printed in *Epitaphes en rondeaux de la royne . . . par maistre Andre de la Vigne* (BnF Rés. Ye 1371).

84. According to Jodogne, 136–37, Lemaire witnessed Anne of Brittany's funeral and wrote a eulogy in honor of the queen, but the work did not survive. In addition, he offered Claude of France a copy of the *Traité des Pompes funèbres*, which he had begun earlier for Margaret of Austria, doubtless in an effort to secure the patronage of Anne's daughter.

85. See above n. 24 regarding Lemaire. As for La Vigne, he was hired on by Francis I and redacted an incomplete chronicle of the king's life up to his coronation (see BnF nouv. acq. ffr. 794), but he disappears from the records after January 1516 (see La Vigne, *La Ressource de la Chrestienté*, 10–13).

86. See the the the BnF copy, Rés. 1371. This edition contains no publication information. Because this is the only extant edition that announces the author's name on the title page, it is probable that La Vigne played some role in its publication.

87. In his account, Choque identifies La Vigne as author of these three poems along with "La Déploracion au Chasteau de Bloys" (37).

88. Choque identifies the author of this rondeau in his account (51).

89. The two latter poems, associated with the procession's stop at Orleans and Estampes, appeared anonymously in Choque's account (60, 65).

90. Although the title page of the *Epitaphes en rondeaux* advertises the inclusion of the "Déploration du Chasteau de Blois" in the collection, this poem is actually missing from the printed volume; it seems to have been either erroneously titled or replaced, perhaps mistakenly, by the above-cited quatrain relating to the Château de Blois. Since this latter poem begins at the end of a quire on folio 4v, the publisher or printer may have decided to limit the imprint to four folios, based on economic exigencies, instead of overflowing into another quire. Although these 6 rondeaux and 1 quatrain appeared simultaneously in Choque's manuscript accounts, 4 poems in the *Epitaphes en rondeaux* edition ("Traistresse mort" [fol. 2v], "De mort, d'envie" [fol. 3r], "Povres servans" [fols. 4r–4v] and "Aprés la mort" [fol. 4r]), were never integrated into Choque's *Récit*. Note the fascination with the fact that the poem "Povres servans" was interred with the queen; it is announced both on the title page and in the preceding rubric.

91. See the BnF copy, Rés. Ye 4286.

92. See v. 23 on fol. 1v and the prose passage on fol. 6r, in which "nostre royne Anne" has been modified to "nostre royne amye."

93. In addition, the 7th verse of "A la garderobe" is borrowed from La Vigne's original quatrain. The reviser of these verses retained the first verse of the first "regret," that of the bedchamber, as well as the four final verses of the last three stanzas ("A la terrace," "A la chapelle de St. Yves," "A la chapelle St. Calais).

94. See above n. 85.

95. See the copy at the BnF, Rés. 1432, which lacks any publication information. A woodcut of two angels holding up royal arms with fleurs de lis decorates the title page.

96. "En ce monde," "Cruelle mort," and "La deploration du chasteau de Bloys des lieux ou plus frequentoit la Royne," in which the first verse has been changed from "Neuf jours apres le froit moys de decembre" [Nine days after the cold month of December] to "Neuf jours apres le chault moys de juillet" [Nine days after the hot month of July], which, as Montaiglon and Rothschild, XII, 125, n. 3, point out, ignores the rhyme in "chambre" as well as the correct date of Claude's death, 20 July 1524. The second hemistich of verse 3 of the *Déploration* (v. 277 in Montaiglon and Rothschild, 125) has been changed from "royne et regente" [queen and regent] to read "royne et duchesse" [queen and duchess], a modification that likewise ignores the rhyme with "gente."

97. See Montaiglon and Rothschild, XII, 120–21, 126–27.

98. The copy at the Bibliothèque municipale in Versailles, G 8° 164 [E 473 c] bears a woodcut of Anne of Brittany's (not Claude of France's) arms on the title page; but no publication information is to be found in the volume.

99. "En ce monde" (fol. 1v), "Cruelle mort" (fol. 1v–2r), "La deploration au chasteau de Blays des lieux ou plus frequentoit la royne" (fols. 4r–4v), "Rondeau double clos de l'esprit & du cueur du roy sur le trespas de la dame en forme de dialogue" (fols. 5r–6r), "Traistresse mort" (fols. 6r–6v), "Le rondeau que mist ledit de La Vigne a Sainct Saulveur de Bloys le jour que la dicte dame y fut portee pour estre menee a Sainct Denys" (fol. 6r), "Cueurs desolez" (fol. 7r), "Plourez humains" (fol. 7r), "Povres servans," "De mort, d'envie" (fols. 6v–7r), "Mort inhumaine" (fol. 7v) and "Aprés la mort" (fol. 8v).

100. The first verse now reads "Droit en juillet affin qu'on s'en remembre" [Right in July so that one remembers it], a modification that acknowledges the rhyme with "chambre" and correctly alludes to the date of Claude's death.

101. For editions of these poems, see Montaiglon and Rothschild, XII, 120–27.

102. In Le Jugement poetic de l'honneur femenin, ed. Armstrong, 299–300.

103. As Wilson-Chevalier, who calls for the urgent need for more research on Claude of France, points out in "Claude de France in Her Mother's Likeness." Bertière, Les Reines de France au temps des Valois, I, 205, calculated that Claude was pregnant 63 of the 122 months of her reign. Compared to Anne of Bretagne, significantly fewer books were written for or dedicated to Claude of France as queen during her lifetime. For a listing of some of these, see, C. Brown, "Like Mother, like Daughter," n. 20. See also C. Brown, "The Patron."

104. See Merlet and Gombert, xxvii, who state: "Plusieurs copies, ornées de belles miniatures en furent faites par ordre de Louis XII."

105. Bloem, 132. See also Jones, "Les manuscrits d'Anne de Bretagne," 79–81, for details on the specific dedicatees. Since Choque's position at Anne's court was at stake following the death of his patroness, he doubtless sought to benefit himself from this print-like diffusion of his work. Indeed, in each dedication he identifies himself as Anne's "herault et roy d'armes." At least one of the books postdates the death of Louis XII, namely the volume dedicated to Louise of Savoy, who is addressed as "Mere du Roy" (BnF ffr. 5094).

106. Dutuit ms. 665, currently housed in the Musée du Petit Palais, also offers an account of Anne's funeral ceremonies, but this manuscript bears a different title (Le Trespas de l'Hermine Regretee) and contains a different text than that of Pierre Choque.

107. Second wife of René II, duke of Lorraine.

108. Third wife of Jean de Bourgogne, count of Nevers, who had died in 1491. Françoise of Albret lived until 1422.

109. She was the widow of François de Bourbon, count of Vendôme.

110. Both were queens, daughters and wives of kings, as described in the opening line of the dedication.

111. Françoise de Foix, wife of Jean de Laval, lord of Châteaubriant, also received a copy of this work (Saint Petersburg, National Library ms. Fr. Q.v.IV.3), but I have not

been able to examine it. Margaret of Austria also owned a copy of the work, although, after Mary of Hungary inherited it in 1530, it eventually ended up in the Escurial Library in 1576, where it burned in a fire in 1671 (Debae, *La Bibliothèque de Marguerite d'Autriche*, 92). A number of manuscripts were also dedicated to Anne's male relatives, including her cousins Jean d'Albret, lord of Orval, the count of Lautrec, Henry VIII, king of England, and the count of Penthièvre and of l'Aigle; her relatives Charles de Bourbon and Guy XVI, count of Laval, the barons and counts of Vertuz, and the queen's *escuyers* (Guillaume de Loyon and le sire de Betton) also received commemoration copies of the funeral. I am most grateful to Elizabeth A. R. Brown for information on several works I have not been able to examine, especially the two Saint Petersburg manuscripts, and for biographical details on several recipients of the *Commémoration*.

112. In a personal communication several years ago, Myra Orth suggested that this artist was the Master of the *Chronique Scandaleuse*.

113. See the manuscripts of Louise of Savoy (BnF ffr. 5094) and Catherine of Foix (BnF ffr. 5095).

114. See the manuscript of Louise of Coëtivy (BnF ffr. 23936).

115. See the manuscripts of Renée of Bourbon (BnF ffr 5100) and an unnamed lady of the House of Bourbon (Nantes, Bibl. Mun., ms 653). See also the dedications to Françoise d'Albret (BnF ffr. 5150), Catherine of Aragon (?) (BBR IV 521), Philippa of Guelders (BnF ffr. 18537)—in this dedication Choque invokes the lady's personal visual experience during the funeral ceremonies—and Claude of France (BnF ffr. 25158).

116. Of the 6 dedications addressed to men that I have examined, 2 contain no reference to reading, hearing, or seeing in the verses (BnF ffr 5098 [Jean d'Albret]; B.L. Stowe 584 [le seigneur de Beton]), one refers only to hearing and seeing (BnF nouv. acq. ffr. 74 [Guy VI, count of Lanval], while 3 include references to reading (BnF ffr 5096; [Charles de Bourbon]; BL Add 6277 [the nobles of Vertuz], BL Cotton Vesp B.III [an unidentified "noble duc"]).

117. No references whatsoever to reading, hearing, or seeing are found in Marie of Luxembourg's dedicatory verses (Arsenal 5224), but Choque mentions in his dedication to Louise of Coëtivy (BnF ffr. 23936) the activities of "hearing" and "seeing" in conjunction with her "reading" the work.

118. See also 42–43, 51, 71, 91. Additional references appear in BnF ffr. ms. 5094, fols. 28, 49.

119. Mention is made of Anne's renown in the dedications Choque addresses to her male relatives as well.

120. See also BnF ffr. 5051, 5094, 5095; BBR IV 521.

121. See the dedications to Renée of Bourbon, Françoise of Albret, and the unnamed Lady of Bourbon.

122. The different poetic forms range from an 8-verse decasyllabic stanza (Claude of France) to stanzas of 9, 10, 12, 13, and 15 verses in decasyllables, with the occasional appearance of alexandrines.

123. Some copies bear neither a miniature of the queen's arms and insignia nor dedicatory verses. See, for example, Lyon, Bib. Mun. ms. 894, BnF ffr. ms. 5099, BnF ffr.

ms. Clairambault 483, and Grenoble, Bibl. Mun., ms 1024. Ms. Dutuit B 664 bears a conventional miniature of Anne's arms, but the space for the dedication remains blank except for a decorated capital "N." The dedication in BnF ffr. ms. 5097 has been excised and BnF ffr. ms. 5099 offers only an abbreviated version of Choque's account, without dedication or miniatures.

124. Claude's copy, therefore, must have been one of the first completed and dedicated to a recipient, since it had to have been transcribed and decorated sometime between June 1514 and January 1515.

125. My analysis of this scene and identification of the figures in it differ from those of Didier Le Fur, *Anne de Bretagne*, 117; Turias, "L'héritière d'Anne de Bretagne?" 114; and the description accompanying this illustration in Chotard, ed., *Anne de Bretagne*, 184. For additional commentary, see C. Brown, "Like Mother, like Daughter."

126. They are presumably the two other Breton heralds, *Vannes* and *Hennebont*, that Choque mentions in his account (7).

127. I am grateful to Lori Walters and Elizabeth A. R. Brown for suggesting this interpretation of the miniature.

128. Some of the ideas in this section are based on an earlier version in "Books in Performance."

129. Since Choque refers to Louise as queen mother, we can conclude that this dedication postdates 1 January 1515.

130. Choque's description of the burial of Anne of Brittany's heart in Nantes (91–111) includes a description of the display of her arms at the Église des Carmes that seems to have served as the model for the miniature accompanying all of Choque's dedication.

131. This genealogy is similar to Symphorien Champier's tribute to Anne of France that prefaces his *Nef des dames vertueuses*. It also recalls Penguern's *Genealogie d'Anne Duchesse de Bretagne*, cited in the Introduction.

132. Choque pointed out earlier in his account that Gabriel de la Châtre was one of six masters of ceremonies in charge of organizing the procession of mourners (47).

133. Elizabeth A. R. Brown discusses this issue in "Order and Disorder in the Life and Death of Anne de Bretagne."

134. The order of the highest ranked members of the procession from the Château of Blois to the St. Sauveur Church was, for example: Francis of Angoulême, heir apparent, Charles d'Alençon, Anne of France, Louise of Savoy, her daughter Margaret of Navarre, and Anne's lady of honor Madame of Mailly. During the procession through Paris, Françoise of Vendôme and the countess of Vendôme (Marie de Luxembourg) were placed before Madame of Mailly (74).

135. For reproductions of other similar miniatures, see Bloem, 149–60, and Pächt and Thoss, *Die illuminierten Handschriften*, II, Ms. S. n. 12733, figs. 3–9.

136. See McCartney's distinction between the king's "full sovereign authority" and the queen's "symbolic form of that power" (193). Although she enjoyed privileges derived from her marital and maternal status, the French queen could not exercise temporal authority like the king (190).

137. See Giesey, *The Royal Funeral Ceremony*, 111, who states that the French king was treated as if he never died.

138. See 28, 29, 32, 62, 65.

139. The processions surrounding her body into Orleans are actually described as an entry (62–63).

140. The chronicler employs the word "corps" much more rarely, although the term comes to dominate the description once the procession arrives in Paris (79).

141. See E. Brown, "Refreshment of the Dead."

142. Choque, alias *Bretaigne*, also stages himself on a number of other occasions (47, 50, 55, 85–87, 89).

143. In BnF ms. ffr. 5094, the arms of Blois (fol. 28r), Orleans (fol. 30v), Janville (fol. 31v), Étampes (fol. 32v), Paris (fol. 37v), and Nantes (fol. 50v) are displayed.

144. In at least three cases, Choque stipulates that these verses were inscribed on *escripteaulx*, presumably public-notice displays similar to the posters in allegorical stagings during a royal entry. Other descriptions are not quite as specific. See descriptions about Janville (61), Angerville (62), Monlhéry (65), and Notres Dame (67).

145. Only Notre Dame des Champs is addressed in the *vous* form, perhaps for versification reasons.

146. See Choque's record also for descriptions of the extensive mourning decorations of interiors in which the body rested and urban exteriors through which it passed, such as that of Notre-Dame-des Champs (73).

147. Choque failed to include mention or a transcription of "Poures seruans," the poem La Vigne placed in Anne's grave, perhaps because it would have upstaged his own role during these events.

148. For details, see Chapter 4, n. 106. Much of the implicit tension that I have uncovered in Louise of Savoy's copy of the funeral account of Anne of Brittany likely characterized the destroyed copy once owned by Margaret of Austria as well, although she would not have been involved in French court politics to the same degree as Louise of Savoy.

149. There is no evidence that Choque's account was also printed around the time of Anne's funeral, although Montaiglon and Rothschild, XII, 106–7, seem to imply this. Godefroy included it in his *Cérémonial de France* of 1619 under the title, *L'Ordre observé à l'enterrement de la reine Anne, duchesse de Bretagne, femme des rois Charles VIII et Louis XII, l'an 1513 par Bretagne, roy d'armes.*

150. The word "blason" may refer to "arms," to a "poem in praise," or to both.

## APPENDIX. MANUSCRIPT AND PRINTED BOOKS
### ASSOCIATED WITH ANNE OF BRITTANY

1. Dated by Avril et Reynaud, no. 143.

2. I am grateful to Diane Booton for these details.

3. Borland, *Western Medieval Manuscripts*, 82–83.

4. This work, which formerly figured in the Séguier library, is now lost.

5. This manuscript copy, formerly at the Hermitage Museum in St. Petersburg, is now lost.

6. Thanks to Diane Booton for the BnF reference.

7. This work is now lost.

8. Many of these fragments are now lost, although one, exhibited in 2007 at the Musée du Château des ducs de Bretagne (Chotard, ed., *Anne de Bretagne*, no. 97), is currently housed at the Musée Dobrée in Nantes as ms 994.3.1. Thanks to Diane Booton for this information.

9. Willard and Hicks, eds. *Le livre des trois vertus*, xxiii–xxiv.

10. Although decorated manuscript copies, they contain no signs of Anne of Brittany's ownership.

11. Date established by Deuffic, "Les Livres manuscrits d'Anne de Bretagne."

12. It is improbable that this manuscript was the one Marot dedicated to the queen.

13. This manuscript contains a dedication miniature featuring a female (Anne? Claude?), whereas the dedication miniature in Paris, BnF ffr. 1672 (LD13, MJ18, PT 28–30) depicts a nobleman.

14. Signature of Charles VIII (1r), reference to Louis XII's ownership (A), reference to the king, queen and dauphin (8v), stamp of the *Bibliotheca Regiae* (8v).

15. Attribution of this manuscript to Anne of Brittany and Louis XII has not been confirmed.

# BIBLIOGRAPHY

## PRIMARY MANUSCRIPT SOURCES

Buckinghamshire, Aylesbury, Waddesdon Manor, James A. Rothschild Collection ms.
  22: André de la Vigne, Description of the Coronation of Anne of Brittany (1504)
Bern, Burgerbibliothek ms. 241: Jean Lemaire de Belges, *Troisième livre des illustrations et singularitez de France orientalle et occidentalle*
Brussels, Bibliothèque Royale (BBR)
  ms. 9509: Giovanni Boccaccio, *Des cleres et nobles femmes*
  ms. 3441: Jean Lemaire de Belges, *La Couronne margariticque*
  ms. IV 521: Pierre Choque, *Commémoration de la mort madame Anne . . . Royne de France*
Chantilly, Musée Condé ms. 856: Boccaccio, *Des cleres et nobles femmes*
Grenoble, Bibl. Mun., ms 1024: Pierre Choque, *Commémoration de la mort madame Anne . . . Royne de France*
Lisbon, Fundação Gulbenkain ms. L. A. 143: Boccaccio, *Des cleres et nobles femmes*
London, British Library (BL)
  Harley 4431: Christine de Pizan, Collected Works
  Royal 16 G V: Giovanni Boccaccio, *Des femmes nobles et renommees*
  Royal 20 C V: Giovanni Boccaccio, *Des femmes nobles et renommees*
  Stowe 584: Pierre Choque, *Discours des ceremonies du sacre et mariage d'Anne de Foix*
Lyon, Bib. mun. ms. 894: Pierre Choque, *Commémoration de la mort madame Anne . . . Royne de France*
Nantes, Musée Dobrée, ms. XVII: Antoine Dufour, *Les Vies des femmes célèbres*
New York, Pierpont Morgan Library ms. M381: Boccaccio, *Des cleres et nobles femmes*
New York, Public Library, Spencer Collection ms. 33: Boccaccio, *Des cleres et nobles femmes*
Paris, Bibliothèque de l'Arsenal (Arsenal)
  Ms. 1096: Cattaneo, Alberto, [History of the Kings of France from Francion to Charles VIII in Latin]
  Ms. 3635: Robert du Herlin, *L'Acort des mesdisans et bien disans*
  Ms. 5224: Pierre Choque, *Commémoration de la mort madame Anne . . . Royne de France.*
Paris: Bibliothèque nationale de France (BnF)
  ffr. 90: Pierre Choque, *Discours sur le voyage d'Anne de Foix*

ffr. 133: Giovanni Boccaccio, *Des cleres et nobles femmes.*

ffr. 138–39: Guillaume Fillastre, *Histoire de la Toison d'Or*

ffr. 225: Francesco Petrarch, *Les Remèdes de l'une ou l'autre Fortune*

ffr. 598: *Livre des femmes nobles et renommees*

ffr. 599: Giovanni Boccaccio, *Des cleres et nobles femmes*

ffr. 873: Octovien de Saint-Gelais, *Les XXI Epistres d'Ovide*

ffr. 875: Octovien de Saint-Gelais, *Les XXI Epistres d'Ovide*

ffr. 1120: Giovanni Boccaccio, *Des cleres et nobles femmes*

ffr. 1672: Pierre Choque, *L'Incendie de la Cordelière*

ffr. 1683: Jean Lemaire de Belges, *La Plainte du Désiré*

ffr. 1684: Jean d'Auton, *La Complaincte de Gennes sur la mort de dame Thomassine Espinolle*

ffr. 1687: André de la Vigne, *La Ressource de la Chrestienté*

ffr. 1704: Jean Marot, *La Vraye disant advocate des dames*

ffr. 5037: Giovanni Boccaccio, *Des cleres et nobles femmes*

ffr. 5094: Pierre Choque, *Commémoration de la mort madame Anne . . . Royne de France*

ffr. 5083: Jean d'Auton, *Chroniques de Louis XII*

ffr. 5091: Jean Marot, *Le Voyage de Gênes*

ffr. 5095: Pierre Choque, *Commémoration de la mort madame Anne . . . Royne de France*

ffr. 5096: Pierre Choque, *Commémoration de la mort madame Anne . . . Royne de France*

ffr. 5098: Pierre Choque, *Commémoration de la mort madame Anne . . . Royne de France*

ffr. 5099: Pierre Choque, *Commémoration de la mort madame Anne . . . Royne de France*

ffr. 5100: Pierre Choque, *Commémoration de la mort madame Anne . . . Royne de France*

ffr. 5101: Pierre Choque, *Commémoration de la mort madame Anne . . . Royne de France*

ffr. 5750: *Le Sacre, couronnement et entrée de Madame Claude Royne de France*

ffr. 6150: Pierre Choque, *Commémoration de la mort madame Anne . . . Royne de France*

ffr. 12420: Giovanni Boccaccio, *Des Femmes nobles et renommees*

ffr. 18537: Pierre Choque, *Commémoration de la mort madame Anne . . . Royne de France*

ffr. 23936: Pierre Choque, *Commémoration de la mort madame Anne . . . Royne de France*

ffr. 23988: Jean Lemaire de Belges, *La Plainte du Désiré*

ffr. 24043: Disarouez Penguern, *Genealogie . . . d'Anne tresillustre royne de France et duchesse de Bretagne* ffr. 25158: Pierre Choque, *Commémoration de la mort madame Anne . . . Royne de France*

ffr. 25295: Jean Lemaire de Belges, Collection of the author's works

ffr. 25419: Jean d'Auton, *La Complaincte de Gennes sur la mort de dame Thomassine Espinolle*

f.lat. 9474: Jean Bourdichon, *Les Grandes Heures d'Anne de Bretagne*

nouv. acq. ffr. 74: Pierre Choque, *Commémoration de la mort madame Anne . . . Royne de France*

Paris, Musée du Petit Palais

Ms. Dutuit B 664: Pierre Choque, *Commémoration de la mort madame Anne . . . Royne de France*

Collection Dutuit ms. 665: *Le Trespas de l'Hermine Regretee*

Saint Petersburg, National Library of Russia

Fr. F. v. I. 3: Antoine Dufour, *Les épistres de Saint Jérôme*

Fr. F. v. XIV.8: Fausto Andrelini/ Macé de Villebresme, Jean d'Auton, et al., Collection of Versified Royal Epistles

Fr. Q.v.III.3: Plutarch, *Discours sur le mariage de Pollionet d'Eurydice*

Fr. Q.v.IV.3: Pierre Choque, *Commémoration de la mort madame Anne . . . Royne de France*

San Marino, Huntington Library, ms. HM 60: Octovien de Saint-Gelais, *Les XXI Epistres d'Ovide*

Vienna, Österreichische Nationalbibliothek (ÖNB)

ms. 2555: Giovanni Boccaccio, *Des cleres et nobles femmes*

ms. S. n. 12733: Pierre Choque, *Commémoration de la mort madame Anne . . . Royne de France*

Privately owned manuscripts

Breslauer and Grieb Catalogue #109: [Octovien de Saint-Gelais], Poetic anthology

*Ex* Phillipps 3648: Boccacio, *Des femmes nommés* [sic] *nobles et renommez*

Société des Manuscrits des Assureurs français, ms. 85.1: Pierre Choque, *L'Incendie de la Cordelière*

## PRIMARY PRINTED SOURCES

Anne de France. *Les Enseignements d'Anne de France, Duchesse de Bourbonnois et d'Auvergne, à sa fille Susanne de Bourbon.* Ed. A.-M. Chazaud. Moulin, 1878; rpt. Marseille: Lafitte, 1978.

———. *Lessons for my Daughter.* Trans. Sharon L. Jansen. Cambridge: Brewer, 2004.

Auton, Jean d'. *Chroniques.* Ed. R. de Maulde La Clavière. 4 vols. Paris: Renouard, 1889–95.

Beaune, Henri and J. d'Arbaumont. *Mémoires d'Olivier de la Marche.* Vol. 2. Paris: Renouard, 1884.

Boccaccio, Giovanni. *De la Louenge des nobles et cleres dames*. Paris: for Antoine Vérard,1493.

London, BL C.22.c.2

Paris, BnF, Rés. G365 and Rés. Vélins 1223

Manchester, University of Manchester, John Rylands Collection, Inc. 15.E.2

———. *Des Cleres et Nobles Femmes Chap. I–LII (Ms. Bibl. Nat. 12420)*. Ed. Jeanne Baroin and Josiane Haffen. Paris: Belles Lettres, 1993.

———. *Des Cleres et Nobles Femmes Chap. LIII–fin (Ms. Bibl. Nat. 12420)*. Ed. Jeanne Baroin and Josiane Haffen. Paris: Belles Lettres, 1995.

———. *Famous Women*. Trans. Virginia Brown. Cambridge, Mass.: Harvard University Press, 2001.

Bonnardot, François. *Registres des délibérations du bureau de la Ville de Paris*. Vol. 1. Paris: Imprimerie Nationale, 1883.

Bouchet, Jean. *Généalogies, effigies, et épitaphes des Roys de France*. Poitiers, 1545.

———. *Le Jugement poetic de l'honneur femenin*. Poitiers, 1538.

———. *Le Jugement poetic de l'honneur femenin*. Ed. Adrian Armstrong. Paris: Champion, 2006.

Champier, Symphorien. *La Nef des dames vertueuses*. Ed. Judy Kem. Paris: Champion, 2007.

Chartier, Alain. *Quadrilog invectif*. Ed. Arthur Piaget. Paris: Champion, 1923.

Chartier, Alain, Baudet Herenc, and Achille Caulier. *Le Cycle de La belle dame sans mercy: une anthologie poétique du XVe siècle (BNF MS Fr. 1131)*. Ed. David F. Hult and Joan E. McRae. Paris: Champion, 2003.

Choque, Pierre. *Récit des Funérailles d'Anne de Bretagne*. Ed. L. Merlet and Max de Gombert. Paris: Aubry, 1858.

Christine de Pizan. *Livre de la Cité des Dames*. Ed. Eric Hicks and Thérèse Moreau. Paris: Stock/Moyen Âge, 1986.

———. *Le Livre des trois vertus*. Ed. Charity Cannon Willard and Eric Hicks. Paris: Champion, 1989. Vienna, ÖNB, Ink.3.D.19

Commynes, Philippe de. *Mémoires*. In *Historiens et chroniqueurs du Moyen Âge*, ed. Albert Pauphilet. Paris: Gallimard, 1952.

Cretin, Guillaume. *Oeuvres poétiques*. Ed. Kathleen Chesney. Paris: Firmin-Didot, 1932.

Dufour, Antoine. *Les Epistres saint Jerosme*. Paris: for Jean de la Garde, 1519 (n.st.) (BnF Rés. C5984).

———. *Les Epistres saint Hierosme*. Paris: for Jean Bonfons, [post 1519] (BnF Rés. D80287).

———. *Les Vies des femmes célèbres*. Ed. Gustave Jeanneau. Geneva: Droz, 1970.

Foresti, Jacopo Filippo. *De Plurimis claris selectisque mulieribus*. Ferrara: Rubeis, 1497.

Godefroy, Théodore. *Le Cérémonial de France*. Vol. 1. Paris: Pacard, 1619.

Gringore, Pierre. *Les Entrées royales à Paris de Marie d'Angleterre [1514] et Claude de France [1517]*. Ed. Cynthia J. Brown. Geneva: Droz, 2005.

Hicks, Eric, ed. *Le Débat sur le Roman de la Rose*. Paris: Champion, 1977.

La Marche, Olivier de. *Le Chevalier délibéré*. Paris: J. Lambert, 1493 (BnF Rés. Vélins 2231).

La Vigne, André de. *La Ressource de la Chrestienté*. 1494. Ed. Cynthia J. Brown. Montreal: CERES, 1989.

Le Franc, Martin. *Le Champion des dames*. Ed. Robert Deschaux. 5 vols. Paris: Champion, 1999.

Lemaire de Belges, Jean. *Épistre du roy à Hector et autres pieces de circonstances (1511–1513)*. Ed. Adrian Armstrong and Jennifer Britnell. Paris: SATFM, 2000.

———. *Les Épîtres de l'Amant Vert*. Ed. Jean Frappier. Lille: Droz, 1948.

———. *La Plainte du Désiré*. Ed. D. Yabsley. Paris: Droz: 1932.

———. *Le Temple d'Honneur et de Vertus*. Ed. Henry Hornik. Geneva: Droz, 1957.

———. *Œuvres*. Ed. J. Stecher. 4 vols. Louvain: Impr. de J. Lefever, 1882–91.

Leroux de Lincy, Alfred. "Cérémonies du mariage d'Anne de Foix, de la Maison de France, avec Ladislas VI, roi de Bohème, de Pologne et de Hongrie." *Bibliothèque de l'École des Chartes* 21, 2 (1861): 156–85, 422–39.

[Margaret of Austria]. *Complainte de dame Marguerite d'Autriche, fille de Maximilian Roy des Romains*. Antwerp: Gheraert Leeu, 1491–92 (BBR ms. 10926).

Marot, Clément. *Œuvres poétiques*. Ed. Gérard Defaux. Paris: Bordas, 1993.

Marot, Jean. *Les Deux recueils*. Ed. Gérard Defaux and Thierry Mantovani. Geneva: Droz, 1999.

———. *Le Voyage de Gênes*. Ed. Giovanna Trisolini. Geneva: Droz, 1974.

———. *Le Voyage de Venise*. Ed. Giovanna Trisolini. Geneva: Droz, 1977.

———. *Poème inédit de Iehan Marot publié d'après un manuscrit de la Bibliothèque impériale*. Ed. Georges Guiffrey. Paris: Renouard, 1860.

Michel de Tours, Guillaume. "Soulas de noblesse sur le coronnement de la royne de France Claude Duchesse de Bretaigne." In *Le Penser de royal memoire*. Paris: for Jean de la Garde and Pierre Le Brodeur, n.d. [1521], fols. l v recto–n ii verso.

———. *Elegies, thrennes et complainctes sur la mort de tresilustre dame, madame Claude, jadis de son vivant royne de France*. n.p. n.d. [1526].

Molinet, Jean. *Chroniques*. Ed. J-A. Buchon. Vol. 5. Paris: Verdière, 1828.

———. *Les Faictz et dictz*. Ed. Noël Dupire. 3 vols. Paris: Société des anciens textes français. 1936–39.

Montaiglon, Anatole de and James de Rothschild, eds. *Recueil de poésies françoises des XVe et XVIe siècles*. Vol. XII. Paris: Jannet, 1877.

Naso, Publius Ovidius. *Héroïdes traduites en vers français par Octovien de Saint-Gelais Österreichische Nationalbibliothek, Wien, Codex 2624*. Ed. Dagmar Thoss. Munich: Lengenfelder, 1986.

———. *Heroides and Amores*. Ed. Grant Showerman. Cambridge, Mass.: Harvard University Press, 1958.

Nicolaï, Jean. "Sensieult le couronnement et entrée de la royne de France en la ville de Paris [février 1492]." *Bulletin de la Société de l'Histoire de France* (1845–46): 111–21.

Petrarch, Francesco. *Remedies for Fortune Fair and Foul*. Ed. Conrad H. Rawski. 5 vols. Bloomington: Indiana University Press, 1991.

————. *Les Remèdes aux deux fortunes/De Remediis utriusque fortune (1354–1366)*. Ed.
Christophe Carraud. 2 vols. Grenoble: Jérôme Millon, 2002.

*Plutarch's* Advice to the Bride and Groom *and* A Consolation to His Wife: *English Translations, Commentary, Interpretive Essays and Bibliography*. Ed. Sarah B. Pomeroy.
New York: Oxford University Press, 1999.

Plutarque. *Oeuvres morales*. Ed. Jean Defradas, Jean Hani, and Robert Klaerr. Vol. 2.
Paris: Belles Lettres, 1985.

*Le Sacre d'Anne de Bretagne à Saint-Denis en 1492* (BnF Rés. 8° Lb$^{28}$ 13)
In Gringore, Pierre. *Les entrées royales*, ed. Cynthia J. Brown, 195–214.

Saint-Gelais, Octovien de. *Le Séjour d'Honneur*. Ed. Frédéric Duval. Geneva: Droz, 2002.

Saint Martin, Robert de. *Trésor de l'âme*. Paris: Vérard, ca. 1497 (BnF Rés. Vélins 350).

————. *A Critical Edition and Study of Frère Robert (Chartreux), Le Chastel perilleux*. Ed.
Sister Marie Brisson. Salzburg: James Hogg, 1974.

Seyssel, Claude de. *Louenges du roy Louys XIIe de ce nom*. Paris: Vérard, 1508 (BnF Rés.
Vélins 2780).

————. *La Monarchie de France et deux autres fragments politiques*. Ed. Jacques Poujol.
Paris: Libra d'Argences, 1961.

————. *Victoire du roy contre les Veniciens*. Paris: Vérard, 1510. (BnF Rés. Vélins 2776).

Wieck, Roger S. and K. Michelle Hearne. *The Prayer Book of Anne de Bretagne: MS M.50,
The Pierpont Morgan Library, New York*. Lucerne: Faksimile Verlag Luzern, 1999.


SECONDARY SOURCES


Alexandre-Bidon, Danièle and Cécile Treffort, eds. *A réveiller les morts: la mort au quotidien dans l'Occident médiéval*. Lyon: Presses Universitaires de Lyon, 1993.

Aliverti, Maria Ines. "Visits to Genoa: The Printed Sources." In *Europa Triumphans:
Court and Civic Festivals in Early Modern Europe*, ed. J. R. Mulryne et al. 22–35.

Angenot, Marc. *Les Champions des femmes: examen du discours sur la supériorité des femmes
1400–1800*. Montreal: Presses de l'Université de Québec, 1977.

Ariès, Philippe, ed. *Essais sur l'histoire de la mort en Occident: du moyen âge à nos jours*.
Paris: Seuil, 1975.

————. *L'Homme devant la mort*. Paris: Seuil, 1977.

Ashley, Kathleen and Pamela Sheingorn, eds. *Interpreting Cultural Symbols: Saint Anne in
Late Medieval Society*. Athens: University of Georgia Press, 1990.

Aulotte, Robert. "Études sur l'influence de Plutarque au seizième siècle." *Bibliothèque
d'Humanisme et Renaissance* 21 (1959): 606–12.

Avril, François. *La Passion des manuscrits enluminés: bibliophiles français 1280–1580*. Paris:
Bibliothèque Nationale, 1991.

————. *Creating French Culture: Treasures from the Bibliothèque Nationale de France*. Ed.
Marie-Hélène Tesnière and Prosser Gifford. New Haven, Conn.: Yale University
Press, 1995.

Avril, François and Nicole Reynaud. *Les Manuscrits à peintures en France 1440–1520.* Paris: BnF/Flammarion, 1995.

Baldwin, Spurgeon and James W. Marchand. "The Virgin Mary as Advocate Before the Heavenly Court." *Medievalia et Humanistica* 18 (1992): 79–94.

Baskins, Cristelle. "Trecento Rome: The Poetics and Politics of Widowhood." In *Widowhood and Visual Culture in Early Modern Europe,* ed. Allison Levy. Aldershot: Ashgate, 2003. 197–209.

Baumgartner, Frederic J. *Louis XII.* New York: St. Martin's, 1994.

Baurmeister, Ursula and Marie-Pierre Laffitte. *Des livres et des rois: la bibliothèque royale de Blois.* Paris: Bibliothèque Nationale, 1992.

Beaune, Colette. "Mourir noblement à la fin du Moyen Âge." In *La Mort au Moyen Âge, colloque de l'Association des Historiens médiévistes français réunis à Strasbourg en juin 1975.* Strasbourg: Librairie Istra, 1977. 12–43.

Beaune, Colette and Élodie Lequain. "Marie de Berry et les livres." In *Livres et lectures de femmes,* ed. Anne-Marie Legaré. 49–65.

Becker, Philip-Auguste. *Jean Lemaire, der erste humanistische Dichter Frankreichs.* Strassburg: Trübner, 1893.

Bell, Susan Groag. *The Lost Tapestries of the City of Ladies: Christine de Pizan's Renaissance Legacy.* Berkeley: University of California Press, 2004.

———. "Medieval Women Book Owners: Arbiters of Lay Piety and Ambassadors of Culture." *Signs* 7 (1982): 746–68.

Bertière, Simone. *Les Reines de France au temps des Valois.* Vol. 1, *Le beau seizième siècle.* Paris: Fallois, 1994.

Binski, Paul. *Medieval Death: Ritual and Representation.* Ithaca, N.Y.: Cornell University Press, 1996.

Blamires, Alcuin. *The Case for Women in Medieval Culture.* Oxford: Clarendon, 1997.

———, ed. *Women Defamed and Women Defended: An Anthology of Medieval Texts.* Oxford: Clarendon, 1992.

Bloch, R. Howard. *Medieval Misogyny and the Invention of Western Romantic Love.* Chicago: University of Chicago Press, 1991.

Bloem, Hélène M. "The Processions and Decorations at the Royal Funeral of Anne of Brittany." *Bibliothèque d'Humanisme et Renaissance* 54, 1 (1992): 131–60.

Bock, Gisela and Margarete Zimmermann. "Die *Querelle des femmes* in Europa: Eine begriffe- und forschungsgeschichtliche Einführung." In *Querelles: Jahrbuch für Frauenforschung 1997,* vol. 2, *Die europäische "Querelle des femmes": Geschlechterdebatten seit dem 15. Jahrhundert,* ed. Gisela Bock and Margarete Zimmermann. Stuttgart/Weimar: Metzler, 1997. 9–38.

Booton, Diane. *Manuscripts, Market and the Transition to Print in Late Medieval Brittany.* Aldershot: Ashgate, 2010.

Bozzolo, Carla. *Manuscrits des traductions françaises d'oeuvres de Boccacce: XVe siècle.* Padova: Antenore, 1973.

Brejon de Lavergnée, Jacques. "L'emblématique d'Anne de Bretagne d'après les manuscrits à peintures (XVe–XVIe siècles)." *Mémoires de la Société d'Histoire et d'Archéologie de Bretagne* 55 (1978): 83–95.

Bridge, John S. C. *A History of France from the Death of Louis XI.* 4 vols. Oxford: Oxford University Press, 1921–36.

Breitenstein, Renée-Claude. "La Rhétorique encomiastique dans les éloges collectifs de femmes imprimés de la première Renaissance (1493–1555)." Dissertation, McGill University, 2009.

Britnell, Jennifer. "L'Épître héroïque à la cour de Louis XII et d'Anne de Bretagne: le manuscrit fr. F.V.XIV.8 de Saint-Pétersbourg." *L'Analisi Linguistica et Letteraria* 8, 1–2 (2000): 459–84.

———. *Jean Bouchet.* Edinburgh: Edinburgh University Press, 1986.

Brown, Cynthia J. "Allegorical Design and Image-Making in Fifteenth-Century France: Alain Chartier's Joan of Arc." *French Studies* 53, 4 (October 1999): 385–404.

———. "Books in Performance: The Parisian Entry (1504) and Funeral (1514) of Anne of Brittany." In *Meanings and Its Objects: Material Culture in Medieval and Renaissance France*), ed. Margaret Burland, David LaGuardia, and Andrea Tarnowski. *Yale French Studies* 110 (2006): 75–91.

———. "Celebration and Controversy at a Late Medieval French Court: A Poetic Anthology for and About Anne of Brittany and Her Female Entourage." (forthcoming)

———, ed. *The Cultural and Political Legacy of Anne de Bretagne: Negotiating Convention in Books and Documents.* Cambridge: D.S. Brewer, 2010.

———. "Du Manuscrit à l'imprimé: *Les XXI Epistres d'Ovide* d'Octovien de Saint Gelais." In *Ovide métamorphosé: les lecteurs médiévaux d'Ovide,* ed., Laurence Harf-Lancner, Laurence Mathey-Maille, and Michelle Szkilnik. Paris: Presses Sorbonne nouvelle, 2009. 69–82.

———. "The 'Famous Women' *Topos* in Early Sixteenth-Century France: Echoes of Christine de Pizan." In *"Rien ne mest seur que la chose incertaine": études sur l'art d'écrire au Moyen Âge offertes à Eric Hicks par ses élèves, collègues, amies et amis,* ed. Jean-Claude Mühlethaler and Denis Billotte. Geneva: Slatkine, 2001. 149–60.

———. "From Stage to Page: Royal Entry Performances in Honour of Mary Tudor (1514)." In *Book and Text in France, 1400–1600: Poetry on the Page,* ed. Adrian Armstrong and Malcolm Quainton. Aldershot: Ashgate, 2007. 49–72.

———. "Grief, Rape, and Suicide as Consolation for the Queen: Ambivalent Images of Female Rulers in the Books of Anne de Bretagne." *Journal of the Early Book Society* (Summer 2001): 172–201.

———. "Like Mother, like Daughter: The Blurring of Royal Imagery in Books for Anne de Bretagne and Claude de France." In *The Cultural and Political Legacy of Anne de Bretagne,* ed. Cynthia J. Brown. 101–21.

———. "Les Louanges d'Anne de Bretagne dans la poésie de Jean Bouchet et de ses contemporains: voix de deuil masculines et féminines." *Actes du Colloque international Les Grands Jours de Rabelais en Poiton (Poitiers, 29 August–2 September 2001),* ed. Nathalie Dauvois and Jennifer Britnell. Paris: Champion, 2003. 32–51.

————. "Le Mécénat d'Anne de Bretagne et la politique du livre." In *Patronnes et femmes mécènes en France à la Renaissance*, ed. Kathleen Wilson-Chevalier. Saint-Étienne: Publications de l'Université de Saint-Étienne, 2007. 195–224.

————. "La Mise en oeuvre et la mise en page des recueils traitant des femmes célèbres à la fin du moyen âge." In *Les Actes du 3e colloque international du GRMF ("Le Livre ou je met toutes mes choses: le recueil à la fin du Moyen Âge"), Université catholique de Louvain, 10–12 mai, 2007*. Turnhout: Brepols, 2010.

————. "La Mise en œuvre et la mise en page du prosimètre chez André de la Vigne." *Cahiers V. L. Saulnier (Le prosimètre à la Renaissance)* 22 (2005): 87–110.

————. "Paratextual Performances in the Early Parisian Book Trade: Antoine Vérard's Edition of Boccaccio's *Nobles et cleres dames* (1493)." In *Cultural Performances in Medieval France: Essays in Honor of Nancy Freeman Regalado*, ed. E. Jane Burns, Eglal Doss-Quinby, and Roberta Krueger. Woodbridge: Boydell and Brewer, 2007. 255–64.

————. "The Patron." In Roger Wieck with Cynthia J. Brown, *The Prayer Book of Claude de France: MS M.1166 The Pierpont Morgan Library, New York*, Luzerne: Quaternio Verlag Luzern, 2010. 57–70.

————. "Pierre Gringore: acteur, auteur, éditeur." *Cahiers V. L. Saulnier (Les grands rhétoriqueurs)* 14 (1997): 145–63.

————. *Poets, Patrons, and Printers: Crisis of Authority in Late Medieval France*. Ithaca, N.Y.: Cornell University Press, 1995.

————. "The Reconstruction of an Author in Print: Christine de Pizan in the Fifteenth and Sixteenth Centuries." In *Christine de Pizan and the Categories of Difference*, ed. Marilynn Desmond. Minneapolis: University of Minnesota Press, 1998. 215–35.

————. *The Shaping of History and Poetry in Late Medieval France: Propaganda and Artistic Expression in the Works of the Rhétoriqueurs*. Birmingham, Ala.: Summa, 1985.

————. "Textual and Iconographical Ambivalence in the Late Medieval Representation of Women." *Bulletin of the John Rylands University Library of Manchester* 81, 3 (Autumn 1999): 205–39.

Brown, Elizabeth A. R. "The Children of Anne de Bretagne." In *The Cultural and Political Legacy of Anne de Bretagne*, ed. Cynthia J. Brown. 193.

————. "Order and Disorder in the Life and Death of Anne de Bretagne: The Funeral of Charles VIII." In *The Cultural and Political Legacy of Anne de Bretagne*, ed. Cynthia J. Brown. 177–92.

————. "Refreshment of the Dead: *Post Mortem* Meals, Anne de Bretagne, Jean Lemaire de Belges, and the Influence of Antiquity on Royal Ceremonial." In *Les Funérailles à la Renaissance: XIIe colloque international de la Société Française d'Étude du Seizième Siècle, Bar-le-Duc, 2–5 décembre 1999*, ed. Jean Balsamo. Geneva: Droz, 2002. 113–30.

Brownlee, Kevin. "Christine de Pizan's Canonical Authors: The Special Case of Boccaccio." *Comparative Literature Studies* 32 (1995): 135–52.

Bruchet, Max. *Marguerite d'Autriche, duchesse de* Savoie. Lille: L. Danel, 1927.

Brueckner, Thomas. "Octovien de Saint-Gelais' Ovid Übersetzung: Der Pariser Codex fr. 874 (B.N.)." *Wolfenbüttler Arbeitskreis für Renaissanceforschung* 13, 3 (December 1989): 93–101.

Bruster, Douglas. "New Materialism in Renaissance Studies." In *Material Culture and Cultural Materialisms in the Middle Ages and Renaissance*, ed. Curtis Perry. Turnhout: Brepols, 2001. 225–38.

Bryant, Lawrence. *The King and the City in the Parisian Royal Entry Ceremony: Politics, Ritual and Art in the Renaissance.* Geneva: Droz, 1986.

———. "The Medieval Entry Ceremony at Paris." In *Coronations: Medieval and Early Modern Monarchic Ritual*, ed. Janos M. Bak. Berkeley: University of California Press, 1990. 88–118.

Buettner, Brigitte. *Boccaccio's "Des cleres et nobles femmes": Systems of Signification in an Illuminated Manuscript.* Seattle: University of Washington Press, 1996.

———. "Women and the Circulation of Books." *Journal of the Early Book Society* 4 (2001): 9–31.

Callahan, Leslie. "Signs of Sorrow: The Expression of Grief and the Representation of Mourning in Fifteenth-Century French Culture." Dissertation, City University of New York, 1996.

Camille, Michael. "The Book of Signs: Writing and Visual Difference in Gothic Manuscript Illumination." *Word and Image* 1, 1 (January–March 1985): 133–48.

Cassagnes-Brouquet, Sophie. *Un manuscrit d'Anne de Bretagne: les Vies des femmes célèbres d'Antoine Dufour.* Rennes: Éditions Ouest-France, 2007.

Cassard, Jean-Christophe. "Du Passage historique à l'invite touristique: Anne de Bretagne à Morlaix." In *Pour en finir avec Anne de Bretagne?*, ed. Dominique Le Page. 125–30.

Castelain, Marie-France. *Au pays de Claude of France.* Romorantin: Société d'Art, d'Histoire et d'Archéologie de Sologne, 1986.

Catherine, Claude. *La Querelle des femmes.* Pantin: Le Temps des Cerises, 2000.

Caviness, Madeline H. "Anchoress, Abbess, and Queen: Donors and Patrons or Intercessors and Matrons?" In *The Cultural Patronage of Medieval Women*, ed. June Hall McCash, 105–54.

Cerquiglini-Toulet, Jacqueline. "La Femme au livre dans la littérature médiévale." In *Livres et lectures de femmes*, ed. Anne-Marie Legaré, 29–34.

Chombart de Lauwe, Marc. *Anne de Beaujeu ou la passion du pouvoir.* Paris: Jules Tallandier, 1980.

Claerr, Roseline. "Que ma mémoire 'là demeure' en mes livres": Catherine de Coëtivy (vers 1460–1529) et sa bibliothèque." In *Livres et lectures de femmes*, ed. Anne-Marie Legaré, 101–17.

Cluzel, Jean. *Anne de France: fille de Louis XI,, duchesse de Bourbon.* Paris: Fayard, 2002.

Cornilliat, François. "Rhétorique, poésie, guérison de Jean à Clément Marot." In *La Génération Marot: poètes français et néolatins, actes du colloque international de Baltimore*, ed. Gérard Defaux. Paris: Champion, 1997, 59–80.

Cosandey, Fanny. "Anne de Bretagne, reine de France." In *Pour en finir avec Anne de Bretagne?* ed. Dominique Le Page, 83–89.

————. *La Reine de France: symbole et pouvoir XVe–XVIIIe siècle*. Paris: Gallimard, 2000.

Couchman, Jane and Ann Crabb. "Form and Persuasion in Women's Letters, 1400–1700." In *Women's Letters Across Europe, 1400–1700: Form and Persuasion*, ed. Jane Couchman and Ann Crabb. Aldershot: Ashgate, 2005. 3–18.

Coudrec, C. "Les Miniatures du *Voyage de Gênes* de Jean Marot." In *Les trésors des bibliothèques de France*. Paris: Van Oest, 1927. 39–55.

Cowling, David. *Building the Text: Architecture as Metaphor in Late Medieval and Early Modern France*. Oxford: Clarendon, 1998.

Damongeot-Bourdat, Marie-Françoise. "Le Coffre aux livres de Marie de Bretagne (1424–77): abbesse de Fontevraud." In *Livres et lectures de femmes*, ed. Anne-Marie Legaré. 81–97.

Debae, Marguerite. *La Bibliothèque de Marguerite d'Autriche: essai de reconstitution d'après l'inventaire de 1523–24*. Louvain-Paris: Peeters, 1995.

Delaissé, L. M. J., James Marrow, and John de Wit. *Illuminated Manuscripts*. London: Office du Livre, 1977.

Delisle, Léopold. *Les Grandes Heures de la Reine Anne de Bretagne et l'atelier de Jean Bourdichon*. Paris: D. Morgand, 1913.

Dewick, E. S. *The Coronation Book of Charles V of France (Cottonian Ms. Tiberius B. VIII)*. London: Harrison and Sons, 1899.

D'Orliac, Jehanne. *Anne de Beaujeu, roi de France*. Paris: Plon, 1936.

Dörrie, Heinrich. "Die Briefdichtung in Frankreich von etwa 1450 bis etwa 1600." In *Der heroische Brief: Bestandsaufnahme, Geschichte, Kritik einer humanistisch-barocken Literaturgattung*. Berlin: de Gruyter, 1968.

Driver, Martha W. "Mirrors of a Collective Past: Reconsidering Images of Medieval Women." In *Women and the Book*, ed. Jane Taylor and Lesley Smith. 75–93.

Droz, Eugénie. "Notice sur un manuscrit ignoré de la Bibliothèque Nationale." *Romania* 45 (1918–19): 503–13.

Dufresne, Laura. "Women Warriors." *Women's Studies* 23 (1994): 111–31.

Duggan, Anne J., ed. *Queens and Queenship in Medieval Europe*. Woodbridge: Boydell & Brewer, 1997.

Durrieu, Paul and Jean-J. Marquet de Vasselot. "Les Manuscrits à miniatures des *Héroïdes* d'Ovide traduites par Saint-Gelais et un grand miniaturiste français du XVIe siècle." *L'Artiste* (May–June 1894): 1–31.

Eichberger, Dagmar. "Margaret of Austria: A Princess with Ambition and Political Insight." In *Women of Distinction: Margaret of York, Margaret of Austria*, ed. Dagmar Eichberger. 49–55.

————. "Margaret of Austria's Portrait Collection: Female Patronage in the Light of Dynastic Ambitions and Artistic Quality." *Renaissance Studies*, 10, 2 (June 1996): 259–79.

————, ed. *Women of Distinction: Margaret of York, Margaret of Austria*. Davidsfonds/ Leuven: Brepols, 2005.

Engel, Gisela et al., eds. *Geschlechterstreit am Beginn der europäischen Moderne: die Querelle des Femmes.* Königstein/Taunus: Helmer, 2004.

Farrell, Joseph. "Reading and Writing the *Heroides.*" *Harvard Studies in Classical Philology* 98 (1998): 324–27.

Fradenburg, Louise. "Introduction: Rethinking Queenship." In *Women and Sovereignty,* ed. Fradenburg. 1–13.

———, ed. *Women and Sovereignty.* Edinburgh: Edinburgh University Press, 1992.

Franklin, Margaret. *Boccaccio's Heroines: Power and Virtue in Renaissance Society.* Aldershot: Ashgate, 2006.

Gabory, Émile. *L'Union de la Bretagne à la France: Anne de Bretagne duchesse et reine.* Paris: Plon, 1941.

Gelfand, Laura D. "Margaret of Austria and the Encoding of Power in Patronage: The Funerary Foundation at Brou." In *Widowhood and Visual Culture in Early Modern Europe,* ed. Allison Levy. 145–59.

Giesey, Ralph E. *The Royal Funeral Ceremony in Renaissance France.* Geneva: Droz, 1960.

Giordano, Luisa. "Les Entrées de Louis XII en Milanais." In *Passer les monts: Français en Italie—l'Italie en France, 1494–1525,* ed. Jean Balsamo. Acts of Xe Colloque de la Société française d'étude du seizième siècle. Paris: Champion, 1998. 141–42.

Grand, Roger. "Anne de Bretagne et le premier humanisme de la Renaissance en France: miniature inédite des 'Illustrations de Gaule et singularités de Troye' de Lemaire de Belges (1512)." *Mémoires de la Société d'Histoire d'Archéologie de Bretagne* 29 (1949): 45–70.

Grieco, Sara. *"Querelle des femmes" or "guerre des sexes"? Visual Representations of Women in Renaissance Europe.* San Domenico: European University Institute, 1989.

Guenée, Bernard and Françoise Lehoux, *Les Entrées royales françaises de 1328 à 1515.* Paris: CNRS, 1968.

Hablot, Laurent. "Pour en finir—ou pour commencer!—avec l'ordre de la Cordelière." In *Pour en finir avec Anne de Bretagne?,* ed. Dominique Le Page. 47–70.

Hauvette, H. "Les Plus anciens traductions françaises de Boccace." *Bulletin italien* 9, 3 (July–September 1909): 193–211.

Hemptinne, Thérèse de "Lire et écrire, c'est prier un peu: culture écrite et pratiques féminines de dévotion aux Pays-Bas à la fin du Moyen Âge." In *Livres et lectures de femmes,* ed. Anne-Marie Legaré, 151–62.

Hochner, Nicole. *Louis XII: les dérèglements de l'image royale (1498–1515).* Seyssel: Champ Vallon, 2006.

Huneycutt, Lois L. "Female Succession and the Language of Power in the Writings of Twelfth-Century Churchmen" In *Medieval Queenship,* ed. John C. Parsons. 189–201.

Huot, Sylvia. "A Book Made for a Queen: The Shaping of a Late Medieval Anthology Manuscript (B.N. fr. 24429)." In *The Whole Book: Cultural Perspectives on the Medieval Miscellany,* ed. Stephen G. Nichols and Siegfried Wenzel. Ann Arbor: University of Michigan Press, 1996. 123–43.

Jeannot, Delphine. "Les Bibliothèques de princesses en France au temps de Charles VI:

l'exemple de Marguerite de Bavière." In *Livres et lectures de femmes*, ed. Anne-Marie Legaré. 191–210.

Jodogne, Pierre. *Jean Lemaire de Belges, écrivain franco-bourguignon*. Bruxelles: Palais des Académies, 1971.

Jones, Michael. *The Creation of Brittany: A Late Medieval State*. London: Hambledon Press, 1988.

———. "Les Signes du pouvoir: l'ordre de l'Hermine, les devises et les hérauts des ducs de Bretagne au XVe siècle." *Mémoires de la Société d'histoire et d'archéologie de Bretagne* 68 (1991): 141–73.

Jordan, Constance. "Boccaccio's In-Famous Women: Gender and Civic Virtues in the *De mulieribus claris*." In *Ambiguous Realities: Women in the Middle Ages and Renaissance*, ed. Carole Levin and Jeanie Watson. Detroit: Wayne State University Press, 1982. 25–47.

Kamerick, Kathleen. "Patronage and Devotion in the Prayer Book of Anne of Brittany, Newberry Library Ms. 83." *Manuscripta* 39 (1995): 40–50.

Katzenellenbogen, Adolf. *Allegories of the Virtues and Vices in Medieval Art*. Toronto: University of Toronto Press, 1989.

Kelly, Joan. "Early Feminist Theory and the *Querelle des femmes 1400–1789*." *Signs* 8 (1982): 4–28.

Kettering, Sharon. *Patronage in Sixteenth- and Seventeenth-Century France*. Aldershot: Ashgate, 2002.

Kipling, Gordon. *Enter the King: Theatre, Liturgy, and Ritual in the Medieval Civic Triumph*. Oxford: Clarendon, 1998.

———. "Henry VII and the Origins of Tudor Patronage." In *Patronage in the Renaissance*, ed. Guy F. Lytle and Stephen Orgel. Princeton, N.J.: Princeton University Press, 1981. 117–64.

Knecht, R. J. *Francis I*. Cambridge: Cambridge University Press, 1972.

Kolsky, Stephen. *The Ghost of Boccaccio: Origins on Famous Women in Renaissance Italy*. Turnhout: Brepols, 2005.

Korteweg, Anne S. "La Collection de livres d'une femme indépendante: Marie de Luxembourg (v. 1470–1547). In *Livres et lectures de femmes*, ed. Anne-Marie Legaré. 221–32.

Labande-Mailfert, Yvonne. *Charles VIII et son milieu, 1470–1498: la jeunesse au pouvoir*. Paris: Klincksieck, 1975.

Laborde, Alexandre de. *Les Principaux manuscrits à peintures conservés dans l'ancienne Bibliothèque Impériale Publique de Saint-Pétersbourg*. Paris: Société Française de Reproduction de Manuscrits à Peintures, 1938.

Laurens, Pierre. *L'Abeille dans l'ambre: célébration de l'épigramme de l'époque alexandrine à la fin de la Renaissance*. Paris: Belles Lettres, 1989.

LeBlanc, Yvonne. *Va Lettre Va: The French Verse Epistle (1400–1550)*. Birmingham, Ala.: Summa, 1995.

Le Fur, Didier. *Anne de Bretagne*. Paris: Guénégaud, 2000.

———. *Louis XII*. Paris: Perrin, 2001.

Legaré, Anne-Marie. "Les Bibliothèques de deux princesses: Marguerite d'York et

Marguerite d'Autriche." In *Livres et lectures de femmes*, ed. Anne-Marie Legaré. 253–64.

———. "Charlotte de Savoie's Library and Illuminators," *Journal of the Early Book Society* 4 (2001): 32–87.

———, ed. *Livres et lectures de femmes en Europe entre Moyen Âge et Renaissance*. Turnhout: Brepols, 2007.

———. "Livres et lectures de la reine Jeanne de Laval." In *Bretagne: art, création, société: mélanges en l'honneur de Denise Delouche*, ed. Jean-Yves Andrieux and Marianne Grivel. Rennes: Presses Universitaires de Rennes, 1997. 220–34.

———. "Le *Pèlerinage de Vie humaine* en prose de la reine Charlotte de Savoie." In *Illuminationen*, #6/Katalog Antiquariat Heribert Tenschert, no. 51. Ramsen-Rothalmunster, 2004. 182–94.

———. "Reassessing Women's Libraries in Late Medieval France: The Case of Jeanne de Laval." *Renaissance Studies* 10 (1996): 209–36.

Lelièvre, Pierre. "Entrées royales à Nantes à l'époque de la Renaissance (1500–55)." In *Fêtes de la Renaissance*, ed. Jean Jacquot and Elie Königson. Vol. 3. Paris: CNRS, 1975. 81–91.

Lemaire, Jacques. "Note sur la datation du 'Séjour d'Honneur' d'Octovien de Saint-Gelais." *Romania* 102 (1981): 74–78.

Le Page, Dominique, ed. *Pour en finir avec Anne de Bretagne? Actes de la journée d'étude organisée aux Archives départementales de la Loire-Atlantqiue, le 15 mai 2002*. Nantes: Conseil Général de Loire-Atlantique, 2004.

Lequain, Élodie. "Anne de France et le livres: la tradition et le pouvoir." In *Patronnes et mécènes en France à la Renaissance*, ed. Kathleen Wilson-Chevalier, 155–68.

Leroux de Lincy, Alfred. *Vie de la reine Anne de Bretagne, femme des rois de France Charles VIII et Louis XII*. 4 vols. Paris: L. Curmer, 1860–61.

L'Estrange, Elizabeth. *Holy Motherhood: Gender, Dynasty and Visual Culture in the Later Middle Ages*. Manchester: Manchester University Press, 2008.

———. "Images de maternité dans deux livres d'heures appartenant aux duchesses de Bretagne." In *Livres et lectures de femmes*, ed. Anne-Marie Legaré. 35–47.

———. "Penitence, Motherhood, and Passion Devotion: Contextualizing Anne de Bretagne's Prayer Book, Chicago, Newberry Library, MS 83." In *The Cultural and Political Legacy of Anne de Bretagne*, ed. Cynthia J. Brown. 81–98.

———. "Sainte Anne et le mécénat d'Anne de France." In *Patronnes et mécènes en France à la Renaissance*, ed. Kathleen Wilson-Chevalier. 135–54.

Le Verdier, Pierre. *L'Entrée du roi Louis XII et de la reine à Rouen (1508)*. Rouen: Léon Gy, 1900.

Levy. Allison, ed. *Widowhood and Visual Culture in Early Modern Europe*. Aldershot: Ashgate, 2003.

Liepe, Lena. "On the Epistemology of Images." In *History and Images: Towards a New Iconology*, ed. Axel Bolvig and Phillip Lindley. Turnhout: Brepols, 2003. 415–30.

Lowden, John. "The Royal/Imperial Book and the Image or Self-Image of the Medieval

Ruler." In *Kings and Kingship in Medieval Europe*, ed. Anne J. Duggan. London: King's College, 1993.

Mâle, Émile. *Les Heures d'Anne de Bretagne*. Paris: Verve, 1946.

Markale, Jean. *Anne de Bretagne*. Paris: Hachette, 1980.

Martin-Ulrich, Claudie. *La Persona de la Princesse au XVIe siècle: personnage littéraire et personnage politique*. Paris: Champion, 2004.

Marvin, Mary Beth W. "'Regret' Chansons for Marguerite d'Autriche by Octovien de Saint-Gelais." *Bibliothèque d'Humanisme et Renaissance* 39 (1977): 23–32.

Matarasso, Pauline. *Queen's Mate: Three Women of Power in France on the Eve of the Renaissance*. Aldershot: Ashgate, 2001.

Mauny, Michel de. *Anne de Bretagne: ce coeur qui a tant aimé la Bretagne*. Plérin: Brittia, 2000.

McCartney, Elizabeth. "Ceremonies and Privileges of Office: Queenship in Late Medieval France." In *Power of the Weak: Studies of Medieval Women*, ed. Jennifer. Carpenter and Sally-Beth Maclean. Urbana: University of Illinois Press, 1995, 178–219.

———. "The King's Mother and Royal Prerogative in Early-Sixteenth-Century France." In *Medieval Queenship*, ed. John C. Parsons. 117–41.

McCash, June Hall, ed. *The Cultural Patronage of Medieval Women*. Athens: University of Georgia Press, 1996.

McFarlane, John. *Antoine Vérard*. Geneva: Slatkine, 1971.

McGrady, Deborah. "What Is a Patron? Benefactors and Authorship in Harley 4431, Christine de Pizan's Collected Works." In *Christine de Pizan and the Categories of Difference*, ed. Marilynn Desmond. Minneapolis: University of Minnesota Press, 1998. 195–214.

———. "Printing the Patron's Pleasure for Profit: The Case of the *Épîtres de l'Amant Vert*." *Journal of the Early Book Society* 2 (1999): 89–112.

McLeod, Glenda. *Virtue and Venom: Catalogues of Women from Antiquity to the Renaissance*. Ann Arbor: University of Michigan Press, 1991.

Minois, George. *Anne de Bretagne*. Paris: Fayard, 1999.

Mitchell, Bonner. *The Majesty of the State: Triumphal Progresses of Foreign Sovereigns in Renaissance Italy, 1494–1600*. Florence: Olschki, 1986.

Molinier, Henri-Joseph. *Essai biographique et littéraire sur Octovien de Saint-Gelays, évêque d'Angoulême 1468–1502*. Rodez, 1910; rpt. Geneva: Slatkine, 1972.

Moss, Ann. *Ovid in Renaissance France: A Survey of the Latin Editions of Ovid and Commentaries Printed in France Before 1600*. London: Warburg Institute/University of London, 1982.

Müller, Catherine M. "Marguerite d'Autriche (1480–1530), poétesse et mécène." *Cahiers du C.R.I.S.I.M.A.* (*Reines et Princesses au Moyen Âge*) 5 (2001): 763–76.

Mulryne, J. R., Helen Watanabe-O'Kelly, Margaret Shewring, et al., eds. *Europa Triumphans: Court and Civic Festivals in Early Modern Europe*. Aldershot: Ashgate, 2004.

Munn, Kathleen. *A Contribution to the Study of Jean Lemaire de Belges: A Critical Study of*

*Bio-Bibliographical Data, Including a Transcript of Various Unpublished Works*. New York: 1936; rpt. Geneva: Slatkine, 1975.

Nassiet, Michel. "Les Traités de mariage d'Anne de Bretagne." In *Pour en finir avec Anne de Bretagne?* ed. Dominique Le Page, 71–81.

O'Meara, Carra Ferguson. *Monarchy and Consent: The Coronation Book of Charles V of France*. Turnhout: Harvey Miller, 2001.

Orth, Myra D. "Louise of Savoy et le pouvoir du livre." In *Royaume de Fémynie: pouvoirs, contraintes, espaces de liberté des femmes, de la Renaissance à la Fronde*, ed. Kathleen Wilson-Chevalier and Éliane Viennot. Paris: Champion, 1999. 71–90.

Oulmont, Charles. "Pierre Gringore et l'entrée de la reine Anne en 1504." In *Mélanges offerts à Émile Picot par ses amis et ses élèves*. Geneva: Slatkine, 1969. 385–92.

Parsons, John C, ed. *Medieval Queenship*. New York: St. Martin's, 1993.

———. "Family, Sex, and Power: The Rhythms of Medieval Queenship." In *Medieval Queenship*, ed. John C. Parsons. 1–11.

———. "Mothers, Daughters, Marriage, Power: Some Plantagenet Evidence, 1150–1500." In *Medieval Queenship*, ed. John C. Parsons. 63–78.

———. "Ritual and Symbol in the English Medieval Queenship to 1500." In *Women and Sovereignty*, ed. Louise O. Fradenburg. 60–77.

Paxson, James. "Personification of Gender." *Rhetorica* 16, 2 (Spring 1998): 149–79.

Penketh, Sandra. "Women and Books of Hours." In *Women and the Book*, ed. Jane Taylor and Lesley Smith. 266–81.

Phillippy, Patricia. "Establishing Authority: Boccaccio's *De Mulieribus claris* and Christine de Pizan's *Le Livre de la cite des dames*." *Romanic Review* 77 (1986): 167–93.

Poulet, André. "Capetian Women and the Regency: The Genesis of a Vocation." In *Medieval Queenship*, ed. John C. Parsons. 93–116.

Pradel, Pierre. *Anne de France 1461–1522*. Paris: Publisud, 1986.

Quentin-Bauchart, Ernest. *Les Femmes bibliophiles de France (XVIe, XVIIe & XVIIIe siècles)*. Vol. 2. Paris: Damsacène Morgand, 1886.

Quilliet, Bernard. *Louis XII*. Paris: Fayard, 1986.

Quilligan, Maureen. *The Allegory of Female Authority: Christine de Pizan's "Cité des dames."* Ithaca, N.Y.: Cornell University Press, 1991.

Regalado, Nancy F. "Allegories of Power: The Tournament of Vices and Virtues in the *Roman de Fauvel* (BN MS Fr. 146)." *Gesta* 32, 2 (1993): 135–46.

Rigolot, François. *Poétique et onomastique: l'exemple de la Renaissance*. Geneva: Droz, 1977.

Russell, Donald. "Advice to the Bride and Groom" [Translation of Plutarch]." In *Plutarch's* Advice to the Bride and Groom *and* A Consolation to His Wife: *English Translations, Commentary, Interpretive Essays and Bibliography*, ed. Sarah B. Pomeroy. New York: Oxford University Press. 1999. 5–13.

Rutson, Elizabeth. "The Life and Works of Jean Marot." Dissertation, University of Oxford, 1960.

Santinelli, Emmanuelle. *Des Femmes éplorées? les veuves dans la société aristocratique du haut Moyen Âge*. Villeneuve d'Ascq: Presses Universitaires du Septentrion, 2003.

Scheller, Robert. "Ensigns of Authority: French Royal Symbolism in the Age of Louis XII." *Simiolus* 13 (1983): 75–141.

———. "Gallia Cisalpina: Louis XII and Italy, 1499–1508." *Simiolus* 15, 1 (1985): 5–60.

———. "Imperial Themes in Art and Literature in the Early French Renaissance: The Period of Charles VIII." *Simiolus* 12, 1 (1981–82): 5–69.

Scollen, Christine. *The Birth of the Elegy in France 1500–1550*. Geneva: Droz, 1967, 157–59.

Sears, Elizabeth. "Reading' Images." In *Reading Medieval Images: The Art Historian and the Object*, ed. Elizabeth Sears and Thelma K. Thomas. Ann Arbor: University of Michigan Press, 2002. 1–7.

Ségemaud, Edmond. *La Bibliothèque de Charles d'Orléans, comte d'Angoulême au château de Cognac en 1496*. Paris: Claudin, 1861.

Sherman, Michael. "'Pomp and Circumstance': Pageantry, Politics and Propaganda in France During the Reign of Louis XII, 1498–1515." *Sixteenth Century Journal* 9, 4 (1978): 13–32.

———. "The Selling of Louis XII: Propaganda and Popular Culture in Renaissance France, 1498–1515." Dissertation, University of Chicago, 1974.

Smith, Susan L. *The Power of Women: A Topos in Medieval Art and Literature*. Philadelphia: University of Pennsylvania Press, 1995.

Sozzi, Lionello. "Boccaccio in Francia nel Cinquecento." In *Il Boccaccio nella cultura francese*, ed. Carlo Pellegrini. Firenze: Olschki, 1971. 211–356.

Stafford, Pauline. "The Portrayal of Royal Women in England, Mid-Tenth to Mid-Twelfth Centuries." In *Medieval Queenship*, ed. John Carmi Parsons. 143–67.

Starn, Randolph. "Seeing Culture in a Room for a Renaissance Prince." In *The New Cultural History*, ed. Lynn Hunt. Berkeley: University of California Press, 1989. 205–32.

Stein, Henri. "Le Sacre d'Anne de Bretagne et son entrée à Paris en 1504." *Mémoires de la Société de l'Histoire de Paris et de l'Île de France* 19 (1902): 268–304.

Stirnemann, Patricia. "Women and Books in France: 1170–1220." In *Representations of the Feminine in the Middle Ages*, ed. Bonnie Wheeler. Dallas: Academia, 1993. 247–52.

Stones, Alison. "Some Portraits of Women in Their Books: Late Thirteenth–Early Fourteenth Century." In *Livres et lectures de femmes en Europe*, ed. Anne-Marie Legaré. 3–27.

Summit, Jennifer. *Lost Property: The Woman Writer and English Literary History, 1380–1589*. Chicago: University of Chicago Press, 2000.

Swift, Helen J. *Gender, Writing and Performance: Men Defending Women in Late Medieval France*. Oxford: Clarendon, 2008.

Szkilnik, Michelle. "Mentoring Noble Ladies: Antoine Dufour's *Vies des femmes célèbres*." In *The Cultural and Political Legacy of Anne de Bretagne*, ed. Cynthia J. Brown. 65–80.

Tanguy, Geneviève-Morgane. *Sur les pas de Anne de Bretagne*. Rennes: Ouest-France, 2003.

Taylor, Jane H. M. "Translation as Reception: Boccaccio's *de Mulieribus claris* and *Des cleres et nobles femmes*." In *"Or la soie amisté": Essays in Honor of Norris J. Lacy*, ed. Keith Busby and Catherine M. Jones. Amsterdam: Rodopi, 2000. 491–507.

Taylor, Jane and Lesley Smith, eds. *The Book and the Worldly*. Woodbridge: Brewer, 1996.

———, eds. *Women and the Book: Assessing the Visual Evidence*. Toronto: University of Toronto Press, 1996.

———, eds. *Women, the Book, and the Godly*. Selected Proceedings of the St. Hilda's Conference, 1993. Woodbridge: Brewer, 1995.

Thiry, Claude. *La Plainte funèbre*. Turnhout: Brepols, 1978.

Tomalin, Margaret. *The Fortunes of the Warrior Heroine in Italian Literature: An Index of Emancipation*. Ravenna: Longo, 1982.

Toudouze, Georges G. *Anne de Bretagne: duchesse et reine*. Paris: Floury, 1950.

Tourault, Philippe. *Anne de Bretagne*. Paris: Perrin, 1990.

Tournoy-Thoen, Godelieve. "Deux épîtres inédites de Fausto Andrelin et l'auteur du *Iulius Exclusus*." *Humanistica Lovaniensia* 18 (1969): 42–75.

———. "Fausto Andrelini et la Cour de France." In *L'Humanisme français au début de la Renaissance* (Colloque International de Tours [XIVe Stage]). Paris: Vrin, 1973. 65–79.

———. Les Premiers épithalames humanistes en France." In *Mélanges à la mémoire de Franco Simone: France et Italie dans la culture européenne*. Vol. 1. Geneva: Slatine, 1980 [1984]. 199–224.

Turias, Odette. "L'Héritière d'Anne de Bretagne: Claude ou Renée de France ?" In *Anne de Bretagne: une histoire, un mythe*, ed. Pierre Chotard. 112–19.

Vandeweghe, Frank. "*La Complainte de dame Marguerite* dedrukt door Gheraert Leeu." *Hellinga Festschrift/Feestbundel/Mélanges*. Amsterdam: Nico Israel, 1980. 529–94.

Voronova,Tamara and Alexander Stergligov. *Western European Illuminated Manuscripts of the 8th to the 16th Centuries in the National Library of Russia, St. Petersburg*. Bournemouth: Parkstone, 1996.

Walsby, Malcolm. "La famille de Laval et Anne de Bretagne 1488–1514" In *Pour en finir avec Anne de Bretagne?*, ed. Dominique Le Page. 109–23.

Walters, Lori J. "Anthoine Vérard's Reframing of Christine de Pizan's *Doctrine* in His 1497 Edition of the *Trésor de la cité des dames*." In *The Cultural and Political Legacy of Anne de Bretagne*, ed. Cynthia J. Brown. 47–63.

———. "Jeanne and Marguerite de Flandre as Female Patrons." *Dalhousie French Studies* 28 (Fall 1994): 15–27.

———. "'Translating Petrarch': *Cité* II.7.1, Jean Daudin, and Vernacular Authority." In *Christine 2000: Studies Offered to Angus Kennedy*, ed. Nadia Margolis and John Campbell. Amsterdam: Rodopi, 2000. 283–97.

Warren, Nancy Bradley. *Women of God and Arms: Female Spirituality and Political Conflict, 1380–1600*. Philadelphia: University of Pennsylvania Press, 2005.

Watanbe-O'Kelly, Helen. "The Early Modern Festival Book: Function and Form." In *Europa Triumphans*, ed. J. R. Mulryne et al. 3–17.

White, Paul. "Ovid's *Heroides* in Early Modern French Translation: Saint-Gelais, Fontaine, Du Bellay." *Translation and Literature* 13 (2004): 165–80.

Wijsman, Hanno. "Les Livres de la 'damoiselle de Dreux': la bibliothèque d'une femme au seuil du XVe siècle." In *Livres et lectures de femmes*, ed. Anne-Marie Legaré. 67–79.

Wilson-Chevalier, Kathleen. "Claude de France in Her Mother's Likeness: A Self-Assertive Queen?" In *The Cultural and Political Legacy of Anne de Bretagne*, ed. Cynthia J. Brown. 123–44.

———, ed. *Patronnes et mécènes en France à la Renaissance*. Saint-Étienne: Publications de l'Université de Saint-Étienne, 2007.

Winn, Mary Beth. *Anthoine Vérard: Parisian Publisher (1485–1512): Prologues, Poems, and Presentations*. Geneva: Droz, 1997.

———. "Books for a Princess and Her Son: Louise of Savoy, François d'Angoulême, and the Parisian Libraire Antoine Vérard." *Bibliothèque d'Humanisme et Renaissance* 45 (1984–83): 603–17.

———. "Louise of Savoy, 'Bibliophile.'" *Journal of the Early Book Society* 4 (2001): 228–58.

———. "Louise de Savoie, ses enfants et ses livres: du pouvoir familial au pouvoir d'état." In *Patronnes et mécènes en France à la Renaissance*, ed. Kathleen Wilson-Chevalier. 251–81.

———. "Marguerite of Austria and Her *Complaintes*." *The Profane Arts of the Middle Ages/Les arts profanes du moyen-âge* 8, 2 (Autumn 1998): 152–69.

———. "Treasures for the Queen: Anne de Bretagne's Books from Anthoine Vérard." *Bibliothèque d'Humanisme et Renaissance* 58, 3 (1996): 667–80.

Wolfthal, Diane. In *Images of Rape: The "Heroic" Tradition and Its Alternatives*. Cambridge: Cambridge University Press, 1999.

Wood, Charles T. "The First Two Queens Elizabeth, 1463–1503." In *Women and Sovereignty*, ed. Fradenburg. 121–31.

Zöhl, Caroline. *Jean Pichore: Buchmaler, Graphiker und Verleger in Paris in Paris um 1500*. Turnhout: Brepols, 2004.

BIBLIOGRAPHIES, CATALOGUES, DICTIONARIES

*Anne de Bretagne et son temps: documents historiques et iconographiques*. Nantes: Musée Dobrée, 1961.

Bierstadt, O. A. *The Library of Robert Hoe: A Contribution to the History of Bibliophilism in America*. New York: Duprat and Co., 1895. 16–18.

Borland, Catherine R. *A Descriptive Catalogue of the Western Mediaeval Manuscripts in Edinburgh University Library*. Edinburgh: T. and A. Constable, 1916.

Breslauer, B. H. and E. W. G. Grieb. *Catalogue One Hundred and Nine Published on the*

*Occasion of the Ninetieth Anniversary of the Firm of Martin Breslauer, Inc.* New York: Bibliograph, 1988.

Brunet, J. C. *Manuel de libraire et de l'amateur de livres.* Vol. 3. Paris: Firmin-Didot, 1862.

*Catalogue des livres de la bibliothèque de feu M. Le Duc de la Vallière* (Première Partie) Vol. 2. Paris: Guillaume de Bure, 1783.

*Catalogue des manuscrits français.* Vol. 1, *Anciens fonds.* Paris: Firmin Didot, 1868.

*Catalogue of the Stowe Manuscripts in the British Museum.* Vol. 1. London: William Clowes and Sons, 1895.

Chotard, Pierre, ed. *Anne de Bretagne: une histoire, un mythe.* Paris, Somogy, 2007.

Cotgrave, Randle. *A Dictionarie of the French and English Tongues.* London, 1611; Columbia: University of South Carolina Press, 1968.

Delisle, Léopold. *Le Cabinet des manuscrits de la Bibliothèque Impériale.* Vol. 1. Paris, 1868; rpt. Amsterdam: van Heusden, 1969.

Deuffic, Jean-Luc. "Les Livres manuscrits d'Anne de Bretagne." http://perso.orange.fr/pecia/Anne%20 de%20Bretagne.htm.

Dibdin, Thomas I. *Bibliotheca Spenceriana.* Vol. 4. London: Shakespeare Press, 1815.

Dutschke, C. W. *Guide to Medieval and Renaissance Manuscripts in the Huntington Library.* 2 vols. San Marino, Calif.: Huntington Library, 1989.

Greimas, A. J. and Teresa Mary Keane. *Dictionnaire du moyen français: la Renaissance.* Paris: Larousse, 1992.

James, M. R. *A Descriptive Catalogue of the Manuscripts in the Fitzwilliam Museum.* Cambridge: Cambridge University Press, 1895.

Jones, Michael. "Les Manuscrits d'Anne de Bretagne, reine de France, duchesse de Bretagne." *Mémoires de la Société d'histoire et d'archéologie de Bretagne* 55 (1978): 43–81.

Pächt, Otto and Dagmar Thoss. *Die illuminierten Handschriften der Österreichischen Nationalbibliothek: Französische Schule II.* 2 vols. Vienna: Österreichische Akademie der Wissenschaften, 1977.

Ricci, Seymour de and W. J. Wilson. *Census of Medieval and Renaissance Manuscripts in the U.S. and Canada.* New York: H.W. Wilson, 1935.

Santrot, Jacques, Claire Aptel, Nathalie Biotteau, Marie Richard, eds. *Thomas Dobrée 1810–1895: un homme, un musée.* Somogy: Éditions d'Art, 1997.

Santrot, Marie-Hélène. *Entre France et Angleterre: le duché de Bretagne: essai d'iconographie des ducs de Bretagne.* Nantes: Conseil Général de Loire-Atlantique, 1988.

Saxl, Fritz and Hans Meier. *Handschriften in Englischen Bibliotheken.* London: Warburg Institute, 1953.

Shipman, C. *A Catalogue of Manuscripts Forming a Portion of the Library of Robert Hoe.* New York: Privately Printed (University Press, Cambridge), 1909.

Sotheby Catalogue of 25 July 1862. Libri Collection "Reserved and Most Valuable Portion."

Sotheby Catalogue of 9 May 1892. Sale of the late Edwin Henry Lawrence, Esq. F.S.A.

Thibault, Pascale. *Louis XII: images d'un roi, de l'imperator au père du peuple.* Exposition au Château de Blois 18 December 1987–14 February 1988. Blois: Château de Blois, 1987.

———. *Les Manuscrits de la Collection d'Anne de Bretagne.* Cahiers de la Bibliothèque Municipale de Blois 8. Blois: Amis de la Bibliothèque de Blois, 1991.

# INDEX

## ACKNOWLEDGMENTS

I am grateful to a number of individuals and organizations that have made important contributions to the development of my ideas during my research on this project and have helped usher the book to its completion. This work would not have come to fruition without the numerous research grants I received from the UCSB Faculty Senate over the course of the project. I am particularly appreciative of a Senate award to cover the purchase of illustrations and permissions to reproduce the many images in this volume. A Summer Stipend from the National Endowment for the Humanities in 2006, for which I am very thankful, supported research in Europe at a critical stage of this process. The University of California President's Fellowship for the Humanities I received in 2006–7 was absolutely invaluable, for I was able to complete a first draft of my book during this leave.

Many thanks to Lori Walters for her comments on an early draft of the entire manuscript and to Mary Beth Winn for her insightful reading of the material in Chapters 3 and 4. I greatly appreciate the incisive queries of Diane Booton concerning the inventory of books associated with Anne of Brittany in the Appendix. Rogert Wieck, Curator of Medieval and Renaissance Manuscripts at the Pierpont Morgan Library, deserves special thanks for his advice and intercession on my behalf concerning several privately owned manuscripts. I am also indebted to Thierry Delcourt, directeur du département des manuscrits at the Bibliothèque nationale de France, who graciously facilitated my examination of numerous luxury Boccaccio manuscripts, and to Jacques Santrot, Conservateur at the Musée Dobrée in Nantes, who authorized a special viewing of the original manuscript of Antoine Dufour's *Vies des femmes célèbres*.

I am particularly grateful to E. Jane Burns, who played an instrumental role in bringing my project to the attention of Jerry Singerman at the University of Pennsylvania Press. The close readings of my manuscript for the

Press by François Rigolot and a second anonymous reader yielded thoughtful suggestions that have enhanced the final outcome.

A Borchard Foundation Symposium Grant generously supported a colloquium I organized at the Château de la Bretesche on the political and cultural legacy of Anne of Brittany in 2008. Besides the extraordinary opportunity to interact and debate with specialists from multiple disciplines carrying out research on the French queen and issues associated with her two reigns, this meeting provided inspiring feedback on my own project. I am also indebted to the following colleagues who extended invitations that permitted me to present my work publicly in the U.S. and Europe and contribute to edited volumes: Adrian Armstrong, Renée-Claude Breitenstein, Jennifer Britnell, Margaret Burland, E. Jane Burns, Annie Charon, Martha Driver, Laurence Harf-Lancner, Roberta Krueger, David Laguardia, Anne-Marie Legaré, Seth Lerer, Frank Lestringant, Deborah McGrady, Jean-Claude Mühlethaler, Nancy Regalado, Michelle Szkilnik, Andrea Tarnowski, Tania Van Hemelryck, Lori Walters, and Kathleen Wilson-Chevalier. These opportunities provided me with considerable stimulus as I reformulated the ideas that found their way into the final version's pages.

A special thanks to Maura Jess, photographer in Instructional Development at UCSB, for her unusual dedication in formatting many of this book's illustrations for publication. I am also grateful to Zelda Bronstein for her assistance in formulating the title for this volume. The continuous support of my husband Art Ludwig over the years has been immeasurable.

I dedicate this book to my mother, the most influential woman in my life, with gratitude for her abiding sustenance and encouragement.

MUSKINGUM COLLEGE LIBRARY

3 8152 002 252 174